Society and Culture in Northern India
1850-1900

Society and Culture in Northern India
1850-1900

SHIVA S. DUA
Formerly Principal, Kalindi College
University of Delhi

INDIAN BIBLIOGRAPHIES BUREAU
CO-PUBLISHER
BALAJI ENTERPRISES
DELHI   INDIA

Cataloguing in Publication Data
Dua, Shiva S., 1913-
 Society and culture in northern India, 1850-1900.
 Bibliography : p.
 Includes Index.
 1. India (Northern)—History 19th century. 2. India (Northern)—History 1850-1900. 3 India (Northern)—Social conditions 1850-1900.
 4. Social History—India (Northern) 1850-1900. I. Title

ISBN 81-85004-04-8

© 1985 Shiva S. Dua
All Rights Reserved

No part of this book may be reproduced, stored in a retrieval system, or transmitted in any form or by any means electronic, mechanical, photocopying microfilming, recording or otherwise, without written permission from the Publisher.

Published by Sushil Kumar for Balaji Enterprises 2153/2 Fountain, Delhi-110006. Phone 2528597. Printed at Swatantra Bharat Press, Esplanade Road, Dehli-110006.
Printed in India

Preface

Social conditions in northern India in the second half of the nineteenth century is a subject on which much work has not been done, though some aspects of social history of the period have been dealt with singly and severally. I have tried to analyse the different facets of social and cultural life and present a connected picture with special reference to the position of woman. The difficulty of studying social phenomena is great in all countries, partly because of the human factor they involve, and which, if not taken on a sufficiently large scale, presents aberrations that can seriously vitiate the reasoning of any and even the most careful and industrious observer. In regard to India, with territories so vast, people so various and multitudes so numerous, the difficulties are tremendous. There being no well defined units or cells so to say of the social organism, it is difficult to deduce sociological laws. All generalisations are, at best, vague and abundant in pitfalls.

Roughly, I have reckoned the vast stretch of territory to the north of the Vindhya mountains, which cut across the country in the middle, hemmed in by the Himalayas, as northern India, touching Burma in the east and Baluchistan in the west. The latter two have not been included in the study though they were both part of British India during the period of review. The fifty years 1850 to 1900 were unusually rich in world-wide activity. From the Far West to the Far East all countries were witnessing movements of great momentum. India had her share of them. For her the fifty years denoted social and intellectual change which was slow and subtle, impalpable and imperceptible, yet definite and momentous.

Being under foreign domination, she moved within certain ruts. Hence the difficulty of finding correct facts. I have gauged the tone and atmosphere of society through fiction by Indian authors. For facts, I have mainly depended on contemporary literature on social and political subjects, travellers' accounts, biographical accounts of important persons and administrative reports. Government records both published and unpublished have been consulted on matters pertaining to legislation and government share in the state of affairs. Reports on Indian newspapers compiled by the Government as also important newspapers, periodicals and journals of the period have also been consulted.

It was, indeed, no easy job to get the correct picture of the conditions. Official accounts suffered from their inherent defects. Non-official accounts of foreigners smacked of something like the opinion of the six blind men who went to see the elephant,

> 'Each in his own opinion,
> Exceedingly stiff and strong
> Though each was partly in the right
> And all were in the wrong.'

Indian authors are few and not always free from bias. However, I have scanned the material and viewed the situation from a purely objective and inquisitive angle. My findings are, in many ways, at variance with popular impression prevalent generally that social evils were rampant everywhere and that social conditions were immutable.

I have considered all residents of the country, permanent and temporary, Indians and non-Indians, as the people, and have divided them into two sections—the ruling class and the subjugated class. Chapter 2 has glimpses of the social life of the Anglo-Indian society, its Sahib Culture and its social attitude towards the Indian people. In Chapter 3, I have tried to show the over-all affinity in the social attitude of the people, generally considered to be diverse and varied and that the pattern of life was basically the same. In Chapter 4-6, I have examined the basic institutions of the Indian society—caste, family and marriage —and have tried to show how changes were creeping into them though they were not always palpable and tangible. In Chapter 7, I have tried to indicate that the Indian woman was as powerful and influential in the domestic sphere as her sister in the West, her social disabilities notwithstanding. I have also tried to bring out the fact that the social evils connected with woman—infanticide, enforced widowhood, polygamy, etc.—were far from universal. Even among the sections they were found to exist they were being deprecated and eliminated. In Chapter 8, I have tried to point out the harmonising factors in the recreational activities of the people, which acted as binding force in the society. Chapter 9 on education is meant to show that despite the appalling illiteracy, society was not moribund; that even with slow and inadequate efforts to disseminate education, the spark was light and progress was rapid. The impact of western education not only led to fermentation of thought, but stirred up unprecedented activity. I have devoted Chapter 10 to describe the most important result of education, the endeavours of the educated few to reform social deformities and to accelerate progress by removing ignorance, the cause at the root of social abuses. In Chapter 11, I have given an over-all review of the forces that operated, the currents and cross-currents of thought and action and the situation that resulted.

This indeed has been a tantalising job in the process of which I have faltered and floundered but have made an effort to analyse the forces at work in an objective and dispassionate manner. There were occasions, when I was lost in the maze of details far too fascinating to resist the temptation of getting into them and found the task an uphill one, for in the proposed analysis of the vast field only a general picture could be given.

I am greatly indebted to Late Professor Bisheshwar Prasad, formerly Head of the Department of History, University of Delhi for his valuable encouragement, guidance and patient cooperation, as also to the National Archives of India for all the facilities made available to me.

15th August, 1985 **Shiva S. Dua**

Contents

Preface

1.	Nineteenth Century Northern India	1-17
2.	The Anglo-Indian Society and Its Sahib Culture	18-38
3.	The Subjugated Indian People: An Enigma to the Ruling Class	39-62
4.	The Caste System: A Unique Mode of Social Organisation	63-90
5.	The Indian Family: Its Structural and Functional Transformation	91-113
6.	The Institution of Marriage	114-135
7.	The Position of Woman	136-155
8.	Pastimes, Festivals and Fairs	156-178
9.	Perspectives on Education	179-203
10.	Social Reformers at Work	204-230
11.	The Old Order Changeth	231-245
	Bibliography	246-263
	Index	264-272

1 Nineteenth Century Northern India

    1.1 Nineteenth Century Indian Society
    1.2 Decline of the Social Traditions
    1.3 The Caste System
    1.4 Intellectual Stagnation
    1.5 Indian Womanhood
    1.6 The British Policy of Non-Interference in Social and Religious Life of the Indian People
    1.7 The New Wave of Social Reforms: Lord Bentinck and Raja Rammohun Roy
        1.71 Abolition of Sati
        1.72 Abolition of Human Sacrifice
        1.73 Abolition of Slavery
        1.74 Abolition of Self-Immolation
        1.75 Abolition of Thugs
    1.8 Lord Dalhousie's Policy of Consolidation of Dominions
        1.81 Legislation for Widow Remarriage
        1.82 Introduction of Railways
        1.83 Introduction of Postal and Telegraph Services
        1.84 Introduction of City Lighting
        1.85 State-Sponsored Education
    1.9 The Momentous Year 1857
    1.10 Latter Half of XIX Century : A Picture of Paradoxes

The social condition of a people is a subject deeply interesting and important. For India, it is much more so, on account of its antiquity, the long history of the social institutions and the variegated nature of the population. In Northern India, a region which has borne the brunt of foreign infiltration through the ages and hence has witnessed a queer mingling of races and cultures, the social conditions in the second half of the nineteenth century form a theme both fascinating and baffling, revealing contradictory states, posing difficult problems which involved forces of diverse and obscure nature. Besides, the religious element, which forms everywhere an important and necessary factor in the social life, was much more so in India. The Indians, whether Hindus, Muslims, Sikhs or Parsis had their social life prominently intertwined with their religious practices and dogmas. The everyday affairs of life for them, derived their sanction, more or less, from religious injunctions so that they were uniquely sanctified. To change the practices of yore or to introduce an innovation, however small and insignificant, was looked upon as sacrilege. Their devotion to tradition, the commanding influence of custom, the force of habit and the desire to maintain *'status quo'*, amounting to strong aversion to change had been the chief features of their attitude to life. They had given a unique continuity to their institutions, but had at the same time yielded results which were highly paradoxical.

1.1 Nineteenth Century Indian Society

The social conditions in the middle of the nineteenth century reveal, on the one hand, a close identity in many respects with those of the remote antiquity except so far as western influences had begun to affect them and, on the other hand, reveal a complexion of natural evolution and change. In spite of the fact that much had changed in Northern India on account of the successive invasions of the Muhammadans and the Europeans, the multitudinous population could well afford to proclaim against the trite saying, *'Tempora mutantur nos et mutamur-in-illis'*. Indeed,

> "new religions had sprung up and declined, new dialects had grown into existence, new conquerors had invaded the fair land, rivers had changed their courses, earthquakes had swallowed up or cast down once renowned cities ; the sea washed where once the rice fields boomed and the salt marsh or the strand were seen where erst,
> 'old ocean made his melancholy moan'
> the people on the whole were the people of the past."

India of the ancient times and that of the mid-nineteenth century had much in common. They were connected by the unchanging character of the people, the bulk of them, being Hindus. Despite the changes in the religious practices and the accretions through the centuries, there was a psychological identity between the early Aryan followers of the Vedas and the worshippers of new gods and practitioners of magical incantations. This dictum, in general, could apply, just as well to other communities living side by side with each other, for they manifested similar traits.

1.2 Decline of the Social Traditions

And yet, the society had not been static. Nature's inexorable law of change, had operated unsparingly. It had through the centuries, wrought havoc with the social and the religious institutions of the Hindus, the majority community whose customs and mode of living permeated the social climate. Their creed filled everything and was felt everywhere. The general state of their spiritual learning and religion had become stagnant and debased.[1] Hinduism was no more like the simple Vedic religion of its pristine form.[2] It had lost its intellectual rationale. During the millennia of vicissitudes, it had degenerated into a complicated system of polytheistic doctrine and caste usages.[3] Ceremonial idolatry, sacrificial ritual and superstitious supplication had become its striking features. It was principally displayed in endeavouring to avert the anger of evil demons and in doing homage to local divinities supposed to guard the worshippers from the assaults of malignant idols, trees, rocks, stones and shapeless symbols. Great attention was given to private religious usages and to the performance of domestic ceremonies at birth, marriage, funeral, etc. conducted by Brahman priests who had nothing, whatsoever to do with the temples or the worship performed in temples. Nor did they have any professions of learning of scriptures. Moreover, homage to ancestors and to the spirits of deceased fathers, grandfathers and great-grand fathers formed, a large part of their religious rites. The moral and spiritual aspects of Hindu religion with the majority had been lost sight of and in its place the grossest superstitions reigned supreme.

Of popular Islam, or of other religions, as of popular Hinduism the most that can be said is that it verged on idolatory and subsisted on meaningless ritual. Religion, in other words, had for all, become but another name for convention. The social institutions, had lost their original rational form making conditions far from salubrious. People were clinging to dead forms and were trying to draw spiritual sustenance therefrom. Their superstitions and adherence to mere form encouraged by the priestly class whose prestige and power depended upon their continuance. In Bengal, this was fostered further by a class of Brahman preachers called Kathaks, who made their living by giving popular expositions of Hindu mythology often working upon the imagination and credulity of the multitude. Thus the most extravagant mythological stories and false ideas of religion became current and were implicitly believed by the ignorant masses.[4]

The corruption and degeneracy of the priesthood, by and large, was appalling; their ignorance of spiritual teaching was lamentable. Their one obsession was disputes over points of ceremonial and yet their power was a force to reckon with.[5] Next to gods, whom the priest propitiated, he received the honour and the obeisance, in a measure which hurt the vanity of the British officials.[6] Thus, tradition-bound life had become a series of observances and thought moved within the prescribed ceremonialism. The worst of it was that these observances varied from caste to caste, assuming the most degenerate and perverse form among the higher castes.[7]

1.3 The Caste System

Caste as an institution had lost its original essence and in course of time had assumed rather an irrational form. Considerations of artificial purity had made it strictly hereditary and rigidly invidious. But it influenced more than ever, the whole social organisation. Its laws governed the conduct of all, high and low. It controlled the intercourse of the people in every grade and condition of life. It was no longer, as it once was, a broad basis for the regulation of social functions ; nor was it any more a bond of union among large bodies of men.[8] Instead, it tended to split up the social fabric into numerous independent communities, forming very small caste fraternities, some of which were little more than groups of families bound together by peculiar usages. Even the Brahmans were splintered into sub-castes claiming superiority over one another and vying for privileges.

The unit of society, as before, was the family organised on patriarchal basis, and generations lived together under the same roof in strict outward discipline enforced by the head of the family. The laws of property were so devised as to stress the family unit rather than the individual. They gave advantage to men and so did the general code of conduct. Men dominated in every respect, women holding an inferior position.[9]

1.4 Intellectual Stagnation

Education, as an organised system, there was hardly any worth the name. The masses were, on the whole, steeped in ignorance and lived in a blissful state with no realisation of it whatever and hence no aspirations to the betterment of their conditions. The intelligentsia, belonging mainly to the higher castes and educated mostly in the traditional style, were content with some knowledge of their classical literature and moved in their conventional grooves. A handful of youth, educated at missionary institutions on western lines stood ill at ease with their conditions. Sceptical and critical of their environments, they clamoured for change, reform and progress, but without much avail. The spark of the once dynamic society appeared to have been lost.

The intellectual stagnation was reflected in the general degeneration of the whole system, religious and social—a system in which stress was on the community and not on the individual, on mutual obligations and not on rights of individual self. This had helped to create stability which had grown to the extent of inertia, creating a social climate in which the individual was hemmed in on all sides. In the context of the vicissitudes that Northern India had suffered through, the conventional society, especially its upper strata, had, in many ways, become perverse.

1.5 Indian Womanhood

The rigours of the conventional community bore most heavily on women. Wielding irresistible influence on the menfolk in the domestic sphere, despite all their disabilities and handicaps, they were, nevertheless, the greatest sufferers. The invidiousness of race and the desire to preserve purity of blood made the social laws highly stringent for them so that their status had come to be low and condition lamentable. From birth, woman was looked upon as a liability on whose account the family might have to suffer compromises particularly in the matter of marriage which was regarded an essential sacrament performed but once in the life of a woman. The injunctions of the law-givers in respect of marriage had come to be so interpreted as to give rise to highly deplorable customs.

Girls were married at appallingly young age, when they were mere children and this entailed grave ills. Utterly ignorant and the majority of them completely unlettered, for society frowned furiously on their education, considering it entirely unnecessary, women led a life, for all outward purposes, of absolute subjection to the men of the family with no liberty of any description. Curiously enough in the majority of cases, the restrictions and the lack of freedom was not even felt. Life in seclusion, was accepted as the mark of high status and respectability.[10] Nor did a woman, the most virtuous wife, enjoy a real security for if she happened to incur the displeasure of her husband, she could be easily cast aside by him in favour of a more fortunate rival. The law afforded no protection against such a fate. A widow as a matter of course was the worst sufferer. For her there was no hope, no future. Having lost her husband, who was her guardian and God on earth she would, so to say, forfeit her right to live a natural life. Her sentiment, her innate idealism, her implicit faith in her fate, her spirit of self-sacrifice and often her abject helplessness were exploited fully and wantonly by the society dominated by men.

The tyranny of the social laws was most oppressive among the higher castes and the upper classes, financially better placed in life. Society among them had the greatest trammels and taboos, barriers and bounds, with self-created, self-imposed, self-inflicted problems. It presented a mournful spectacle of a caste-ridden convention-ridden and priest-ridden system.

Conditions among the lower castes, however, presented a comparatively brighter picture. With fewer inhibitions and less stringent restrictions, as far as women were concerned, society bestowed fewer shackles on them. And although they formed the vast majority, the general stamp to the social conditions as a whole came from the higher castes.

On the whole the institution of caste, the inferiority of women and the sanctity of the family formed the chief features of the social pattern among the Hindus, the majority community, which were reflected in the social conditions of the entire people. It is in regard to these that the worst form of degeneration had set in, and the most persistent social evils prevailed.

1.6 The British Policy of Non-Interference in Social and Religious Life of the Indian People

Any government would normally have found it hard to tackle such problems as the eradication of social evils. The British colonial rulers could least afford to meddle with them. The circumstances in which the

British had become the rulers of India were such as to make any policy of introducing changes in society absolutely out of the question. The security and the stability of the British Empire demanded that the government follow rather than anticipate or create public opinion. From the first, therefore, it had followed a policy of non-interference with the social and religious life of the people of the British dominions in India.[11] The promises made by the regulations of 1793, "to preserve the laws of the *Shastras* and the *Koran* and to protect the natives of India in the free exercise of their religion", were adhered to scrupulously, in the years and decades that followed. All rites and customs accordingly were to be tolerated; all endowments were left untouched; all religious liabilities created by former rulers accepted as trusts.

The government paid no heed, much less made adequate efforts to eradicate or even to mitigate the horrors of the evils that prevailed. British security was bound up with the maintenance of *status quo* in social and religious matters. Extreme care, therefore, had been taken so as not to disturb the susceptibilities of the Hindus and the Muslims. Their religious usages and ceremonies had been treated with profound official deference. Even troops were posted and salutes were fired on the occasion of their special festivals. The Christian missionaries, on the contrary, as a precautionary measure, for some time, were not given official sanction for their activities. Their work was a matter of apprehension to the government and was closely watched. They had to obtain special licence from the directors without which they were on various occasions deported from or refused permission to land in British India.[12] It was only in the opening years of the nineteenth century that the policy of the government had begun to change. The Charter Act of 1813 favoured definitely the adoption of a policy of promoting religious and moral improvement. Accordingly, in the first instance, the Company's Anglican establishment was, thereafter, placed under the superintendence of a bishop and three archdeacons and the mission work was given the necessary sanction. Missionary activities increased and as a result the number of Christian converts also went up.

1.7 The New Wave of Social Reforms: Lord Bentinck and Raja Rammohun Roy

The spirit of modern statesmanship, however, had been at work, for some time, against the earlier policy of the government.[13] The negative attitude, the standing aloof, being an imperfect and not altogether a well-secured position for a political system founded mainly upon considerations of material interest and well-being, had been declared by high philosophic authority to be unstable.[14] Serious notice was beginning to be taken of the religious practices prevalent among the Indian,— Hindus, Muslims and Christian converts—which, hitherto, had been ignored as matters beyond the pale of British concern. Besides, propaganda by the enlightened had also been going on for some time both in England as well as in India in favour of measures to be taken against customs and usages which were considered to be uncivilised and even immoral, in Christian opinion. In India, this feeling had come to a head during the governor-generalship of Lord William Bentinck, though some of his predecessors had also shown signs of change in their attitude and had also taken certain steps accordingly. The resentment shown by the people to small innovations such as in the case of the removal of castemarks from the foreheads of soldiers, taken as interference with their religion, had served as a note of warning and the government had restrained itself from any further action of the type. Repeated appeals, however, had continued to be made to the government by religious communities to abolish certain practices and "suppress the indecency of the ceremonials of heathenism". The authorities believed that those demands if conceded wholly would amount to a holy war against the whole people of India which if attempted might result in the defeat and destruction of the British Empire in India.

However, the policy of the British Government in India under Lord Bentinck was a clear departure from the traditional policy of virtual "let sleeping dogs lie" in social matters. It was a distant but a distinct echo of the tone of public opinion and its official acceptance in England. It was made possible by the newly emerging consciousness of the desirability of such a policy among certain sections of English educated Indians particularly in Bengal, the province first to come under British rule and effective western impact. It was also the province where high-caste Hindu society happened to be infested with social evils in their worst form.

The central figure of the new trend of thought was Raja Rammohun Roy. It was primarlly due to his single-handed efforts that an atmosphere was created in northern India which encouraged and facilitated the action of the government against the most heinous of the social evils of the period. Raja Rammohun Roy's crusade against the superstitions and the idolatry of orthodox Brahmanism, had begun at the early age of the sixteen with a clash with his father when he wrote a tract against idolatry, resulting in his having to leave his home. His whole life, thereafter, was a series of clashes with the orthodox Hindus exposing the falsity of the prevalent customs, particularly among the social strata to which he belonged—the higher castes.[15]

His researches into the domain of Sanskrit literature had convinced him of the purity of the monotheistic doctrines of the *Upanishads* as contra-distinguished from the prevailing corruptions of Hindu idolatry. To rouse his countrymen to a sense of the superiority of the monotheistic creed became his life's mission and he spared himself no pains to work for it. He translated some of the *Upanishads* into

Bengali and English with a view to propagating the true faith and published them liberally often involving huge personal expense. His prolific writings, quoting from the scriptures, he had studied profoundly, helped to create a climate of reform and change. Having a masterful knowledge of the English language acquired by self-study and diligence, he saw the advantages of western learning and became a staunch advocate of English education. He threw himself heart and soul into the colossal task of rousing public conscience in India to social evils of the time. Primarily concerned with religious practices and energetically prosecuting his religious controversies, he was fully conscious of the degeneration that had set in the whole system and made incessant and arduous efforts to uplift the people and to bring about reform.

As early as 1814-15 when he founded the 'Atmiya Sabha' an association of a few educated men for the dissemination of religious truth and the promotion of free discussion of theological subjects, he also encouraged the discussion of Hindu social customs, like *Kulin* polygamy as it prevailed then among a section of Brahmans in Bengal, caste and idolatry. He set in motion the forces that raised a vociferous cry against many ills widely prevalent in the high-caste Hindu society not only in Bengal but in other parts of northern India also, and led, eventually, to the correction of some of them. The practice of *Sati*, human sacrifice, slavery, infanticide, child-marriage, disabilities of women such as their complete seclusion and unequal rights of inheritance etc., the exposure of the sick on the banks of the Ganges were some of the conspicuous social evils of his time. He realised that the root cause of the degenerate conditions was lack of education; that the future regeneration of society lay in the adoption of the western education and western science. Hence, he threw his full weight in favour of western education. His efforts led to the setting up of the Hindu College at Calcutta in 1817, an institution for educating boys on western lines. This was the beginning of an energetic campaign by the Indians under Indian leadership for scientific education. His endeavours and exertions in this regard, actually met with posthumous success and yielded real fruit only in the later years of the nineteenth century.

1.71 Abolition of Sati

But he lived to see the success of his most ardent and fervent efforts directed to the eradication of the most heinous of the evils, the practice of *Sati*, the self-immolation of a widow on the pyre of her deceased husband. This was protected by religious tradition and priestly authority and was practised openly in public. It required skilled and forceful propaganda to create public opinion sufficiently strong to bring about any change. This was done by the great champion of women's rights, Raja Rammohun Roy, who inaugurated intense propaganda and conducted a furious agitation in his journal *Kaumudi* favouring women's rights. In his tract *The Modern Encroachment on the Ancient Rights of Females according to Hindu Law of Inheritance*, published in 1822, he decried polygamy, showed the abject misery in which widows lived among the high castes indirectly proving that their self-immolation was, in many cases, an escape from greater misery. He suggested that every man desirous of taking a second wife during the life-time of the first should be obliged by law to prove before a court of justice or some suitable legal authority that one of the conditions authorised by the Hindu *Shastras* for second marriage existed in the case. Even this modicum of reform, he felt, would have saved hundreds of women from a miserable lot. His skilled campaign against the practice of *Sati* proved to be a masterly achievement. But for the propaganda he did against it, and in favour of government action, by holding discussions, writing articles, producing tracts in English and Bengali and translating them in two or three current languages of the people, it is doubtful whether the government would have dared to hazard the risk of a departure from the traditional policy of non-interference, a policy more or less of deliberate 'salutary neglect'.

This propaganda, nevertheless, represented the first organised effort made by the educated Indians, however few, to reform Hindu social system. It created an atmosphere and strengthened the hands of the government to undertake legislation. It prepared the ground for reformist activity which sprouted up with zeal in the subsequent decades. The first bold step in the direction of change in the policy of the government came as a master stroke in 1829, with which Lord William Bentinck proclaimed *Sati* or burning alive of a widow the most revolting of the practices among the higher castes in Bengal and the Chiefs of Rajputana, punishable as murder throughout British India.[16]

A laudable act, supported and applauded by the educated and the enlightened few, it was condemned as an encroachment on their religious rights by the conservatives, a vast majority. It encouraged, however, the forces working in favour of reform and facilitated further legislation. The years that followed saw a succession of government measures against several other evils then rampant in society, some of which were more of the nature of crime than merely innocent evils. The era of reform in England had its reflections in the policy of the Government in India and its resonant echoes struck hard against some of the evils.

1.72 Abolition of Human Sacrifice

Human sacrifices to the Goddess of Earth, for securing better crops had been widely prevalent among the *Khonds* or *Kandhs*, an aboriginal tribe in Orissa. Their terrible Earth-God was supposed to send famines and pestilences unless propitiated by blood. According to Hunter "the victims were of either sex and generally of tender age. The detestable office of providing them formed a hereditary privilege of the *Pans*, one of the low castes attached to the Kandh villages. Procurers of this class yearly sallied forth into the plains and bought up a herd of promising boys and girls from the poorer Hindus. Sometimes they kidnapped their prey and each Kandh district kept a stock of victims in reserve,"[17] to meet sudden demands for atonement. Brahmans and Kandhs were the only castes whose purity exempted them from sacrifices and a rule came down from remote antiquity that the victim, must be bought with a price. After a village had purchased a victim it treated him with much kindness, regarding him as a consecrated being, eagerly welcomed at every threshold. If a child, he enjoyed perfect liberty; but if an adult the chief of the village kept him in his own house and fed him well but fettered him so that he could not escape. When the time for atonement came, the Kandhs spent two days in feasting and riot; on the third day they offered up the victim, shouting as the first blood fell to the ground, "We bought you with a price, no sin rests with us."[18] In 1845, government legislation suppressed these horrible sacrifices and established a special agency for enforcing obedience to the order for their abolition.[19]

1.73 Abolition of Slavery

Another evil, the institution of slavery prevailed commonly among the rich of all communities, especially the Muslims and was practised in a peculiar manner. It was just a trifle for the needy members of the humbler classes to sell themselves or their children into slavery in order to obtain a bare subsistance.[20] Curiously enough, purchasers would often restore such children to their parents in better times. There were, however, many of those who indulged in the lucrative vocation of traffic in children, kidnapped for purposes of sale as slaves to the rich.[21] In Muslim families eunuchs were kept as servants, though they were virtual slaves for life. The treatment of slaves, domestic and agricultural, varied in different parts of the country, but in most cases they received human treatment. In 1843, legal recognition of slavery was prohibited,[22] though the keeping of slaves or trafficking in them became a criminal offence much later in 1860.[23] Strangely enough, the act aroused no protest and change was accepted without any questioning whatsoever.

1.74 Abolition of Self-immolation

Queer ideas of immolation in many forms had been commonly prevalent, some of which had been prohibited in the early years of the nineteenth century. The sacrifice of Hindu children in fulfilment of vows assumed many forms. Throwing away a child into the sea at Sagar to be drowned or devoured by sharks was the commonest.[24] The custom was little countenanced either by the religious orders or by the great body of people who, on the contrary, considered it a pious act to rescue and raise a cast-away child. It had, therefore, been easier for the government to forbid it. As early as 1802, child sacrifices of this kind had been declared murder.[25]

In some parts of the country like Gujarat, the votive offering of male child had assumed the form of suicide. The mother in such a case brought up her first born son tenderly, till he attained the age of puberty and then told him the secret of the vow she had taken and urged him to honour and fulfil it. The boy would then as a religious obligation put on the habit of a mendicant, leave home, visit the temples dedicated to the god Mahadev for a year and at the annual fair throw himself from a precipice and be dashed to pieces on the rocks below. This form of self-sacrifice known as '*Bhrigu Pat*' was also forbidden.[26]

1.75 ABOLITION OF THUGS

Not only had notions of religious merit given rise to self-sacrifice and self-torture as means of virtue and chastity ensuring reward in future life, but even crimes were committed under the garb of religious sacrifice. The Government had fought a regular campaign against one of them, committed by the thugs, a brotherhood of secret murderers who in the name of Goddess Kali were out to attack and strangle in lonely places the unwary traveller they had marked out for plunder. This murderous activity had spread widely in Central India and had found its way into the Punjab among the Jats and low caste Sikhs. The rigorous action of the government tracked down hundreds of these thugs, traffickers in human lives in the name of religion and brought them to the gallows. 'Thaggi' was declared illegal in 1837[27], but it was only after 1852 that the practice could be proclaimed to have been effectively checked.[28]

By 1850, however, the government had struck against some of the evils that were apparent and prominent while many others not easily palpable, subtle and elusive, stubborn and unyielding, remained to be contended. These affected mainly the position of women.

1.8 Lord Dalhousie's Policy of Consolidation of Dominions

The second half of the nineteenth century opened with a man of dynamic ability, Lord Dalhousie, at the helm of government affairs in India. His regime 1848-56, striding across the two halves of the century, forms an important period, in that it marked the beginning of a new era. It was crowded with rigorous activity of an unprecedented nature, involving far-reaching effects, contradictory in some respects, but momentous in every way. Lord Dalhousie's policy to do away with abuses, to redress apparent wrongs, to consolidate the dominions he was extending by conquest and annexation, through projects of railways, roads, canals and public works and his schemes to draw forth material resources resulted indirectly in bringing about a strange upheaval in the social conditions. It inadvertantly sowed the seeds of change and laid the foundations of a new social order.

One of the earliest steps in this direction was the law which consummated the efforts made earlier by Lord Hardinge to protect private persons from the forfeiture awarded under the old Hindu codes. The Caste Disabilities Removal Act in 1850 opened the period under review as a happy augury enforcing in the case of converts from Hinduism the righteous principle that no man shall be robbed of his right to property on account of any change in his religious creed.[29] Under the old law every such convert incurred a kind of civil outlawing and became an outcaste from his family and his race, stripped of all rights to property inherited from a Hindu forefather. His wife was forbidden to cleave to him, his children were commanded to shun him as one accursed of gods and men.[30] The Government declared plainly that the state was bound to "keep in its own hands the right of regulating succession to property." The new act secured the convert from the secular penalties attached to his revolt against ancestral usage. An outcast from his kin, his social fellows, he might still be, but of his rights as a citizen and a house-father none could thenceforth rob him with impunity. This was a bold step, followed by another bolder still, when Lord Dalhousie's interference in the state of Udaipur, Alwar and Bikaner took the form of threats against the practice of *Sati* still allowed to continue. In the Rajput State of Doongarpur which passed under British management in 1852, Dalhousie took stern action against those connected with the *Sati* of the Rajput widow of the Thakur.

1.81 Legislation for Widow Remarriage

The suppression of *Sati* in 1829 had resulted in serious implications. The widow, however young and beautiful, was not allowed to marry a second time. Although, the elderly widow, among the enlightened classes was often the wise matron and stern ruler of the household, the young widow, generally, particularly in Bengal, led a life of degrading drudgery. This had aroused the conscience of some of the enlightened Indians and the government was inclined to respond to their suggestion for action to eliminate the abuse and to sanction widow remarriage through legislation. The orthodox sections of higher castes, especially of Bengal, who had denounced the Caste Disabilities Removal Act of 1850 as a measure of sheer tyranny, raised a louder and fiercer outcry against the government for its attempt to afford relief to the widows. Slaves of time-old customs, people who had not yet reconciled themselves to the suppression of *Sati*, considered it sacrilege for any widow to think of remarriage. Conservative elements were at war with progressive forces and legislation regarding grievous wrongs had to be deferred. Nevertheless, undeterred efforts continued to be made to take stock of the situation and collect data regarding the prevalence of evils such as female infanticide. But they were slow and tardy, cautious and wary, so as not to be temerarious.

1.82 Introduction of Railways

Government activity, however, had its full outlet in other directions and eventually had significant bearing on social conditions. Lord Dalhousie's commanding will and unflinching decisions pursued with alacrity the projects which had previously been viewed with diffidence and even apprehension on account of the serious social inhibitions they involved, but which, he thought, would be in the interests of the British dominions. He carefully shaped out his plans for covering India with a network of railways and telegraph lines and launched the scheme with full force. What Lord Ellenborough, only a few years earlier, had pronounced as 'moon-shine'[31] was a *'fait accompli'* in 1853, when on April 16, the first section of the Indian railway line was opened covering a distance of 24 miles and carried 400 people from Bombay to Thanah, and back, at the rate of 20 miles an hour:[32] Early in the following year, the East Indian line was opened from Calcutta to Ranigunj, covering a distance of 120 miles. By August 1854, regular trains were plying between Howrah and Hooghli. The extension of railway lines in other parts of the region, thereafter was brisk. It followed as a matter of accepted, experimented and successful policy. It accelerated literally the pace of life.

1.83 Introduction of Postal and Telegraph Services

The year 1853 also saw the introduction of the new postal scheme. Under the Postage Act, the postal system was organised on the principle of cheap uniform postal rates. As a result, half an anna, could carry a letter anywhere in the country. On newspapers, pamphlets, books, a low uniform rate was levied varying with the differences of weight only. A complement of this came in the form of Dalhousie's efforts to bind the British dominions together by a girdle of telegraph lines. His countenance to Dr. William O'Shaughnessy's plan resulted in the setting up of the first part of telegraph line from Calcutta to Agra. By the end of January 1855, the wires had been carried from Agra to Bombay in the West and Attock on the Indus in the North, and from Calcutta in other directions southwards also. As early as 1856 O'Shaughnessy's computation of miles of electric telegraph was in thousands.

1.84 Introduction of City Lighting

Simultaneously with this had come O'Shaughnessy's pioneer lighting post, lighting the city of Calcutta with gas by a private company.[33] The Bombay traders did not lag behind in welcoming the new lighting scheme and initiating a similar one in their city.

1.85 State-Sponsored Education

The crowning measure of these opening years of the period under study was the Educational Despatch of 1854 which laid on the Government of India the duty of educating the people of India.[34] Until then the duty, so far as it had been fulfilled at all, had been discharged by the Pandits and Maulavis of the ancient learning and by Christian missionaries. Efforts under government auspices had been made, but to little avail. The Despatch inaugurated a new era of enlightment, mental and intellectual along with the literal physical lighting of the streets started in Calcutta and Bombay.

The organisation of education, thereafter, on secular basis, even though on a very small scale, yielded results not only in the annually augmenting figures, but also in the upheaval in the realms of thought, in the generation of ideas and in the creation of new forces which, in many ways, ushered changes and caused considerable flutter in the placid dovecots of the Indian social set-up.

Immobility as attributed by Europeans, was no longer the chief feature of the Indian society. The introduction of the three engines of social improvement—the railways, the uniform postage and the electric telegraph—gave a new and unforeseen turn to things. They proved at once, that prejudices were not invulnerable. It had been at one time surmised that the priesthood would take umbrage at these innovations and that the unchangeable habits and traditional prejudices of the Hindus would present a serious obstacle to the success of the rail. But these apprehensions were dispelled before the first line had been six months in operation.[35] Some of the Brahmans, with all their religious conservatism, hailed it with delight, folded up their caste prejudices and travelled third class with those whose touch was pollution. Even the Dharma Sabha in Calcutta, the great Sanhedrim of Hindu orthodoxy which had petitioned the Privy Council for the restoration of the 'sacred rite' of *Sati*, unanimously decided in favour of pilgrims availing themselves of the rail. Travelling by rail became at once a national passion. The number of passengers within a decade could be reckoned in millions, majority of whom were of third class. This, in itself, was a revolution in the social conditions.

1.9 The Momentous Year 1857

The crusading zeal against the evils of social life, manifested in the government policy initiated by Lord William Bentinck, followed in general principle by his successors, and consummated under Lord Dalhousie received a serious set-back with the uprising of 1857. A deadly threat to the very existence of the British in India, partly ascribed to causes arising from interference with social and religious practices, the mid-century uprising formed a real landmark in regard to the policy followed by the government thereafter. The greased cartridge, apart from other causes, had touched the most delicate and sensitive cord of the Indian social pattern. It interfered with the social and religious ethos of the two major communities of the people, the Hindus and the Muslims. Soldiers from among both of them felt alike the threat and the danger to their faith and conviction, usage and practice. The cataclysm of 1857, thus stands as a watershed between the two halves of the nineteenth century. It was followed by an emphatic and explicit statement of the policy of non-interference in the Proclamation of 1858, which reiterated the pledges made to the people by the East India Company whose "firmest article of faith was that all the customs of the natives should be scrupulously respected and nothing should be done to give umbrage to their religious prejudices."[36] In 1877, the pledge of 1858 was repeated and reconfirmed and the policy was, thereafter, in the main consistently adhered to throughout the period. Even when justice and humanity clamoured for action, the government showed reluctance to move and was disinclined to act on the plea that the measures proposed were ahead of public opinion, which it was not prepared to offend. Changes in public opinion, it need hardly be stressed, are usually impalpable in character, imperceptible in progress, difficult to discover and their significance almost impossible to realise.

1.10 Latter Half of XIX Century : A Picture of Paradoxes

The apparent result of this was that progressive forces were discouraged, dispirited and were disconsolate; social institutions seemed to assume a static and stereotyped form. In reality, however, the period witnessed tremendous change widespread, far-reaching and momentous, but not uniform. Government activity, motivated by interests of the dominion had gone on unabated, if not accelerated, in fields other than social. In fact, the policy of the government after 1857, was directed, with all the might, towards the consolidation and stabilisation of the Empire. This meant not only political and administrative measures, but stepping up activity in the economic field also, encouraging commercial enterprise in which the Europeans, in the first instance, played a very important role. A few Indians, in Bombay and Calcutta were also beginning to join the new venture.

The mid-century years, thus, crowded with innovations and activities in the different fields—political, social and economic—formed a real turning point. They proved highly potential, in that they yielded results, direct and indirect, immediate and remote, which influenced and affected tremendously, the development of social conditions. The atmosphere created by Raja Ram Mohun Roy which had, hitherto, remained, more or less, passive and receptive caught momentum. The voice raised in favour of change, gained weight. It became strong and stentorian, affecting public opinion of a considerable section among the educated, and obstrusive enough to compel government attention, so that social conditions began to take a new turn. The legacy of reform begun in the early part of 19th century did not, however, remain a monopoly of the Hindus only. It was readily taken up by keen thinkers in other communities also. There grew up a band of kindred spirit and zeal who perceived with regret the degeneration all round and felt the need to eliminate the abuses.

At the same time, the opening up of the Civil Service, the extraordinary development of the internal communications, the building of the rails, roads and canals, the establishment of the postal system and the laying of telegraph lines, the encouragement of settlers, the increase in the number of the mercantile European community, the rapid spread of tea-planting, coffee-planting and other agricultural and commercial speculations, the beginning of popular education and the founding of universities, which entailed numerical expansion of higher education and progressive increase in the class of government employees at the clerical level, had profound bearings, in general, on the social conditions of northern India of the second half of the nineteenth century. They present, consequently, a strange picture of paradoxes, in a conglomeration of people at different levels of development. The majority community, the Hindus, no wonder had a predominant position, but the upper castes among them, who formed a minority had assumed an exaggerated importance giving a stamp to the whole social pattern; the lower castes, a vast majority, though living a life of their own, in many respects different from the upper castes, yet looked up to the minority with aspirations to escalate in the social status, and hence drew cues from it.

The English and other European residents formed yet another important element in the population, alien and incongruous, adding thus to the complexities of the social conditions.

References

1. Monier-Williams, (1878), p.161.
2. Basu, Vol. I, p.45.
3. Monier-Williams (1878), p.161.
4. Sastri, Siva Nath, p.2.
5. Monier-Williams, (1878), p.161.
6. Cotton, Henry John Stedman, p.213.
7. Holderness, pp.119-20 ; *Indian Spectator* (June 27, 1886), p.513 ; *Quarterly Journal of Poona Sarvajanik Sabha* 9, (July, 1886), pp.1-8.
8. Monier-Williams, (1878), p.162.
9. Basu, Vol. I. p.123 ; Ishuree Dass, p.115.
10. Fuller, (Mrs.) Jenney, p.97.
11. Nolan Vol. I, p. (i) (1859) ; Tucker, pp.354-55.

12. Stock, p.1.
13. Trotter (1866), Vol. 2, p.400.
14. Lyall, pp.298-306.
15. Sastri, Siva Nath, pp 16-17 ; Collet, pp.33-34, 115.
16. Regulation No. XVII of 1929.
17. Hunter (1875-77), Vol. XIX, p.235.
18. Ibid.
19. Government of India Act, No. XXI,1845.
20. Peggs, p.407.
21. Home Public Proceedings September 8th, 1864, Nos. 27-28 A.
22. Government of India Acts No. V, 1843.
23. Indian Penal Code, 1860.
24. Marshman (1864), p.75.
25. Regulation VI, 1802.
26. Sleeman (1844), p.133 ; Monier-Williams, (1878), p.71.
27. Government of India Act, No. XVIII, 1837.
28. Trotter (1886), Vol. I, p.260.
29. Government of India Acts No. XXI, 1850.
30. Trotter (1886), Vol. I, p.257.
31. Marshman (1867), p.783.
32. Trotter (1868), p.347.
33. Trotter (1868), p.348.
34. Richey, p.364 ; Hunter (1903), p.30.
35. Marshman (1867), pp.786-87.
36. Proclamation of 1858, Home (Public) Proceedings No. 2, dated November 5, 1858.

2 The Anglo-Indian Society and Its Sahib Culture

    2.1 Two Divisions of the Indian Population
    2.2 Civil and Military Sections of the English Community
    2.3 The Mercantile Class
    2.4 The Sahib Culture
    2.5 Indian Hill Stations : The Haven of the White World
    2.6 Attitude Towards Indians
    2.7 Accentuation of Estrangement
    2.8 Relations at Crossroads

India, a vast country and the home of about one-fifths of the human race, exhibits a large variety of people. The heterogeneous nature of the population and the consequent complexities in the modes of living, have led many foreigners to deny India the status of a single and whole country.[1] Indeed, many European writers have often spoken of this country as a continent; others have even compared the different provinces of India with the small countries on the continent of Europe with regard to their size, population and the languages spoken; and even some of them have referred to India as an ethnological conglomerate. Conceding the diversity one gets baffled at the underlying remarkable unity.

    "It is the peculiarity of the Indian population that it is one in many respects. The same system and manners and divisions of the people prevail throughout the country. And yet in every part there is a great variety of different classes dwelling together, but in points altogether dissimilar."[2]

The different races, that have entered the country during the course of centuries have fused, mingled, blended and united in the common culture notwithstanding the fact that different degrees, in which the different elements have been mixed, produced the extraneous differences. Nevertheless, the fact remains that the population of India does consist of diverse elements seemingly incompatible and irreconcilable. It was much more so in the mid-nineteenth century.

2.1 Two Divisions of the Indian Population

The population at that time was not only divided between rich and poor, town and country, employer and employee as one would find in any society, but the differences were subtle and intriguing. Centering around lass, caste, creed, race and language the diversities were responsible for the creation of myriads of groups. Though no hard and fast principles could be laid down to determine the basis of the divisions which appeared to be constantly merging, overlapping or disregarding the barriers, one group stands distinctly apart from all the rest of them together, creating thus, two uneven divisions of the population—the rulers and the ruled. The divergences between these two were definite; the differences distinct and the contrast sharp. In fact, the gulf that separated the two, gaped wide and appeared unbridgeable.[3] Curiously enough, the two groups were utterly unequal in strength and numbers, unbalanced in influence and uneven in distribution. Hardly visible in places other than the centres of government—central, provincial and district, big cities and towns in the plains as well as hills—the rulers constituted an infinitesimal minority, a mere sprinkling among millions.

The coterie of colonial rulers thus consisted, of those who ran the government—civil and millitary—and their associates, though for all practical purposes it embraced in its folds, all westerners who happened to be in the country for, however, short periods and multifarious purposes, official and non-official, such as trade and commerce, personal business, religious and missionary professions, etc. Unknown to and unseen by millions, no doubt, the existence of the ruling group in the country was indeed a *fait accompli* and a force to reckon with. It served as the pivot around which the rest of the people revolved; the axis on which everything else turned, the factor that determined the course of all the others. Contemporary, historical, literary and official sources abound in terms of all kinds, used to designate this community, as Europeans, Eurasians, Anglo-Indians, etc., the last being the most common and convenient to style the community which covered a wide variety of westerners. Since the census figures of the period do not classify the European population according to their occupations, it is not possible to determine the proportions in which this populations was supported by government service or by each of the various vocations in which the non-officials were engaged. However, one thing is clear that the Europeans lived in India only as 'birds of passage' and their numbers remained surprisingly small.[4]

2.2 Civil and Military Sections of the English Community

On the official side, the English community could be divided into two sections, the civil and military. Since the very foundations of the British dominion in India rested on conquest, the most important and the major portion of the European population consisted of the army personnel—army officers, their families and some 80,000 white troops—and this formed nearly one-third of the Indian army. On the civil side it covered the entire hierarchy of officials, the covenanted civil servants, by whose agency the Indian Government maintained law and order, supervised the collection of revenues, administered justice and gave effect to all its policies. Then there was an important class of officers drawn from the army for civil and political employ. The greater part of the diplomatic or political appointments in the country were held by them. In addition, there were other classes which, though not having the official style of covenanted appointments, were yet under covenant with the government, having been sent out from England under this condition. In the latter part of the nineteenth century, these classes had grown much in importance and their members were filling places of consequence in the public service, such as education officers, civil engineers, forest officers, scientific officers like geologists, botanists, chemists, meteorologists, astronomers, etc.—all appointed from England. The civil engineers constituted the bulk of the officers serving in the Department of Public Works, a branch of service which grew very rapidly with the construction of railways and the extension of canals. Then there were the clergy consisting mainly of the English Church in the employ of the Government who ministered among the European soldiery and among all the servants of the state, both civil and military. There were also Presbyterian ministers and Roman Catholic priests who attended to the troops and other establishments of their respective denominations.[5]

2.3 The Mercantile Class

As for the non-official section of the Anglo-Indian community, it was growing both in numbers as also in the influence it wielded. It comprised a class of people who followed a wide variety of pursuits, besides the original one of trade which in the first instance had been restricted to those who came within the purview of the Charter. The East India Company, it might be mentioned, had resisted all along the efforts of private traders. But after 1833 when the Indian trading ports were made free to all who wished to do business in them, the European traders found free and uncontrolled entry into the country which offered immense scope in many directions. The French were not as numerous as they once had been, but the Germans were fast growing in importance and the Americans were developing their enterprises. Added to these, the Greeks, Armenians, Jews, with all their differences of creed and language, yet included in the English-speaking community, enjoyed much mercantile repute. Industrial undertakings, though not exclusively financed by Europeans, drew much support from them.

The planting industry had offered a great attraction to the Europeans, and in Bengal, the European planters formed a very important class, owning broad acres posssesing large leasehold interests and dwelling in fine country seats. The widespread agitation against the indigo planters in 1860, no doubt, led to their abandoning eastern Bengal, but in Bihar where the people were less resentful and numbers of Indian landlords themselves engaged in the business sympathised with it, the indigo planters survived and formed colonies of their own.[6] Their busy factories, extensive establishments, picturesque houses, gardens and parks constituted some of the most remarkable and interesting sights in that province. As tea-planters, the Europeans, chiefly British, increased considerably during the period and formed quite a formidable group. They covered the slopes of the mountains which hemmed in Assam, a portion of the hills bounding Bengal on the east, the territory ceded by the Bhutan State, the greater part of Darjeeling and British Sikkim, much of Kumaon and Garhwal and some of the Kangra valley in the Punjab. The mining industry, particularly of coal, had attracted another set of investors from the western world. So had the cotton and jute industries in Bombay and Bengal Presidencies. All of them formed their own groups. Then there were English lawyers who, despite the fact that Indians were qualifying as lawyers and taking up the profession, were still held in much esteem. The Anglo-Indian newspaper press as an institution had always flourished and claimed a fair portion of the Anglo-Indian community.

2.4 The Sahib Culture

So great was the prestige attached to the word 'officer' that every white man from the Brigadier to the private soldier or a lay man, was an officer of some sort or other and was called a *Sahib*. The community of whites or the Anglo-Indians was collectively referred to as *Sahibs*, who as members of the ruling race inspired fear rather than awe, adulation rather than admiration.[7]

To the resident *Sahibs*, India was seldom or never a home. However long the tenure of their office and however much some old retired officers might struggle to postpone departure from the country so as to secure as long as possible an easy living, their sojourn, at best, remained temporary, guided and controlled by duty and self-interest. "To make a fortune and return home was the grand object with all of them."[8] The planters and merchants might dwell for long years in one place, but even they went 'home' at intervals. To the bachelors, the quest for mate, as India could hardly offer much field for choice, to the married with children, not satisfied with the educational facilities and highly concerned about the future of their children, the pretexts to go 'home' were not difficult to find even during the term of service. The military officers were continually moving and so were the officials of the civil hierarchy. Hence, the kaleidoscope of Anglo-Indian society was constantly changing.

Nevertheless, the basic pattern of their life and attitude to the country and its inhabitants was one and uniform, with rare exceptions that proved the rule. The number of visits 'home' and the periods of absence from the country made no difference whatsoever. True, the life of the *Sahibs* in the capital and other big cities showed marked differences when compared with those whom duty obliged to make homes in muffassil towns. Yet, these were differences of degree and not of kind. The *Sahibs* lived a life of comfort and luxury enjoying a standard of living far above, and utterly out of proportion with that of the masses of people overwhelmed with poverty and suffering penury.

The easy manner in which the men and women of the white official world took life, as though the whole universe existed for them, assumed at times rather grotesque and bizarre forms. The caricature of social life of the English officers, both civil and military, at a station not of any outstanding importance, in normal times, drawn in 1860 by George Franklin Atkinson, a captain in the army, is significantly illuminating.[9] Giving appropriately befitting but euphonious appellations to the station and its resident *Sahibs* who evidently were out to eat, drink and be merry, Atkinson professed to describe only the sunny side of the picture of Anglo-Indian life. Calling the station, *Kabob* in the plains of *Dekchi*, the judge, Mr. Turmeric, the magistrate, Mr. Chutney, he talks of the visits by Lords Coriander and Tamarind. Describing different aspects of life, Atkinson touches humorously on the foibles and idiosyncracies of the officers of the station. Wit and humour apart, which is hilarious, even the exaggerated vein of fun does not conceal the basic attitude of the *Sahibs* to the land of their career.

A place where the English settled to stay was known as a station, with its two sections, the cantonment where the troops and the army officers lived and the civil lines where the personnel required to run the civil administration dwelt. The section where the native population swarmed was referred to by the dignitaries of the ruling race as the town or the city. Alluding to the contrast that two parts of an Indian station presented, Russell wrote in 1859:

"Between the two there is a great gulf fixed; to bridge it over is the work reserved for him who shall come to stabilitate our empire in the east, if ever he comes at all. The European station is laid out in large rectangles formed by wide roads. The native city is an aggregate of houses perforated by tortuous paths, so that a plan of it would resemble a section of worm-eaten wood. The Europeans live in detached houses, each surrounded by walls enclosing large gardens, lawns and outhouses ... The natives live in packed and squeezed up tenements, kept from falling to pieces by mutual pressure. The handful of Europeans occupy four times the space of the city which contains tens of thousands of Hindus and Mussalmans."[10]

Lord Beveridge said

"The European quarter is like the electric light. It only throws into deeper shadow the unlighted places."[11]

Among the members of the Anglo-Indian community of the station, strict etiquette was followed observing rigidly the distinction of position and status. At solemn dinners, the lady of the highest rank went away first and it was not considered good etiquette for any one else to make the first move for any reason whatever.

Many resident *Sahibs* knew only that part of India situated within a limited radius of the place where they lived and the road to the nearest port.[12] Utterly ignorant of the surroundings and completely indifferent to them they assumed airs and showed unconcerned conceit. Independently of any official relations, thus, their attitude to Indians was not of a character to inspire confidence. They rarely knew the people of India as such. Their interests were confined only to what touched them and their efforts were limited by what they derived from them. This attitude perhaps could be explained when under the old system of nomination inferior men, as regards diligence and capacity, education and culture, having no openings whatsoever in their own country, crept into the service of this land of tremendous opportunities where, as members of the ruling race they could hold important positions.[13] It was no wonder if such Englishmen with faulty training and imperfect education, fresh from the study of Mill's history, affected a supercilious air of conceit and failed, at times, to maintain a dignified balance.

The change in the mode of recruitment and the introduction of the system of open competition resulted, as was expected, in raising considerably the calibre of the civil servant, but no proportionate change in the attitude that would have been desirable. To the average Englishmen, wherever they might be stationed, life in India continued to be a source of much satisfaction for it meant not only power and prestige, it also implied comfortable living and comparatively affluent circumstances. In big cities like Calcutta, Bombay and other centres of activity in northern India, each *Sahib* lived like a feudal lord with spacious premises furnished on western lines and swarming with trains of servants unheard and undreamt of in the land from which he hailed.[14] There seemed to be some one at the beck and call of all, not only the master and the lady of the house, but some one to dance attendance on the children as also the pets and domestic animals. Russell's graphic description of Anglo-Indian life as he saw it in one of the camps is interesting :

"A luxurious little baby was carried forth for a walk under the shade of the trees ; it was borne in the arms of a fat *Ayah*, besides whom walked a man, whose sole business it was gently to whisk away the flies which might venture to disturb baby's slumbers. Another man wheeled a small carriage in which lay another little lord of Indian creation, asleep likewise with his human flapper by his side, whilst two *Ayahs* followed the procession in rear; through the open door could be seen the lady mother reading for her husband; a native servant fanned her with hand *pankha*; two little terriers, chained to a tree, were under the care of a separate domestic. A cook was busy superintending several pots upon fire in the open air, a second prepared the curry paste, a third was busy with plates, knives and forks. In the rear of the servants tents were two small tents for the *syces*, grass-cutters and camelmen or *doodhwallas*, behind which were picketed three horses, three camels, and a pair of bullocks and ere we left another servant drove in a few goats which were used for milking. I was curious to know who this millionaire could be and was astonished to learn that it was only Capt. Smith."[15]

At the residence of a *Sahib*, the service started right at the entrance where the *darwan* or the gate-keeper occupied a hut so as to be on guard all the time, and it extended to all parts of the house and all hours of day and night. This round the clock service was indeed a luxury, the *Sahibs* could afford in India and that too of the bygone days only.

A peep into an average establishment of an English officer's home in a big city in northern India would surely be interesting. For his personal service, the *Sahib* required a bearer or valet who had an assistant to do subordinate work since the *Sahib* called for attention both like a child as also a royalty. There was a similar set besides, if there was a lady, with an *Ayah* a maid servant to take on the responsibilities. Another bearer or two would be required for the house, besides *chaprasis* or messengers for out-door commissions. Then there had to be a cook who required an assistant as also a steward who bought everything necessary for the house. If the *Sahib* kept a carriage, there had to be a driver, a 'coachman', and for every horse a *syce* or a groom as well as a grass-cutter. A washerman was another necessity and an extra one, if there be a lady, for the fine things. A tailor or more than one, to mend the things, coarse and fine, and to make such articles of apparel as it might not be considered necessary to get from Europe. In summer if the *Sahib* could not go to a hill station for some reason or the other, a number of coolies to pull the '*pankhas*' or fans were needed; *bhishtis* or water-carriers were employed to supply the house all the year round and in summer to keep sprinkling water on the '*khas tatties*' to keep the house cool. If the house happened to have a garden, which it almost always did, one or two *malis* or gardeners were necessary. In case the *Sahib* chose to keep his own conveyance for travelling around, it meant additional servants. In the early part of the mid-century, it was not unusual for an officer to maintain his own travelling equipment such as a *palki* or a palanquin and the necessary staff.[16] The expenses of such an establishment, though considerable, were by no means so great in the then currency as might be supposed. Comforts and luxuries were more easily obtained on a moderately large income in India than in England. One would get less in India out of Rs. 300, but more out of one or two thousands[17] with the result that a person of any consequence in India had usually a considerable number of servants of various kind so that his compound constituted a sort of a village or a small municipality of which he was the chief authority, Lord

Paramount, *Sahib* or the master.[18] The mounting cost of living in the closing decades of the nineteenth century notwithstanding, the account of house-keeping that one reads in the diaries of some of the officers' wives are illustrative of the lavish style in which *Sahibs* lived. Mrs. Robert King who sent home detailed description of her household establishment and the manner in which she ran it, mentioned thirty-two servants at the total wages of Rs. 194 per month only.[19]

List of Servants	*English Equivalent*	*Monthly Wages*
Khansama	Butler	Rs. 10
Khidmadgar	Footman	Rs. 8
Bavarchi	Cook	Rs. 10
Masalchi	Scullion	Rs. 5
Bearer	Valet, etc.	Rs. 10
Mate-bearer	Assistant valet	Rs. 6
Ayah	Lady's maid	Rs. 10
Dhai	Wet nurse	Rs. 10
Mehtarani	Low-caste Ayah or sweepress	Rs. 4
Mehtar	Sweeper	Rs. 5
Dhobi	Washerman	Rs. 13
Bhishti	Water-carrier	Rs. 5
Darzi	Tailor	Rs. 10
Murghiwalla	Fowl-keeper	Rs. 5
Goala	Cow-man	Rs. 5
Chowkidar	Watchman	Rs. 5
Coachman	Coachman	Rs. 8
Syces (Three)	Grooms	Rs. 15
Ghasiaras (Three)	Grass-cutters	Rs. 15
Pankha coolies (six)		Rs. 24
Garden coolies (Two)		Rs. 24
Mali	Gardener	Rs. 6
Total 32		Total Rs. 194

Besides these private servants, she mentions five orderlies in attendance on her husband for official work. But they were government servants. This list of servants varied but slightly according to the circumstances of the officer and place of his service. This was a moderate and rather modest household as compared to many other earlier accounts in which the number of servants mentioned entered three figures.[20]

Women, wives of the officers, on the whole, had the best out of life, in India. Normally, they had no work to do, there being no housekeeping worth the name. A set of servants headed by the *ayah* looked after all their needs and demands from their persons to the wardrobe, the repairs and mending of articles as also the washing of fineries. Generally speaking, they were too indolent even to go out shopping, so the shop came to them. An assortment of goods covering all possible requirements would be carried in a box to the house of the *Sahib* for the lady of the house to choose the articles she needed.[21]

An establishment in a muffassil town followed practically the same pattern though at less cost; it meant larger and more spacious bungalows with huge compounds on one side of which ran rows of houses for the servants and stables for houses and provision for any other needs of the *Sahib*. The living conditions of the servants presented a contrast sharp and even ugly.

"The quadrupeds it must be confessed are as well provided for as bipeds; and as for the *syces* they generally share the horses beds sleeping between the feet of their charges in a manner which appears to be mutually agreeable."[22]

On a tour, an officer's entourage appeared to be a regular caravan transporting the whole outfit in some way or the other. The discription of a District Collector's camp is suggestive of a mobile miniature Mughal Court or brings back the idea of the paraphernalia of the Bourbon Court of the eighteenth century France. The camp provided for every aspect of the Collector's life, private, domestic and official. Speaking of the Collector of Kaira's camp in the Bombay Presidency, Monier-Williams wrote:

"The camp consists of about a dozen tents all under large spreading trees with which the whole park-like country round is beautifully wooded ... Under one mango tree is a large pavilion like erection for the collector and his wife. Then there is another double tent which serves as a dining room and drawing room of ample dimensions, fitted up with carpets, tables, book-cases, easy chairs, sewing machines and harmonium. Two or three others for visitors, another for the baby and its *Ayahs*, another for the Portugese butler and of course a capacious tent with annexees, which together serve for the collector's *Kutchery*, the magisterial court, and other offices."[23]

His description of the stately dinner in the camp, where he was visiting the collector as a guest, is particularly impressive.

"I have a French menu placed before me. I eat a dinner cooked with Parisian skill. I drink wine fit for an emperor and am waited on by a stately butler and half a dozen stately waiters in imposing costumes, who move about with noiseless tread behind my chair and anticipate every eccentricity of my appetite. I am evidently on enchanted grounds and can only think of Aladdin in the Arabian Nights."[24]

It does not by any means indicate that camp life was always easy and comfortable. It only suggests that the *Sahibs* meant to get the best of life, if and when possible. The cost, the labour and the discomfort of the staff involved being no consideration whatsoever.

Life in big cities was definitely on a large and lavish scale—the habits of the city-life being traditionally expensive, and the society in such places being in a whirlpool of great fluctuation—there was not much sociability though there was no dearth of formal parties and entertainment. Official duty, generally speaking, in normal times, being light, evenings were spent at clubs or were occupied by 'At Homes', dances and balls. Gossip, irresponsible chatting, implying scandal-mongering, and light flirtations were indeed the necessary concomitants of such a mode of life. "I am sick to death at times of the vapidity of the Anglo-Indian life and of the stupid talk of the club men" was the reaction of Lord Beveridge to such a life.[25] It was felt by many among them that the Anglo-Indian society composed too exclusively of the servants of the government, civil, military and ecclesiastic, and lacked much of the freshness, variety and intelligence of cultivated societies otherwise constituted.[26] In large cantonments, there was always activity, something 'going on' all the time, even during the hot winds.[27] Sometimes the civilian officers would get together and give a ball to the staff of the Regiments and *vice-versa*.[28] In Calcutta, tennis and badminton parties were popular, exclusively confined to their own ranks and circles originally, the later years of the nineteenth century saw startling changes in the conventional practices. In 1876, at one such party, some Bengali ladies were seen for the first time.[29] Balls arranged in honour of the Governor-General being events of special importance were attended by officers and their wives coming long distances. Parties at the Government House, on occasions such as welcoming the new Governor-General or bidding farewell to the out-going one, were big affairs with all the pomp and show, the ceremonial paraphernalia smacking of royalty. The invitees to such parties comprised high officials—civil and military, princes of the ruling houses and the elite from among the Indians consisting of those who had received titles from the Government in lieu of some service rendered by them, distinguished scholars, men of outstanding abilities, lawyers, advocates, rich merchants and bankers, etc. Many of the princes and rich Indians used such opportunities to flaunt their wealth through expensive costumes and jewels, but went about without getting any notice or honour as guests if not ignored and humiliated. The strict etiquette, the punctilious ceremony, the formal procedure observed at such functions displayed fully the authority of the rulers as well as the callous and wanton extravagance on their amusement.[30]

As for amusements the *Sahibs* made full use of all possible opportunities. Shooting, considered recreation par excellence, engaged the leisure hours of many. A wide variety of this sport was easily available within reasonable distance of a civil station or cantonment though the best chance for shooting was during tours, in camp. Tiger-shooting, hog-hunting and pig-sticking were common; snipe-shooting, though dangerous was enjoyed; polo playing was popular and boating was practised a a good deal.[31] Other games like cricket, quoits, rackets, billiards had their votaries among the energetic while backgammon, cards and chess attracted the more sedentary. Gambling under many different forms was more than prevalent and large sums of money were often staked on very trifling matters, for instance, heads or tails, the longest or shortest straw drawn from a thatched house, high points at cards, high stakes on horses to run at the Derby and betting upon any circumstances that admitted of a bet.[32]

In muffassil towns, the pace of life was much slower, the gaieties simpler though the pattern was no different. Dinner parties would break up earlier, balls would not go on through the night, amateur theatricals as would occasionally induce late hours; a billiard-table at a military mess or elsewhere might keep stray men going till twelve or so, but normally, there being few amusements out of doors to tempt keeping late hours, officers would be back to their premises at a reasonably decent hour.

2.5 Indian Hill Stations : The Haven of the White World

In the hill stations used as summer resorts by the Government—central and provincial—by the army for cantonments, and by others, for purposes of rest and enjoyment, the tone and tempo of life assumed a different colour and pace. The diversity of conditions at the hill stations of northern India, such as Simla, Murree, Mussoorie, Nainital, Darjeeling, Shillong, Pachmarhi and Mount Abu did not by any means change the contours of the *Sahib* culture. It appeared, somehow, to have developed certain traditions and the grooves once formed were followed all over in more or less uniform pattern with only slight variations.[33] Actually, it was at these places that some of the worst foibles of the social life of the white world in India revealed themselves and often received not only disapprobation but definite reproach from all quarters.

Of all the northern Indian hill stations where the worn and weary *Sahibs* thronged for rest and recuperation, Simla and Mussoorie had become centres of special attention, the former primarily on account of its being the summer seat of the Central Government as also that of the Government of the Punjab and the latter perhaps for its easy access and slightly less rigid officialdom which permitted greater freedom and latitude to the young subalterns and the non-official visitors. Not that it curtailed its social rigidity or distinctions. Far from it, a caste system peculiar to them, existed beyond question. Discussing Anglo-Indian society in the mid-nineteenth century, the famous *Times* correspondent D.W.T. Russell wrote :

> "Social distinctions are by no means lost sight of in India. On the contrary they are perhaps more rigidly observed here than at home and the smaller the society the broader are the lines of demarcation. Each man depends on his position in the public service which is the aristocracy and those who do not belong to it are out of the pale, no matter how wealthy they may be or what claims they may advance to the consideration of the world around them ... women depend on the rank of their husbands ... wealth can do nothing for man or woman in securing them honour or precedence in their march to dinner or on their way to supper table or in the dance. A successful speculator or a merchant prince may force his way into good society in England. He may be presented at court and flourish at court halls, but in India he must remain forever outside the sacred barrier which keeps the non-official world from the high society of the services."[34]

Whatever extenuating circumstances may be produced to soften the poignancy of such society, it has not been possible for any supporter or sympathiser to blink completely at the laxity of discipline that prevailed at almost all such centres, particularly those at Simla and Mussorie, reputed for their endless festivity, comic frivolity and to a certain extent light foppery.

> "There can be no more convincing proof of the very lax notions of discipline and decency of these young men than the excesses of their conduct which would not be endured in any place where a sound public opinion existed or indeed any public opinion at all."

Disapproval, definite censure and sometimes even disciplinary action by the authorities led, no doubt, to some betterment of conditions, yet there remained ample scope for improvement of the tone of the Anglo-Indian society throughout the period under consideration. Balls and dinner parties, spiced with gossip, back-biting, light flirtations and long drinking sessions were normal features of the social life of the *Sahibs*, more particularly at hill stations where in the absence of any pressure of work or duty they could aimlessly wander and relax. Although duelling had been considerably checked, gambling still continued to be a favourite source of relaxation, assuming many forms sometimes rather formidable. In Simla in the sixties, '*Loo*' the unlimited brand flourished like a green bay tree in the highest circles. A select coterie would assemble in a private house most evenings and play the game at high stakes. The chits often ran into four figures though the payments were mostly made in kind and seldom in cash. To those who went to Simla seeking enjoyment, wrote W.H. Carry in 1870, amusement was the '*sine qua non and conte que conte*'.[35]

2.6 Attitude Towards Indians

This attitude to life was not peculiar to those who would trek up the heights of mountains for pleasure and then feel justified that they had earned special privilege. It was obvious among the Anglo-Indians as a community all over the country. The self-centred egotistical attitude that the community displayed has not only been admitted, but even disapproved and condemned by many members of the community itself.[36] The utter disregard shown to the best interests of the Indian people, either spiritual or temporal, provided they could achieve their own worldly objectives and leave the country at the earliest was adjudged to be one of the worst features of the European society at Calcutta.[37]

The acceptance of gifts, called *dalis*, from Indians, often subordinates of not much means, on occasions of festivals was common among the *Sahibs*. Interesting accounts of such presents are found in the diaries of officers' wives. Describing Christmas of 1879, Mrs. Robert King wrote :

> "Christmas day was marked by the usual '*dalis*' or offerings of oranges, raisins, apples, almonds, pomegranates, grapes packed between layers of cotton in little round boxes, plantains and other fruit and toys for the boy...."[38]

The recipients of these presents, a subtle form of bribe, no wonder, blinked at a highly undesirable practice prevalent among their servants, the custom of *dastoori*.[39] According to this a certain percentage, two pice in a rupee on the price of the article purchased for the master was allowed by the seller to the servant. This was an open secret and no *Sahib* objected to it. Even when a hawker called trudging and carrying his load to the house he was made by the servants to pay the *dastoori* even though they had nothing to do with the purchase. The hawkers paid it thinking that otherwise they would never be allowed to enter the gate of the bunglow.

It required, perhaps, effort alongwith sterling character and education for men, who enjoyed power and prestige, as members of the ruling party, to keep their poise and not to allow their position and status to get the better of them in regard to their relations with the Indian people. This, however, was rare. With few exceptions, the general attitude of the *Sahibs* to the Indians smacked of official pride, a superiority complex.

The haughty superciliousness, arrogance and even insolence of behaviour which the generality of the English thought it necessary to adopt towards the Indian's by way of keeping their dignity was extremely great. It was not at all uncommon to hear a young Englishman, who had been in India for a year or two, though totally ignorant of the character and language of the Indian people beyond a little Anglo-Hindustani jargon picked up and made up through servants, say that he "hated the natives", that they did not have a single good quality, but possessed almost every bad one.

The use of indecent language was more of general practice than a matter of exception. Commenting on the usual expressions used by the Englishmen, such as, "he liked to beat a black fellow", or "damn these niggers", John Shore wrote:

"In England such a language as this in regard to the inhabitants of any country, particularly if the speaker were a young man, unacquainted with language and customs of that country would procure for him the reputation of an illiberal blockhead or perhaps, worse. But so far from this being the case in India, a man who speaks in this way, of the natives, often has the greater part of the society in his favour and hears himself supported by sundry observations corroborating what he says. A person who does know something of them and consequently does not see so very great a difference between them and himself can only venture to say a word in their favour with the almost certainty of being ill-spoken of by the majority of his countrymen...one would suppose the principle adopted was to treat the people as a degraded inferior race."[40]

This feeling showed itself consciously or unconsciously at every step and pervaded more or less every thought and action of Englishmen in India, not including among them the high level thinkers and planners. Few of them returned the greetings of a native; they could hardly bring themselves round to speak to them civilly.[41] The slightest fault of a servant would lead often, if not as would frequently be the case, to blows, to the most gross abuse... "The language of Billingsgate is in hourly use towards servants in the situation of butlers, footmen and even clerks; and very often for no fault beyond not understanding what their master said who probably spoke unintelligibly."[42] Servants were frequently beaten and turned away without paying their wages for the universal reason and fault alleged that they were insolent. Newspaper reports of the period are full of instances where servants, coolies and *pankha* pullers were beaten cruelly and in many cases fatally.[43] In this respect, the non-official *Sahibs*, on the whole, were more at fault, their conduct being much more objectionable than that of the officials whom they tried to copy.

2.7 Accentuation of Estrangement

The attitude of the average Englishman towards the people of the country did not show any marked improvement throughout the 19th century. If anything, it showed deterioration. Serious and open-minded critics, even among the English, admitted their lack of sympathy with the Indians and pride of superiority. This gradually came to the state that there was no human relationship worth the name between the English and the inhabitants of India,[44] "neither that of master and slave, nor that of patron and client, nor until 1857 even that of open foe—a hard misunderstanding and mutual distrust subsists which but a few individuals on either side can break through."[45] True, the Parsis appeared to be on seemingly better relations, but it was no rapprochment; in fact, there was an actual barrier which neither desired to cross.[46] One important result of the British supremacy firmly and surely established after 1858 and the consequent rapidly diminishing reliance on the Indian agency, was the augmentation of the general contempt of the English towards the people. Unmindful of all the provocation on the part of the governmental authorities and their policies that contributed to the 1857 conflagration, the average English officer and whiteman, felt frustrated and fretted over the effort that had well-nigh shaken the very roots of the so-called British dominions in India. The memories of the excesses, the English thought had been perpetrated on them, not keeping in mind the resultant vindication, embittered still more the relations between the rulers and the ruled with the result that distance between the two was getting more and more stretched.[47]

In fact, things were changing fast. The opening of the Suez Canal, it is said, brought England and India closer only to separate them the more,[48] for as the distance between them shrank from months to days, the European in India became less Indian and more English in all his habits and in all his feelings.[49] With increased facilities for visiting England, English officials grudged every hour of Indian service. Home yearnings increased and their sojourn in India bore more and more the character of an exile affecting adversely their attitude towards the Indian people as a whole. The larger number of Englishmen in India, strangely, led to a 'greater alienation' from the Indians. When they were few, isolated and scattered, they were constrained by force of circumstances to associate with people. But, in proportion as they were able to find companions among their own kins folk, they shrank from all avoidable communication with others.

True, in the upper strata of Indian society, European and Indian, some half-hearted attempts to bring about social intercourse were not wanting, but in the lower ranks of life there were no signs of it, no drawing together real or feigned.[50] Ambitious and pushing Indians naturally desired to keep themselves as much as possible before the eyes of the higher English officials—dispensers of government favours, rewards and honours—and these well paid officials on their part posing as liberal-minded administrators, devoted disinterestedly, heart and soul to the welfare of the country, were constrained to encourage any movement that might reasonably be thought conducive to the welfare and improvement of what, with fine humility, they styled their native fellow subjects. Under the promptings of such people and their efforts, associations were formed for the special object of promoting social intercourse between Europeans and Indians, but their influence remained merely on the surface. These associations would arrange some functions during the year such as garden parties or receptions for the formal get-together of the Europeans and the Indians. A few English officials would attend and respond with pleasant, but condescending civility, the attentions of the Indian gentlemen present. No Hindu or Muslim women would attend these functions. Their absence could, no doubt, be ascribed to the social inhibitions which regulated their society, but even in the case of Christians it was only occasionally that a few Indian Christian ladies would be seen at these mixed gatherings in northern India. A fair attendance of English ladies might be counted upon, all of them, with very rare exceptions, quite unacquainted with the Indian gentlemen amongst whom they moved about with unconcealed indifference during a brief hour or two.[52] The tension and boredom that prevailed at these functions indicated the hollowness of these attempts and the utter lack of sociability. A few Indian gentlemen of high position, Rajas and Maharajas and Nawabs, also made efforts in this direction and extended their magnificent hospitality to highly placed English officers and their ladies. The hosts and male members of the family left no stone unturned to entertain their guests, organising shooting parties, races and sports of all kinds. The Maharaja himself, some of his relatives and high officers of the State might even dance with the English ladies, but no Indian ladies would participate in these festivities.

Business relations often brought the two classes together when both happened to be mutually interested in some special deal. Wealthy businessmen would now and then invite Europeans to their homes to see a *nautch* or perhaps the tricks of Indian jugglers, and on such occasions provide their guests with sumptuous repasts and champagne *ad libitum*. Such parties remained confined to men only.[53] As the century advanced, no doubt, a certain amount of daily intercourse took place between the men of the different races as far as official, professional and commercial life was concerned. In administrative departments of the state, in the universities and colleges, in government, railway and commercial offices, in banks, markets and business places of every kind, Europeans and Indians met apparently as fellow workers. At higher levels, even sports, in which both Europeans and Indian met in friendly rivalry, afforded opportunities, though not very numerous, for the men of the two races to understand and appreciate each other. Nevertheless, the two classes remained far apart. The English officers looked disdainfully on the generality of the educated Indians, who adopted western mannerism and spoke English well.[54] The term 'Bengali Babu', they used for the English educated Indians in Bengal, serving mostly as clerks was far from complimentary.[55] There is enough evidence to indicate that the average Englishman in all spheres, official and non-official, was averse to mixing on intimate terms or on a footing of social equality with the Indians, even of the best class, while

Indians on their part had not the least incentive or the remotest intention of admitting westerners to the intimacy of their home life.

Scant regard was shown to Indian visitors, who would with much difficulty find their way through for it was no easy task to have access to an officer round whom the innumerable attendants formed a formidable barrier which gave way only under the warm pressure of gold or silver. Discourteous language or slighting treatment even to dignitaries like Indian princes was a common practice.[56]

2.8 Relations At Crossroads

The want of consideration for the feelings and opinions of the people of India was very great on the part of the English and appeared to be increasing in the closing years of the century. It appeared as though there was a regular competition among the civil and military officers as to who showed the greatest skill in insulting the Indians. Instances are not wanting when Englishmen would enter mosques or temples without taking off shoes. Should the attendant priests protest, they would be abused and not infrequently beaten. To satisfy their sporting instinct they would go to any length. Often they would be angling in the ponds and rivers considered holy by Brahmans or even go treading on the corn and other crop ripe and ready for harvest while in search of quail.[57] Members of the ruling race, in short, could brook no impediments in the pursuit of their wilful plans for anything. Their arrogance assumed indignant and ludicrous bounds and is eloquent in instances where, they not only expected, but demanded that every Indian should stop while passing by an Englishman to make way and pay homage by greeting courteously. On one occasion an assistant master of a high school in Satara is reported to have been stopped by a military officer, rebuked for not saluting, and given orders that in future it was to be taken as law that he was to greet him. The matter did not end here for trouble arose a few days later when the same military officer objected to the said teacher not saluting properly. He went to the extent of slapping him with the indignant remark, "You must know how to salute a man of the ruling race."[58]

Strangely enough even the collector of the district gave his opinion on the matter that the Indians should salute superior European officials.[59] It would be interesting to note that there had been suggestions earlier in Bengal, of an enactment to this effect. Mr. Agnew's new bill known as the Salaaming and Spitting Act defined the *sahib* as including such persons who were fair in complexion, strong, vested in a coat and pantaloons, enjoying a large pay, possessing the monopoly of all high places in this country and labouring under the influence of "Punchusat Bayoo". The gist of the bill provided :

"Whenever a native meets a *sahib* on the roads and highways, he must *salaam* him. Should the *sahib* not be able to hear this salutation it will be the duty of the native to present himself before the *sahib* and cry out *salaam* in a loud voice. If a native meets a *sahib* on horseback he should run after him and cry *salaam, salaam*. It will be incumbent on all school masters to instruct their scholars in this act every morning before taking up any other subject. Should any person fail to abide by, this act, the *chowkidar* of that man's village shall be liable to imprisonment with hard labour for a term not exceeding six months. Should any school boy neglect to obey this act, the Inspector of Schools belonging to that circle shall be sentenced to transportation for life."[60]

With the coming of the trains, the white world had still another field in which they could show their whiteness in its absolute crystal form. Indeed it was when travelling that the east and the west were treading on each other's toes. Indians met with a great deal of rudeness from the English who resented the intrusion of a native into their carriage.[61] Reservation of compartments for the *sahibs* was a normal practice, but if an Indian happened, per chance to board it, he would immediately be ejected under most humiliating conditions with such remarks, "I say guard there is a native in this compartment; he must go somewhere else".[62] Even big dignitaries were not spared. It was common to find at railway stations seats and water closets bearing the inscription 'For Natives' while others were marked 'Gentlemen', which signified a European. The treatment meted out to the coolies and labour employed by the indigo and tea-planters, to say the least, was appalling Press reports of the period are full of cases where the white man committed inhuman and unreasonable assaults on the poor labourer for minor lapses and did not spare even women workers whose honour and chastity were not infrequently violated.[63] The saddest part of the situation was that the much eulogised law under the British regime had no relief to offer. If anything, it afforded preferential treatment to the Anglo-Indians since there were special provisions to deal lightly with the Anglo-Indian offenders, whose derelictions, acts of ommission and commission were lightly blinked at.[64] With very few exceptions the Anglo-Indian offenders either escaped scot free or with a most inadequate and ridiculous punishment.[65] Curiously enough even the highest authorities acknowledged, on occasions, the failure of law to administer justice to the sufferer where the offender happened to be an Anglo-Indian. But beyond the sympathetic regrets there were no practical amends. In fact, attempts at bringing about equality before law were highly resented.

The introduction of the Ilbert Bill in 1882 was in a way an acknowledgement of the anomalies that existed, a step to rectify certain wrongs; an effort to create a slightly more amiable atmosphere. But the uproar from the Anglo-Indian community with which they protested against the measure, suggesting equality before the law for all, got the better of the good sense with which the higher level statesmen alone could be credited. The members of the ruling race in India proved once and for all that even they ridiculed and contemptuously derided the groupings in the Indian society. They, on their own part, suffered from complexes of a somewhat similar nature. They stood as one solid block above all others, impregnable and impervious. As far as their interests and privileges were concerned they were to be considered sacrosanct. Whatever equality before the law had to be established was to be confined exclusively to the subject people only. The rulers as a group were not to be touched. They formed, thus, a community among others, with distinctions of class, caste, creed, race and language of perhaps less pronounced nature and may be on a different basis. They stood cemented as one compact unit for the simple reason that they were in a foreign country as conquerors. Being attached in some way or the other to the governmental machinery, organised to keep the country in subjection, they shared the common objective.

One section of the community of *sahibs*, the missionaries, appeared to make some amends for the general lack of sympathy and warmth towards the Indians. Although their objective, evangelisation, could hardly be concealed, the fact remains that their willingness to serve the poor and the suffering endeared them to the people with whom they came into contact. They found it easy to mix with them and to move among them. In this regard, the women missionaries were able to cross hurdles which appeared to be insurmountable barriers to men.[66] Lady doctors and women teachers, with their pleasing dispositions, winning manners, courteous behaviour and sympathetic attitude found admission into the homes of the Indians at different levels, rich and poor, even orthodox, who were most unwilling to allow members of the fair sex from their families to step out or be exposed to outsiders.[67] It was only with diligent efforts and persistent endeavour that ladies of Christian missions were able to induce Indian women to let them impart knowledge of the three Rs or teach needle-work or make them interested in some hobbies or handicrafts. Some European ladies of the highest position took the initiative to have contacts with Indian women by holding receptions exclusively for them and organising functions to draw them out.

References

1. Ward, Vol. 1. p. 461; Strachey, p. 2; Lyall, p. 152.
2. Campbell (1852), p. 36.
3. Shore, pp. 10-12 ; Russell, William Haward. pp. 105, 160; Monier-Williams (1878), p. 176; Muller, pp. 34-35.
4. Del Mar p. 3; *Census Report 1901*, p. 80; Fuller, p. 196.

5. Temple, 'Richard' pp. 60-53.
6. Temple, 'Richard' p. 56; Fuller, p. 203.
7. Del Mar p. 3; Cox, p. 11.
8. Nolan, (1878-79) Vol. III, p. 521.
9. Atkinson, 2, 3, 6
10. Russell, William Haward p. 180; Monier-Williams, (1878) p. 176.
11. Beveridge, William Henry, p. 354.
12. Del Mar : p. 3.
13. Temple, Richard p. 45.
14. Blanchard, p. 35 ; Buyers, p. 55.
15. Russell, William Haward, pp. 159-160.
16. Blanchard, pp. 38-39.
17. Blanchard, p. 45.
18. Buyers, p. 55.
19. King, Vol. 1, p. 129.
20. Acland, pp. 8-9.
21. Ibid.
22. Blanchard, p. 46.
23. Monier-Williams, (1878), p. 31.
24. Ibid.
25. Beveridge, William Henry, p. 251.
26. Sleeman, p. 586.
27. *Calcutta Review 1857*, p. 16.
28. King, p. 36.
29. Duff, p. 173.
30. Nolan (1878-79), Vol. III, pp. 516-18.
31. Thomson, F.S. p. 125.
32. McCosh, p. 174.
33. Temple, 'Richard' p. 12.
34. Buck, Edward John, p. 207-8.
35. Ibid., p. 209.
36. Cotton, J.H.S., pp. 14 and 22 ; Digby, pp. 2-3 ;
37. Buyers : p. 56.
38. King, Vol. II, p. 23.
39. Hunter, *Rural life in Bengal*, p. 71.
40. Shore, Vol. I, p. 11.
41. Report on Native Press, Bengal, 1883, *Samaya*, May 28th ; Also Report on Native Papers, Punjab. 1889, *Durbin*, June 11 th.
42. Shore, John, Vol. I, p. 11 ; Now rozjee Furdoonji : A paper read before the London Branch of the National Indian Association in Aid of Social Progress in India, January 24, 1874, pp. 3-5.
43. Report on Native Press, Bengal, 1883, *Sohkh-i-Oudh*, 1st February 1883. Also, *Samaya*, January 28, 1884.
44. Oman, p. 72; Also, Report on Native Papers, Punjab, 1881, *Durbin* 18th June, 1889 : Digby, pp. 1-3.

45. Bell (1859), p. 54.
46. Russell, William Haward, p. 105.
47. Bell (1859), p. 43 ; Cotton H.J.S., pp. 44-45.
48. Cotton, H.J.S. p. 44.
49. Strachey, p. 17.
50. Oman (1907), p. 229 ; Report on Native Press. Bengal, 1880, *Sadharani*, 15th February 1880, p.8.
51. Oman, (1907), p. 229.
52. Oman, (1907), pp. 229-30.
53. Oman, (1907), p. 231.
54. Cotton, H.J.S., p. 58.
55. Bose, pp. 190-91.
56. Shore, Vol. I, p. 12.
57. Shore, Vol. I, p. 12-14.
58. Report on Native Papers, Bombay, *Mahratta*, 24th April, 1898. p. 22.
59. Report on Native Press, Bombay *Indu Prakash*, 28th April; 1898. *Dhyan Prakash*, 27th April.
60. Report on Native Press Bengal, 1871, p. 4, para 22.
61. Elwin, p. 228.
62. Report on Native Papers Bengal 1887, *Som Prakash*, p. 895; *Sanjivani*, 11th June, 1887, p. 625; Also, Report on Native Papers, Bombay, 1876, *Dnyanodaya*, 27th July, 1876.
63. Report on Native Papers Bengal, 1877, *Hindu Ranjika*, 21st March. p. 2 ; also, Bengal 1887, *Sahchar*, 9th November, p. 1141 ; also Bombay, 1871, *Native Opinion*, 7th May ; also Punjab 1897, *Paisa Akhbar*, 11th December, p. 1050.
64. Report on Native Papers Bengal 1883, 8th January : also 1887, *Srimant Sadagar*, 19th August, p. 898 ; also, Bombay 1890; The *Bombay Samachar*, 6th August 1890, p. 9 ; also Punjab 1890, p. 307, *Khair Khwah-i-Kasamir*, 10th August, 1890.
65. Dennis, Vol. III, pp. 108-11.
66. Dennis, Vol. III, pp. 108-11.
67. Oman (1907), p. 234.

3. The Subjugated Indian People : An Enigma to the Ruling Class

    3.1 India : An Enigma to the Western World
    3.2 Northern India : A Physiognomical Kaleidoscope
    3.3 Varieties of Indian Dress
    3.4 Diversity in Languages
    3.5 The Land of Many Religions
        3.51 The Hindus
        3.52 The Buddhists
        3.53 The Jains
        3.54 The Sikhs
        3.55 The Muslims
        3.56 The Parsis
        3.57 The Christians
        3.58 The Ascetics
    3.6 Some Salient Distinctions of Religious Groups
    3.7 The Unifying Force of Social Institutions
    3.8 Pattern of Urban Life
    3.9 Pattern of Rural Life

In contradistinction to the small Anglo-Indian ruling class, there was the vast mass of people—The Indians, the ruled—an immensely mixed multitude at different stages of material and moral growth as also of intellectual and cultural achievement living in rural and urban areas. The people of India, in the latter half of the nineteenth century, presented a picture of extraordinary diversity in almost every respect.

3.1 India : An Enigma to the Western World

To the westerners, the Indian expanse of land covering some 1,766,597 sq. miles involving all possible varieties of climate and physical conditions with their effects upon the dense population ranging between two to three hundred million souls during the period of purview had always been an enigma. It was difficult for them to comprehend the unique composition of the heterogeneous Indian populace exhibiting varieties of race, creed, language, custom and mores. The extreme reactions were commonly noticed among them. The ordinary untravelled European, on first arriving in India, found it difficult to distinguish people of one part of the country from another. To his untrained eye all Indians appeared to be alike.[1] On the other hand, a discerning eye could spot nothing else but diversity, dissimilarity and multiplicity. The fact, however, is that truth lurks somewhere between these two extremes.

True, India during the period 1850-1900 presented, as it does even now to a certain extent a diversity unknown and unseen in any other part of the world. A traveller in northern India would, indeed, have been struck by an all-round variety more conspicuous than what he would have found while travelling through Europe. The differences between the Dutch and the Greeks or the Spaniards and the Germans, would not have appeared to be as pronounced as those between the Punjabis and the Bengalis or between the Rajasthanis and the Assamese or between the inhabitants of the North West Frontier Provinces and the Gujaratis. The very immensity of the distances in India with its varying physical conditions accounts to a certain extent for the variety exhibited by its people.

Her long history and the influx of different races at different times through the millennia and the consequent inevitable intermingling, although restricted, explains further some of its diversities. But the fact that race has a great resisting power appears at the same time to have added much to the complexities in India, by qualifying the general dictum that man is the product of his surroundings with the result that the qualities and peculiarities of the race persisted in many cases in the face of adverse circumstances. By a rigid prohibition of inter-marriage, the races that constituted the population of India had maintained some of their distinctive characteristics and despite the fact that they had lived side by side with each other for centuries, they had preserved some of their individuality. Nevertheless, India had stamped them with a common seal and had wrought out a "recognisable type amid a great profusion of species."[2] The underlying similarity that ran through the apparent diversity has, however, been generally overlooked and stress is mostly laid on dissimilarity. Yet, "the more one studies the subject, the more identity one finds in the state of things in all the different parts of India."[3]

The people of northern India, an area most densely populated, containing more than half the total population of the country during the later half of the nineteenth century, shared all the complexities of the population as a whole and displayed differences of a varied nature. A gathering of people from the different parts of northern India would certainly have appeared a motley host of diverse types. Stressing the points of difference only, there would be no end to the process of splitting them into small groups. A few striking lines of dissimilarity will elucidate the heterogeneous character of the people. They could be grouped under heads based on differences of a varied nature such as physical appearance and dress, forms of human speech, profession of faith and mode of living. This grouping, however, could, at best, be of a very rough and general nature. No strict and rigid lines could be

THE SUBJUGATED INDIAN PEOPLE 41

drawn either for types or localities in which they were found or the languages they spoke. Nor could creeds or customs be strictly associated with particular localities or languages. All groups appeared somewhere to be overlapping or merging into each other.

3.2 Northern India : A Physiognomical Kaleidoscope

The most obvious differences which would strike even a casual visitor were those of physical types, the costumes they wore and the languages they spoke. The variety of physical appearance due partly to differences of climate and environment and partly to racial admixture gave a unique picturesqueness to the population. Differences in stature, features and appearance, such as shapes of head and nose, colour of hair and shades of complexion from fair to dark produced an interesting medley spread all over northern India. A great deal of attention has been given by skilled observers to classifying and grouping the different physical types. Seven main types are generally accepted as to make up the people of India specimens of which, were found scattered in Northern India.[4]

1. Beginning with the extreme north, the part which came to be known as the North West Frontier Province, the people mainly represented the Turko-Iranian type and could be easily recognised by their distinctive features—stature above mean ; complexion fair, eyes mostly dark, but occasionally grey, head broad, nose narrow, prominent and very long. Normally, they were not found in other parts of the country.
2. Kashmir, Punjab and Rajputana showed a striking type, the Indo-Aryan with stature mostly tall, complexion fair, eyes dark, hair on face plentiful, head long, nose narrow and prominent. They could be spotted as a distinct group anywhere.
3. People in the western parts of India had their own special features of the Scytho-Dravidian type—broad heads, fair complexion, nose moderately fine, hair on face rather scanty and stature medium.
4. A good part of the region including United Provinces of Agra and Oudh, parts of Rajputana and Bihar had the Aryo-Dravidian type scattered all over. They showed their own curious combination of features. Their head form was long with a tendency to medium ; their complexion varied from light brown to black; the nose ranged from medium to broad and the stature rather short.
5. The lower and eastern parts of Bengal, Assam and Orissa showed a different type, the Mongol-o-Dravidian. Their medium stature with broad head, complexion dark, hair on face usually plentiful, nose medium with a tendency to broad, gave the people in these parts of northern India, a distinctive appearance of their own.
6. The hill areas at the foot of the Himalayas, from north-west to north-east, had yet another type, the Mongoloid, with equally distinctive features, such as broad head, dark complexion with a yellowish tinge,

hair on face scanty, stature small, nose fine to broad, face characteristically flat and eyelids often oblique. These people could be recognised as hill people in any mixed crowd anywhere.

7. The parts bordering on the two regions, the northern and southern, showed still another variety, the Dravidian type. Although this group was mainly confined to the southern parts of the country, yet they were found sprinkled in other areas also such as Central Provinces, parts of Bihar and most of Central India. They could be easily picked from any medley for their short stature dark complexion, approaching almost black, hair plentiful with an occasional tendency to curl, eyes dark, head long and nose very broad.

It would be interesting to note that while a purely ethnical grouping was not possible, the said physical types could be distinguished from each other in the roughly defined areas. But they could not, however, be always kept distinct. In fact, they melted into each other, insensibly and imperceptibly while passing from one part of northern India to another, though, where exactly the transformation took place could never be determined. Again, the different types enunciated had nothing whatsoever to do with religion or language. The fact that a person was of any particular type or a blend of types was no certain guide to his creed or tongue. They were all, curiously enough, mixed up, not only with physical environments, but also with the social strata. The fair skinned with sharp features having a sort of aroma about them were considered the higher classes while the dark complexioned flat featured forming the lower levels.

3.3 Varieties of Indian Dress

The variety in physical appearance became more pronounced because of the variety of dress. The traditional costume of the people in India was simple consisting of three unsewn pieces of cloth—the loincloth or *dhoti*, the *shawl* or *chaddar* and the turban. This simple dress was commonly worn by the orthodox throughout the country with minor variations in different localities, particularly in the form of the *dhoti*, differing in its length and voluminousness from province to province and in some ways with communities, etc. In towns and cities, among the upper classes, generally, the *shawl* had given place to the more convenient coat which began to be made in European style, fitted with buttons and provided with pockets and could be long or short. In its original form it was fastened with tapes.[5] But perhaps the most striking differences of costume between one part of the region and another were in the shape and colour of the turban.[6]

In the North West Frontier where Afghan fashions prevailed men wore very baggy trousers and covered their heads with a large turban folded round a conical skull cap.[7] In the Indo-Gangetic plain the turban was smaller and often discarded for a small rounded cap of muslin. In the eastern parts, Bengal, Orissa and Assam many went bare-headed. The style and the type of the dhoti also changed, in that it became voluminous. In the western parts, the turbans were mostly coloured. Among the Mahrattas they were coloured as well as of a very large size and of peculiar shape somewhat of a cart-wheel shape. In Gujarat and Rajasthan also, men wore bright-coloured turbans, though they were smaller in size and in winding were given a peculiar twist.[8]

Among the Hindu and the Parsi women, the typical garment was the *sari*, a long piece of cloth some five yards in length. It was wrapped round the waist with a loose end carried round in a variety of ways over the head so as to form a hood. Among the higher castes a bodice was also worn. Parsi women wore silk vest with short sleeves called *kanchari* or *choli*. They also observed a peculiar customs of tying a thin white cloth on their heads called '*mathabana*' or head-binder thus concealing the hair completely. Village women wore a skirt petticoat in place of the *sari* and wrapped a broad scarf or a *shawl* or a *chaddar* to cover the upper part of the body. Muslim women wore either long *pyjamas* or skirts, speaking generally, according to the upper or the lower classes they belonged to. The children among all were rarely clad before the age of eight or nine.[9]

On the whole, the Indian costume, despite the many specific varieties had a generic resemblance. Plain and simple ordinarily, on festivals a gay crowd in some parts of the region, say near Banaras or Lahore or Jaipur, with its sea of turbaned heads would present a brilliant and varied mass of colour. Among the upper and middle classes "on gala occasions the dresses were quite resplendent with gorgeous colour."[10] The aristocracy, consisting of the princes of the ruling houses and the *Rajas* and *Nawabs*, etc., needless to say, were most extravagant and flashy in their dress and adornment, particularly at public functions.

3.4 Diversity in Languages

Broadly speaking the different types among the people represented the principal races of the world and indicated the effects of the successive influx and admixture even though it had been in a limited and restricted manner. The diverse races had maintained not only some of their distinctive features of physiognomy, but had also retained in many cases, their tribal language causing thus a diversity which far surpassed that of physical appearance. Linguistic affinity among people, divided by other prejudices, racial and sectarian, served, however, as a unifying force and formed the basis of another set of groups. The decennial census reports of the period lay great stress on the variety of languages and enumerate several families of human speech prevalent in northern India. To a traveller across northern India in any direction, the polyglot people might well have appeared a babel of sounds, highly baffling, for the form of speech changed within short distance, even though the change was largely dialectic.[11]

The identification of the boundaries of a language is not an easy matter anywhere. In fact, it is impossible to circumscribe a language by any bounds of region or ascribe it strictly to any group of people and "in a huge country like India, with a long stretch of history and civilisation" it is much less so. As a rule, unless separated by great ethnic differences or by some natural obstacle such as a range of mountain or a large river, Indian languages merged into each other as they do even now and could not be separated by any hard and fast line of demarcation. Nevertheless, certain languages could be associated with certain people in certain areas though they could neither be taken as guides to race or religion, nor could they be taken to indicate any set pattern. The vagaries of language were just confounding. In one locality, sometimes, more than one languages were spoken. In the district of Malda, in Bengal, for instance, there were certain villages where three languages were spoken. The village tribes had, however, evolved a kind of *lingua franca* for themselves to facilitate inter-communication while each adhered to its tongue for conversation among its fellows.[12]

Again, in many parts, the same language was spoken by people professing different religions, for instance, Punjabi in Punjab, Bengali in Bengal, Kashmiri in Kashmir. The religion of the speaker would sometimes be revealed when any reference to God or allied subjects came up and the terms used changed such as *Ram* by the Hindus and *Allah* by the Muslims. The tribal names of the dialects prevalent in certain areas were also no index to special tribes or races, there being several instances where the name of the language spoken by the people had no connection with the tribe to which they belonged. In the hills north of Murree in the Punjab, for example, there were a number of dialects varying according to locality. One of the important tribes living in these hills was the *Chibb*, who spoke the dialect of the place where they lived and not necessarily the Chibhali language. The term was employed to mean the language of the hills of Murree and *Chibbs* were not the only tribe who spoke it.[13] Such instances can be cited from different parts of northern India. Notwithstanding the confounding vagaries of language, the people of certain areas were associated with certain languages, a vast majority of which belonged to the Indo-Aryan family of which the Sanskritic group predominated.

The people of the North West Frontier Province, in the extreme north spoke Pashto akin to Persian and those on the outer fringe on the north west spoke Baloch. Leaving the frontier districts and entering Punjab one would hear the people speaking another language *Lhanda*, in many forms. Akin to Sanskrit, it assumed still more dialectic variations in Sindh.[14] Thence eastward, down the Indo-Gangetic Plain to a line some distances within the frontier of Bengal proper on one side and Gujarat on the western side, the people spoke varying dialects of Hindi such as **Braj, Kanauji, Purabi, Awadhi, Bhojpuri, Newari,**

Bagheli, Chhatisgarhi, etc. and Hindustani, which when it abounded in Persian words was termed Urdu and was commonly considered the Muslim form of it.[15]

East of the Hindi area in Bengal, the language of the people was Bengali, closely akin to which were Assamese and Oriya, spoken in Assam and Orissa, parts to the east and south of Bengal. Passing through the central parts to the south of Indo-Gangetic Plain and moving to western regions one would hear Marathi. Reaching Gujarat there would be heard Gujarati with its dialects. Thence moving up northwards to Kashmir through an easterly route, one would meet with people in Rajasthan and Kashmir speaking Rajasthani and Kashmiri respectively with many dialects. The hill people at the foot of Himalayas and the north-eastern parts had their assortment of languages. Of these some belonged to the Indo-Tibetan family and some to the Indo-Chinese.[16] The inhabitants in the areas bordering the northern and southern regions of the country spoke languages of the Dravido-Munda family.[17]

The baffling linguistic variety notwithstanding, it is interesting to note that speaking Hindustani abounding in either Hindi or Urdu words was understood more or less throughout northern India. Capable of being written both in Persian and Devnagari characters and without purism, avoiding alike the excessive use of either Persian or Sanskrit words, Hindustani a modification of Hindi and Urdu served as a bond of union. Being a highly composite form of speech it reflected the composite character of the people.

As the century rolled and English education spread, English was becoming the language of yet another group—the educated, a group that was small, but scattered all over the region and was growing fast both in numbers and in importance, especially in towns and cities where much of the official work was done in English.

3.5 The Land of Many Religions

The chief bond of union among the diverse people, however, was religion which served as the basis of the most important set of groups but which did not necessarily correspond with either of race or language. India was, during the period of study, as it is even now, the home of many faiths. "There is no land comparable with India in the variegated expression of its beliefs which add picturesqueness to the country and diversity to the people."[18] It may, however, be asserted that Hinduism and Islam were the two main religions of the people, Up to 1881 even the census was conducted on this basis.[19] It was only in the closing decades of the nineteenth century that stress began to be laid on efforts to find out the minor differences of faith and modes of worship, though it did not alter in any substantial manner the position of the religious groups.

3.51 THE HINDUS

Although some variation is found in the numbers during the period of study, Hinduism stood unquestionably as the religion of the majority in India. Of the total population of India at the close of the nineteenth century, it claimed no less than 207 million votaries. In other words, it was professed in one or other of its multifarious forms by 70% of the people.[20] It predominated practically everywhere except in the most inaccessible tracts in the heart and on the outskirts of India where it had hitherto either failed to subjugate the earlier faiths of the aborigines or succumbed soon to the reforming zeal of its own followers or later still failed to combat the proselytising forces of more aggressive faiths such as Islam and Christianity.[21] In northern India, it was only in the Punjab and the North Western Frontier Province where it was the faith of less than half the population, being 40.74% only. In Bengal where its followers were found in the largest number being 45, 452, 806, they did not, however, form the largest proportion to the total population which was 65.37% only. An overall picture of northern India does, nonetheless, show that the Hindus were in the majority. Their numerical strength province-wise was in the following order :

Rajputana 87.50%; North Western Frontier Province 86.27%; Baroda 84.80%; Central India 84.22%; Ajmer 81.62%; Central Provinces States 81.02%; Bombay States 79.62%; North West Province States 77.68%; Central Provinces 74.80%; Bengal 65.37%; Assam 62.74%; Punjab States 54.94%; Punjab 40.74%.

Basically rational and highly intellectual, Hinduism founded on the *Vedas* with their *Brahmans* and *Upanishadas*, rested on a series of post-Vedic sacred literature, chiefly the laws of Manu, the *Ramayana* and *Mahabharata* and the *Puranas*. Unbound by any dogmatic code or rigid tenets it had over the millennia evolved to be largely a social system, highly accomodating, absorbing readily the rites and superstitions of others and finding cheerfully, among its divinities, place for other strange gods. Excepting the less ignorant who constituted a comparatively very small proportion of the community, the religion of the masses of the Hindus might more properly be termed Brahmanism. Having degenerated considerably it had little resemblance with the Hinduism described in ancient Sanskrit literature, some in broad outline. The basis of the whole fabric appeared to be divine rights of the Brahmans making it a highly complicated sacerdotalism.

To the westerners it is inconceivable that there be a religious system like that of the Hindus, with no single founder, no high priest such as the Pope, no authoritative council to pronounce decisions or prescribe rites, no organised community and no ecclesiastical capital. And yet its is in all this that there lay the strength and potency of Hinduism. It gradual growth, reflected in the vast, but rather disjointed sacred writings, equipped it with a compromising faculty and a unique catholicity and elasticity. In the words of Monier-Williams, Hinduism in the prevalent form during the period was like

"an ancient overgrown fabric with no apparent unity of design—patched, pieced, restored and enlarged in all directions inlaid with every variety of ideas, and although looking as if ready at any moment to fall into ruins, still extending itself so as to cover every hole and corner of available ground, still holding its own with great pertinacity and still keeping its position securely because supported by a hard foundation of Brahmanism and caste."[23]

Then there were certain groups of people professing faiths closely allied with Hinduism. According to the *Census Report of 1901*, there were some $8\frac{1}{2}$ million souls who were supposed to follow faiths for which it was difficult to find an appropriate name though it was taken to be the oldest of the religions. The medley of heterogeneous and uncomfortable superstitions representing it were denoted by the name, animism—the amorphous collection of crude and confused conceptions.[24] It had also been referred to earlier by the term fetishism—the worship of tangible inanimate objects believed to possess in themselves some kind of mysterious power.

The animists were found to be gradually falling under the influence of Hinduism which on account of its accomodating and elastic tenets could easily be stretched and extended. In fact, it was found difficult to determine where animism ended and Hinduism began. Being the faith, primarily of the ignorant, animism had adherents in almost all the religious groups. Actually, the masses in many cases had two religions, one to profess, the other to practice. The largest number of animists, some one-thirds of the total, were found in Bengal, more than one-fifths in Central Provinces, one-eighths in Assam, one-ninths in Central India Agency and very small proportion comprising some 100,000 of them in Rajputana. In proportion to the total population, the animists were most numerous in Assam and Central Provinces. In Bengal, the proportion for the province at large was only one in 29, but in the tracts where they were chiefly found, it was much higher, and in two districts of Chhota Nagpur nearly half the population was thus classed.

3.52 The Buddhists

Then there were the a faiths which had apparently dissented from the Hinduism. Of these Buddhism was one of the earliest. Its followers, the Buddhists, had been, during the period of study, reduced tremendously, both in numbers as also in influence, almost to a non-entity.[25] They were found sprinkled in certain parts of north-western and north-eastern India mainly in parts of the Himalayan and Sub-Himalayan areas. Some 237,893 adherents were found in north Bengal on the borders of Nepal Bhutan and Sikkim in places such as Darjeeling and Jalpaiguri. In parts of Bengal they were for the most part immigrants from China. The only professed Buddhists of local origin were found among a small colony of Saraks in the tributary states of Orissa whose number was less than 1,000. In Assam, there were some 9,000 Buddhists many of whom were cold weather visitors from Bhutan. The Punjab had some 7,000 Buddhists in the Himalayan area in the north east chiefly in Spiti, Lahaul and Kinnaur where many of the inhabitants were of Tibetan origin. In the Himalayan districts of the United Provinces, Buddhism was conspicuously non-existent. It is a striking fact that only three Buddhists were registered in Garhwal and 217 in Almora at the end of the century. The comparatively higher number of Buddhists, 35,000 in Kashmir, were found mainly in the province of Ladakh. The religion practised by the Buddhists in these areas had deflected much from its pristine form and had assumed a pattern much more debased and superstitious than the parent religion against which centuries before it had revolted.

3.53 The Jains

Belonging originally to the same period as that of the Buddhists and having close affinities with them there was another group, the Jains. Having lost much of their importance and influence they were in many parts prone to describe themselves as Hindus. Of their total numerical strength of $1\frac{1}{3}$ million at the close of the nineteenth century, some were found in Bombay and the adjoining state of Baroda, 27 percent in Rajputana, $8\frac{1}{2}$ percent in Central India and over 6 percent in United Provinces. The rest were scattered in other parts of Northern India. Punjab had a fair share of this sprinkling, but Bengal and Bihar where the faith had originated were singularly devoid of any representation and so was Orissa.

3.54 The Sikhs

The Sikhs, originally a small religious sect, dissenting from the Brahmanic Hindu religion, being theoretically monotheists, who did not believe in idolatry and caste distinction, had in course of time assumed importance other than religious, having developed martial qualities and acquired political significance. Easily distinguished as such from any mass anywhere by their distinctive characteristics, long hair and beards, iron bangle and steel quoit, the Sikhs were mainly found in the land of their birth, the Punjab. Of their strength 2,195,339 at the end of the nineteenth century all but 64,352 were confined to their homeland, the rest being scattered in Kashmir, United Provinces and Sindh.[26] The line between Hinduism and Sikhism was vague and often members of the same family were found to be followers of these two different faiths without in any way affecting the amicable family or social relationship. The separatist tedencies among them became more distinct when in the military service stress was laid by the authorities on small ceremonies and rites such as that of initiation to be performed by the Sikhs.

Besides these faiths allied to Hinduism, representing the voice of reform in the past from the remotest times, new groups were coming into being, drawing inspiration from western thought and claiming votaries of considerable numerical strength from among the educated Hindus. Of these, the followers of Brahmo Samaj mainly in Bengal and of Arya Samaj in the Punjab and United Provinces were notable.

3.55 The Muslims

The second major religious group was that of the Muslims. The total number of the votaries of Islam came to be about $62\frac{1}{2}$ millions, the largest aggregation of the adherents of the faith under any one dominion[27], and the bulk of them was found in northern India.[28] They were most numerous in North West India and in the eastern districts of lower Bengal. On the whole, the province of Bengal contributed $25\frac{1}{2}$ million; Punjab and Frontier Province 14 million; and the United Province 7 million; Bombay contained $4\frac{1}{2}$ million; Kashmir had $2\frac{3}{4}$ million; while Assam had $1\frac{3}{4}$ million. In proportion to the total population, Islam appeared to be most strongly represented in Kashmir where it was the religion of 74 percent of the inhabitants; next came the Punjab with 53 percent, Bengal with 32 percent, Assam with 26 percent, Bombay 18 percent, and United Provinces with 14 percent. The proportions, however, were not uniform, their being thick pockets in certain parts. For instance, in Bengal half the total number of Muslims were found in the eastern parts where two-thirds of the population were of this faith compared with only $9\frac{1}{2}$ percent in the south Bihar, $4\frac{1}{2}$ percent in Chhota Nagpur and $2\frac{1}{2}$ percent in Orissa. Some Muslims being of foreign origin showed it in their features, but the vast majority were the descendants of Indian converts mainly from the lower strata of the Hindus. Although the Muslims were a closely knit group with a definite and dogmatic religion, the vast majority of them, particularly the agricultural population among them was nominally Muslims. They were as fanatical as they were ignorant. Like the masses of any community, they had hardly any knowledge of the pure tenets and principles of their religion. For all practical purposes their religion was a compound of animistic superstitions and Hindu customs. They were as much imbued with caste prejudices as their Hindu brethren. In the Punjab, where rural society was organised on the tribal system, it was a common thing to find one section of the tribe to be Hindu, and the other Muslim.[29] In the towns and the cities and among the educated classes, the religion of the Muslims, however, was comparatively less affected by the Hindu practices and superstitions.

3.56 THE PARSIS

The followers of Zoroastrianism, worshippers of fire, the Parsis formed yet another group. Numerically a small minority, they had, on account of the rigidity of their dogmas and relentlessness of their customs, maintained the purity of their community which, curiously enough, showed some increase in their ranks during the period of survey.[30] Between 1881 and 1891, for instance, they increased by 5.3 percent yet their total strength at the end of the nineteenth century did not touch one hundred thousand. Numbering only 9,400, of whom all but 7,000 were in Bombay,[31] the Parsis, nevertheless, were a notable group known to contribute to the industrial, commercial and public life of the country in an infinitely greater measure than their proportion to the total population. Successful as businessmen to an unsurpassable degree, they had thus acquired an influence far beyond their numbers during the period of study, specially in Bombay where philanthropy and education owed greatly to them. Largely influenced by the Hindus of the western parts of India, where they had settled after their exodus from Persia. Their religious practices and social usages, generally speaking, showed close affinity with those of the Hindus. However, they responded more readily and cheerfully to western education. The closing decades of the ninteenth century saw them taking rapid strides towards change, save in one prejudice, the invidiousness of their race. Forming the vanguard of the advanced sections of society, adopting western ways of life, the higher classes among the Parsis appeared to be a group closely akin to Christians, half-way between the Europeans and the indigenous populace while the less fortunately placed among them continued to be more like their Hindu brethren.[32]

3.57 THE CHRISTIANS

Then there were the Christians, forming a group which numbered some 2,923,241 at the close of the century in the whole country. About one-third of the total strength was found in northern India and of these they were most numerous in Bengal. Their distribution, however, was most uneven. The majority of the Christians being converts from the lower strata of the Hindus and the poorer sections of the Muslims they mostly formed pockets in areas where the Christian missionaries were active. Half the Indian Christians of the eastern parts were thus found in one district of Chhota Nagpur, Ranchi, where Luthran, Roman Catholic and Anglican missions were busily engaged among the aboriginal tribes. Bombay accounted for 220,000 of whom 181,000 were Indians ; United Provinces had 103,000 Christians of whom 69,000 were Indians ; of the 72,000 Christians in the Punjab only 39,000 were Indians ; Assam had some 36,000 of whom 34,000 were Indians.[37]

3.58 The Ascestics

While all these religious groups had their respective sects, rites and priests they also had an interesting *'non-official'* personnel—the ascetics which formed a familiar group in any Indian scene. The ascetics covered a variety of devotees and mendicants, *sadhus* and *faqirs*, *pirs* and *ghazis*.[34] Popularly respected for their piety and wisdom, knowledge of astrology and privileged possession of divine powers, many among them were no better than pretenders and imposters exploiting the sense of devotion and the implicit credulity of the ignorant. Although not confined strictly to any one community they came largely from among the Hindus. Scantily clad, almost naked, sprinkled and smeared with ashes, wearing long plaits of jetted hair, often false, they were found wandering in groups from shrine to shrine or congregate in large companies at bathing festivals and fairs. Many of them were found waiting for alms at roadsides or outside temples and other religious places. Others would settle themselves in shrines and many more formed part of the general community, but subsisted on the charity of the people around, not necessarily too well-placed financially.

With the object of getting admiration or extorting alms or under the simple delusion that their self-torture was an act of religious merit, some of them would mortify their flesh with unsparing severity. Holding up an arm until it withered in its socket or habitually sleeping on a bed of sharp prongs were common sight feats which attracted the ignorant masses of all communities with all the devotion and reverence they could command. They received charity from all irrespective of caste, creed or even status.

3.6 Some Salient Distinctions of Religious Groups

Each of the religious groups had their places of worship with priests and levites and followed formally the precepts of their faith from which they derived a general code and sanction for the social life of their members. In a mixed social gathering, generally speaking, the adherents of the diverse faiths could be distinguished from each other by some external characteristics, mode of behaviour, dietary, manner of living, etc. peculiar to each group. A few instances by way of illustration might be interesting.

Generally speaking, the very name of a person gave a clue to his religious denomination, being associated with its religious literature having Sanskritic origin in the case of Hindus and Arabic in that of the Muslims. The Sikh names invariably ended in Singh. The mode of salutation was equally distinctive of the chief religious groups though there was a wide variety in that. The Hindus and Sikhs normally folded their hands and bowed hailing God by the name, they worshipped Him, for instance, *Jai Ram* or *Ram Ram* or *Jai Deva* in the case of the

Hindus and '*Sat Sri Akal*' in the case of the Sikhs. The Muslims raised the right hand and touched the forehead. In towns, this had become the general mode of greeting among men of equal status. The lower classes, in greeting the higher classes, as also officials, explicitly addressed the person as '*sahib*' while saluting.

The Hindus venerated the cow and would not normally kill animals. Generally, they abstained from meat; the Sikhs were, perhaps, even more particular in their reverance for the cow, but ate other animals. The Muslims abhorred pig and dog but killed and ate most other animals. The Buddhists and Jains respected all animal life. Vagrant and outcast tribes did not abstain even from the impure animal. Again, the Sikhs scrupulously abstained from tobacco but substituted spirit and narcotics. Muslims were supposed to be forbidden to the spirits. The Hindus were not forbidden, any of these as such. The orthodox Parsi had leanings towards Hindu ways while the advanced among them adopted the practices of the English in India.

The exterior make up and grooming, if any, of the individual also indicated, more or less, the religious group to which he belonged. The Hindus cropped their hair close with the exception of the scalp lock called *choti*; the Sikhs grew hair uncut, untrimmed; the Muslims mostly flourished their beard. Even the dress of a person gave some clues to the faith he professed. In the Punjab, for instance, the Hindus, Jains and Sikhs buttoned their coats on the right, and the Muslims on the left. The loincloth or the *dhoti* worn by the male Hindu or Jain would be tucked up between the legs; the Sikhs wore short drawers, reaching up to knees. The Muslims wore the *dhoti* or the loincloth like a kilt. Among towns people, they wore trousers loose and baggy *shalwar* or *pyajamas* tight to the skin. Particular head dresses and types of caps stood for particular religious groups. Special colours were associated with the different groups. The Sikhs wore white or blue, the Hindus considered red as auspicious, and the Muslim colour was green.

The Hindus and Jains might cook in, but not eat out of an earthen pot which might have already been used once for the purpose. Their earthen vessels might be ornamented with stripes and the metal ones would be brass or bell metal. A Mussalman might use his earthen vessel over and over again for eating purposes, but it would not be striped and his metal vessels would be of copper. The Sikhs followed the Hindu practices mainly, but were comparatively less particular. The Hindus and Sikhs observed the daily ablutions which the Muslims did not consider a matter of necessity. The Hindus, the Jains and the Sikhs married by circumambulation of the sacred fire; the Muslims by consent of the two parties formally given in the presence of witnesses; the Parsis by their priest giving the nuptial benediction to the couple in the presence of their relatives and friends. The Hindus, the Sikhs and the Jains cremated their dead ; the Muslims and Christians buried them; the Parsis exposed the dead on high towers to be consumed by vultures while the Buddhists used all the three methods to dispose off the dead.

3.7 The Unifying Force of Social Institutions

The differences, among people, indeed, were striking and innumerable. But they were more of a formal nature; the divergence was superficial and so was the distance among the adherents of the diverse creeds. In practical life, the masses, regardless of the faith they professed, by virtue of the simple ignorance common to all, were governed by long-standing customs. Tradition bound, convention controlled, they were much closer to each other than was perceptible from distance to any foreigner, save when political and economic forces worked and placated matters.

The religions, in their social functioning, merged into each other so that social life assumed a pattern to which all conformed more or less generally, but which showed a preponderating influence of the majority group, the Hindus. Essentially and innately simple, with few needs and hardly any stress on comfort in the western sense of the word, except in urban centres, and that too in a very moderate manner, the general mode of life reflected the chief features of the Hindu social structure—the institution of caste, the joint-family, and the general inferior position of woman. Society, on the whole, appeared to be conditioned by trends common to all—the domination of custom, respect for the principle of toleration and disposition of charity and hospitality. The unostentatious benevolence of all grades of society, with which, throughout the year, a stream of charity flowed unceasingly from most households, in proportion to their means, to look after not only the needy relatives, but also the orphans of the caste, was considered as one of the most beautiful traits of Indian social conditions.[35] There being no 'Poor Law' in India, large number of persons, "independent of work", as the Census Reports designate them, mostly mendicants, subsisted on the charity of all irrespective of any sect or creed. The cities had a greater share in it since this class was two and a half times more numerous in urban areas than rural.[36]

The general trend of hospitality was conspicuously manifest in many ways. The fact that many temples and mosques, *gurudwaras* and Parsi *Atash Baharam* (the free temple) served not only as places for worship, but had some rooms attached to serve as travellers' rest-houses, speaks for it. In rural areas, most villages had their *dharamsalas* for Hindus and *taqiyas* for Muslim travellers which were maintained by the village community.

3.8 Pattern of Urban Life

There was, however, one overall difference, conspicuous and striking, determined by circumstances depending primarily upon the functional and vocational activities dividing the people into two main, but very unequal sections, urban and rural.

As a whole northern India conformed to the general pattern of the whole country and was primarily agricultural. The urban element, despite the augmentation it witnessed due to the improvement of railway communication, the development of trade, the growth of industry and the working of the mines, all crowded in the decades following 1850, formed, at the end of the century but a small fraction barely one-tenths of the whole population.[37] The majority of the towns reckoned their inhabitants between five to ten thousand; some between 10 to 20 ; a few between 20 to 100 and fewer still had a population more than 100,000. Those towns that had more than 200,000 denizens could be counted on finger-tips. Of these centres of urban life, Calcutta was the largest with 1,100,000 people followed by Bombay, Lucknow, Delhi and Lahore. The tendency to live in towns, however, was most marked in Bombay, Berar and Rajputana, least so in Bengal. It was still less in tracts on the borders of the region such as Kashmir and Assam. Elsewhere the proportions of the town-dwellers were fairly uniform. The majority of the denizens of towns lived by occupations other than those pertaining to agriculture, which in all cities taken together was the means of support of only one-twelfths of the inhabitants as compared to two-thirds of the general population.[38]

In some big cities. the proportion was even lower. For instance, in Bombay 1 in 30 and in Calcutta 1 in 28 was thus supported. The city, dwellers followed vocations which, unlike the villagers, were determined- not by the characteristic principle of heredity, but by aptitude and ability and often by aspirations to rise in the social scale. An educated Brahman in town, for example, would not want his son to be a priest but rather have him trained for some other career.

Government policy—administrative, economic and educational—was leading to the opening up of new avenues which encouraged occupational mobility. According to the Census of 1901[38], one-fourteenth of the urban population derived livelihood from government service, one-eighth from commerce, one-eleventh from unskilled labour and two-fifth were engaged for living in the preparation and supply of raw materials. There were, however, variations in these average proportions in the important cities. Occupations in regard to commerce rose, for instance, in Calcutta to 1 in 4 ; in Bombay, Delhi, Lahore and Amritsar to 1 in 6 ; in Karachi to 1 in 12 ; Ahmedabad and Kanpur 1 in 13 ; and Allahabad 1 in 27.

The urban populace thus presented a medley of professions such as government service of a wide variety, ranging from administrative and judicial jobs to clerical work, excepting the highest post reserved for the personnel from among the rulers, technical jobs connected with trade and industry such as engineers, overseers, supervisors, managers and independent professions like law, medicine, education, etc.[39] The new vocations in the cities, developing into new social classes in contrast to the hereditary castes, served as the nuclei of the new middle class of which three groups were most prominent, government servants, those connected with commerce and industry and English-educated found in the so-called learned professions. Life in the cities, which were witnessing change during the period of study on account of commercial and administrative development, indicated a struggle for adjustment of old habits to new forces, the putting of 'new wine in old bottles'.

Conditions in the cities, however, were far from uniform. There were decaying cities like Lucknow and growing cities like Kanpur; old cities like Delhi and new cities like Calcutta; cosmopolitan cities like Bombay and sombre cities like Banaras and Allahabad. Social life in each of them was marked by its own peculiar needs and characteristics. But the one outstanding feature common to all, in contrast to the villages was the absence of a corporate life. The population of cities was drifting into groups, and a conglomerate of fortuitous forces appeared to be working often in opposite directions.[40] There was no central point on which the activities of the different sections of the population could be focussed, no common measure of social conduct and no combining force or personality to which the different strata of society could look up as in some way setting a standard. For all practical purposes the ruling class served as the focal point.

The upper classes of all communities, the wealthy and the affluent, the aristocracy lived or aspired to live in style like the *Sahibs*, some in huge estates, others having big establishments, but assuming a sort of dual manner of living, an outer one in relation to the British officials from whom they secured advantages, and the other in regard to their own community, caste and the family. Even their living abodes showed it. The house would have a drawing room fitted in European style to receive visitors accustomed to western mode of life to entertain high officials of the government. Another would be fitted in the oriental style. In their private life, the majority of them were most conservative and real sticklers to the orthodox observances. Many of them would even have bath or at least wash hands after mixing with the foreigners.

Life among the middle classes revealed rather a fluid state. Semi-westernised and sophisticated in certain respects, depending on the extent of the contact with the westerners, most of them were struggling to adjust their ideas imbibed through education and the requirements of their professions, with usage at home. Life in the family was regulated by custom and convention as practised by women, majority of whom were uneducated. As a result, while some social restrictions among men in regard to their life outside the family were relaxing others were tightening up. Thus urban life revealed a queer crystallisation of social institutions. The upper and the comparatively better placed classes among the different groups followed their customs most zealously. Even the educated whose ideas had undergone change and were in some ways introducing innovations were unable, generally, to disregard customs. In fact, the observance of customs, irrational and distorted, though they might be with gusto and enthusiasm, involving extravagance was the determining factor of status. Social taboos were stiff and restrictions rigid in important matters like marriage. The lower classes, as is everywhere the case, looked up to the higher for cues and endeavoured to adopt their ways of life in order to gain by way of statue.

3.9 Pattern of Rural Life

The vast majority of the people, nine-tenths of the total population, in the rural areas, showed, in contrast to the urban, the characteristic Indian living, preserved as of yore to a very great extent, simple, untouched and unaffected by the western style.[41] And although there was a wide variety in the conditions of villages, they revealed, on the whole, a common pattern forming a sort of "joint interest, joint property, joint trade and joint income". Every village had a corporate life in which differences of religion hardly mattered. In a way village life had no mystery about it ; "every one lived in the open, every one talked in the open, every one slept in the open."[42]

A village in northern India was not merely a collection of houses, but a rural commune or territorial division of cultivable land highly interesting in its bearing on the condition of rural society. The whole village system was based on principles of self-government which had its origin in the simple patriarchal constitution of society when the family of brothers, joint-owners of the family land, lived together and cultivated the soil as co-partners under a paternal head. Every village large or small was a collection of such families united in intimate relations. And as each family was held together by a close interdependence of interests under the father, so the members of each village community were united in close association under a headman or a chief. The majority of the inhabitants of a village, normally 200 to 300, were the actual tillers of the land, and a bare minority consisted of the various functionaries. Men of distinct employment, indispensable to any society so as to minister to its needs, included a variety of workers such as the village priest (*purohit*), the barber (*nai*), the potter (*kumhar*), the carpenter, (*barhai*), the blacksmith (*lohar*), the washerman (*dhobi*), waterman (*bhisti*), tailor (*darzi*), cobbler (*mochi*), oilman (*teli*), weaver (*julaha*), dyer (*rangrez*), etc. Each of these formed a separate caste and followed strictly the principle of heredity in occupation. Larger villages added other functionaries such as the astrologer and the village apothecary and the teacher. All these were paid in kind, a few sheaves of grain and cakes of sugar-cane jaggery, according to the value of the service rendered.

The details of rural organisation were not absolutely uniform, but each village formed a unit, self-contained and self-sufficient, a social world in itself. There was close inter-mingling of communal relations in every village so that the separate existence and independence of any individual community was barely recognised. Large villages frequently consisted of five or six rural communities each under a distinct headman. Sometimes a village would be inhabited conjointly by Hindus or Muslims or even other religious communities who lived side by side amicably and congenially forming an organised society subsisting harmoniously in comfort on the produce of the village lands. Formal profession of any faith was no impediment in the adoption of any custom or mores which satisfied the emotional wants of the ignorant.

Hindus and Muslims, the two major groups, commonly considered the antithesis of each other not only tolerated and respected each other's customs, but often adopted them and actively participated in each other's festivities and celebrations.[43] Sir Denzil Ibbetson's description of the Musalmans of the east Punjab, which might equally be applied to the Musalmans of Bengal, is an eloquent testimony to the happy co-mingling of the two communities and the prevalence of a common pattern of life. He wrote in 1881:

"The Musalman Rajput, Gujar or Jat is for all social tribal, political, and administrative purposes as much a Rajput, Gujar or Jat as his Hindu brother. His social customs are unaltered, his tribal restrictions are unrelaxed, his rules of marriage and inheritance unchanged and almost all the difference is that he shaves his scalp lock and the upper-edge of his moustache, repeats the Muhammadan creed in a mosque and adds the Musalman to Hindu wedding ceremony... The local saints and deities still have their shrines even in villages held wholly by Muslims and are still regularly worshipped by the majority though the practice is gradually declining."[44]

The Census Report of 1901 had identical notes on Muslims of U.P., Rajputana, Bengal and even Baluchistan which was predominantly Muslim.

"The unreformed Muhammadans of the lower and uneducated class," the note ran, "are deeply infected with Hindu superstitions and their knowledge of the faith they profess seldom extends beyond the three cardinal doctrines . . . and they have a very faint idea of the differences between their religion and that of the Hindus. Sometimes they believe that they are descended from Abel while the Hindus owe their origin to Cain."[45]

Innumerable instances can be cited to elucidate the close affinity among the common people, which revealed itself, unimpeded and unhampered in the day to day life, in the emotional outlets, in moments of concern and distress, joy and jubilations. The Hindu priests were kept up by the Muslims and were consulted as of old for anything important and were fed on important occasions, not infrequently functioning along with the Muslim priests. The faith in the astrologer (*jyotishi*) and his pretensions was implicit and unshaken among all, regardless of the creed, and governed all important decisions of life.[46]

In regard to ceremonial, as distinct from actual worship, it prevailed in exactly the same way both among the Hindus and the Muslims. In some cases, the Muslims carefully preserved the idols even if they were not actually tended and regularly worshipped. An instance in point, reported from a Muslim village in Hissar in the Punjab, might be interesting. On one occasion the Muslim headman of the village was found refreshing an idol with a new coat of oil while a Brahman repeated the holy texts. The explanation given for this un-Islamic act was that the villagers had been constrained to bury the idol under orders of their *Mullah* and so after he had left they were trying to console and assuage the god for the rough treatment given to him.[47]

In these matters, the Hindus reacted equally, if not more readily. There were no scruples or compunctions of any type in accepting Muslim saints or proper objects of veneration although this was more true of the lower classes, including some Brahmans.[48] Hindu saints, often had Muslim names. Among the peasantry, regardless of their creed, saints of widespread renown occupied a very important place. They were generally Muslims, but were worshipped by the Hindus and the Muslims alike with the most absolute importiality.[49] In the Punjab, thousands of worshippers, belonging to both religions flocked yearly to the sacred shrines of saints, chief among them being those of Sakhi Sarwar Sultan, Baba Shakar Ganj, Guga Pir, Baoli Qalandar and Panch Pir. Even their origin was mixed up. Some were claimed by both Hindus and the Muslims ; others were accepted by both.[50] The implicit faith in the efficacy of the worship of saints and the belief in the value of offerings at certain holy places for obtaining temporal blessings was far too strong for any differences of caste or creed. They receded, easily into the background if not total oblivion. Thus the shrine of Saiyad Salar at Bahraich was resorted to by both the Hindus and the Muslims if a wife was childless or family quarrels could not be composed. Disease could be cured by a visit to the shrine of Shaikh Saddo at Amroha in Moradabad, while for help in legal difficulties Shah Mina's *dargah* at Lucknow was renowned. Each of these had its appropriate offering, a long embroidered flag for the first, a cock for the second and a piece of cloth for the third, and was accepted without any reservations.[51] This exemplified the extraordinary manner in which religions intermingled in the social sphere.

Rivers were held in reverence by all and not only was river-bathing a common practice, but places on the river-side, considered especially holy, had shrines dedicated to saints by the different religious communities. At Sakhi Sarwar in the Punjab, for instance, the Muslims visited the tomb of one of their saints, Sikhs a monument of Guru Nanak, and the Hindus went to bathe in the holy water.

Again, the idea of the efficacy of pilgrimage was commonly shared and was as unsectarian as river-veneration. All had their respective places of pilgrimage. A rich devotee among Muslims would go to Meeca, while a person with ordinary means would be content with a visit to the tomb of one of the saints at Ajmer, Fatehpur Sikri or Pak Patan. For the Hindu men and women, a visit, once in the life-time, to one at least of the many places of pilgrimage scattered in the different parts of the country was the greatest ambition for the satisfaction of which no pains were spared. The Sikhs were equally keen on visiting their holy places.

Belief in exorcism and charms, divination and possession by spirits, the influence of the evil eye being concomitants of ignorance were common to all though witch-craft was confined to the lowest castes only.

Illness was generally attributed to the malignant influence of a deity or to possession by a spirit. Recourse was taken by all, to the soothsayer, the wise, the devotee, in the Punjab known as the '*Sayana*' or the '*Bhagat*' as to who was to be appeased and in what manner. The malignant spirit was appeased by building him a new shrine or making offerings at the old one. The offerings at the shrine took many forms. The simplest form of an offerings say in the case of a sick person, was to tie a rag taken from the patient's body to the sacred tree beneath which the shrine stood. Such trees covered with remnants of those offerings in green and red denoting the two communities, Muslims and Hindus respectively, were a very common sight in rural areas.

Building of a new shrine, sometimes gave rise to delicate questions as the Hindu temple faces the east and the Muslim shrine faces south. Controversies of this kind between the Hindus and the Muslims of a village were settled amicably making convenient compromises to satisfy both. In a village, for instance, in the Punjab, where one section of the community had become Muslim, the shrine of the common ancestor required to be rebuilt and there was much dispute as to its shape and type. The problem was solved by building a Musalman grave facing south and over it a Hindu shrine facing east.[52]

Village deities were honoured by all alike. In the Punjab, for instance, Bhumia or the god of the homestead often called *Khera* (village) was the most honoured deity and as such, he was worshipped after the harvest, at marriages and on the birth of a male child; Brahmans were commonly fed in his name; the first milk of a cow or a buffalo was offered to him; women considered it auspicious to take their children to his shrine to receive blessings.[53] In fact, women were especially susceptible to such influences. A Musalman mother who had not sacrificed to the small-pox goddess *Sitala*, known to others as *'mata'*, the eldest of a band of seven sisters by whom the *'Pustular'* group of diseases was supposed to be caused and so were most dreaded, would feel exactly like her Hindu sister, that she had wantonly endangered the life of her child.[54]

Actually the customs of the masses on important occasions of joy and sorrow, pleasure and pain, involving emotional expressions were practically the same. When disease was prevalent, *Sitala* and *Rakshya Kali* were worshipped and *Dharmaraj Manasa*, and *Bishahari* were venerated by all alike. In Bengal Shashthi was worshipped when a child was born. In Bihar, the Muslims joined in the worship of the sun and on the birth of a child they observed customs commonly ascribed to the Hindus, namely, lighting a fire and placing cactus and a sword at the door to prevent the demon from entering and killing the infant. At marriage the bridegroom often followed the practices of smearing the bride's forehead with vermillion. In the Santhal Parganas, the Muslims were often seen carrying sacred water to the shrine of Baidyanath and as they could not enter the shrine they would pour it out as a libation on the outside verandah.[55]

The most puissant common factor among the people, however, was the superstitions they observed. The Hindus and the Muslims alike, particularly the less enlightened among them, were highly subject to their influence. They were very particular about omens and auspicious days and nothing could be done, from cutting a bamboo or the commencement of the building of a house or undertaking a journey or fixing the date of a wedding, without consulting the Hindu almanac.[56] Among the peasantry, as a whole, the superstitions conncected with cattle and agriculture were endless. A few examples might be interesting by way of illustration as to how life assumed one general pattern. Special days were considered auspicious for particular work. No horned cattle or anything pertaining to them such as butter or leather was bought or sold on Saturdays or Sundays; if one died on these days it was buried and not given away to menials. All field work, cutting of grass, grinding of corn and cooking of food was stopped on Saturday morning. The annual extraction of sugar-cane or digging a well was started on Sunday. When women began to pick the cotton they would go round the field eating rice-milk, the first mouth-full of which they spat on the field towards the west and the first cotton picked was exchanged at the village shop for its weight in salt over which they prayed and which they kept in the house till picking was completed.[57]

Many fairs and festivals, even some of the fasts and feasts were commonly shared. In Bengal, the Muslims considered the festival of Durga Puja just as much an occasion for festivities as the Hindus, and spent money on new clothes and feasts. On the occasion of the Muslim festival of *Muharram*, many Hindus, not infrequently, participated in the celebrations with enthusiasm, beating their chests like pious Muslims. The Hindu women particularly considered it auspicious for small children to walk across underneath the *'Taziyas'*.[58] The crowds collected in the streets on such occasions were far from sectarian and the respect shown for each other's sentiments was mutual.

Endless examples can be cited to elucidate the fact that despite wide varieties, the pattern of life, basically, was more or less the same. A "moral monotone" was perceptible in all the varieties of men and manners, habits and observances, their ideals and attitudes. And, amidst their 'grovelling superstitions' and contacts with the western civilisation, the people of India, regardless of the religious denominations, were the same in disposition, sympathy, tastes, capacities and the genius of their customs and social life.[59]

References

1. Risley, (1915) p. 5.
2. Holderness. p. 8.
3. Campbell, (1852) p. 37.
4. Risley, (1915) p. 32-35.
5. Fuller, Joseph Bamyfytde (1909) p. 148 ; Bose, p. 192.
6. Ishuree Dass, p. 134.
7. Fuller, Joseph Bamyfytde (1910) p. 52.
8. Fuller, Joseph Bampfytde (1910) p. 148.
9. Ishuree Dass, p. 138.
10. Temple, Richard, p. 21.
11. *Census Report 1861*, Vol. I. p. 248.
12. Ibid.
13. Ibid., p. 249.
14. Ibid., p. 311.
15. Ibid; Fuller, Joseph Bampfytde (1910) p. 52-65; Monier-Williams (1878), p. 154.
16. *Census Report 1901*, Vol. I, pp 323-24 ; Monier-Williams (1878), p. 153.
17. *Census Report 1901*, Vol. I, pp. 323-24.
18. Jones, P. John p. 30.
19. *Census Report 1881*, p. 17.
20. *Census Report 1901*, Vol. I, p. 392.
21. Ibid, p. 395.
22. Ibid, p.
23. Monier-Williams (1878), p. 157.
24. *Census Report 1901*, Vol. I, pp. 378-79.
25. Ibid, p. 382.

26. Ibid. p. 381.
27. Temple, (Richard), p. 89.
28. *Census Report 1901*, Vol. I, p. 383.
29. Holderness, p. 128.
30. Framjee, (1884) pp. 53 and 55.
31. *Census Report 1901*, Vol. I, p. 392.
32. Framjee (1858), p. 123.
33. *Census Report 1901*, Vol. I, p. 387-88.
34. Fuller, Joseph Bampfytde (1909) p. 164.
35. Holderness, pp. 142-43.
36. *Census Report 1901*, Vol. I, p. 200.
37. *Census Report 1901*, Vol. I, pp. 25 and 27 ; Chailley, pp. 127-28.
38. *Census Report 1901*, Vol. I, p. 199.
39. Ibid, p. 200.
40. Ibid, p. 30; Yusuf Ali (1907), p. 38.
41. Chailley, p. 128.
42. Yusuf Ali (1907), p. 71.
43. *Census Report 1901*, Vol. I, pp. 373-75.
44. *Census Report 1881, Punjab*, Vol. I. p. 176.
45. *Census Report 1901*, Vol. I. p, 374.
46. *Calcutta Report, 1887*, p. 273.
47. *Census Report 1891*, Vol. I, p. 168.
48. Strachey, p. 292.
49. *Census Report 1881, Punjab*, p. 143.
50. Ibid.
51. *Census Report 1901, N.W.P.*, Part I, p. 94.
52. *Census Report, Punjab*, p. 117.
53. Ibid, Appendix B, p. IX.
54. Ibid.
55. *Census Report 1901*, Vol. I, p. 375.
56. *Census Report 1881*, Punjab, Appendix B, p. IX.
57. *Census Report 1881*, Punjab, Appendix B, p. IX.
58. Ibid.
59. Nolan, Edward Henry (1878-79), pp. 465-66.

4 The Caste System : A Unique Mode of Social Organisation

    4.1 The Permeability of Caste System
    4.2 Some Salient Features of Caste System
        4.21 Heredity
        4.22 Heirarchy
        4.23 Caste Restrictions
        4.24 Commensal and Food Restrictions
        4.25 Contractual Restrictions
        4.26 Restrictions of Privileges
        4.27 Occupational Restrictions
        4.28 Connubial Restrictions
    4.3 Types of Castes
        4.31 Tribal Castes
        4.32 Territorial Castes
        4.33 Functionl Castes
        4.34 Sectarian Castes
        4.35 Castes formed by Miscegenation
        4.36 Castes of National Type
        4.37 Castes formed by Change of Custom
    4.4 Caste-Government
        4.41 Forms of Punishment
    4.5 Peripheral Changes in Caste System
    4.6 Caste and other Communities
    4.7 Social Reforms Inimical to Caste System

The social life of the vast multitude of the people of nineteenth century northern India manifested a strong and dominant influence of the customs and usages of the majority community, the Hindus. The general pattern of life, therefore, notwithstanding the distinctive features of other communities, appeared to be influenced by their social institutions. Out of which, the caste and the joint-family, formed the nucleous around which the whole of the social structure revolved.

    The institution of caste stood at the root of the social set-up of the people of northern India, giving it a unique character. Its antiquity, ubiquity and oddity, indeed, marked a contrast to the social grouping prevalent in other countries of the contemporary period. Its obtrusive nature has, no wonder, attracted the attention of foreign scholars to whom it has proved baffling, tricky and almost enigmatic. Not a few among them have, even after long, detailed and intensive study, pronounced it as an institution peculiar to India only.[1] There are others who contend, and rightly so, that the social pattern based on the grouping of people into classes was not confined to India only.[2]

Such divisions were probably common to the majority of ancient nations. The Egyptians, Sumerians, Assyrians, for instance, all had caste divisions in their own form. The Greeks and the Romans too were very much governed by somewhat similar institution at the helm of their society. Even in the middle ages, human society, in practically all parts of the world, was subject to some sort of social differentiation with its concomitant demarcation of groups involving grades of status of individual's achievements in the fields of activities which were prized by those communities. The differentiation showed itself in the special rights and privileges or the disabilities and the stigma attached to certain groups. In certain communities the status of an individual was determined by birth.

The system of caste as practised and maintained by the Hindus through the ages has, however, been adjudged to be unique and incomparable to any other social organisation, not because of its being inherently different, but because of its development on certain peculiar lines. Instead of moving with times, changing and becoming simplified as it did elsewhere in India, on the contrary, it assumed a complicated form. It is no wonder that the system has been but imperfectly understood by the westerners among whom the primitive need for social divisions had, in course of time, taken a turn for simplification so that the social strata and trammels of the early stages of civilisation have almost disappeared.

It is difficult to convey the extraordinary complexity of the social system involved in the word caste. Enthoven of the Bombay Census Report called caste "a puzzling amorphous collection of anomalies and anachronisms,"[3] while Ibbetson of the Punjab Census felt that he famous words of an agnostic, "the only thing I know is that I know nothing and I am not quite sure that I know that" might very well apply to caste.[4] Indeed the subject of caste is so vast and complicated, albeit, fascinating, that it has remained a matter of uncertainty and debate. It has aroused much thought and speculation, "some wild, some ingenious but all inconclusive." Attempts to define and describe caste have, at best, met with partial success.

Actually, authorities have found it easier to give the derivation of the word caste indicating its foreign origin than to furnish an appropriate definition of it. Instead of making it easier to understand the subject, this has naturally augmented the difficulties. The vague and uncertain use of the term according to the sense in which the foreigners chose to interpret and stress it could not but add to the complexity of the phenomenon. Moreover, the indiscriminate use of the term, both for the main group as well as for its sub-divisions, caused confusion, since the connotation and the denotation of the term would change with the sense in which it was used. Scholars have laboured hard and delved deep into the subject for analysis and exposition. Yet authorities have remained at variance regarding much concerning it. Its origin itself has remained a topic of wide controversy.

Renowned scholars have expounded theories laying stress on the aspect of the institution which impressed them most. Consequently, the religious, the tribal, the social and occupational and crossing theory, at best, bring out only one of the many aspects of the caste system. They fail simply to explain the real spirit underlying the institution of caste, which in actual working showed all these aspects welded into one mighty whole. What appears to be a reasonable hypothesis is that perhaps caste originated in India, as it must have originated in all other countries where it might have prevailed, as one of the necessities of an early stage of society.[5]

4.1 The Permeability of the Caste System

Be it as it may, the caste as it manifested itself in northern India in the later half of the nineteenth century was far from simple. Being the outgrowth of millenniums, it was the saturated resultant of multifarious forces and tendencies at work. It was the cumulative effect of the impact of political vicissitudes and so had evolved into a highly complex and intricate system, resulting in the segmentation of the population into an infinite number of mutually exclusive aggregates regulating their life strictly in all spheres by inexorable social laws, dictating every detail of human relationship and controlling the whole destiny of its members. This stratification into classes on the basis of social status determined by birth, however, was the most striking feature of Indian society even up to the close of the nineteenth century. In other words, the universality of caste and the pride of birth and descent, carried to the extreme, were the controlling factors of the Hindu society.

"To a Hindu, caste was as much a necessity as food to eat, as raiment to wear, as a house to live in", wrote an eminent writer in 1880. The comment continued, "Indeed he can often dispense with raiment and during most of the year prefers the court outside the house to the hot rooms within, but he can never free himself from caste, can never escape from its influence. By day and night, at home, abroad, in working, in sleeping, eating and drinking and in all the customs of the society in which he moves and the events governing his entire life, he is always under its pervasive and overmastering influence."[6]

True, a Hindu was necessarily known by his caste. "A man without caste was an insulting epithet."[7]

A premium appeared to have been placed on the religious aspect of the sanction behind caste. For the unsophisticated, caste was of super human origin. The mass mind consistently declined to recognise any distinction between the social and the religious, which were looked upon as the obverse and the reverse, both yielding to and enforced by the same authority. In fact, religion as understood and practised in the popular sense appeared to permeate the whole social domain. The ruling principle of existence being the doctrine of transmigration of soul, the sanctions of caste were accepted to be not only social but spiritual as well extending beyond death.[8] The orthodox theory—that found strength in the new tendency of the Neo-Hindus to justify and find rational explanations for every custom of the Hindus, which propounded that society was divinely ordained, that the Indian social order was regulated by religious injunctions and that forms and rituals were enforced by religious penalties—appeared to be generally accepted.

The common belief was that the basis of the caste was the original division of society into four major groups, *Brahmana, Kshatriya, Vaisya,* and *Sudra*. Whether the fourfold division of society was ever a reality in practice, is today a matter of grave doubt.[9] Some scholars pronounce it as only ideological and not in any manner based on facts of the social system and hold that it was only a schematic arrangement by theorists who visualised society as organised on a horizontal basis.[10] Whatever be the position one thing is certain that society in the nineteenth century did not conform strictly to the fourfold division of the days of the Purushsukta (*Rgveda*, Book X, Hymn 90) or even Manu. From the four primal classes, if that view may be held, had descended through myriads of permutations and combinations, mingling and miscegenation, multitudinous caste organisation, which had no uniformity except the lack of it, and the amazing influence it exercised over all including the non-Hindus. The *Census Report of 1901* mentions hundreds of castes, each with its own code of conduct regulating the life of its members with a relentless rigidity. Wilson sums up very comprehensively the extent to which caste rules governed every member of a caste. Caste he writes,

> "gives its direction for recognition, acceptance, consecration and sacramental dedication and *vice versa* of a human being on his appearance in the world. It has for infancy, pupilage and manhood its ordained methods of sucking, sipping, drinking, eating and voiding; of washing, rinsing, anointing and smearing; of clothing, dressing and ornamenting; of sitting, rising and reclining; of moving visiting and travelling; of speaking, reading, listening and reciting; and of meditating, singing, working, playing and fighting. It has its laws for social and religious rights, privileges and occupations ; for instructing, training and educating for obligation, duty and practices ; for divine recognition, service and ceremony : for errors, sins and transgressions ; for inter communion, avoidance and excommunication ; for defilement, ablution and purification for fines, chastisements, imprisonments, mutilations, banishments and capital executions. It upholds the ways of committing what it calls sins,

THE CASTE SYSTEM 67

accumulating sin, and of putting away sin ; and of acquiring merit, dispensing merit and losing merit. It treats of inheritance, conveyance, possession and dispossession and of bargains, gain, loss and ruin. It deals with death, burial and burning and with commemoration, assistance and injury, after death. It interferes, in short, with all the relations and events of life and with what precedes and follows life."[11]

To describe an institution with such social implications is indeed difficult. Much more is it so to define it. It was too capricious even to be termed a system.

4.2 Some Salient Features of Caste System

It varied in its character and manifestations in different locations. Its picture in the countryside was considerably different from that found in towns and cities where again it appeared at times to show kaleidoscopic scenes. The rules of a caste affecting the same tribe might be, to some extent, different in the same neighbourhood. It often happened that among members of the same caste what was unlawful in one place was lawful in another only a few miles distant. It may also be observed that the status of the same caste varied considerably in different districts. Accidental and merely local circumstances might give to a particular caste an importance in one locality which it did not have in others. In other words, the social status of a caste varied in the different parts according to its natural strength and political importance. Thus, a caste which dominated a particular tract of country enjoyed in that area a position denied to it in other places where it occupied a subordinate position. For instance, in Bharatpur and Dholpur in Rajputana, where the ruling chiefs were Jats, some of the Jats were considered to be socially of as high a standing as Rajputs ; in Alwar, Bharatpur and Jaipur the Minas, who in ancient times were the actual possessors and rulers of a large part of the country, held in public opinion a much higher social position than they did in Marwar and Sirohi.[12]

In Bengal, wrote Buchanan, "by a strange caprice bankers and goldsmiths are excluded from the pure castes of Sudras and blacksmiths and weavers are admitted, while in other districts this rule is reversed and the goldsmith ranks higher than the blacksmith." This position does not appear to have altered even at the close of the century.[13] Notwithstanding the seeming vagaries, it is, however, possible to state certain basic features of the caste system.

4.21 HEREDITY

Each caste was a group with a closely knit and well-developed life, membership of which unlike that of voluntary associations or groups was determined not by choice or selection, but by the accident of birth.

Once born in a caste one belonged to it for ever unless thrown out for some default which did not allow expiation or pardon. No new member could be recruited in the place of one so outcast. There was no possibility of changing one's caste; raising it by an individual was impossible; degrading it was not difficult; losing it was not only possible, but quite easy. The social status of a person thus depended not on his wealth or achievements in any field, but mainly on the traditional importance of the caste in which he happened to be born. Caste, thus, was involuntary, inexorable and arbitrary.

4.22 Hierarchy

The caste groups based on birth formed a sort of roughly graded hierarchy, each group having a particular position and commanding a certain status of superiority or inferiority in relation to the others.[14] The principle of social inequality thus appeared to be the normal basis of the entire system in which the concept of social distance was developed to its extreme length. The order of social precedence among the individual sub-castes of any of the main castes is not easy to establish. It is practically an insoluble problem because of the ever multiplying number of sub-castes as also the lack of common principles by which they might be graded. Besides, not only was there no ungrudging acceptance of such ranks at all levels, but also the ideas of the people on this point were very nebulous and uncertain. Moreover, they varied from place to place, and within the same caste the ranks of different sub-castes were controversial. Aside from the rough grading of the main groups, which also varied from region to region, the only assertion that can be made with a fair amount of certainty is that Brahmans stood at the head of the hierarchy.

Originally a sacerdotal class, the Brahmans, during the period of study, had lost the vocational solidarity and although they still enjoyed a distinct identity as a group, they neither formed a compact whole nor could they command respect of a uniform nature. It varied in depth from province to province, as also in regard to the functions discharged by them. The Brahmans at best denoted a multitude of castes and sub-castes, which were as marked from each other as those of any other series of castes, graded in order of social precedence, and were governed by rules just as strict and intricate as those that regulated any other group, if not more stringent in some respects. The lowest of the Brahmanical castes were looked down upon disdainfully by some of the higher Brahmans themselves and were held in very little respect by the upper castes of the other groups.[15] But by the lower and ignorant classes, almost every Brahman, whatever his rank or status, was regarded with a feeling of instinctive respect such as no other caste could ever expect to inspire. He was addressed as *Maharaj* (Your Highness) and was greeted in respectful terms.

THE CASTE SYSTEM

The prominent position which the Brahman held was not a peculiarity of the Indian society as such. The extravagant claims which the priest makes are well-known to be co-existent with certain stages of social advancement. The story of ancient nations such as the Persians and Egyptians bear testimony to this. Even in Europe till the nations were emancipated from the temporal control of the Pope, the clergy was always superior to the temporal authority. The noteworthy point in this regard is that the Brahmans had managed, even in the nineteenth century, to maintain their position at the apex of Hindu society, despite the challenges from time to time for nearly two thousand years.

The Brahmans served as the central point from which the social precedence, as recognised by public opinion, of other castes, as representatives of one or the other of the main castes of the theoretical Hindu system was determined. For instance, Brahmans would take water from certain castes; that Brahmans of high standing would serve particular castes; that certain castes though not served by the best Brahmans had, nevertheless, Brahmans of their own whose rank varied according to circumstances; that certain castes were not served by Brahmans at all, but had priests of their own.

The belief in the traditional fourfold division of society, especially in regard to the social precedence involved in it, however, undoubtedly held sway in a general fashion and was wide-spread. It was manifest in the general, aspirations and strivings of the castes to be considered as the descendants of the higher groups, the Kshatriyas and the Vaishyas, though the bounds to which each of these extended were vague and uncertain.*

Interestingly enough, these two orders, in actual practice, did not appear to exist as separate classes; the very names were unknown as conveying their original meaning. Nor could the term Sudra be applied to any set of sub-castes in any definite manner. Yet the lower castes, vaguely denoted by the term Sudra, were generally accepted to be at the base of the social pyramid, even though they performed duties which were most essential. Whatever be the mutual relationship and the relative position of the higher groups towards one another, they enjoyed certain privileges and honours in common, which were deemed to the lower classes.

There was, however, no uniform scheme of graded castes for general application. Different provinces, had in course of time evolved their own groupings, depending on their circumstances, but mainly in accord with the essential spirit of the hierarchy. In Bengal, for instance, only two main groups—Brahmans and Sudras—were recognised.[16] For Brahmans all others were Sudras though they conceded a difference in

---

*Several memorials and petitions were sent by many astes to the Superintendants of Census 1901 in many provinces with appeals to be placed as descendants of Kshatriyas and not as Vaishyas. The Khatris of U.P. and Punjab were chief among them.

the degree of their inferiority. Hence the divisions and sub-divisions of the Sudras, establishing a hierarchy of several groups. The controversy over the status of the Baidyas and Kayasthas of Bengal led to the verdict of the Calcutta High Court that the Kayasthas were Sudras.[17] In the Punjab, *Khatris, Rajputs, Jats* and *Banias* were distinguished as the main groups[18] while in Bombay the *Vanis, Marathas* and *Lingayats* stood as the chief castes, each with its sub-sections.[19] For practical purposes, a broader but vaguer grouping appeared to be prevalent—the privileged, unprivileged and the untouchables.

4.23 Caste Restrictions

Each caste in the general hierarchy built up elaborate rules for its members, guiding them specifically for almost everything important in life, developing thus a code of conduct. This led to definite taboos, resulting generally in rigid isolation and insulation of caste groups. It is through these restrictions that caste manifested its vital existence and maintained its hold.

4.24 Commensal and Food Restrictions

There were detailed rules as to what sort of food or drink might be accepted by a person and from what castes, although there was great diversity in this matter. In most parts of northern India all food was divided into *Kachcha* and *Pakka*, the former being food in the cooking of which water had been used and the latter being cooked in *ghee* without the addition of water. All castes in regard to food were divided into five groups—the twice-born castes; castes from whom the twice-born could take *Pakka* food; castes at whose hands the twice-born could not accept any kind of food, but might take water; castes that were not untouchable, yet were such that water from them could not be used by the twice-born; and last came those castes whose touch would defile not only the twice-born but any orthodox Hindu.[20]

Generally speaking, *Kachcha* food could not be eaten unless prepared by a fellow casteman, which meant a member of his own endogamous group. The more punctilious among the higher castes would not take *Kachcha* food from one another even among themselves. In practice, most castes appeared to take no objection to *Kachcha* food from a Brahman. A Brahman could accept *Kachcha* food at the hands of no other caste. Some of them like the Kanaujia Brahmans were punctilious to the extent of being ridiculous as is indicated by the trite proverb.

"Nine Kanaujias require no less than thirteen hearths".[21]

As for the *Pakka* food, Brahamans could take it from some castes only. Rules in this regard were just as complicated as the whole question of caste, and were liable to vary from one locality to another. No general rule could be laid down, nor any scale of correspondence between social

THE CASTE SYSTEM

position and strictness of observance be specified. In eastern Punjab, for instance, "a Gujarati Brahman would eat '*Pakki Roti*' from a Gaur, a Gaur from a Taga, and Brahman or Taga from a Rajput, any Brahman, Taga or Rajput from a Jat, Gujar or Ror."[22] In west Bengal, a Kurmi would not take food cooked by any Brahman except his own *Guru*, and his wife would not take the food her husband's *Guru* cooked[23]. As a general rule, it might be said that a person could never accept *Kachcha* food from caste lower than himself. Among the lower castes, there were fewer such inhibitions. Jats, Gujars, Rahbaris and Ahirs ate and drank in common without any scruples.[24] Again, areas like the west Punjab, were comparatively freer from commensal taboos.

The handling and cooking of the articles of food and their source had their importance. Some articles of food such as fruit, milk, *ghee* were not subject to pollution, others were highly so.[25] Cooking counteracted all pollution. Hence the importance of who cooked the food.

Then again different castes prescribed different articles of food in different localities, particularly types of meat. As a rule, no Hindu except the lowest castes like Doms and Chamars would eat beef. Some castes were purely vegetarian. Even where meat was eaten, most respectable castes, especially in Bengal, eschewed the domestic fowl and even more the domestic pig. Mutton and game were eaten freely. As regards fish, custom varied greatly perhaps by locality than by social position. Thus, most respectable castes ate fish in Bengal, whereas in the dry and sandy deserts of Rajputana the idea was most repugnant. In some cases, even some vegetables were tabooed. Certain castes would not eat turnips, carrots, and onions, and some sub-castes would bar turmeric. Restrictions were also placed on the material of which eating and drinking vessels were made. Earthenware, for instance, was tabooed by all higher castes, unless it was thrown away after using it once.[26]

In the western Punjab, the distinction of *Kachcha* and *Pakka* food was not observed and the restrictions regarding food were much less stringent. In Bengal, castes for this purpose were divided into two main groups, Brahmans and Sudras, who were further split into four sub-classes indicating in regard to food and water. First among these were, the *Sat-Sudra* group including such castes as the *Kayasthas* and the *Nabasakh*. Then came the *Jalcharnlya-Sudras*, being those castes not technically belonging to the *Nabsakh* group from whom Brahmans and members of the higher castes could take water. The third group was the *Jalabhyabhachariya-Sudras* from whom the Brahmans could not take water and the last were the *Asprisya-Sudras* from whom nothing could be accepted.[27] In certain respects, the food restrictions in Bengal were even more stringent than in other parts of northern India. Certain castes would not accept any *Kachcha* food even from the hands of a Brahman. In certain parts of Bengal and Gujarat where no distinction was made between *Kachcha* and *Pakka* food, the general rule was that food could be taken from a caste higher in status and not from one lower in social scale. Thus a Brahman could not accept water, much less cooked food, from any caste, but his own. As a rule, the lower castes had no scruples in accepting cooked food from any higher castes. Thus all castes could take food from Brahmans.[28]

In addition to these, there were equally strict restrictions on smoking also. Generally speaking, smoking was treated in the same way, as taking water or *Kachcha* food. In the countryside at the time or large and mixed gatherings small rags of different colours were tied to the *hukkas* to indicate which castes might use them.[29] These restrictions sometimes displayed themselves in a ludicrous manner. Servants working for English officers in their homes would refuse to eat food from their table even if it was untouched by any one. In camps, with officers on tour, the servants would cook their food separately on improvised hearths within small demarcated areas, square or round blocks depending on the space available. So did the *sepoys* or soldiers coming from high castes such as the Brahmans or Rajputs. The only place where these restrictions were relaxed was at the temple of Jagannath at Puri in Orissa.[30]

4.25 CONTRACTUAL RESTRICTIONS

Normally, no Hindu would touch any person of the so-called lower castes such as a Dom or a Chamar. Some of the low castes were tough sticklers about it. For instance, "the Bansphor and Basor themselves branches of the Dom caste would touch neither a Dom nor a Dhobi," whilst the Basor would extend his objections to Musahar, Chamar, Dharkar and Bhand.[31] In this respect contact with members of other communities such as Muslims and Christians of even the highest social rank and position was not permissible. Even educated people, with few exceptions in big cities, observed these restrictions. "The High caste Hindu washes his hands the moment your back is turned if he has had the misfortune to touch you", remarked Duff in 1876.[32]

4.26 RESTRICTIONS OF PRIVILEGES

There were certain privileges which the higher castes arrogated to themselves and denied to the others. The twice-born were entitled to the ceremonies performed by the Brahman priest initiating them to the second birth. The sacred thread was the emblem of the superiority and chief distinction of the high caste Hindus. The Sudras were debarred from many privileges. They were not supposed to study the scriptures and were not even allowed to perform the Vedic ritual. The impure castes could not even have a Brahman priest minister to them. They had to look to some Pseudo-Brahman or an apostate.

Although northern India was not too strict about the segregation of the lower castes yet in certain parts such as the Central Provinces, the impure castes lived on the outskirts of the villages. In one respect, they suffered almost everywhere; they were denied access to the village well used by other castes for drawing water. Even in the Punjab where restrictions of this nature were much less stringent than in other parts, a sweeper while walking through the streets of the larger towns was expected to carry a broom in his hand or under his armpit as a mark of his being a scavenger and had almost to shout out to people warning them of his presence.[33] It appears that the Brahmans as the highest class enjoyed the greatest privileges, even to an unjustifiable extent. For instance, a Brahman would expect others to salute him, but would not bow to a non-Brahman. Some of them were so conscious of their superiority that they would not condescend to bow even to the idols of gods in a Sudra's house.[34]

4.27 Occupational Restrictions

Generally speaking, caste regulated the vocation of its members. Certain callings were considered to belong to certain castes and any change in the traditional practice was looked upon as a violation of the caste rules. Thus a Brahman's profession was to be a priest, a washerman's work to do the washing, a blacksmith's job to work on iron; a Chamar's function to handle hides and skins. This, however, was only generally true, for there were occupations such as trading, agriculture, labouring in the fields, army service, clerical work in offices etc. which were practised at this time by any caste.[35] The restrictions in regard to vocations were more palpable in rural than urban areas. Castes there were exceedingly touchy and sensitive about change of hereditary occupation by members of any group. Taking up a calling associated with a lower caste was considered almost a sacrilege. It was not only the moral restraint and the social check of the caste-fellows that restricted the choice of one's occupation, but also the ban imposed by other castes on the entry into their profession of outsiders. Such restrictions were jealously imposed by Brahmans particularly on their claimed profession of priesthood. All priests were Brahmans, but all Brahmans were not priests. Curiously enough they were found engaged in almost any secular calling, including trade, agriculture and even army. Their multiplying numbers were responsible for many of them becoming cooks. It does not, however, mean that the traditional hereditary occupations were being given up. Perhaps the occupation which was common to the caste was the traditional one; it was not necessarily that by which all or even most of the group made their living.

4.28 Connubial Restrictions

The major field of life where caste restrictions were most minutely detailed, rigid and relentless were in regard to marriage. It is here that the multitudinous ramifications of caste came into obtrusive prominence. Rules of all kinds were in operation restricting the field for choice of a mate. The principle of endogamy was applied with meticulous care to most caste-groups, so that a caste was almost invariably endogamous in the sense that a member of the large circle denoted by the common name might not marry outside that circle. But within the circle there were usually smaller circles each of which was also endogamous. For instance, a Gaur Brahman had to find a wife not only from among the Brahmans, but she must belong to the Gaur Brahman group.[36] In fact, this rule was the *fons et origo* (the source and origin) of caste perpetuity.[37]

In the North Western Provinces and in Rajputana the endogamous groups were often divided into exogamous groups who had to look for matrimonial relations beyond their closely limited circle. The division into exogamous groups sometimes presented the phenomenon of isogamy and hypergamy.[38] Some castes had exogamous groups which were strictly hypergamous. On the whole, the principle of endogamy held ground. Some sociologists have even been driven to regard endogamy as the chief characteristic of caste since it is in this regard that caste trammels were most tenacious. Any violation of rules regarding marriage alliances meant severe censure leading invariably to expulsion from the group with no possibility of finding admittance to any other respectable group.

4.3 Types of Castes

Within the hierarchy, while the predominance of the traditional system of the fourfold castes was vaguely believed in the ramifications of the subcastes with their distinctive names were greatly obtrusive. This was the result of a process of fission and formation of new castes which had been going on for a long time and had by no means come to an end. It was still going apace. The baffling names of the innumerable sub-castes in the consequent medley pose a tremendous problem in an attempt at categorising them under the traditional system. They had outgrown that simple pattern and were far too complex to be fitted into it. The Brahmans were the only group that could be discerned as such despite the variety of callings followed by them and the countless sub-castes that had spun out. The nomenclature of the sub-castes, however, is suggestive of the forces and trends in operation, on the basis of which a rough classification may be drawn up.

Contrary to the popular idea that caste is immutable, facts prove that caste is *varium et mutabile semper* (is ever a fickle and changeable thing). A trivial cause would be sufficient to produce fission within a caste giving rise to a new group. The bases, thus, of distinction leading to the exclusive marking off of these groups were several. Of these, tribal, territorial, occupational, sectarian, of miscegenation, dissimilarity of customs and even adventitious, circumstances were prominent.

THE CASTE SYSTEM

Illustrative examples of all these groups could be found in different parts of Northern India.

4.31 TRIBAL CASTES

Initially tribes, some of them had in course of time developed into regular castes, preserved their original names and many of their characteristic customs, but modifying others in the direction of orthodox Hinduism and adjusting their manner of life in accordance with the same model. The Ahir, Dom, Dosadh of U.P. and Bihar; the Gujar, Jat and Meo of Rajputana and Punjab ; the Koli, Mahar and Maratha of Bombay ; the Bagri Bauri, Kaibartha, Pod of Bengal are typical examples of the tribal type.[39]

4.32 TERRITORIAL CASTES

The sub-castes bearing the name of some ancient city or locality were very common. In U.P. and Bihar most of the sub-castes of the Brahmans had names of the locality to which they belonged or came from originally. The Kanaujia Brahmans from Kanauj, Maithil from Mithila, Saraswat after the river Saraswati and Gaur from an old name of a large part of northern India. In Bengal, Radhia Brahmans took their name from Radh, the old name of western Bengal, and Barendra from the northern part of Bengal.[40] The Ahirs of Central Provinces had, among others, the Narwaria sub-caste taking its name from Narwar ; Kosaria from Kosala, and Jijhotia from Jijhoti, the classical designation of Bundelkhand.

4.33 FUNCTIONAL CASTES

The occupational or the functional type of caste bearing the name of the function were the most common. They were so numerous and widely spread that community of function has often been taken to be the main force behind the process of evolution. Any change in the traditional occupation, especially among lower castes tended to give rise to a sub-division which ultimately developed into a distinct group.[41] If a Chamar took to weaving instead of leather working he would become a *Chamar-Julaha*. The Sadgops of Bengal broke away from the pastoral caste to which they originally belonged and took to agriculture; the Madhunapitias who were barbers became confectioners ; the Chasadhobas originally washerman took to agriculture.[42] The Sahansars of Hoshiarpur were admittedly Rajputs. but began to be known as Arains when they took to growing vegetables.[43] Actually most castes bore names of their occupation. Barber, weaver, *kumhar* or potter, *dhuniya* or cotton-carder, Basor are common instances. Sub-castes within many of the occupational castes bore names derived from the special branches of the occupation. Some sub-castes carried the name from some special activity such as the *Gargapari* who derived the name from the occupation of using magic to avert hailstorm.[44] Even peculiarities connected with the apparatus or technique of an occupation gave names to castes. The *kumhars*, for instance, in Central Provinces distinguished between those who made pots by hand without a wheel, and those who used a big wheel. The former were known as *Hathghade* and the latter *Thorchake*. Examples may be multiplied from every area which may not be necessary here.

4.34 SECTARIAN CASTES

Though small in number, the castes bearing names of religious sects were pretty noteworthy. The *Atith, Goshain, Bishnoi* and *Sadhs* of U.P.; the *Saraks* of western Bengal, Chotta Nagpur and Orissa, and *Lingayats* of Bombay are good examples. Even the reforming sects of the Brahmos and Aryas, opposed to the principle of caste, could not withstand this tendency and many of their followers assumed those names to indicate their sects. They did not, however, crystallise into castes perhaps on account of their rational and intellectual programme.

4.35 CASTES FORMED BY MISCEGENATION

In case of marriage not permissible by caste rules, the off-spring formed a separate caste, the name of which often denoted the precise cross by which it was started.[45] The *Shagirdapesha* or *Sagarpesha* caste of Bengal, *Boria* caste of Assam, and *Vidurs* of Central Provinces are typical instances. In spite of the rigidity of caste and the *jus connubi*, left-handed marriage were either permitted or connived at if the progeny of such unions formed groups distinct from the original. Many of the occupational castes were also the result of mixed marriages.

4.36 CASTES OF NATIONAL TYPE

Certain groups cherished traditions of bygone sovereignty and clung to traces of an organisation of a rather elaborate kind. The Marathas and Rajputs may be cited as examples.

4.37 CASTES FORMED BY CHANGE OF CUSTOM

Differences in custom and usage were important cause of fission and many new groups were the outcome of either neglect of some usage or adoption of new practices. In this respect the most potent influence during the period under review was the practice of widow-marriage. Some castes clung jealously to their customs and considered the suggestions of widow-marriage as highly reprehensible. Consequently, they severed relations with those who adopted the practice. In the Punjab, the Gaurava Rajputs, having taken to widow marriage, were for all practical purposes considered a distinct group with whom other Rajputs would not have any relations.[46] Another instance may be cited from the hill Rajputs of Kangra where the Rathi Rajputs separated from the Thakkar

Rajputs because they allowed widow marriage.[47] New habit, new caste, appeared to be the guiding maxim.

4.4 Caste-Government

In every caste, there was some authority charged with the duty of compelling obedience to customary laws. Among the twice-born that authority was often nothing more tangible than public opinion. But most castes or rather sub-castes had a regular system of government of which the ruling body was a council or assembly or tribunal known as the *Panchayat*. In Bengal, this council was known as *Dal*. Literally meaning a quintette or a body of five members, a *Panchayat* was more often than not, a much bigger group depending on the nature of the particular purpose for which it met. Generally, every adult male in an endogamous group had the right to speak and vote ; sometimes the *Panchayat* consisted of representatives selected on one basis or another, but mostly in greater number than five. There was, however, in most *Panchayats* a smaller group of elders of the village who guided its deliberations. The number of this committee was mostly five. The chairman was known as the *Sarpanch* or the *Dalpati*.

Its powers and functions varied both in nature and in extent. Generally speaking, it enjoyed some measure of judicial and executive powers. Proper observance of customs as also investigation and punishment of offences, thus, were its main duties.[48] In certain cases it acted as a licensing authority, permitting acts or omissions which by custom required sanction such as adoption of children and marriage contracts. In other words, the caste-council sat more to adjudicate than to legislate. It pronounced judgment upon the conduct of particular individual on particular occasions. It acted primarily as a judicial tribunal, with rather indefinite jurisdiction entirely unrecognised by law. The substantive law at the basis of the verdict being custom and usage, a mass of floating opinion as interpreted by the wisest elders. "Immemorial custom is transcendent law" as pronounced by Manu was still the guiding principle not only of the rank and file but also the *Panchayat*. Caste, no doubt, became a factor of legal importance and even more when its custom happened to be contrary to the general principles of law.[49]

The group which the *Panchayat* ruled was not the caste as such but the smaller group, a sub-caste or more properly an endogamous group of a caste so that the *Panchayat* of one endogamous group was completely independent of the *Panchayat* of another similar group within a caste. The decentralisation in this matter was considerable, there being not one *Panchayat* only to each endogamous group, but one Panchayat to each independent local section of that group, known as the *Biradari*. The local boundary of the jurisdiction of each such *Panchayat* was clearly demarcated and specifically stated. Sometimes it covered part of a village or town, sometimes a whole village or town, occasionally it stretched over a group of villages. These jurisdictions were known by different terms such as *ilaqa* (estate), *tat chatai* (mat from the tribal mat used at the meetings of the brotherhood), *ghole* or circle.[50]

In the network of the *Panchayats* exhibiting endless variations, two main types might be mentioned, the permanent and the impermanent. The former had one or more permanent officers whose duty was to bring offences to its notice and who also had the power to convene it whenever necessary. The latter had no such officers nor any committee save such as might be found for any particular purpose for the duration of a particular time. Among the higher castes, though there was no *Panchayat* as such, discipline was generally maintained by the elders of the caste who commanded respect and whose verdict on any controversial issue was honoured with respect and implicit faith in their judgment. Normally, the *Panchayat* would meet when convened by the headman either by himself or at the suggestion of an interested party. Such meetings were convened through the official summoner failing whom the barber (*Nai*) acted as such.

There were other interesting ways in which the meetings of the *Panchayats* could be convened. At a feast of the brotherhood, any person who had a complaint to make could use the opportunity by raising the point and the whole assembly would change from conviviality to business. A remarkable sense of decorum and consideration appears to have existed since controversial questions were seldom raised at marriages, so that the harmony of occasion might not be disturbed. Funeral gatherings often resolved themselves into courts of enquiry. Again on fixed occasions, usually a fair or religious festival at which large number of members of the brotherhood were likely to be present, the opportunity would often be used for a meeting of the *Panchayat* also. On such occasions several brotherhoods would assemble to discuss matters of general interest. Questions like the prohibition of liquors, curtailment of marriage expenses, abandonment or reprehension of such customs as widow-marriage were beginning to be mooted openly during the waning years of the nineteenth century.

The procedure followed by the *Panchayats* was more or less based on that of a court of law. The elders, under the guidance of the *Sarpanch* or the *Dalpati*, would take evidence, examine witnesses, hear what the accusers and the accused had to say and pronounce judgment. The judge and the jury, however, were potential witnesses since every member present had the right to speak and vote. Some castes insisted on a unanimous verdict, others accepted decisions of majority.

The scope of a *Panchayat's* jurisdiction was extensive. Violation of any of the caste restrictions was normally considered a cognisable offence. Hence, breaches of the convivial and commensal law, including

THE CASTE SYSTEM

restrictions on drinking and smoking, disregard of caste customs of trade and occupation, neglect of caste regulations regarding social privileges and violation of caste connubial rules which were elaborately minute and specific, formed the chief transgressions. The connubial restrictions covered breaches of marriage law in every aspect such as seduction or adultery, immorality or concubinage; refusal to carry out marriage after agreement; refusal to carry out the '*gauna*' ceremony (finalising marriage by sending the girl to the groom) refusal to maintain a wife; marrying a widow without permission and other allied matters.[51]

4.41 Forms of Punishment

Common punishments were fines and feasts to the brotherhood or to Brahmans. For certain offences pilgrimages, begging and various forms of degradation were imposed. A fine would normally be spent on sweets, drinks or feasts for the assembled brotherhood. High fines were contributed to projects of common public interest such as the recitation of *Katha*, the feeding of Brahmans or the purchase of cooking vessels for the use of the community.[52] In all cases, whether serious or trifling, the penalties imposed would normally be proportioned to the enormity of the offence committed as measured by caste standards and might range from a mere reprimand to final expulsion from the community, which could be temporary or permanent, depending on the offence. This, without doubt, was the most dreaded punishment for social ostracism had serious implications. As Sister Nivedita puts, "the church excommunicates, the law imprisons, but society merely cuts the offender in the street".[53] It meant not merely a suspension of or severance from all those good offices between man and man which the social code prescribes; it was not merely a cessation of the pleasures of social gatherings or reunions, but was infinitely worse than all these. It symbolised living death of the outcast. The ceremony as prescribed in the laws of Manu, a solemn and imposing proceeding. was performed with all seriousness, at least by the lower castes in the villages.

The decisions of the *Panchayat* were normally accepted as final verdict and punishments were borne with patience and fortitude. Caste penalties provided a very powerful moral sanction. In Sister Nivedita's words, "It is true of London as of Banaras that caste law is the last and the final that controls a man for it comes into operation at that point where tribunals fail. It takes cognisance of offences for which no judge could inflict penalties."[54] The reality of its dread and efficiency is too obvious from popular terms such as *Panch Parmeshwar* which means the caste-council is God. Actually, the power of caste custom could be even superior to law.

The equity of the pronouncements of the *Panchayat* and the extent to which the punishments were meted out is a matter open to doubt especially when the culprits happened to be rich and influential. There were ample means by which the offender against caste-rules could expiate his misdeeds and retrieve his caste-status. These means such as performance of religious rites and purificatory ceremonies, the feasting of Brahmans and bestowing of suitable presents on them and banqueting the members of his caste involved expenditure of money. Naturally, therefore, re-admission to the privileges of caste was a comparatively easy matter for the rich. A Bengali millionaire, none too scrupulous, discussing the subject of caste is reported to have remarked emphatically that caste was in his iron chest.[55] The infringement of caste rules by the poor meant terrible hardships on the delinquents, often leading such men and women to crime and even suicide. For many, with a less sensitive nature and more a calculating and practical outlook the easier way to face their predicament was to let themselves break away from the original caste, and in course of time constitute a new one. Curiously enough, the new groups thus formed, developed and observed trammels no less stringent than those of which they had been the victims.

4.5 Peripheral Changes in Caste System

This overall picture of the caste system as it prevailed in northern India during the period of study was more true of the rural areas than urban. The citadel of caste with all its fortifications of rules and regulations, taboos and penalties, was showing signs of giving way to the exigencies of life under changed conditions in cities and towns. It exhibited cracks, crevices and chasms of a varied nature. Diversity, here again, was the essence adding to the caprice and eccentricities so that the system appeared at times rather grotesque and ludicrous on account of the conflicting and contradictory practices. Not that it had been static; like any social institution it had ever been growing and changing. In fact, the additions and accretions over the centuries had so moulded it that the system, as it exhibited itself in towns and cities, presented a considerably different picture from what it is supposed to have been in its primal shape. The principle of heredity was perhaps the only aspect in which it had remained unchanged. All else saw change and readjustment.

The roundly stated hierarchy was considerably shaken. It was losing ground mainly because of the fission and formation of new castes. The change in the position of the Brahmans was most conspicuous. Although in many places, particularly villages, the Brahmans were still generally regarded as little less than divines and received their dues by way of respect as well as material gifts, they could no longer command the universal reverence of yore associated with the priestly duties. The 'earthly gods' did not meet with unqualified reverence which they once received.[56] Nominally one class, for the Brahmans held together better than any other caste, they did not form a single compact body which could be identified with the sacerdotal profession. Nor did they conform to the ideal life of a Brahman as prescribed in the Hindu Law books. There were exceptional cases, no doubt, of those who passed through the traditional four stages of the student, the householder, the meditative and the ascetic, but what was commonly practised was a very much modified scheme. Occasionally some Brahmans, when growing old would hand over their property to their heirs and go to some place like Banaras, Gaya or Haridwar on the banks of the sacred rivers to await their end in peace.[57] But this was by no means a universal practice. The old idea that it was derogatory to the dignity of a Brahman to sell his services had given way to the pressure of circumstances. Instead, therefore, of the traditional single calling of priesthood they were found in all professions and occupations that can be named. Not only did they seek employment as priests and teachers, but also as soldiers, physicians and artists. A great many of them were farmers and merchants. Not a few of them were employed as domestic servants particularly as cooks even in the homes of Sudras rich enough to pay them for their services.[58] They suffered no qualms of conscience in serving the English officers whom they considered *mlechhas*. They were found among beggars as also among criminals. In the general scramble for employment, in fact, they had to compete and fight their way among other classes as equals and not by any divinity or advantages of belonging to a privileged order. The pride of their birth was no longer for them the cause of compunction in accepting jobs of any kind. In short, the prestige of the Brahman was on the decline and was maintained at its ancient pitch only in the remote villages and in the fastness of superstition in big cities.[59]

The conception of the hierarchy was getting confused on account of the multiplying ramifications of new castes accelerated by the exigencies of modern life. Not only were new needs giving rise to new occupations, but changes were coming over the occupations of many craftsmen. For instance, the national ox-cart in which the village land-owner or the portly merchant rode was in many places being replaced by the dog-cart or the barouche. Again the development of the original crafts accounts in a great measure for the constant change which was ever going on in the occupational groups. Thus the old occupation of the *kunjra* or the green-grocer broke up into that of *mewa-farosh* or fruit-seller and the *sabzi-farosh* or dealer in greenstuff; that of the carpenter into those of the farrier, joiner, cabinet-maker, coachbuilder, carver and guilder. The new groups that were coming into being did not all develop into regular castes. Some remained as vocational groups only, but the factor of birth and heredity counted much. In short, as the new civilisation developed, fresh wants had brushed aside some of the old practices, there was found a curious admixture of occupational groups. One reads of "earpickers, tattooers, makers of caste-marks, twisters of the sacred thread, tooth-stick sellers, markers of henna and carmine, exorcists, hail-averters, astrologers, casters of horoscopes, genealogists, side by side with watch makers, photographers, journalists missionaries, astronomers, meteorologists, firemen and shutters, electroplaters, and ice-manufacturers."[60]

With the rise of new occupations naturally the inveterate idea that caste tied a person down unalterably to the station of life in which he was born and that the son must invariably follow the occupation of the father without the possibility of ever deviating from it or rising above it, was changing. Excepting priesthood which continued to be the monopoly of Brahmans, almost every occupation was open to any one. Nor was there in practice any obstacle in the way of Sudras from rising to the highest rank. Many Kayasthas, considered Sudras in Bengal, were in the vanguard of society as members of learned professions such as lawyers, teachers, doctors, etc. Many castes took their names from the ordinary trade or profession of the members and that was in many cases hereditary, but it did not necessarily denote their vocation. For instance, the *Ahirs* in Bihar were herdsmen by tradition but eighty percent of them were engaged in agriculture. The same was true of the *chamars* of Bihar of whom not more than eight percent lived by working in leather, their hereditary occupation, and of the *telis* (oil-pressers) only thirty two percent followed their traditional profession.[61] Thus, there were ample cases of men belonging to different castes engaged in the same trade or profession. In urban areas, the administrative services and other learned professions were a real medley of different castes and creeds, and in rural areas agriculture displayed a similar mingling.[62] Many castes took their names from the ordinary trade or profession of the members and that was in many cases hereditary. But there were ample cases of men belonging to different castes engaged in the same trade or profession.

The traditional restrictions separating class from class by impassable barriers, and keeping all, for ages in certain relative positions, had considerably lost their former rigours. With the exception of the connubial restrictions, which appeared to be getting more rigid, all other taboos were losing their hold. The disabilities from which certain classes suffered were often ignored. Even in Bengal where caste restrictions were most stringent, a considerable softening was noticeable. The position of mixed castes had improved. The Kayasthas and the Vaidyas, leaders of the Sudras, were no longer treated with contempt, but were considered equal in importance with the Brahmans[63]

The strictness of caste-regulations in matters of food and drinks though constantly in evidence was permitting convenient relaxations to suit the exigencies of changed conditions. In cities like Calcutta, it was possible for the more advanced people to set aside rules which at no distant age were most rigorously observed, though this was looked down upon as something undesirable. They could, if they chose to eat meat, drink wine, wear shoes made of cow-hide, sit down at table with Europeans without losing their position in society. In fact, public dinners were given in European hotels where Hindu gentlemen of various castes publicly partook of food together. The conservatism was proving too weak to resist the temptation of self-interest and material advantages that might be derived from social intercourse with the official and the ruling classes. It was flexible enough to make adjustments. Even in the countryside rich landlords relaxed their prejudices to entertain government officials, serving meat with the meals and engaging Muslim cooks for the purpose. In travelling, convenient adjustments were being made; water might be permitted from the pitcher of a man of low caste, light refreshments such as biscuits and sweets were purchased and eaten without too many enquiries. *Pakka* food in any case could be taken. Ice and soda water at railway stations were considered permissible by many save the most conservative. The introduction of water-works in larger cities shows how practical conveniences overcame all caste prejudices in the matter. In Calcutta, the orthodox Hindus attempted to boycott the water-taps to which all castes had free access or to have separate taps set up for the different castes, but when this was found to be impracticable, the *Hindu Dharma Rakshini Sabha* (Society for the Preservation of the Eternal Religion) determined that although it was contrary to the precepts of Hinduism for men of different castes to drink water which came from the same vessel, yet as the people had to pay taxes for the water supply, the money payment should be considered sufficient atonement for violation of the ordinances of the Hindu religion.[64]

The caste-councils in their turn were often lax and allowed violation of their rules to pass lightly. They devised ways and means by which the process of purification to be gone through by the defaulters was considerably modified and punishments made lighter. The tampering of caste rules by the rich and the better educated, thus, was becoming frequent.

The growing laxity of caste in this period may be ascribed to many factors. Railways stand out as one of the chief forces inimical to caste, showing no favour whatever to the institution. Promiscuous travelling by them, throughout the country brought thousands of the twice-born classes in contact with the Sudras, out-casts and *mlechhas*. Public hospitals and jails were institutions which in their own way proved unpropitious to caste for no regard was paid by them to its claims. The system of administration of justice by the law courts under the British government with its recognition of the rights of the individual, irrespective of the caste or creed, added a subtle influence to the undermining of the caste prejudices. The advancement of education had its effect also. The schools and colleges that began to multiply, as decades moved, brought persons of all creeds and castes, except the lowest, to sit together in the same class rooms, join in the games on the play-fields and sometimes reside in the same boarding houses attached to these institutions. All these forces exercised a subtle influence which, by the end of the century, had, indirectly and inadvertantly but surely and definitely, modified the inveterate caste prejudices of the people. The educated people who, interestingly, were forming a class by themselves, were beginning to realise that caste had not only become outdated, but was also responsible for many ills of the society. Many of them were openly criticising and censuring it, though they did not have the courage to abjure it.

4.6 Caste and other Communities

Essentially a Hindu institution, caste had not remained confined to the Hindus only. Its contagion had spread to others too but in a relatively mild form. The intricacies and the irrational commensal restrictions were not found among them though a fussy and discriminating trend was palpable among some of them. The Muhammadans of India were deeply imbued with the prejudices of caste. This was more particularly the case in the districts where they were numerically a small body and were lost in the denser Hindu population. It was more the case in Bengal than in the upper provinces at places such as Dacca and Bhagalpur than at Agra and Delhi. Muhammadan converts from Hinduism naturally retained many of their old prejudices and more often than not clung to them most tenaciously.[65] Caste restrictions regarding marriage had full force. Laws of endogamy and exogamy, as also rules prohibiting eating or drinking with strangers to the group were observed.[66]

The gradation of rank too was very similar to that of the Hindu society so that some Muhammadan families enjoyed a higher hereditary rank than others. They formed a kind of gentry, refused to intermarry with families of lower rank and abstained even in extreme poverty from menial service and degrading trades. Not only were there particular families placed in these superior circumstances, but there were whole clans among whom there were degrees of dignity and social position.[67]

The Musalmans in India were popularly divided into four groups. The *Sayyaids*, a term meaning lord and also known as *Pirzada* were taken to be the descendants of the Prophet and so were the highest in rank. Next in line came the *Shaikhs*, claiming descent from the gentry of Arabia. Mostly husbandmen they would not become artisans or engage in common trades. The term *Shaikh*, however, was becoming common and was being assumed by Hindu converts to Islam as a title of courtesy. The third in rank were the *Mughals*, a term originally denoting those who had invaded India and was applied to the followers of Mughal Emperor Babar but was assumed by certain agricultural groups as also converts to Islam. The *Pathan*, a corrupted form of *Pashtana* (speakers of Pashto) was a name given to certain tribes on the North West borderland. All these claimed to rank with the gentry.

Popularly however, the Muslims had two main divisions, the *Ashraf* or *Sharaf* and the *Aliaf* or *Kamina*. The former section consisted of all undoubted descendants of foreigners and converts from the higher castes of Hindus. The rest of the community fell under the latter section. The change in the status and the title of these groups, perhaps, was not impossible. From the saying. 'Last year I was a *julaha* or weaver; this year I am a *shaikh*, next year, if prices rise I shall be a *sayyaid*', it appears this was not difficult.

Even Christianity could not escape the subtle contagion of caste. It failed to obliterate caste prejudices from among the converts, there being a clear tendency on their part to group themselves according to the castes to which they originally belonged. They retained their caste names and clung to their time old usages particularly in regard to matters pertaining to marriage. In cases of church discipline, the system of caste was occasionally imitated in the Christian church When for any misconduct a man was put out of fellowship with his church the members would refuse to visit him, or give him their *hukka* (the smoking pipe). The exclusion from the friendly offices would lead to penitence and restoration to the fraternity would follow An Indian Christian headmaster of a mission school while giving evidence in a court of justice is reported to have given his religion as Brahman Christian. When questioned as to what that meant, he is believed to have repeated rather strongly and scornfully, "I cannot call myself simply a Christian when that *choorah* (sweeper) there is also a Christian. I am a Brahman Christian, Sir."[68] This was said by way of asserting his claim to caste superiority not desiring that it should be forgotten because he had adopted a new creed. At the missionary conferences the question of caste observances among the Indian Christians was frequently brought forward and discussed. Christian opinion was by no means unanimously in favour of doing away with caste

Even the British who laughed at caste, and in theory condemned it, disdainfully appeared to have adopted some features of it, without subscribing to it in theory wherever their own interests were concerned. It may not be an exaggeration to say that in "India they formed a distinct caste, the most exclusive and haughty *varna* in the land."[69] So thought some among the Englishmen themselves. In a way, they formed a group which might as well be considered to stand at the apex of the 'society in India', to which the elite, particularly the educated looked up in adulation. European society in India was practically divided into endogamous groups with just a little bias in favour of exogamy in regard to bringing brides from 'home'. They rarely had matrimonial relations with Indian Christians.

4.7 Social Reforms Inimical to Caste System

Caste society thus assumed rather an interesting though highly baffling picture which appeared to be getting more so as the century rolled towards its close. The currents and cross-currents of conflicting tendencies both on the part of the people as well as the government led to an anomalous situation. In one sense, the rigours of caste appeared to be losing their vigour, in another they seemed to be establishing their hold more firmly. The impact of English education and western civilisation served as stimulus for thought. The educated few, however small their number, were beginning to perceive not only the responsibility of caste for many ills of the society but also the way in which it had deviated from its pristine shape. A dual activity of reform and revolt was going apace simultaneously. The bold and the courageous among the educated were not only treating caste authority with scant regard but often flouting it.

There had always been revolts against caste from time to time. The principle of caste had often been called in question when the Hindu founders of new religious sects manifested a decided hostility to the system by admitting men and women of all castes indiscriminately into those communities on a footing of equality; but the practical result of such latitudinarianism had in the long run been merely the creation of new castes and not the abrogation of the system. No wonder, the serious-minded people felt the crying need for reform in the social set-up. The movement started earlier in the century by Raja Ram Mohun Roy caught momentum. Along with the move to liberalise religion, the Brahmo Samaj in Bengal, the Prarthna Samaj in Bombay and the Arya Samaj in the Punjab and United Provinces had the repudiation of caste as part of their programme. Swami Dayanand, the leader of the Arya Samaj movement, spoke of a resuscitation of Hindu society and preached the restoration of the original four-fold division based on occupation rather than on birth, instead of the manifold ramifications of caste. Movements of a more militant nature against caste, were not slow to arise. The force was being directed against the supremacy of the Brahmans and the general disabilities suffered by the lower castes.

The inroads on the solidarity of caste were not confined to the reformers only. They came from the government too, though not in a direct manner. In fact, the role played by the government appeared to be a dual one. As judicious and prudent administrators, the government would not interfere with the social life of the people. For all outward purposes, therefore, while the professed policy was in favour of equality of status, they also recognised the integrity of caste for its internal affairs. This did not protect the institution completely from forays on some of its vital powers. The establishment of British courts, administering a uniform criminal law removed from the purview of caste many matters that were at one time adjudicated by the caste-council. Questions of assault, adultery, rape and the like began to be taken to the courts of law for decision. The caste-councils in proportion lost their former importance. In matters of civil law, such as marriage and divorce, despite the avowed intention of the government to be guided by caste-custom and usage, the decisions of the High Courts slowly but surely set aside the authority of caste.

Furthermore, some of the administrative measures of the government were not in line with the caste spirit. The first official blow to it came with the Caste Disabilities Removal Act of 1850. The Widow Remarriage Act of 1856 served a second blow as it contained clauses practically violating the customs of some of the castes. The Special Marriage Act of 1872 was another incursion on the sacred bounds of caste in regard to matrimonial affairs. The Act made it possible for an Indian of whatever caste or creed to enter into a valid marriage with a person belonging to any caste or creed provided the parties registered the contract of marriage declaring *inter alia* that they did not belong to any religion. While these Acts were not in consonance with the spirit of caste, they were not sufficiently inimical to bring about its abrogation. The Acts proved ineffective and remained just passive avowals of policy and principles on the part of the government which, in actual practice, was unable to afford any relief to those who exposed themselves to the wrath of their caste or community for having indulged in the latitude provided by these Acts.

Yet the caste appeared to be stronger than law. It existed regardless and independent of the government, particularly during the post-1857 revolt period, since the government followed a policy cautious and wary to avoid adverse effects on its own security. Caste, as an institution received not only a tacit recognition as an internal affair, but active abetment also in many ways. The uprising of 1857 had opened the eyes of the British Government in regard to the potentialities of caste. The policy followed, thereafter, to recruit men of different castes in the army and to keep out the higher castes, Brahmans and Rajputs, was certainly the result of the realisation by the British rulers that caste might be useful in preventing rebellion. Kerr's remarks are an eloquent testimony to this.

"It may be doubted if the existence of caste is on the whole unfavourable to the permanence of our rule. It may even be considered favourable to it provided we act with prudence and forbearance. Its spirit is opposed to National Union."[70]

The progressively elaborate treatment of caste in the Census Reports since 1872 did much to consolidate caste groups. True, the government never avowed their intention of helping any caste to retain its number and prosperity. Nor did they at any time help any particular caste if it showed a numerical decline or economic dislocation. Yet the active interest of the officers conducting the census operations and their efforts to make a social phenomenon a scientific one by giving it a systematic classification and a nomenclature, where no names existed, did much to keep the caste spirit alive. In fact, it encouraged the strivings of the castes to escalate the social hierarchy. This some of the census superintendents have acknowledged.

Again, although the government did not recognise caste as a unit empowered to administer justice, it would not normally set aside the customs of a caste in matters of civil law. The cultural integrity of the caste, therefore, remained intact. In this respect, the responsibility of the *Panchayat* must also be noted. Even in its normal functioning the *Panchayat* helped in the perpetuation of caste keeping alive among members of a group a close interest in their affairs. Serving as a force for the maintenance of a better moral standard and for the strict observance of caste customs, it could not but foster the caste spirit at the same time.

The system of caste as modified by English civilisation and new ideas, had thus attained a more unique form that it ever did. Waning and waxing at the same time, it appeared both to be losing ground and growing into a stupendous system. Perhaps it had shifted its ground and assumed a shape different which appeared highly anomalous. The spirit of exclusiveness, however, pervaded the society of an inchoate mass of small units, isolated and insulated by elaborate rules. And while the vitality and tenacity of caste appeared to be still growing unabated in certain ways, there were encouraging signs of its decadence also. The growing and unwieldy multiplicity of its sub-divisions was in its own way causing the relaxing of its grip and the softening of its asperities.

References

1. *Census Report 1901*, Vol. I, p.496.
2. *Calcutta Review* Vol. LXXI, 1880, p. 26 ; Wilson, J. (1877). Vol. I, p 9 ; Dubois (1906). pp. 31-32.
3. *Census Report 1901, Bombay,* Vol. I, p. 175.
4. *Census Report 1881, Punjab*, Vol. I, p. 172.
5. Bower, Vol. 2, p. 17.
6. *Calcutta Review*, Vol. 71, 1880, p. 26.
7. Dubois (1906), p. 39.
8. Bower, Vol. 2, p. 17.
9. *Calcutta Review*, Vol. 55, 1872, 382.
10. Panikkar, p. 7 ; Wilkins, p. 158.
11. Wilson, J. (1877). Vol. I, pp. 13-14.

THE CASTE SYSTEM

12. *Census Report 1901, Rajputana*, Part I, para 219.
13. Kerr, p. 290.
14. *Census Report 1901*, Vol. I, p. 539.
15. *Calcutta Review*, Vol. 84, April 1887, 257.
16. Kerr, p. 252.
17. Risley (1915), p. 116 ; Ram Kumar Lal vs. Bisesar Dayal 1884, 10 Calcutta 638.
18. *Census Report 1901, Punjab*. Vol. I, p. 302.
19. *Census Report 1901, Bombay*, p 178.
20. *Census Report 1901, N.W.P.*, p. 227.
21. Ibid., pp. 212, 227 ; Chintamani, p. 154.
22. *Census Report 1881, Punjab*, Vol. I, p. 184.
23. *Census Report 1911, U.P.*, p. 328.
24. *Census Report 1881, Punjab* Vol. I, p. 184.
25. *Census Report 1901, N.W.P.*, p. 212.
26. Kerr, pp. 252 and 288 ; Hutton, p. 77 : Ishuree Dass p. 48.
27. *Census Report 1901, Bengal*, p. 367.
28. *Census Report 1901, Bengal*, p. 367. *Ibid.*
29. *Census Report 1881, Punjab*, p. 184.
30. Kerr, p. 309; Fuller, B., p. 163.
31. *Census Report 1901, N W.P.* Vol. I. pp. 212-13.
32. Duff, p. 266 ; Risley (1915), p. 111 ; Russell, Vol. I, pp. 72-73, Yusuf Ali (1907), p. 315 ; Also *Census Report 1881, Punjab*, pp. 173-74 ; Report on Native Press N.W.P., p. 364, *The Rohilkhand Akhbar* 11 July, 1868.
33. *Census Report 1911, Punjab* p. 413.
34. Bhattacharya, pp. 19-20.
35. Kerr, p. 258.
36. *Census Report 1901, Punjab.* p. 301.
37. Jones, p. 43.
38. *Census Report 1901, N.W.P.*, p. 814; *Census Report 1901. Rajputana*, p. 211.
39. *Census Report, 1901*, Vol. I, p. 519.
40. Bhattacharya, p. 35.
41. *Census Report 1901*, Vol. I, p. 522 ; *Census Report Punjab, 1881*, Vol. I, p. 175.
42. *Census Report 1901*, Vol. I., p. 522.
43. *Census Report Punjab, 1881*, Vol. I. p. 175.
44. Risley (1915), p. 77.
45. *Census Report, 1901*, Vol. I., p. 523.
46. *Census Report, Punjab, 1881.* p. 240.
47. Risley (1915), p. 94.
48. *Census Report 1911, U.P.*, p. 337 ; Blunt, (1931), p. 104.
49. Blunt (1931), p. 104.
50. Ibid.

51. Bhattacharya, p. 17 ; Risley, (1915), p. 78.
52. Oman (1907), p. 46.
53. Nivedita, Sister (1904), p. 128.
54. Ibid.
55. Oman, p. 47.
56. *Calcutta Review*, Vol. 15, 62.
57. Wilkins, (1887), p. 160 ; Bower, Vol, 2, pp. 18-19.
58. Kerr (1907), p, 269.
59. Sherring, Vol. I, p. 4 ; Bose, p. 187.
60. Crooke (1897), pp. 208-10.
61. *Census Report, 1901, Bengal*, Vol. I, p. 486.
62. Risley (1915), p. 77.
63. *Calcutta Review*, Vol. 15, p. 165.
64. Wilkins (1887), p. 163.
65. Kerr, p. 334.
66. Crooke (1921), p. 9.
67. *Imperial Gazetter of India,.* Vol. I, p. 329.
68. Oman (1907), p. 74.
69. Ibid., p. 70 : *Kayastha Samachar*, 16 January 1902, pp. 60-61.
70. Kerr, p. 361.

5 The Indian Family : Its Structural and Functional Transformation

- 5.1 The Hindu Joint-Family
  - 5.11 The Karta
  - 5.12 The Grihini
  - 5.13 Other Members of the Family
- 5.2 The Fissures in the Joint-Family
- 5.3 Muslim, Parsi and Christian Families
- 5.4 The Dwelling Place of the Family
- 5.5 The Family Ceremonies
- 5.6 Omens and Superstitions
- 5.7 Conclusion

If the caste system in India was the axis on which the social organisation moved, its basic unit was the family. Descending through generations, the institution of the family had survived the vicissitudes of the country's fortunes and maintained through the centuries its uniformity in a remarkable manner with slight local differences only. No political or religious change had in any vital manner altered its basic features.

5.1 The Hindu Joint-Family

All accounts indicate that the system of family prevalent in northern India among the Hindus, the majority community during the period under review, was based on the old idea of the *Pater-familias* (the Father of the Family). It was more or less a reproduction of the ancient patriarchal group of which the chief characteristics were the supremacy of the eldest male, the agnatic kinship and the resulting law of inheritance, ancestral worship of the patriarchal group and the exclusion of the females from inheritance. It was the patriarchal group that gradually developed into the Hindu joint-family system. The conception of family, however, it might be pointed out, was widely different both in character and aims from what is understood by it from the western stand point, today, even in India.

While the western countries had discarded all that represented the characteristics of primitive stages such as the need of defence against enemies, the obligation of common family worship etc., in India the Hindu joint-family system continued relatively unchanged. It was an institution of the early agricultural communities which was common to many races and peoples and had its origin in the necessities of a remote age when the protection of person and property and reparation of injuries suffered did not form the duty of an organised central authority. It had retained many of its old distinctive features even with the passage of time. The family organisation now had no longer to defend itself against outside aggression, nor was it kept together for common ancestor worship. These were, perhaps, concomitant and incidental. The family, on the whole, was an organisation chiefly for the building up of common property. Its plain and simple object was to provide for the maintenance of a number of persons connected together by some sort of relationship. It brought together under the roof of a common *pater-familias*, a number of persons who did or did not have a legal or moral claim on his support. It undertook not only the support of the old parents, but also that of needy sisters, brothers, cousins, uncles, aunts and other relations. Three generations, if not even more, living together, enjoying a community of life and interest was a normal feature particularly in Bengal.[1] There was no limit to the number of persons of whom a Hindu joint-family consisted, nor to the remoteness of their descent from the common ancestor and consequently to the distance of their relationship from each other. Instances were common when a single family consisted of nearly a hundred persons or even more—men, women, children, servants.[2] Daughters born in the family were its members till their marriage and women married into the family were equally members of the joint family. The whole body of such a family constituted a sort of a corporation, some of the members of which were co-parceners, that is to say, persons who on partition would be entitled to demand a share while others were entitled only to maintenance. Each person was merely entitled to reside and be maintained in the family house. When he died his claims ceased and as others were born their claims arose. The claims of each member sprang from the mere entrance into the family and not from taking the place of any particular individual.[3]

The Hindu joint-family system has been described by some as a sort of joint-stock company in which the head of the family was the managing director with almost unlimited powers; or as a little kingdom in which he was an almost absolute sovereign. The sons, grandsons or nephews, who formed the family regarded all their earnings as belonging to the common treasury and their expenditure was under the direct control of the head. If and when some members of the family happened to be engaged in work away from home the balance of their salaries and profits was remitted to the head of the family. This worked well as long as the family depended mainly on land for its subsistence. But in proportion as the livelihood of the family ceased to be derived from land alone and was obtained from other occupations as well, the unwieldy constitution of the family was beginning to be shaken. As the upper classes, especially in towns, though few in number, began to fill public service, flock to learned professions or adopt occupations of trade and commerce, it was becoming obvious to them that they could not live together in the same place or that the earnings of different members could not be pooled for common use. This, in a way, received encouragement from the Hindu Gains of Learning Act, which allowed educated members of the family to treat their earnings as personal acquisitions.[4] Members of the family, in some cases, were being separated, each living in a place to which his avocation called him. The necessity of change was an inevitable blow to the traditional constitution and spirit of the joint-family, though it affected only a very bare minority in urban areas. In the villages, the system of joint-family existed more or less undisturbed by the changes in towns and cities.[5]

5.11 THE KARTA

The head in a joint-family, known as the *Karta*, as a general rule was the father or the grandfather, if alive, or in his absence, the senior male member of the family. He was entitled to, and was presumed to manage the joint property and family affairs. With the consent of the others, a junior member of the family might become the manager of the family property. The managing member was entitled to full possession of the joint-family property and was absolute in its management. He had the power and the right to represent the family in all transactions relating to it. He was to act on behalf of the family without the consent of the other members and even in spite of their dissent; and when his act was within his legal authority and for family purposes, it also bound the others. The other members, as long as the family was undivided, had only a right to maintenance and residence. They could not call for an account except as incidental to their right to partition, nor could they claim any specific share of the income, nor even require that their maintenance or the family outlay should be in proportion to the income. An absolute discretion in this respect vested with the *Karta* whose position was *sui-generis*. The relation between him and the other members of the family was not that of a principal and agent or of partners. It was more like that of a trustee *cestui que trust*[6] (that is what may be called a trust).

Although his powers as the chief captain, the high-priest and the sole magistrate which convention had allowed to him, had no legal force during the period of study still in orthodox families he continued to wield them with the implicit acceptance of other members. In matters affecting the health and comfort, education and training of the subordinate members, his rule was absolute.[7] He was the final authority in all matters. If a son or a daughter were to be married his voice was indispensable. The *Karta* could almost dictate what friendships the dependent members would form. In other words, the *Karta* exercised supreme control over the whole family so that no domestic affair of any importance was undertaken without his consent or knowledge. The management of finances was almost entirely regulated by his judgement ; it seldom or never exceeded the available means at his disposal. Property acquired by the subordinate members was managed by him with absolute authority; the honour, dignity and the reputation of the family wholly depended on his prudence and wisdom weighed by age and matured by experience. His own individual happiness was completely identified with that of the other members of the household. As the supreme head, he was not only to look after the secular wants of the family, but also to watch the spiritual needs of all the members, checking irregularities by the sound discipline of earnest admonition.[8] On the whole, with some exceptions, the *Karta* was a great disciplinarian.

The exceptions, however, manifested the change, differing in degree, that was creeping into the general set up particularly in big cities. In many cases, the substance of the power and control of the head of the family, as such, was gone. His position rested more or less on what his juniors or even dependents were, out of reverence to his age or gratitude for his past services or even fear of public opinion, vehemently in favour of the old order, disposed to concede. In some cases he was the head only on sufferance.[9]

5.12 The Grihini

Next in point of importance in the domestic circle was the *Grihini*, the wife of the *Karta* or the mother or the grand-mother, if alive, the *mater-familias*. The position of the *Grihini* was a responsible one and her duties were alike manifold and arduous. What the *Karta* was to the whole family, the *Grihini* was to the female members. In orthodox families, she was looked upon with awe and reverence. She was the sole arbiter where female members were parties to a cause. Her decisions were final unless she chose to refer any particular matter to the *Karta*. She was looked upon as the source of all knowledge and authority and honoured almost like the goddess *Saraswati* or *Lakshmi*.[10] She ministered to the internal life of the family, looking after the needs of all, young and old. Food, its procurement and preparation, were her special concern. More often than not, the *Grihini* was an excellent cook and acted as the goddess *Annapoorna* providing food for the family. There was a sort of a religious purity observed in the Hindu kitchen to which the *Grihini* gave a finishing touch. She organised the team-work among the younger women and supervised it with meticulous care. In well-to-do families where women were beginning to show their disinclination to do the cooking and paid cooks were engaged, the need for her supervision was still greater and so also her responsibilities. In the management of the commissariat, she was all economy and frugality, avoiding all waste and yet taking care that full hospitality was extended to the guests, the poor, and the helpless.[11] In the days when Home Economics Colleges were unknown in India, it appears, the home itself served as a centre where the young ladies acquired practical knowledge of domestic economy.

The *Grihini* and that was true of the *Karta* as well, generally led a simple life of self-denial. Working from dawn till midnight, she would be satisfied with the coarsest of meals and commonest of raiment, would observe fasts, keep vigils for securing the blessings of the gods towards her children.[12] Instinctively and naturally affectionate, she would often be indulgent to her children to a point not in keeping with the needs of discipline.

5.13 Other Members of the Family

As for the other members of the family, there could be a wide variety. The number of the incidental members did not depend on the means of the householder, but on his generosity and liberalism. No wonder, English officers were often amazed at the charitable attitude of the Indians towards their poorer relations. To them an Indian home was an asylum for the poor and destitute relations. One renowned English officer wrote in wonderment, "A young clerk of mine provided sixteen persons with food and raiment, his wife, his widowed mother, four younger brothers for whose education he paid, two widowed sisters with young families and a cousin out of employment."[13]

All members of the family, directly related or indirectly connected were subordinate to the *Karta* and the *Grihini*. Even the sons and the daughters-in-law, who came next in the order of importance, enjoyed a subordinate status. The sons might earn the money by which the family was supported and the daughters-in-law might have a fare share of the daily work of the home, but in the management of the affairs they had little power. In carrying out instructions in accordance with their ability, no wonder, some would earn more regard and favour of the *Karta* and the *Grihini*. Discontent on this account would naturally be there but that did not normally disrupt the joint-family. It was only when the sons got to the middle age, had large families of their own and the father became too old to be able to so manage the affairs as to check disaffection that they would begin to have separate kitchens. Parents would then join the son kindest to them. Sometimes they would find it convenient to eat together, but have expenses regarding other needs separate. Each son would pay a certain portion of his earnings for his family's support. Even when the sons separated they did not always part entirely, but most generally lived in the same enclosure. The father, as long as he was physically fit to do so, would exercise a general control over them. Even after complete separation the sons would generally continue to live in the same yard. Rarely would a man leave his brothers to live in another part of the town or village for it was considered much more convenient to be near each other so as to be of help in case of sickness or any other emergency. In case a brother was absent from home, his family would be under the immediate protection of his brothers or any male relations living in the same place.

The daughters in a patriarchal system, had a temporary place till their marriage only, when they became members of another family. Naturally, they were treated with more indulgence than the daughter-in-law. The privacy and the punctiliousness with which the young women of the family were guarded, undoubtedly, applied to all. They enjoyed, but little freedom of movement. However, in the general surveillance over them and the strict observance of etiquette expected of them, the daughter enjoyed greater liberty than the daughter-in-law, who in a respectable family, was subject to a very strict code of conduct. She was confined to an exclusively female section of the house.[14] Should she venture to go out or be seen in the men's part of the house, it would be considered highly immodest and unmannerly. If, per chance, she became so loud as to be heard by the men in their part of the house she would earn a severe censure and be admonished to behave better. Even the *Grihini* would not escape censure for a like offence.

The children of the family formed an important link in the great chain of the domestic circle. Looking upon each other, the cousins, boys and girls, as sister and brothers, they grew up in an atmosphere of practical socialism where they received equal attention and care from all—parents, uncles and aunts.

The incidental members consisting of distant cousins, relations by marriage and other caste-men formed quite a bulk. "Their mission in the family varied from active cooperation in the discharge of household duties to 'masterly inactivity.'"[15] When co-operation was real it was either rendered in the form of accountant or steward's services or, where the family was not prosperous, in the purchase of daily requirements etc. Where the family had landed property, the distant cousins took up the duty of collecting rents. The female relations helped in the kitchen, in preparing the daily offerings for worshipping or in looking after the children of the family.

The family was, thus, managed almost on the lines of benevolent despotism. The needs of each member were tenderly ministered and duties of each person fairly allotted. The system, nevertheless, suffered from its inherent weaknesses, A despotism, however benevolent, implies resentment of some kind. In a family also, with the spread of education, in the closing decades of the period of study, the tendency to question authority, to assert individual opinion and even to revolt against the will of the head, were more than palpable.

Besides all these, there were some important functionaries who were of the family and yet not in the family. The barber and the midwife rendered indispensable services for which they were adequately rewarded and were considered as part of the family.

The family priest, the astrologer and the *guru* were honoured dignitaries who wielded tremendous influence on the family and enjoyed a fat share of the resources through claims of all types. Guests in the family received hospitality.

Wealthy families would have a host of servants; though paid workers, those who had been with the family for a long time were treated as part of the family was would even be addressed as uncle or aunt. The family midwife was called *ma* by the children.

All expenses were justly considered to be the legitimate expenses of the whole family. For instance, one member of a joint-family might have a larger number of daughters to marry than the others. The marriage of each of these daughters to a suitable match was an obligation incumbent upon the whole family and discharged ungrudgingly.[16]

5.2 The Fissures in the Joint-Family

Normally, the relationship among members of the family under the benevolent influence of the *Karta* and the *Grihini* would be reasonably cordial except when the depravity of human nature did not allow it to remain so. Often the antagonistic influence arising from dissimilar idiosyncracies or individual designs of self-aggrandisement vitiated the otherwise congenial atmosphere in a family. Sometimes an unaccountable coldness would spring up between a daughter-in-law and a daughter to whom the parents would be partial. This would seriously affect the domestic felicity. The bickerings among the daughters-in-law often strained the relations of the brothers also and on that score, sometimes, separation from the family ensued. In towns and cities where education, however insignificant, and western ideas, brought with it alongwith the changes in the economic set-up, were beginning to show their influence, particularly in the closing decades of the nineteenth century. Instances of this nature were not too uncommon. In fact as the livelihood of the family ceased to be derived from land alone and was met through other occupations as well, the unwieldy construction of the family was also being shaken.

In Bengal, the system was rigidly traditional and uniform both in the urban as well as rural areas, except in Calcutta where the new forces of western ideas had affected it otherwise. The large undivided family comprising in some cases of no less than 300 or 400 individuals, including servants, living and having all things in common and cultivating under the guidance of a single head, was the general rule.[17] Among *kulin* Brahmans the numbers were particularly large since sisters' children had to be maintained for they had no parental home. In the Punjab, the system was slightly different in that it was the confocal group that formed the family which was not too large. In certain parts of the province such as Kangra and Rohtak, the average family consisted of 4.87 and 4.75 respectively. In Spiti, the familles were smaller still consisting of 3.3 members. The position in other provinces was not very much different from that of Bengal.

It may be broadly said that where the hamlet was the unit of habitation the familes lived in separate houses; where the large compact village was the rule they inhabited joint courtyards. Again in the western parts of the Punjab, the tendency was for the families to separate while in the eastern districts they were inclined to live together in common enclosures. On the whole, numerically the undivided family of the Punjab did not compare with that of Bengal. To the Punjab peasant, the tribe or the village community supplied the place of the undivided family,

> "the young men of the village are his brothers and the grey beards his fathers, the children following the village herd as he drives the cattle to their rest in the common pen his nephews and nieces, the field is his home and the settlement his undivided family,"[18] was the verdict of the Superintendent of the Census in 1881.

Although the basic pattern of the joint-family was the same, the tendency was to separate as soon as sons and daughters-in-law grew up and were able to look after their children. This tendency was on the increase in towns and cities where education was spreading. Each family would receive a part of the common house or a separate building in the common courtyard, cooking its meal and managing its income and domestic expenses separately. When the parents grew old, they would either live with one of the sons or live with all of them in turns. After some generations when the group of families became too large for the house, another would be built and a further separation would take place, the more closely related families living together. Sometimes the separation of the sons would be deferred till the death of the father dissolved the common tie, but it was more usual for it to take place as soon as the sons were grown up and dissensions began among their wives. The separation of confocal families was a purely domestic arrangement and extended only to expenditure on food, clothes etc. resulting almost invariably from disagreement among women and did not as a rule affect the land in the management of which they had no voice.[19]

5.3 Muslim, Parsi and Christian Families

The system found in the other communities—Muslims, Parsis and Indian Christians, did not differ considerably from that of the Hindus joint-family.

Among the Muslim converts, clinging to the old customs, looking upon cousins as brothers and sisters, the related families were inclined to live together. Among others who practised the very limited restrictions which the law of Islam interposed on inter-marriage and according to which marriage with a first cousin was allowed, no wonder the tendency of the families was to keep apart.[20] Nevertheless, the general tone in the family was that of a patriarchal system in which the master and the mistress received the utmost veneration from the members of the family. "The undeviating kindness to aged servants no longer capable of rendering their accustomed service, the remarkable attention paid to the convenience and comfort of poor relatives, even to the most remote in consanguinity; the beamings of universal charity ; the tenderness of parents and the implicit obedience of children are a few of the traits."[21] The Parsis, undoubtedly, followed the joint-family system practically on the same lines as the Hindus and the Indian Christians were no exception to the general trend among converts to cling to their old usages.

5.4 The Dwelling Place of the Family

The dwelling houses for the large families were designed to meet their normal requirements. With slight differences on account of climatic conditions, they were typically uniform in the general outlay. For all intents and purposes an Indian house was a regular sanctum not easily accessible to the outside world. Generally speaking, it was built in the form of a quadrangle with an open courtyard in the centre and among the well-to-do and the middle class, two distinct divisions, the outer and the inner apartments. The former had more open space with sitting and reception rooms exclusively for the male members of the family. The open court-yard, meant for the celebration of festivals, family gatherings and entertainments on occasions of domestic ceremonies was a very necessary feature. The inner apartments were meant exclusively for the ladies and were constructed with great care and scrupulousness. Few, or no windows, would open on the outside and often, specially in the case of high caste Hindus and Musalmans, there would be an inner courtyard so that strict privacy of the women's section would be maintained. Wealthy people living in towns and cities had fairly big buildings made of stone and baked bricks often two or three storeys high, sometimes ornamented with gaudy frescoes of historical or mythical scenes and personages,[22] but invariably having the same pattern of room arrangement around a courtyard.

The houses in the countryside were mostly of mud only one storey high. Four or five or more houses would be in a little yard laid out in the form of a square or a triangle or a circle with an open space in the middle where the members of the different families, related to each other, would sit and talk and where the cattle would be kept in the cool of the day in the hot season. Each house had two or three small rooms, one of which was used for kitchen and the others for sleeping and keeping things. Generally there would be a *verandah* in front of the rooms where women would sit during the day. A room at the entrance of the yard served as a sitting room for the men when not at work and for receiving strangers and visitors. No outsider could go, unaccompanied by an older member of the family to the inner section of the house, the sanctity of which was maintained to a great extent even in the villages, by the well-placed in life. Wealthy landlords or better class yeomen had comparatively larger houses, imitating the urban pattern, considered more respectable and dignified especially in respect of the inner section reserved for the women of the family.

The dwelling place of a smaller cultivator or artisan was of a simpler type made of mud walls and thatched roof. It was ordinarily a 'single room sleeping hut' outside which the housewife did her cooking, if possible under a small thatch near which the oxen stood, the cow, buffalo or the goat tethered and milked.[23] The prevailing note of village life was the absence of domestic privacy and the publicity amidst which the people lived. Life was largely spent in the open air and there was none of the isolation of the family. On the whole, the dwelling of a poorer tenant or artisan was surprisingly cleaner and less exposed to insanitary conditions than that of his richer neighbour; the floor and the outer cooking place would be carefully plastered with thin mud; the fewer possessions inside meant less stuffy frowziness.

The mode of living, on the whole, was simple. Excepting the light bedsteads, which could be easily moved in and out, the houses had hardly any furniture save in wealthy homes, in places like Calcutta where European style furniture was beginning to make its appearance. An average home would have some wooden boxes or baskets with covers and locks, depending on the income of the family, for the clothes and the jewels, cooking vessels and other utensils, brass plates and tumblers etc. A person was known to have wealth and be in comfortable circumstances by the house he lived in and the quality of the raiment he and his family wore, by the jewels that the women used and the number of the cooking vessels and utensils the family possessed.[24]

In the villages, the small peasant's possessions consisted of a few rickety cots, some brass cooking utensils, a store of earthen pottery for storing water, a stool or two for the children, a box for clothes or other valuables and an earthen granary in which the grain supply of the household was stored. The only difference shown by the household of a yeoman was that brass pots were in greater abundance and the women owned more heavy silver jewellery. The food and habiliment were also simple except on ceremonial occasions when the villagers dressed gorgeously, particularly the women.

In wealthy houses, the culinary arrangements and the cuisine were somewhat elaborate. The preparation and serving of the food on account of the caste restrictions which left limited scope for servants to handle it, kept the women busy most of the time. The feasts given on ceremonial occasions were sumptuous, involving expenditure often beyond the means of the family concerned. Women were not invited to these formal feasts, whether they were given to the Brahmans or the caste community on any occasion, happy, sad or punitive, except in the case of weddings and other domestic celebrations when they also partook of the feasts, though served separately. In the case of the rites and ceremonies conducted entirely by women, the feastiug was confined to them only.

5.5 The Family Ceremonies

Life in the family was regulated completely by custom and tradition, closely associated and bound up with religion. It is in regard to this aspect of life that the incidental members who were of the family and yet not in the family came into prominence. The priest, the *guru* and the astrologer, whose duty might be combined in one person in a village, each vying with the other for importance, had distinct roles to play, though their functions often overlapped and were confusing. The astrologer was, by far, the most important functionary for nothing could be done unless he fixed the auspicious day and the moment.

Generally speaking, the house of a Hindu was his sanctuary where the tutelary god had its niche to which daily worship was offered. In fact, there was hardly and event connected with home life which was not interwoven with religious ceremony in some form or the other, performed with an implicit faith in the presence of the dead ancestors to bless them. At the basis of all this was filial piety which made god of a man and assigned to father and grandfather a place next to God only in rank. The priest presided over these and conducted the ritual.

From birth to death, a Hindu would go through a mass of ceremonies and ritual which necessarily took up a large part of his life. The influence of this was seen in the family life of other communities also. Whatever the theoretical differences in the faith professed by them, the Muslims, the Parsis, and the Indian Christians, the pattern of their domestic life appeared to be similar to that of the Hindus. The ritual connected with the main events of life showed a striking similarity. They differed only in detail or in respect of the religious aspect involved in the ceremony. The ritual, controlled mainly by women, curiously enough, displayed a marvellous community of ideas springing from common faith in superstitions and omens, essentials of no religion whatever, but the result of intellectual backwardness. In the tortuous complexities of the ceremonies observed by the different communities, the Hindus were, undoubtedly, giving the lead. Some usages were common to all castes even to all faiths; others were confined only to the higher classes, so that the wealthier the family the more minute and meticulous the observance. The dominant factor at all events in the family being the feeling of commonness or oneness, sharing the joys and sorrows of each other. No ceremony could take place, normally, without the whole family being present regardless of occasional differences or unpleasantness among some members. In fact domestic ceremonies served as good opportunities for clearing up differences and patching up minor quarrels and thus reassuring and re-cementing the family solidarity.[25]

The domestic ceremonies began even before birth. Whether this was due to the faith in the theory of transmigration of soul, which could be, in the case of the Hindus only or merely to the realisation of the risk involved in the physical phenomenon of birth, is beside the point. The fact remains that the pre-natal ceremonies were considered important not only by the Hindus, but by practically all, and were celebrated with equal meticulous care. These being mainly ladies' functions, much feasting and gaiety, singing and dancing was done by them alongwith trifling ceremonies, important in their view to the well-being of both the expectant mother and the baby. The first ceremony began some four months before the birth of the baby and the other two that followed came at intervals of two months each. The auspicious time and hour for each being fixed by the astrologer. The nature of the ceremonies performed indicates that the expectant mother was closely watched and the family took interest in her progressive condition. The first three ceremonies were connected mainly with the diet of the expectant mother. Gradually and successively, restrictions respecting food observed rigorously in the earlier months, were removed and she was allowed to eat normal food. The last of these ceremonies, known as the '*Satsanka*' ceremony among The Hindus in Bengal and by different terms in other provinces, came one month before the birth. The expectant mother, on this occasion, would be gaily dressed and brought out among the gathering of the ladies. She would be seated in the centre, with a lamp lighted in front and offerings would be made to gods on her behalf so that she might have a safe delivery. Presents would be given to her and much merry-making would go on. Similar ceremonies were observed among the Muslims and the Parsis also.[26]

At the time of birth the midwife would be sent for to attend on the mother who would be segregated since she was regarded ceremonially unclean for three weeks after child-birth if she had a son and for a month if her child happened to be a girl.[27] Generally, she would not be allowed to mix with outsiders for forty days. Often a shed would be provided as her temporary home. In poorer families, the lumber-room would generally be vacated, whilst in larger houses among well-to-do families, a special room would be reserved for the purpose. The birth of a girl generally would pass without any fuss if it did not mean sorrow and gloom in the family, while particular rejoicing would be made if the child be a son. The parents would be congratulated, women would sing songs suitable to the occasion, eunuchs would come and dance and receive gratuity, the astrologer would be sent for and the new-born's horoscope be cast to predict his fortune. The male issue was prized both for the continuance of the family as well as for the performance of funeral rites and offerings. The desire for male offspring was, therefore, universal.

On the host of ceremonies following child-birth, some were common to all, while a few were peculiar to some communities only. The most important of the ones common to all was celebrated on the sixth day and was known as *Chhati* or *Shashthi* after the name of the goddess *Shashthi*, the guardian of children. The mother and child would have bath and the goddess *Shashthi* would be worshipped, since she was supposed to write that night the child's destiny on his forehead. The child would then be dressed in clothes, rings on wrists and ankles, and a chain round its waist, if it be a boy. The whole night merry-making would go on so that a proper vigil be kept.

The credulity of women, especially in Bengal, is reflected in the details of the preparation for the writing of the destiny. A palm leaf, pen and ink, a snake's skin, a brick from a temple of Shiva, fruit, wool and money would be kept in readiness. A regular watch would be kept during the night lest the deity should feel slighted and in anger write a long list of calamities.[28] The Parsi ladies, perhaps, exceeded the credulity by adding to the details of the ceremony.

In Bengal, on the eighth day, came the *Atkauri* ceremony when eight kinds of peas, rice, etc. were distributed. Children from the neighbourhood would come with winnowing fans, knock at the door of the room of confinement, make enquiries after the baby's health and have a few jokes at its father's expense. Sweets would be distributed to them and they would go away.

In certain regions in case of a birth under a certain starry constellation, another curious ceremony was performed on the 27th day when "water was brought from twenty seven wells and leaves of twenty seven different kinds were put into a small earthen jug of twenty seven tubes which the potter made for them for the purpose."[29] Incense would be burnt and an awning of blanket would be made under which the parents would sit with the child. The water of the earthen jug would be poured on the blanket through which it would fall on them; when the whole water would be poured, they would come out, have bath in separate places and change their clothes. On the fortieth day after child-birth was celebrated, another ceremony known as *Chhillah* in some regions and *Maswara* in some parts of the North Western Provinces. It indicated the completion of the period of segregation as also the safe emergence from the risks of delivery. The mother and child would have bath and dress in gaudy clothes. Women relations would get together and give presents to the mother and the child. The young mother, after this ceremony was allowed to move about freely.

Giving the child a name was an important ceremony, though it varied greatly, as to the time when it was celebrated from region to region and from people to people. It could be performed on the 11th, 13th, 21st, 40th day or even later. The essential part of the matter was the choice of the name by the astrologer. Curiously enough his authority was recognised by all, regardless of religious differences. He suggested the name after proper calculation and consideration of the influence of the position of the planets at the time of the birth. The baby could, however, have other names besides the one chosen officially. Such a name would often have a whole history of years of disappointment, weary-waiting, sorrows, the final joy and perhaps fears and apprehensions of a chance unkindness of the gods.

At the age of five or six months the *Annaprashana* ceremony was performed when the child would have his first taste of grain-food. This would generally be rice cooked with milk and sugar. Among the Muslims, the equivalent of this was the ceremony known as the *Namakchashi* when the child was given the taste of seasoned food for the first time.

In the first, third or the fifth year or on an auspicious day the child would be shaved for the first time. This might be done at home or in a temple or on the river bank, etc. Besides the feast to relations and friends on this occasion, the barber would get a good share of presents.

At eight or sometimes later in the early teens, came the ceremony of initiation for the boys when the child was supposed to enter the sacred pale. This rite was performed by the *guru*. Among the twice-born the *vagyopaveet* or *upnayan* for boys only was performed at this time. In the closing decades of the period of study, the Arya Samajists were advocating the performance of the *upnayan* ceremony for girls also. No instance of the actual performance of the ceremony has, however, come to my notice. The ceremony involved a thorough ritual for the boy to be initiated. He had to fast, bathe and appear in spotless garments before the *guru*, who would then in private, select a special deity as also a text which he would teach the child. This he would thereafter repeat daily a certain number of times, but keep it a profound secret.

Similar ceremonies, varying in their religious aspects, were performed by other communities also. The higher classes among the Muslims had it in the form of '*bismillah*', the creemony of pronouncing the name of God, and beginning of education. When the child, boy or girl, was about five years of age the family teacher would perform the religious rites and receive presents in return. In the case of girls, the hair was plaited for the first time on this occasion. The Parsis had an equivalent to this in the form of the ceremony of investiture with the '*Sudra* and *Kasti*', both for boys and girls. The priest performed it with all the religious injunctions.

The Muslims performed another ceremony, the circumcision (*khatna* or *sunnat*) for boys at the age of about eight. It could be any time between seven and twelve years of age, though it was considered lawful to have it even seven days after birth. The performing of the minor operation by the barber was attended by many trifling ceremonies. Some tribes in certain parts of the Punjab and North Western Frontier Provinces practised female circumcision also.[30]

Next in importance came the ceremonies connected with marriage, undoubtedly an important event in life. Months before a marriage, the family would be in an uproar making preparations for it. There was a wide variety of ceremonies connected with it among different castes, which also varied from region to region. Yet, the basic pattern was the same in which the family priest and the barber played an important role. Not only did the barber carry the overtures of matrimonial alliance between the families and helped in settling the preliminaries, he also acted as an invitation card in flesh and blood when the auspicious time for the celebration approached. The priest performing all the rites and ceremonies extending over days acted as the main figure. Mingling fun and jubilations with custom and usage as well as religious ritual, the members of the two families participating in full strength, women holding steadfast at the helm of affairs, a marriage was a long-drawn out affair. The actual marriage ceremony was, undoubtedly, a religious rite but its sanctity was shrouded, often completely eclipsed, by a horde of unessential and trifling ceremonies. Among the Hindus, giving of the daughter by the father as a gift to the bridegroom, going round the fire by the couple, invoking the ancestors and the gods as witnesses and soliciting their blessings being the core of the ceremony, it was performed by the priests of the parties concerned in accordance with the prescribed rites accompanied by the recital of the religious text. All this was, however, interposed with ceremonies in which the closer relations of the couple had special parts to play. Some of these were curious, inexplicable and irksome, while others were the result of the peculiar ideas about marriage as an institution in India.

The other communities were equally prone to revel in the nupital ceremonies, most of which were adopted from the Hindus, whose influence was most markedly manifest in this regard. Excepting the actual marriage ceremony which was performed strictly in accordance with the religious injunctions all other customs were not very much different from those of the Hindus. In the case of some classes among the Muslims, in some regions, the marriage ceremony after it had been performed by the *Qazi* or the *Maulavi* had to be finalised by the *Padha*.

All these ceremonies connected with important events in the family were occasions for the relatives, friends and acquaintances to get together. The dominant note in all the celebrations was the merry-making and the feasting, the latter being the most essential concomitant without which no ceremony could be complete. The generosity and hospitality of the host, on such occasions, extending even to casual visitors was remarkable, though this trait was not so marked among the educated in urban areas towards the end of the nineteenth century.

If the ceremonies on happy occasions were prolonged those at the time of death were no less so. Among The Hindus, they began when a person, ill and suffering, appeared to be approaching his end. A place in the room would be plastered with cowdung and consecrated; some *kusha* grass (considered sacred) would be spread on it and the dying person would be laid on it. On this occasion charity would be given to the Ganga Putra sub-caste of the Brahmans. Those who could afford would give a cow as also large sums of money. The leaves of the sacred plant of Tulsi (Basil) and the holy water of the river Ganges would be put into the month of the dying person and the name of God, *Ram*, would be repeated.

It was generally believed by the Hindus that death near the holy Ganges or any of its tributaries was desirable for a speedy entrance into heaven. Those living anywhere near the holy river would, therefore, remove the sick for whom the doctors held out no hopes of recovery to its banks. The sick would be kept close to the waters of the Ganges despite the risks of exposure. A few minutes before death, the person would be brought to the brink of the river, where half-immersed in water he would be expected to have his last breath.[31] This the family did for the beatitude of the departed soul. Perhaps in this period, the custom was losing its intensity.

The disposal of the dead body by cremation among the Hindus involved a regular ceremonial, some meaningless, yet grim and glum, adding to the gloom of bereavement. The basis of these ceremonies being the belief in the life before and after; great regard was shown to the ancestors at each step. The range of variety in the funeral ceremonies was wide, though the general pattern was more or less the same.[32]

The son, failing him the person who was to light the funeral pyre, would be the central figure along with the priest giving directions and the members of the family participating according to the closeness of the relationship. He would make a small ball of barley flour and put it into the right hand of the dead body which would then be wrapped in clean white cloth, laid on a bamboo framework, covered then with better cloth depending on the means of the family and carried on the shoulders by the male members of the family helped by fellow-caste men to the river side or the burning place. Arriving on the spot, the body would be placed with its head towards the north and its feet to the south. The body would be given its last dip in the river or bathed, with the covering sheet on it before placing it on the fire when a little gold and *ghee* would be put into its mouth. The person to set fire would have himself completely shaved if the deceased was older than him, otherwise he would be allowed to leave the whiskers untouched. When the body would be half consumed a little *ghee* would be poured on the head and the skull broken with bamboos; when it would be almost consumed, the fire would be extinguished with the water of the Ganges and the remains of the body would be immersed in the river. The cremation spot would be cleaned and consecrated with the words 'Ram' 'Ram' written on it. At a little distance, the barber would stick a blade of *kusha* grass over which the gathering would throw *tilanjali*—a handful of sesame—after they had bathed. The whole party then would go to the door of the house of the deceased, chew the bitter leaves of *neem* and a few grains of barley then wash their mouths and go back home.

Those who did not have access to the river would leave the ashes and remains on the spot to be collected two days later by the male members of the family and closer relations. The bones picked would be kept at home in an urn till such time, as possible, at the earliest, for some one of the family to take it to be immersed in the holy Ganges.

For elevan days, the bereaved family, particularly the chief mourner, the son, would follow a very strict code of conduct in every respect, including the diet. For ten days he would make a *pind* or ball of flour and on the eleventh day would take them all to the river, temple or a grove, where rice and milk would be cooked and made into balls. The whole thing with some more additions of sweets would be put on the ground, milk poured on it, incense and *ghee* burnt and a lamp lighted.

During this period the closer relations including women would bathe and offer *tilanjali*, burn a lamp in an earthen pot and suspend it on a *peepal* tree. A large earthen pot full of water with a small hole through which the water would drip would also be suspended. On the eleventh day, the *Ekadhash* ceremony would be performed when the *Maha-Brahman* would come and be given presents consisting of all possible things which a man would use in his life, the quality and quantity of these depending on the means of the family concerned. Incense would be burnt in the house and the chief mourner then would don his formal clothes and greet relations and friends. On the thirteenth day, The Brahmans would be fed and given presents. For a whole year, the family would remain in mourning and no festivals would be celebrated. On the darkest night of the month, during this period of mourning special ceremonies would be performed and on the last day of these special dinner would be given to twelve Brahmans who would also get presents of vessels and clothes. On one of such nights in the fourth year after the death again a dinner would be given to four Brahmans with the usual presents.[33]

The dead of the family, the ancestors received special commemoration throughout life. One whole fortnight of the waning moon, known as the *Pitri* or *Pittir Paksha* in the month of *Ashwin*, (September-October), was dedicated to this purpose. On the dates of the deaths of the ancestors special offerings known as *Shradhas* were performed. Brahmans would be invited and fed in the name of the dead. Relations and friends were also be invited to partake of the meals. The *Shradha*, the superstitious garb which shrouded it aside, was important as a special institution. It was the keystone of succession to property. Being worship of ancestors this rite exacted an unqualified submission to the authority of the deceased patriarch, an unexampled appreciation of his services, a manifestation of love and reverence, gratitude and obedience and a natural passion for the welfare of his departed soul.

Those who had the means would go to Gaya to perform the *Shradha* at the Vishnupad Temple. The process of performing *Shradha* at Gaya was neither simple nor rapid. Its efficacy was beyond doubt for the credulous and it could be secured only by performing the rites of offering the *pinds*, balls of flour, to the ancestors and presents to the Brahmans at about fifty distinct places around Gaya, besides at the renowned temple.[34]

The rites observed by the other communities differed no doubt in respect of their religious faith. The Muslims buried their dead and the Parsis carried them to the Towers of Silence and left them there exposed, to be devoured by birds and consumed by elements. But the ceremonial shrouding those rites manifested not only a similarity in many ways, but a strong influence of the Hindu customs.

Among the Muslims, the putting of water from the holy well—Zamzam—into the mouth of the dying, the elaborate preprations of the dead body for its internment into the grave and the post-burial custom of visiting the grave on the third day are points in instance. Again, the mourners among Muslims also observed for some days a special conduct in regard to diet abstaining from meat, fish or savoury food. A lamp would generally be lighted at the place of death where the body was washed and sometimes on the grave for three, ten or forty nights. On the fortieth day, the *Chehalum* ceremony would be performed.

The commemoration of the dead throughout the year, at short intervals, with an elaborate ritual, besides the annual ceremony, is another instance reflecting Hindu influence. Among the Parsis, the ritual was not only more elaborate and complex but strictly administered by their priest and staunchly adhered to by the persons concerned.

THE INDIAN FAMILY

Death as elsewhere meant deep sorrow and grief, to which women mostly gave unrestrained expression by loud wailings. This assumed painful and ghastly sights in that they beat their chests as they wept, joined by friends and distant relations. Voice against this practice of *siapa*, as it was called in certain regions was being raised by the reformers towards the end of the nineteenth century.

5.6 Omens and Superstitions

Not only were the main events of the human life enshrouded by ceremonies, but even the trifling day-to-day happening such as the building of a house, going out on a journey, undertaking a new project of work, were not free from them. At each stage in life and at each step towards it, there was the ritual that had to be gone through. So staunch and deep-rooted was the faith in the supernatural that life in the family appeared to be completely guided by superstitions and omens. This was not peculiar to the Hindus only. In fact if there was anything common to all it was this credulity and backwardness. Nothing was the result of natural laws; no happening could be reckoned as a chance occurrence, no rational or scientific explanation would satisfy either the rustic or the average town-dweller. Surprisingly, even the educated, whose faith in the ritual was, perhaps, no longer implicit could not break away from the customs, partly on account of the influence of the women of the family and partly of public opinion as also the hold exercised by their caste. Hence, the elaborate ritual in everything, including the daily routine.

Normally, a Hindu would adore the household god daily, offer *Tarpan* (oblations of water) to his ancestors before taking his meals, and for anything important invoke the ancestors and the gods, both of whom were treated with equal respect almost on the same plane, to protect, bless and ward off the danger.

Superstition governed life hourly and the belief in omens restricted thought and action. It is difficult to distinguish as to which of these belonged particularly to which community, such being their all-pervading. A few examples from a very wide variety will illustrate their fantastic nature.

If a person was to commence a new task or was about to set out on a business and somebody sneeze, he would stop for a few moments otherwise he was sure to fail in his task. If one heard the word monkey, although it was considered a sacred animal, in the morning it was believed that he would get nothing to eat during the day. If a shopkeeper started the day's first deal on credit, it meant the whole day would bring no earning. If one shoe happened to fall on top of the other, when taken off by some one to sit down, it indicated imminent travel. The evil eye was firmly believed in and iron was considered the sovereign safe-guard against it. If a house under construction, an iron pot would be kept on the works. At child-birth some sort of iron was kept near the child to frighten the evil spirits.

In certain parts of the Punjab, superstition of the evil eye had curious manifestations. On the birth of a child an invisible spirit was sometimes supposed to be born with it and unless the mother kept one breast tied up for forty days while she fed the baby from the other, in which case the spirit died of hunger, the child grew with an endowment of the evil eye. Whenever a person so endowed looked at anything constantly, something evil, it was believed, was bound to happen.[35] Admiring a child's health or looks was not considered good and mothers would often put a little black mark on the face of the child to ward off the evil eye. Good and bad omens were innumerable. Black was unlucky; if on beginning to dig for the construction of a house, the first spade turned up charcoal the site would normally be abandoned; owls portended desolate homes and cuckoo (*koil*) was especially unlucky.

Chief among good omens was *dogar*, two water pots one on top of the other. To sneeze, in itself, was considered auspicious as one would not die immediately after sneezing. Odd numbers were lucky, though three and thirteen were not. Hence if a man wished to marry a third wife, he would first marry a tree so that the new wife could be reckoned as the fourth. Number five and its aliquot parts ran through most religious and ceremonial customs. For instance, the shrine to Bhumia was made of five bricks, five blades of the sacred grass were offered to him after child-birth, five sticks of sugar cane were offered with the first fruits of the juice to the god of the sugar-press. Offerings to Brahmans were always $1\frac{1}{4}$, $2\frac{1}{2}$, 5, $7\frac{1}{2}$, whether rupees or seers of grain.

The south was a quarter to be specially avoided as the spirits of the dead were believed to live there. Hence, the cooking hearth in a house could not face the south; nor could any one sleep or lie with feet in that direction except in death. Certain days were associated with the demon of the four quarters known as the *Dishashul* living in certain directions. A wise and cautious person would not only avoid taking a journey, but avoid even ploughing in these directions on those days. The position of certain planets had to be ascertained before undertaking a journey lest their influence should prove to be harmful. If Venus were in declension a bride would not go to her husband's house nor would one return thence to visit her parents.

The peasants observed many additional superstitions connected with their agricultural activities. They would sow only on certain days ; so also begin and complete the harvest on certain days considered auspicious.

The belief in charms and amulets was common. Not only would small children often have an amulet put around their neck to shield them from danger, but even older persons would resort to this measure as the only recourse against misfortune. This was most marked among the Muslims.

The faith in all superstitions and omens naturally gave the astrologer, the priest and the *guru* a dominant position with a tremendous influence on all, young and old, in the family. The functions of these three dignitaries were absolutely indispensable to the family, though they could not always be distinctly demarcated. The priest who presided over all the ceremonies often combined in him the functions of an astrologer. As such, he practically dictated the activities of the family. Nothing could be done without his approval and sanction; He cast the horoscope of the new-born and predicted the events of life, warning against the misfortunes as also suggesting the precautions for averting imminent dangers. This involved propitiation of gods and offerings to Brahmans. He fixed the time for everything in accordance with what the stars indicated to be auspicious and laid down the procedure. Disregard to his dictates meant deliberate invitation to misfortune.

The priest or the *Padha* as he was known in the Punjab was the officiating Brahman and was expected to be acquainted with the Hindu ritual in ordinary use or weddings, funerals and other domestic ceremonies and be able to respect the sacred text used on those occasions.

The *Guru*, normally, enjoyed a very dignified position in the family. Respect to the *Guru* was enjoined by the scriptures. In theory, every Hindu was supposed to have a *Guru* or a spiritual preceptor; in fact the great mass of the peasantry did not even pretend to possess one: But those who profess to have a *guru* showed him the utmost honour, and served him with great veneration. In the long list of the festivals that the family celebrated, the one dedicated to the *guru*, known as *Vyas Puja* or *Guru Puja* (worship of the *guru*) had quite a prominent position. The preceptor on this occasion was offered special honour by way of presents. In many cases, this was converted into a most lucrative position since the Hindus, influenced by superstitious fears, gave lavishly to such men who were believed to wield divine powers and solve all problems. The *Guru* would visit his disciples about once a year and if he be really earnest, as some were, he would use the opportunity to teach them some portions of Hindu mythology or some lessons in religion. But often they were ignorant and selfish; their chief object in visiting the disciples was to obtain the customary share. Nevertheless the visit of the *Guru* caused great excitement in the family and all, young and old, men and women would be up in his service.

Then there was a group of Brahmans, purely levitical, being potential priests, but exercising no sacred functions beyond the receipt of offerings. A considerable number of them were *purohits* or hereditary family priests who received as of right the alms and offerings of their clients, and attended upon them when the presence of the Brahmans was necessary. Some of them—perhaps, a large number of them—were associated with families for purposes of being fed only. No child was born, named, betrothed, married ; nobody died or was burnt ; no journey was undertaken or auspicious day selected ; no house was built; no agricultural operation of importance begun or harvest gathered without the Brahmans being fed. In short they were feasted by the family in sorrow and in joy.

The other communities had the equivalents of these dignitaries discharging almost similar duties. The Hindu astrologer, however, appeared to hold sway among all. He was consulted regardless of religious differences, though not always openly by the higher classes.

5.7 Conclusion

Generally speaking, thus, the traditional family-system supported by the religious injunctions prevailed almost unchanged, unquestioned and unchallenged. Yet cracks in the system began to appear as the century rolled towards its close. As new ideas filtered in through education on western lines, as contacts with the western world increased, as the economic set-up, particularly, in cities began to alter, though very slightly, the sense of values began also to be changed. The educated urban society, though small and insignificant numerically, just a speck in a vast ocean, was beginning to view the system with scepticism. It was no longer, for them, a heaven of peace and felicity. The force of religion and tradition which had kept the several branches of the family structure, was losing, considerably, its moral cohesiveness so that the advantages of the joint-family were beginning to be eclipsed by its disadvantages. Its redeeming virtues were being supplanted by vices of an abnormal degree and magnitude. Sincere sympathy and harmony which were the normal features of a joint-family were beginning to give way to stolid indifferences, jealousies and rivalries. The control over extravagance which the family normally exercised, at best encouraged idleness and killed all initiative and desire for progress and advancement. The benevolent despotism of the parents under which, individualism was sublimated and self-interest completely subordinated to the interests of the family as a whole was beginning to be looked upon as a tyranny under which the young felt fettered and restless while many a patriarch felt frustrated and longed for the halcyon of the old times. The protection and the asylum to the dependent women especially the widows of the family was becoming a drudgery from which there was no salvation for them except through death. The implicit trust among members was beginning to be undermined. Family feuds, litigation and waste of resources were no longer too uncommon. The Hindu family in cities, where more openings for jobs for young men were arising, was beginning to show signs of change from a convenient social unit into an incoherent and cumbersome mass, as though the domestic instincts were undergoing change. However, small and insignificant the signs, they were, perhaps, the harbingers of a revolution of its own kind.

References

1. Jones, p. 246 ; Wilkins, p. 21.
2. Chintamani, p. 127.
3. Mayne, p. 271.
4. Mayne, pp. 290-92.
5. Ishuree Dass, pp. 115-16.
6. Mayne, p. 308.
7. Mullick, p. 17.
8. Bose, Shiv Chunder, p. 2.
9. Mullick, p. 10.
10. Ibid., p. 40.
11. Bose, Shiv Chunder, p. 4.
12. Mullick, p. 42.
13. Fuller, Joseph Bompfylde (1910), p. 166.
14. Bose, Shive Chunder p. 67.
15. Mullick, p. 138.
16. Mayne, p. 308.
17. *Census Report 1881, Punjab*, p. 42.
18. *Census Report 1881, Punjab*, p. 42-43.
19. Ibid.
20. *Census Report 1881, Punjab*, p. 41.
21. Crooke (1897), p. 2.
22. *Ferozpur District Gazetter* 1883-84, p. 38 ; Ishuree Dass, pp. 118-19.
23. Crooke (1897), p. 267.
24. Ishuree Dass, pp. 119-20.
25. Crooke, *Mrs Mir Hassan Ali's Observations*, p. 199.
26. *Ibid*, p. 210 ; Karaka, pp. 153-59.
27. Ishuree Dass, p. 186 ; *Allahabad Gazetter*, 1884, p. 1730.
28. Wilkins, p. 10.
29. Ishuree Dass, p. 188.
30. Harklots' *Jafar Sharif's Islam in India*, pp. 48-50.
31. Wilkins, p. 446.
32. Ishuree Dass p. 189 ; Monier-Wiliams, (1878) pp. 97-99.
33. Ishuree Dass, pp. 192-93 : Wilkins, p. 459.
34. Monier-Williams, (1878) p. 102.
35. *Census Report 1881, Punjab*, p. 117-119.

6 The Institution of Marriage

6.1 Marriage as a Religious Injunction as well as a Civil Contract
6.2 Three Forms of Hindu Marriage
6.3 Marriageable Age
6.4 Child Marriage
6.5 Social Restrictions in Match-making
6.6 Matrimonial Bargaining
6.7 Dowry System
6.8 Marriage Expenses
6.9 Auspicious Time for Marriage
6.10 Marriage Rituals
6.11 Monogamy and Polygamy
6.12 Polyandry

Marriage, as a basis of family and as one of the most important human institutions in all civilised societies, held a position of singular significance in India of the nineteenth century. The pervading influence of this institution, indigenous to the majority community, the Hindus, was such that a good many of its special features had been adopted by most of the others that came into close contact with them, even though the orthodox prescriptions of their own system were opposed to them.[1] Curiously enough, the heterogeneous public opinion appeared to be at one in regarding marriage as one of the most prominent human duties. Its universality, thus, regardless of caste, creed and status, with slight variations here and there was remarkable. The statistics of the period bear eloquent testimony to the fact that marriage was more a rule than an exception, particularly with the Hindus.[2]

6.1 Marriage as a Religious Injunction as well as a Civil Contract

Among them, it was the most important of the *samskaras* and was regulated not merely as a social necessity, a natural instinct, but a religious injunction. It was a duty to be performed by all unless desirous of a celebate life of renunciation. Hindu popular opinion undoubtedly upheld the marriage system as regulated by the Hindu lawgivers and writers of the *Smritis*, chief among them being Manu. According to his ideals, marriage was a necessity for purposes of the performance of obsequies by the son. Without such ceremonies the father's soul could not be delivered from the hell called '*Pūt*'. This was also connected with the law of inheritance which was to some extent binding on the masses.³ Marriage, thus, was a sacrament, a religious rite and not a civil contract. It had to be administered by a priest, in the presence of the house-hold god and not merely to be registered by a state agency.

The conception of marriage as an essential duty was shared, to a very great extent, by the other communities also, including the Muslims even though they did not regard it purely as a sacrament. Their marriage rites were performed by their religious preceptors—the *Qazi* or *Mulla* for the Muslims, *Dasturji* for the Parsis and the Christian minister of the particular sect concerned. All Hindu marriages were ecclesiastical marriages and as far as the state is concerned were not registered. Regarded as a social institution, marriage under the Muhammadan law was essentially a civil contract and rested on the same footing as other contracts.⁴ The principle of registration was first introduced during the period in the case of Christians as much confusion arose from the practice of their marriages being performed by ministers of different sects. There being enough scope for irregularities, the validity of some marriages was open to question. The Christian Marriage Act of 1852 (Government of India Act V of 1852) was passed specifically to systematise their marriages. This Act accepted the idea that marriage, whatever else it may be, is a civil contract and that it is only in this respect of it that the law regards it. The Act of 1852 was applicable only to Indian Christians.

Among the Muslims, it was commonly believed that marriage was enjoined on every Muslim and celibacy was condemned by the Prophet; hence, the generality of the marital state among them also. The proportion of the married and unmarried among the Muslims as compared with the Hindus differed but slightly.⁵ The difference was most notable amongst the very young of both sexes. Under the age of five, the proportion of Muslim girls, for instance, who were unmarried was much more than a quarter of the corresponding figures for the Hindus and between the ages of five and ten it was only a half. The age period 15-20 showed an equality between the proportions of the two communities.

Marriage as a religious injunction had important implications. It was irrevocable and indissoluble among the upper class Hindus, however ill-sorted and unhappy it might be. The bulk of people among the high caste Hindus appeared to accept with unstinted faith the ordinance of the Hindu law-givers even if they were proved to be unjust distortions or irrational contradictions of law in its pristine form. A thin minority of the educated people, mainly in big cities like Calcutta were beginning to give serious thought to this aspect of the accepted conception of marriage leading to grievous customs and the resultant problems of unhappy marital adjustments.⁶ Their voice, though soft, yet sonorous, raised in favour of reform of the marriage system was also beginning to fructify. Public opinion, although of a very small section of the educated people, indicated a definite change in their attitude to the whole concept of marriage. The Native Marriage Act of 1872 was the outcome of a demand from this section of the intelligentsia led by Keshav Chandra Sen.[7] Intended originally to be a general measure for all, except Christians governed by the Act of 1852, who might expressly object to be married with rites of any recognised religion, it was, when passed, applicable only to a small community, the Neo-Hindus, as would object to marry according to ordinary Hindu rites. The orthodox Hindu community, a vast majority, took alarm and complained vociferously that such a measure would strike at the very foundation of social organisation. So strong was the opposition that the Act was restricted in its application only to the progressive Brahmos, a group numerically far too insignificant. The Act fixed the minimum age for a bridegroom at eighteen and for a bride at fourteen, but required the written consent of parents or guardians when either party was under twenty one. Higher ages would have been preferred, but it was considered expedient to defer it, for lack of favourable public opinion. The marrying parties, moreover, had to make a declaration that they did not profess any of the religions, Hinduism, Islam, Sikhism, Jainism, Christianity, Zorastrianism, etc. The Civil Marriage Act of 1872 (Government of India Act III of 1872), at best, was a minor crack in the otherwise solid and invulnerable system. The vast majority of the Hindus continued to regard marriage as of yore, a sacrament irrevocable and indissoluble.

6.2 Three Forms of Hindu Marriage

A necessary corollary of this system of marriage was that a consenting mind was not essential. Its absence, whether from infancy or incapacity was immaterial. Of the eight archaic forms of marriage sanctioned in the Hindu scriptures and approved even by Manu, accepted as the Paramount authority, all, but three—*Brahma, Asur* and *Gandharva*, were obsolete.[8] The essence of the *Brahma* form of marriage, one that was held in the highest esteem and was practised mainly by the higher castes, was a gift of the daughter in marriage. The distinctive mark of the *Asur* form, prevalent generally among lower castes was the payment of money for the bride; and the basis of the *Gandharva* marriage which was very rare, prevalent mostly among primitive forest and vagrant tribes as also among the people of the hills, was the agreement of the parties concerned. Marriage rites were implied in all the three forms. The gift of a maiden in the *Brahma* marriage signified transfer of the ownership, but the girl did not become a wife until the rites were performed. So too in the *Asur* form wherein the payment of money for the bride or the sale without the rites did not complete the marriage. These rites were mainly identical in all the forms of marriage whether

THE INSTITUTION OF MARRIAGE

it was *Brahma*, *Asur* or *Gandharva*. Though in the case of some forest and vagrant tribes, *Gandharva* marriage assumed forms which had no similarity whatever with Hindu rites.[9] The sanctity of the religious rites of marriage was upheld not only by the Hindus, but by all communities though much of it was shrouded by long-practised custom and usage.

The very nature of the two forms of marriage, *Brahma* and *Asur*, commonly found in practice precluded the possibility of free mutual choice on the part of the wedding couple, so that the sentiments of love scarcely entered as an element in the transaction. It was not usual for the young people even to see each other until the marriage was performed. Not only was the whole affair managed by the parents, their authority was implicitly and imperatively accepted. The nature of the marriage makes it understandable to a certain extent at least. In the case of the *Brahma* marriage the father or the guardian would, as of right and duty, select the most deserving and suitable recipient of the gift of the daughter, one whom he would deem fit to look after, protect and honour her. So, too, in the *Asur* form where money was accepted for the bride. The father or the guardian played the major role, since efforts were made to strike the best bargain and get the highest price for the daughter. Marriage thus, in either form, was arranged by the elders of the family assisted by professional match-makers, family barber or common friends who acted as media of communication between the families. The final word rested with the astrologer who gave the verdict not in consultation with the young couple but with their horoscopes instead.

6.3 Marriageable Age

There could hardly be a question of discretion or consent on the part of the couple as the age for marriage, accepted generally, was very young, notwithstanding slight variations in this respect in the different parts of the country and among different castes. Men as a rule married early and remarried as their circumstances permitted.

In regard to women, as a general rule, the tendency was in the direction of earliest marriage and less re-marriage and no re-marriage among certain classes. The figures of the period, even at the close of the century show that a considerably large percentage of children were married in the age group 0-5 years. Normally, however, most boys got married between 15 and 20 and most girls between 10 and 12.[10] The diversity of practice that prevailed in this respect was due mainly to local rather than merely caste or social customs.[11] For instance, the lowest grades of the community in some parts of Northern India married habitually at an age below that of the upper ranks.[12] In the east of the Punjab where Brahmanic influence prevailed even the Muslims followed the practice of their neighbours and *vice versa* in the west of the Punjab. Again, there was a great difference in this respect between the frontier and western plains and the more settled tracts of the central and eastern India which resembled North Western Provinces where the age of marriage was much younger than usual. On the whole, the Punjab population married at a comparatively maturer age.[13] In Bengal, too, locality was the main factor in determining the age of marrige, but the tendeney to conform more and more to Brahmanic orthodoxy was very marked amongst the castes that were on the border-land of respectability. Social status was exercising greater influence in determining the age for marriage so that the higher the social position the lower the age for marriage.[14] The lower castes, in most cases, were consciously adopting the customs of the higher castes to satisfy their vanity.

Among the Indian Christians, the custom of the early marriage prevailed even to a greater extent than amongst the Hindus. The Parsis followed more or less the same pattern in matters relating to marriage. The animistic sections of Orissa, where otherwise the percentage of early marriages was lower and those of Chhota Nagpur, were encouraging early marriage of boys and girls with a view to establishing a better social position.[15] Figures of the period indicate the largest percentage of juvenile marriages in Bihar and Bengal with North Western Provinces lagging not too far behind. In this respect girls were greater sufferers. The Vedic ideals of marriage which gave as much option to women as to men to marry or not to marry and by which it was normally contracted after the attainment of the years of discretion had gone completely into desuetude. The guiding authority in the matter during the period under study was Manu and other authors of *Smritis* who regarded marriage as one of the *samskaras*, the earliest for the girls like the *upnayan* for the boys or baptism for the Christian infant.

Parents would, therefore, naturally be anxious to see their daughters married at an early age, even if it be to take advantage of the eligible matches for worldly considerations only. The belief in the almost mandatory declaration of the *Smritis* that it was the duty of the father to see his daughter married before puberty was undoubtedly the motive force in determining their attitude. The ideal age according to the scriptures, which held sway over popular mind, was eight, nine or ten at the most. Early marriage for girls was not only prevalent but had become so compelling that a departure from it was a matter of social disapproval and even of social calumny, disgrace, obloquy to the family and of damnation to the ancestors. Such was the faith in the religious injunctions.

The sentiments which the orthodox were ever watchful to exploit for the continuance of this practice not only made marriage after puberty inconceivable, but helped the process of degenerating pre-puberty marriage among many sections into infant marriages. The anxiety of the parents to secure matches for their daughters led to customs which were far from desirable, One of these was the betrothal of babies, even before birth at times. There were castes who observed this custom known as *Petmanganiya* (pre-natals betrothal), a custom by which, children yet unborn were promised in marriage on condition that they turned out to be of opposite sexes.[16] For all practical purposes, it was as binding an arrangement as marriage since betrothal, as a general rule, was looked upon as a contract, a preliminary of the religious rite of marriage and as such could not be annulled. In fact, the term marriage among many sections included both the formal betrothal, an important ceremony and the subsequent handing over of the bride. The interval between the two being dependent on local custom and social rank. The two, marriage and betrothal, however, were distinct ceremonies and must not be confounded with each other. One was a completed transaction, the other was a promise for a deed, a contract to be fulfilled. It was an indissoluble agreement save in extraordinary circumstances.

In certain regions, such as the Punjab, among certain castes some curious customs arose out of this idea about the betrothal. If either the boy or the girl became dangerously ill a special ceremony known as the *Mathe Lagawan*—touching the forehead—was performed to cancel the betrothal. The boy would go to the girl's death-bed or *vice-versa*, with some sweets and offer to her addressing as sister which she would accept as from a brother. Every effort was made by the ailing child's relations to prevent the other child from coming to perform this ceremony at their house, because if once this happened no other family would marry with them while on the other side strenuous efforts, which sometimes resulted in severe affrays, were made to get to the sick child. Occasionally, even disguise had to be resorted to if other means did not assure success. If all these efforts failed it was sufficient to effect *Sawan* or striking the head against the wall of the sick child's house. In case the child died, this could be done within four days of the death. If neither was performed the surviving child could not get a second spouse. If, on the other hand, the sick party survived after the breaking off of the contract the betrothal could be renewed. The idea underlying these rites perhapes was that the betrothal was virtually a marriage, that the death of one party before the contract was cancelled made the other a widow or a widower and that the survivor as such was so ill-starred that, he or she could not obtain a new alliance.[17]

Another objectionable custom resulting from the anxiety of the parents to secure matches at the earliest was the inequality of the age of the couple. The authority of Manu prescribing age of the groom as twenty-four for a girl of eight and thirty for a girl of twelve was enough sanction for further perversion. In certain parts of northern India, specially Bengal, the disparity in the ages of the wedding couple was often disgracefully wide. This involved problems of widowhood. While girls of tender age were not infrequently united in wedlock to men of mature age, it was unheard of that a young boy would be married to a woman considerably his senior in years except in very rare cases among the *Kulin* Brahmans of Bengal.[18]

At any rate, marriage among the Hindus was not necessarily or even usually followed at once by co-habitation. More often than not, it signified only the performance of an irrevocable ceremony and did not result in the beginning of conjugal life till after another ceremony, called *gauna* or *bida* or *rukhsat* in the N.W.P. and *muklawa* in the Punjab, was completed. This was done usually after the brides attained puberty, after an interval generally of three, five, seven or even nine years depending on the age at which marriage was contracted. Till then, the bride lived as virgin in her father's house. *Gauna*, however, did not necessarily mean the commencement of conjugal relations. The time for this was normally determined by the parents of the bride when she attained maturity, after consultation with the astrologer. In some parts of the country, this ceremony was performed only to remove the restrictions, against the bride going to her husband's house. Normally thus, the earlier the marriage, the later the second ceremony when cohabitation was allowed. For instance, in the eastern districts of the Punjab, Jats generally married between five to seven years of age and Rajputs at fifteen or sixteen. The Rajput couples began their married life thereafter while the former deferred the second ceremony for several years to allow the girl to mature. In fact, the Jat parents often found the daughter so useful at home as she grew up that some pressure had to be put on them to give her up to her husband. For all practical purposes she began her married life later than the Rajput bride.[19]

In the south-eastern parts along the plains of the Ganges, ceremonies, irrational and irksome, were prevalent on a very large scale. In the North West Provinces the three highest castes—Brahmans, Rajputs and Kayasthas—permitted the bride to be sent to her husband's house immediately after the wedding although it was considered better and wiser to wait for the second ceremony, the *gauna*. In most cases, better sense prevailed and the child bride was allowed to enjoy a short span of childhood in her parents' home. Few girls bore children before their fifteenth year, cohabitation of the couple began generally between the fifteenth and the twentieth years.

What was the exception in the North West Provinces and most other parts of Northern India, tended unhappily to become the rule in Bengal where the influence of women's tradition was dominent and "overlaid the canonical rites of Hindu marriage with a lot of senseless hocus-pocus". This led to monstrous abuses, so that girls of the upper classes began married life at very tender age, often at nine and became mothers at the very earliest time that it was physically possible for them to do so. The ignorance and superstitious beliefs of the parents unconsciously encouraged the practice and made it almost unavoidable. On the second day after the marriage was held the 'flower-bed' ceremony which accepted the fact that conjugal relations were permitted from that time. Furthermore, within eight days of her marriage, the girl had to go back to her father's house and return to her father-in-law's or else she was forbidden to go her husband's house for a year. In a few families, the bride was not brought for a year but in the majority of cases this was considered most inconvenient and the eight day convention was followed.[20]

Among Muslims, the normal age for marriage was slightly higher than among the Hindus and betrothal was not regarded as part of the marriage. Consequently, married life commenced immediately after the wedding. But the bulk of them being converts from the Hindus, for most part they retained the old customs and indulged in such practices as were considered respectable among the castes to which they originally belonged.

6.4 Child Marriage

The vitiated system of marriage in Bengal became more and more rampant and by the third quarter of the century was beginning to arouse a sense of disapproval among the educated. Like most other matters this remained for some time a topic of discussion and at the utmost academic agitation. Press and platform though restricted in their scope were both active in the field. Repeated demands were being made, though by a very small section of the vast population, for banning child-marriage by law. Matters came to a head when a specific case of a pathetic nature occurred, This was the death of one Phulmani Dassi, an eleven year old wife, as a result of the excesses committed by her thirty year old husband. This proved to be crucial and a storm of open denunciation of the custom of infant marriage broke out. The agitation took a turn for a definite demand for practical steps to raise the customary age of marriage and its consummation.[21] The opposing forces of innovation and reform came to open blows, with those for the maintenance of the *status quo* and the result of the duel was the age of Consent Bill of (1891) Government of India Act No. X of 1891. A compromise at best, the Act was a tiny step towards change for it laid down officially the age for conjugal relations at twelve instead of ten as was customary on the basis of the religious sanction. It was the result of the labours of gentlemen like B.H. Malabari, who felt vividly the sin, the folly and the grievous harm of the custom of infant marriage. Tracing the woes of of womanhood and social degeneration in India to this cause, Malabari had proposed that the evil be combated through legislation. The issue became countrywide, there being much opposition to the proposal for enactment. The press was full of comments on it both for and against, the latter, no doubt, appeared to be expressed in large number of papers.

The Government invited opinions from all sections of the public including medical men. The opponents of the measure argued that Phulmani Dassi was a solitary case of its kind and was not enough justification for interference on the part of the Government in the social and religious customs of the people. Even some of those who admitted the evils of infant marriage were against legislation which, the protagonists of it felt, was the only way to remedy the state of affairs. Eventually, despite the acrimonious controversy and propaganda both for and against, the measure became an Act. It was, however, far from successful in rooting out the evil. Child marriage remained very much in practice, though a little stealthily where it clashed with the letter of the law or was likely to be punished. At best, the Act had only raised the age of consent from ten to twelve and that mitigated the evil effects of the system in Bengal to a very small extent. At worst, the controversy over the issue revealed the dismal fact that public opinion, by and large, was still determined blindly by custom and long established usage. Even the few open to reason did not possess enough courage of their convictions to defy social conventions. Curiously enough, some of the politically progressive among the educated formed the vanguard of opposition on the issue over the age of consent. Yet, despite the bitter fight, the Act did prove to be the thin end of the wedge. The figures at the close of the century indicated a change, however slight and meagre, in lowering the percentage of infant marriages.[22] This was partly due to the Age of Consent Bill and partly to many other forces at work which influenced, though imperceptibly, the question of infant marriage. Actually, the situation appears to be uncertain and fluid. Even figures show lack of uniformity. Among the uneducated and lower classes of Hindus, especially those that allowed their widows to remarry, the tendency appeared to be towards a more extensive resort to the practice; but among certain sections of the better classes a feeling was springing up against it partly because parents disliked exposing their daughters to the risk of a long period of widowhood and partly on account of the influence of western and reformist ideas. The educated few were being influenced by the voice of two sects Brahmo Samaj and the Arya Samaj who laid great stress on the desirability of girls marrying at a maturer age. The last decade of the nineteenth century saw the rise of many caste organisations which recognised the evil effects of child marriage and made efforts to introduce reforms within their respective castes. The Walterkrit Rajputra Hitkarini Sabha fixed the minimum age for marriage for girls at fourteen and for boys at eighteen.[23]

In the case of Muslims, infant marriage was regarded with disfavour, particularly among the educated classes. Even amongst the more ignorant sections of the community, with whom the practice was a relic of the customs they had followed before their conversion to Islam, the influence of the *Mullas*, who were doing propaganda to purge their system of the customs alien to their religion, was helping to bring it into disfavour. The animistic tribes, however, showed a tendency in the opposite direction. They were beginning to discountenance their custom of favouring adult marriage coupled with considerable pre-marital sexual freedom, and, being impressed by the example of the Hindus, some of them were substituting it by the system of early marriage. This was in conformity with the general trend of the period among the different castes to adopt such customs as would help them to acquire higher social status.

For all practical considerations the system appeared to continue mainly unchanged. The figures show but a most infinitesimal difference in the proportions. The disparity of age between the couple as also other concomitant evils, so to say, remained substantially unmitigated.[24]

6.5 Social Restrictions in Match-making

Although marriage was accepted as an imperative obligation for all, more particularly the Hindus, it is surprising that it should have been subjected to all kinds of restrictions in the matter of the choice of the mate. To a certain extent, it is intelligible, for in all societies there exist, to this day, some it is restrictions on marriage, however implicit or explicit they may be. These restrictions are normally prescribed by religion, custom or law and are enforced by corresponding sanctions. In the West during the period under review, the field from which a man could choose his wife was practically unlimited. The restrictions based on consanguinity were few and all but an insignificant number of marriages were determined by the free choice of persons who had attained physical maturity and believed that they knew their minds.[25] In India, on the contrary, marriage was hampered by numerous conditions of a varied nature. Sets of rules, negative and positive, operated intricately so as to conspire and limit strictly the scope for the choice of the spouse. The freedom in this regard according to Vedic ideals had become a matter of the hoary past. The general restriction on inter-marriage, which allowed *Anuloma* marriage, marriage of high caste man into a lower caste and not *vice versa*; the *Pratiloma* marriage in ancient India, had, in course of time, become so distorted that marriage during the period under review was completely fettered by taboos and trammels, of all types, legal, religious, tribal or social. Religious restrictions were comparatively lax, but this was more than made up by the complexity of others. According to Hindu law-givers, marriage could take place between *non-sapinda* persons only, that is to say, those who were not related directly by blood. This prohibited the union of any two persons who had a common ancestor not less than six degrees removed on the male side or four degrees removed on the female side. The twice-born castes were very particular about these restrictions. Roughly, a man could not marry a girl of the same *gotra*, petronymic or *pravara*. In other words, a girl who was a *sapinda*, *sa-gotra* or a *samanapravara* could not acquire the status of a wife. Among Musalmans, only the sister, niece and aunt were excluded in addition to the direct line of descent. These restrictions applied even to an adopted son who would for all purposes pass from the *gotra* of his father into that of his adoptive father and acquire the full status of a son in the adoptive family. For purposes of marriage, the prohibitions continued to be applicable to him as if he still belonged to his natural family so that the *gotras* to be avoided were those of the two families. Foster kinship was as great a bar as blood relationship. The *sapinda* rule was very wide in application and excluded a large number of relatives, many of whom would not even be available for matrimonial purposes since they would be dead. This only reflects excess of caution. Many castes in northern India forbade unions with any person in the line of the paternal and maternal uncle and aunt. This barred all marriages between any kind of uncle and niece or aunt and nephew.

The tribal restrictions were of a more rigorous nature and operated much more rigidly than the religious or legal injunctions. Throughout the eastern Punjab, the masses of Muslim converts, Gujars, Rajputs and the like were as much bound by them as their Hindu brethren and the Indian Christians did not follow any different set of rules either. These restrictions were based on two laws, endogamy and exogamy, closely and intricately connected with the hierarchical segmentation of the castes.

Endogamy or 'marrying in' was the custom which forbade the members of a particular caste or a social group to marry anyone who was not a member of that group. An endogamous division, therefore, was a group within which its members must marry. For instance, a Jat would marry a Jat only, a Gujar would marry a Gujar ; a *Kanyakubja* Brahman would marry a *Kanyakubja* Brahman; in Central Provinces the *Deshashtha Kankanashtha* and *Karbada* Brahman would not inter-marry. The divisions so based were innumerable. A few outstanding types might be mentioned to illustrate the lines on which the principle of endogamy worked. These could be ethnic, linguistic, territorial, functional, sectarian and social though they were not found in all the parts of northern India in any uniform pattern.

The ethnic groups consisted of compact tribes like the Rajputs of Rajputana or Santhals of Chhota Nagpur. The linguistic groups, such as the Bengali, Punjabi, Bihari, Oriya etc, were large and vague and included whole castes which were broken up into endogamous sub-castes. The territorial or local groups such as the *Rarhi* and *Barendra* Brahmans, the *Uttariya* and *Dakshini Doms* of Bihar, the *Shikharbhumi Bhumij* of Manbhum etc. The functional or occupational groups were the largest in number and were being multiplied at the slightest instance. As a rule, groups based upon religious differences, within Hinduism, did not tend to become endogamous, and the evolution of a caste from a sect was not too common. Yet the *Bishnois* of Upper Provinces and *Lingayats* of Bombay are typical examples of such grouping. The social groups consisted of those who marked themselves off by abstaining from or practising some particular social or ceremonial usage like the *Sagahut* and *Byahut* sub-castes of the *Sunris* in Bihar. Another example of the same type is that of the Chauseni and Barahseni, two groups from among the mercantile castes of the United Provinces who were endogamous. The endogamous groups were in many cases further subdivided into smaller groups of the same nature so that sometimes they were broken up into exogamous sections.

Exogamy or 'marrying out' was the custom which forbade the members of a particular social group, usually supposed to be descended from a common ancestor, or to be associated with a certain locality, to marry anyone who was a member of the same group. An exogamous group, therefore, was a group of persons related by blood between whom inter-marriage was forbidden. Such group could be of many types such as the totemistic, eponymous, territorial, communal or family and titular.[26]

Members of a totem group regarded themselves as relatives just as much as those of a *gotra* which was, at best, an exaggerated family, a group of relations tracing descent from the same ancestor. So also did the residents of a village look upon each other as relatives in some sense, referring to each other as village brother, *gaon ka bhai*. As such in many castes a villager usually looked outside his villages for his wife. In most cases, perhaps, all the members of a caste living in the same village probably were as a matter of fact members of the same exogamous group which would compel them to go outside it for their brides.

These sets of rules, working in two different ways, produced the same result that of restricting the field of choice of the mate. Endogamy restricted inter-marriage in one direction by creating a number of artificially small groups within which people must marry. Exogamy artificially enlarged the circle within which they could not marry.

The third set of restrictions, based upon social status and pride of rank, operated even more stringently as also more widely touching all communities. Beyond the nominal limitations on marriage imposed by the law of Islam, these might be said to be the only restrictions observed by the Muslims, especially in the Punjab. The social laws which governed inter-marriage, however, were not binding so as to make a marriage void and its offspring illegitimate as would be the case if it were contracted in opposition to the tribal rules. They had at their back the whole weight of public opinion and that the hereditary pride of descent which was very strong, especially among the higher classes. Any infringement of these rules would reduce the family which committed it to a lower level in the social scale.

The social restricions, involving pride of status, were based upon two laws, isogamy and hypergamy and were followed by the majority of the upper castes in most parts of northern India during the period of study, with slight variations only. The system of caste being essentially hierarchical, the law of isogamy had developed into very stringent restrictions. It allowed the parents to give the daughter only to a man of the same status and explicitly forbade her being given in marriage to a man of any group lower than theirs. This law governed marriage, as a natural course, among the highest classes irrespective of their creed. It was punctiliously practised by all the dominant Muslims and other well-placed people of the Western Punjab.

Hypergamy, the law of superior marriage or 'marrying up' was the custom which forbade a woman of a particular group to marry a man of a group lower than her own in social standing and compelled her to marry in a group equal or superior in rank. A hypergamous division, therefore, was a group forming part of a series of groups governed by the rule that, 'a group of higher rank will take brides from, but will not give brides to a group of lower rank'. In other words, the men of a group could marry in it or below it; the women could marry in it or above it. Instances of the hypergamous divisions were most conspicuous among the Rajputs, *Kanyakubi* Brahmans, Khatris, Agarwals, Aroras, Marathas and the *Kulin* Brahmans of Bengal, though it was observed by many other castes such as the Bhat, Byar, Dharkar, Gujar, Jat, Jijhotiya Brahmans, Kharwar Khatri and Patwa. Indeed, amongst all Hindus there was a tendency towards hypergamy.[27] Perhaps, a segmented hierarchical social structure could not be free from such a trend. The Rajput chiefs of the ruling houses, would not give their daughters, under any circumstances to non-ruling families. The Maratha families belonging to groups such as Kadam, Bande, Bhonsle etc. whose ancestors rose to power during the Maratha ascendancy would not marry their daugthers to Marathas of lower position.[28] The Khatris of United Provinces were divided into *Dhaighar, Charghar, Barghar* and *Bawanjati*. A *Dhaighar* man could take a wife only from the *Dhaighar* or *Charghar* groups, while a *Dhaighar* woman could marry only a *Dhaighar* man. The *Dhaighars*, therefore, were exogamous as regards men and endogamous as regards women. Among the *Kulin* Brahmans of Bengal, the custom of hypergamy assumed its worst form; thus giving rise to many evils of the Hindu society.

The law of hypergamy greatly complicated the marriage system of the castes who observed it. New trends in the closing decades of the nineteenth century were making it more so. One curious development of this was noticeable among the educated people. In the districts near Calcutta, the *Pods* who were originally a cultivating and fishing caste were taking to English education and becoming clerks, doctors and lawyers. These educated *Pods* were developing an attitude of superiority setting up for themselves a special *jus connubii* assuming the right of taking girls, but not giving to classes other than their own group.

The influence of hypergamy was not only that of complicating the system, it was responsible for many evils also. Husbands were at premium in the upper groups and so were the cause of vigorous competition, the bride-price of early usage was replaced in many cases by the bridegroom-price paid by the higher castes. The rich got their daughters married above their proper rank; poorer people were driven to reckless borrowing or in the last resort to other undesirable means, just to avoid their daughters to grow up unmarried. Unhappily the efforts made to combat the situation arising out of these restrictions instead of improving had only made it worse. Evils of a varied nature such as infanticide, polygamy and *kulinism* appeared to be threatening the Hindu society with complete demoralisation. Hypergamy among groups which were of a low rank and found it difficult to obtain wives produced a shortage of marriageable women. This had deplorable effects on the age at which marriage took place as also on the esteem in which women were held. These restrictions were further augmented by the custom of virgin marriage, that the religious rite of marriage could be performed but once in the case of a woman. Naturally the choice of a bride would be restricted still more as all widows, however young, would be eliminated. This was more particularly a problem in the case of the higher classes, lower classes not being so finical about it.

6.6 Matrimonial Bargaining

Varied restrictions were greatly responsible for the practical problem of the shortage of matches—the bride or the groom as the case might be. Hence, matrimonial bargains. Among the lower castes payment for the bride and among the higher castes for the groom were usual. The custom of exchange marriage was also the outcome of this practice. Where money was not conveniently forthcoming naturally an agreement to provide a bride in return was the easiest way to get one. Primitive, though the practice has been dubbed, it was very much in existence among certain sections of people.[29] The custom was called '*gurwat*' or '*adla badla*' in United Provinces and '*batta satta*' in the west Punjab. Chief among the castes which practised it were the *Brahais*, *Bhuiva*s, *Dharkara*, *Ghasiya*s, *Musaharas*, *Tarkibars*, etc. in United Province, the *Arora* caste in the Punjab and many hill castes.

The payment of bride-price could be in cash or kind. One way to do that was to pay in the form of labour for a certain stipulated period during which the prospective bridegroom would live with the bride's family and work as their servant. During his service which usually lasted three years the bridegroom had no rights over his prospective bride and no claim on her father's property; all he got was maintenance. This custom known as *Beena* marriage prevailed among certain low castes, *Bhuivar, Bind, Chero, Ghasiva, Majhmar,* etc.[30] Strictly speaking, the payment of bride-price was forbidden by the Hindu law, but the exigencies of a practical nature had given the practice a kind of tacit sanction. It was common among low castes, but no longer formed a business transaction except in some regions. The amount, generally small, was fixed by tribal custom.

6.7 Dowry System

The bridegroom price took the form of dowry and was usual with the better classes. Partly a distortion of the injunctions of law-givers by which the bride was to be adorned and provided with the necessities when given over as a gift to the groom, the custom of dowry, in the exaggerated form it prevailed, was, to a great extent, the outcome of the restrictions on the choice of the match, particularly, hypergamy. The bride's family, according to this, being of an inferior social position, had to pay for marrying her to a man above her rank. Then again the desire to make a show of wealth as a set off to the groom's social advantages as also the satisfaction of their vanity cannot be entirely eliminated from the custom of giving large dowries. The amount of the dowry was generally regulated by the social prestige of the families concerned. In certain provinces, especially Bengal, dowries were becoming unreasonably excessive and were often the cause of unhappiness, too infrequently with tragic and ruinous effects. The closing decades of the nineteenth century witnessed the appearance of yet another factor in this sphere. The educational qualifications of the bridegroom became the most important determinant of the dowry which often included large sums of money to meet the further education of the groom, besides the usual presents to his relatives, in cash as well as in kind. Again, during the year, following the marriage it was customary with the bride's father to make periodical presents to his son-in-law in the shape of sweets, clothes and money. Every important festival meant expenditure of this nature, which only the rich could afford without a pinch. Public opinion was then, as it is now, a hard task-master and, should the presents be trite, the giver was stigmatised as stingy. The daughter eventually was the sufferer as she had to bear the most tantalising remarks on this score.

6.8 Marriage Expenses

Apart from the custom of dowry, marriage was, as it is even today, among all classes on the whole an expensive affair as compared with the means of the family. A person, in other respects, thrifty and parsimonious, would grudge no outlay at the celebration of a child's marriage. This was often a grievous burden; the rich felt it, but a poor man was just overwhelmed. It devoured in a few days the labour of years past as well as future. Large sums were squandered on festivities, feasting and entertainments on a large scale lasting for days. Not only would all the relations and friends collect, but also a host of Brahmans, idle and ignorant, a number of bands who would chant the praises of the family, strolling minstrels with dancing girls and wandering *sanyasis* would be there to the expected feast. Most of these self-invited guests would be feasted by the host and presented with money and other gifts at an expense often disproportionate to his resources. It was considered a matter of pride and honour to feed all the poor and low caste people of the neighbourhood who would flock to the house where a marriage was being celebrated. Interestingly enough, the bars of caste and creed would give way on such occasions.

Even low caste Muslims would go to take advantage of the feast and be fed ungrudgingly. It was not unusual for groups of *faqirs* and mendicants even to make demands and use objectionable tactics for their gratification. Oman's account of an incident of the type is an interesting illustration.

"At a wedding... a number of *Sanyasis* presented themselves and insisted upon having not less than one rupee each. The host declared that he could not afford so much as that, but offered to give half a rupee to each man. The offer was indignantly spurned. As the host held out, the *Sanyasis* resorted to their usual tactics. One man hit his forehead with a sharp stone till the blood flowed. In this state he moved about amongst the assembled guests while his companions chanted a funeral dirge. These tactics effected the purpose of the unscrupulous *Sanyasis* and to get rid of them their demands were satisfied as quickly as possible."[31]

Much of the expenditure incurred, thus, was needless and large sums were recklessly squandered. In certain regions, the burden of marriage expenses was lighted by the custom of 'tambol' by which friends and relations attending the wedding brought money and presents which were repaid eventually on like occasions in their families. Proper records of the 'tambol' money were maintained, though occasional bickerings on this score could not be avoided. In certain parts of the Punjab, among low castes the custom of 'tambol' was so common that a marriage was almost a paying speculation. In Rajputana, among higher castes, the 'tambol' money tended to become higher so that it was becoming a burden to those who gave it. Before the nineteenth century closed a move to remedy this had started. Some Rajputs got together and formed an organisation Walterkrit Rajputra Hitkarini Sabha in 1898 under which rules were laid down to check the unreasonable expenses and also to reform marriage customs particularly in regard to the age of the couple. Ignorance, superstition and convention all conspired to drain the resources of the parents by giving undue importance to what had hardly anything to do with marriage as a religious rite and an imperative duty—the ceremonies eclipsing the essence of the rite proper.

6.9 Auspicious Months for Marriage

Among the Hindus, the marriages were normally celebrated only in certain months, considered auspicious—March, April, May and June being the most favoured ones, They did not take place in the rainy season because the gods were supposed to be asleep and could not be invoked to bestow blessings on the happy couple and also doubtless because the marriage parties could not travel about the country except at great inconvenience and discomfort. The months of *Chait* (15th March to 15th April) and *Kartik* (15th September to 15th October) were considered especially inauspicious for marriage. Among cultivating classes, the favourite time for wedding was after the spring harvest had been gathered so that they could command their resources and the leisure to the utmost. In certain regions marriages could be performed only at special times often at long intervals covering years. The actual dates were fixed by astrologers. There were, however, certain auspicious days such as *Baisakhi, Dussehra*, on which marriages could be celebrated without the necessity of consulting astrologers. Some castes like the *Jats, Gujars, Ahirs, Minas, Sunar, Nai*, etc. fixed their marriages on festivals like *Akka Teej*, third day of the second half of *Baisakh, Janam Ashtami, Deo Uthni Gyaras* in November etc. Often they would celebrate their marriages on the dates fixed for the marriages of the *Jagirdars* and chieftains to whom they were subordinate. Muhammadans married at any time during the year except *Muharrum*. Some people considered the first thirteen days of the month Safer, which follows the *Muharrum*, to be unlucky.

6.10 The Marriage Rituals

Although marriage customs showed a wide variety from region to region and among caste, class, creed and community, yet they, no doubt, revealed a common pattern. The principal ritualistic performance of the community, in all cases, whether it was a religious sacrament as in the case of the Hindus or a civil contract as among Muslims, was overlaid by a host of ceremonies spread over days. The main ceremony among the Hindus was the '*Sapt-Padi*, seven steps round the sacred fire by the bridal pair while the priest read out the religious text. The Muslim ceremony '*Nikah*', performed by the *Qazi* consisted in the promise made by the couple that they accepted each other as husband and wife in the presence of witnesses. The groom agreed to pay a certain amount of money in case of separation. The Parsi ceremony conducted by the *Dustoor* was also the reading of the pledges in the Zend and Sanskrit by the couple that they accept each other as husband and wife, The underlying note, however, was the spirit of gaiety and pageantry, mirth and pleasure, feasting and festivity for all concerned. The couple, mostly too young to grasp the seriousness and the implications of the rites, were engrossed in the fun of the whole show. The bride, in the majority of cases, a mere child, enjoyed the gorgeous clothes, jewellery and the fuss made over her; the bridegroom felt elated with the importance and the attention he received.

6.11 Monogamy and Polygamy

Generally speaking, monogamy was the rule with exceptions to it, though in certain areas and among small sections of people, these exceptions assumed the form of polygamy and polyandry.

Polygamy was restricted mainly to the richer classes, the chiefs and the ruling houses, though the sundry hill tribes were also found to be indulging in the custom. In actual practice, it was more common among the Mohamadans than the Hindus among whom a second wife was rarely taken unless the first one was barren or suffered from some incurable disease. Even then a Hindu had, generally, to take permission from his caste *Panchayat* and, formally at least, from his first wife also.[32] In the Punjab, polygamy was common among the lower castes such as the *Chamars, Churhas, Darzis, Nais* and several other menial and artisan castes. It was also prevalent among the lower agricultural tribes especially those of the hills, The *Kanets, Ghirths, Gujars* and *Jats* practised it somewhat extensively.[33] Among the *Kanets* of Kulu, polygamy was a form of investment as most of the field work was done by women, and a man's wealth depended on the number of his wives, This applied to the Ghirths of Kangra also but in a less degree. Among the *Jats*, it was partly the result of the custom of widow remarriage they followed. Among the polygamous tribes of Assam, the practice extended far beyond its Punjab limits. For instance, the heir to a *miri* estate inherited with it the whole body of his father's wives who were numerous in proportion to his means, an exception, however, was made of the actual mother of the successor.

Among the higher Hindu castes, polygamy, on the whole, was uncommon, but certain castes of Brahmans, such as the Audichyas of Gujarat and Chaubes of Mathura indulged in the practice to a considerable extent. The *Kulin* Brahmans of Bengal in this respect out did every other section and thus presented a sad and outrageous picture. In other words, the number of men with more than one wife in most of Northern India was very small except, among the *Kulin* Brahmans of Bengal, who indulged in the practice to a shocking extent and magnitude. *Kulinism*, as it began to be termed, was the hotbed of Hindu polygamy. At its root was the custom of hypergamy which regulated the marriage of *Kulin* or high rank Brahman girls. These rules being cruelly stringent, *Kulin* girls could not on any account be given to any person, but of an equal or superior rank so that a girl's hereditary honour among the *Kulins* became her worst misfortune. Great difficulty was experienced in settling her in life. The only circle from which a husband might be selected would be in quest every where and by every body. The effort to outbid each other had become a sort of a cut-throat game among the different sections of the *Kulin* Brahmans.

Originally divided into two divisions in Bengal, the *Rarhi* and the *Barindra*, according to the part of the country they settled in, they had n course of time been split into several sub-divisions, chief among them, during the period of study being three – *Kulins, Shrotriyas aud Bangashaias*—who in their turn had smaller sub-sections like other sub-castes. The *Kulins* alone had no less than 36 of these sub-sections known as the *melas* which had strict and detailed rules prohibiting marriages between two different *melas*. Besides these, there were other obstacles, those of the *Prajya* system, placing further restrictions on the field of choice of the match. In order to keep up the genealogy of the *Kulins* there had grown up a class of men known as *Kulachariyas, Ghataks* or matchmakers who played an important role in the *Kulin* marriages.

A *Kuliu*, therefore, considered it a great honour and advantage to marry the daughter of a good *Shrotriya*, who as a group enjoyed important social position on account of the wealth and property they owned. He would, however, lose his *kulinism* if he married a daughter of a *Bangashaia* or any one in contravention of the *Prajya* system.

Owing to the great difficulty of finding a suitable husband for their girls, the *Kulins* were compelled sometimes to marry four or five of them to one and the same husband at the same time. It was very common for a *Kulin* husband even though not placed in affluent circumstances to have a large number of wives, sometimes thirty, forty even fifty[33], with all of whom he surely could not make a home. The wives, naturally, continued to live in their parental homes waiting for a visit from the husband whenever he chose to do so. The *Kulins*, thus, led a roving life feasted, worshipped and enriched by the family of the bride and when the honeymoon would be over they would go away, perhaps never to return, to enter into similar engagements with other families. On their conjugal tours, they would be "leaving at every halt a penelope in her teens to lament for the loss and despair for their return." Being destitute of finer susceptibilities of human nature and looking upon matrimony as a matter of traffic, a *Kulin* husband regarded his wives as so many automatons whose happiness was not at all identified with his own. Influenced by a sordid love of gain and brought up in ignorance and laziness, pampered by effiminate habits, he undoubtedly led a profligate life of utter demoralisation. The sufferers of this, for sure, were his wives, the women and ultimately the society.

Where the number of wives was large he could not even recognise them all simply because he had seldom or never seen their faces. Even if he kept a register of the number of his wives, he could keep no record of his children. When he needed money he could descend on such a father-in-law as could satisfy him. If he kept one wife at home it was not necessarily from warmth of affection, but merely for his own convience and comfort, for she would take care of all the household duties and drudgeries like a servant.

The vices of *kulinism* were of no inconsiderable magnitude. Not only were most of the polygamous unions due to it, but the abominable disparity of age of the couples also. An octogenerian marrying a girl of eight and a youth of sixteen united to a woman of twenty were not unknown happenings. The death of one *Kulin*, for sure rendered at once several women, girls, some of them were children, widows, to suffer the hardships imposed on them by an unkind society. *Kulinism*, as such, a system of monstrous polygamy and perhaps without a parallel in the history of human depravity prevailed only in Bengal for the most part of the nineteenth century. It was only towards the end of it that public opinion was becoming hostile to the practice The educated, at best, were becoming aware of its evil consequences and marriages according to Kulinism were getting rare.[34] The press was becoming vocal on this issue as early as the sixties and suggestions began to be made openly in the newspapers during the decades that followed that the government should legislate to put an end to this execrable practice even though it was prevalent only in Bengal and that too in one section of the Brahmans.

6.12 Polyandry

Polyandry was practised among certain tribes inhabiting the sub-montane regions of the Himalayas. Of the two types of polyandry, the fraternal form in which a woman married several brothers, was found in the Himalayan area from Kashmir to the eastern extremity of Assam.[35] It existed as a recognised institution chiefly in the case of people of Tibetan affinities, along the Tibetan border, such as Ladakh in Kashmir, Lahul and Spiti in Punjab, the hill parganas of Jaunsar Bawar in Dehra Dun district, in N.W.P., and in Sikkim and Darjeeling in Bengal.[36] In Ladakh, the woman was apparently regarded as the wife of all the brothers and the children called them all father. In the Spiti and Lahul areas, the practice was rather uncertain. According to some accounts, it was similar to that prevailing in Kashmir while, according to others, it differed slightly in that the first born child was regarded as that of the eldest brother, the second born of the next, so on and so forth. In Sikkim, Darjeeling and the neighbourhood when a woman married a man she was regarded as the wife of the *de jure* husband and also of his younger brothers; in rare cases cousins also, though it did not necessarily follow that she cohabited with all of them. In this matter, the choice rested with the woman and in any case she was visited by the younger brothers only when the man who actually married her was away.[37]

The *Khasis* and *Garos* of Assam practised polygamy of the matriarchal form in that they adhered to the rule of succession through the females. In the Punjab, polyandry as an avowed institution was confined to the Spiti and Lahul *parganas* of Kangra, Chamba, Lahul, Kanawar and Seoraj or highlands of Kulu and Mandi, though it was doubtlessly also practised more or less openly by the lower castes throughout the hill areas and as a matter of fact, though the custom was not admitted by the *Jats* of the plains.

"Polyandry in Seoraj is in reality a mere custom of community of wives among brothers who have community of other goods. In one house you may find three brothers with one wife, in the next three brothers with four wives, all alike in common, in the next house there may be an only son with three wives to himself. It is a matter of means and of land, a large farm requires several women to look after it."[38]

In Kanawar step brothers or cousins could also marry one wife. Indeed in rare cases men not related became '*Dharma Bhai*' or ritual brothers and took a joint-wife usually making their property joint also.[39] Among the Jats of the eastern plains or the Jama zone, it appears from the reports that by the end of the century the custom was gradually waning and was not practised openly although there existed among them a feeling that a woman brought by marriage into the family remained the property of the family and on the death of her husband she was claimed almost as by right of inheritance by a surviving brother. In the Dehra dun district, stress was laid on the fact that husbands must be sons of the same mother or by the same set of husbands. Sometimes a brother might take a separate wife and might continue to enjoy the common wife as well if the other brothers did not object. Often a household had several wives in common. Such customs in regard to marriage did not by any chance denote an exalted status of woman.

References

1. *Census Report, 1891*, Vol. I, p. 59.
2. *Census Report, 1901*, Vol. I, pp. 436-37.
3. *Census Report, 1891*, Vol. I, p. 59 ; Mayne, p. 70.
4. Amir Ali, p. 270.
5. *Census Report, 1901*, p. 438.
6. Sastri, S.N., pp. 220-29.
7. *Calcutta Review*, Vol. 54, 1872, p. 286.
8. Mayne, pp. 85-86.
9. Mayne, pp. 85-86 ; *Calcutta Review*, October 1883, p. 381.
10. *Census Reports, 1881* p. 92 ; *Census Reports 1891* Vol. 1, p. 60 ; *Census Reports, 1901* Vol. I, p. 437.
11. *Census Report 1891, Bengal*, Vol. III, p. 181.
12. *Census Report 1891, Bengal*, Vol. I, p. 264.

THE INSTITUTION OF MARRIAGE 135

13. Ibid.
14. *Census Reports, 1901,* Vol. I, p. 334.
15. *Census Report, 1891,* Vol. I, p. 267.
16. *Census Report, 1901, N.W.P.,* Vol. I, p. 116.
17. *Censes Report 1901, Punjab,* Part I, p. 217.
18. *Census Report 1901, N.W.P.,* Vol. I, p. 79.
19. *Census Report 1931,* Vol, I, p. 733.
20. *Census Report 1901,* Vol, I, p. 434.
21. Government of India. *Legislative Proceedings,* Nos. 1-73 pp. 1-3.
22. *Census Report 1901,* Vol. I, pp. 442-43,
23. *Report of the General Committee of the Walterkrit Rajputra Hitkarini Sabha, 1889.*
24. *Census Report, 1901,* Vol. I, p. 443.
25. Risley, p. 155.
26. Risley, p. 161.
27. *Census Report, 1901,* Vol. I. p. 425.
28. *Census Report, 1901, Bombay.* Part I, p. 183.
29. Chintamani, p. 152.
30. Blunt, p. 70.
31. Oman, p. 174.
32. *Census Report, 1891,* Vol. I, p. 254.
33. *Census Report 1901, Punjab, Part I.*
34. Bose, p.231; Strachey, p.354; Wilkins, p. 184.
35. *Census Report, 1901,* Vol. I, p. 448.
36. *Indian Antiquiry,* Vol. V, 1876, p. 161.
37. *Census Report, 1901,* Vol. I, p. 448.
38. *Census Report 1882, Punjab,* para 698.
39. *Census Report 1901, Punjab,* Part I, p. 220.

7 The Position of Woman

7.1 Aspects of Social Inferiority of Woman
7.2 Female Infanticide
7.3 Attitude of Sufferance towards Girls
7.4 Seclusion of Woman
7.5 Female Attachment for Ornaments
7.6 Male Child as a Source of Female Security
7.7 The Stigma of Widowhood
7.8 Rise of Immoral Trafficking
7.9 Widow Remarriage
7.10 Economic Conditions of Woman
7.11 Right to Inheritance and Property
7.12 Social Reformers at Work

One sure measure to gauge the refinement of society in a given age and clime is the status enjoyed by women therein. The better their status, the more cultured the society. Judged by this yardstick, society in northern India in the second half of the nineteenth century could not boast of a complimentary degree of refinement. The high status known to have been enjoyed by Hindu women in the Vedic age had become practically a myth. It had, through the centuries, completely degenerated so that the condition of woman was at the lowest ebb during the greater part of the nineteenth century. Ideologically, women were considered absolutely inferior to men, having no significance, no personality. They were, by and large, ignorant and illiterate. Reading and writing were deemed superfluous for them, if not completely pernicious. Sentiments regarding their capacity, uses and dispositions were contemptuous and brutal in the extreme. In no field other than the one concerning women, perhaps Manu's so-called injunctions were more punctiliously observed, reducing women merely to physical and mechanical entities, owned and regulated by men for the satisfaction of their physical happiness. For the purpose of this study, a probe into Manu's motivation to stress only the bad qualities of woman and so to ordain stringent regulations to keep her under check may be out of place. But his injunctions such as, "Day and night should women be kept by the male members of the family in a state of dependence. In pursuits to which they are too devoted they should be restrained under the husband's power. The father guards them in childhood, the husband guards them in youth; in old age the son guards them. A woman ought not to be in a state of independence", are significant in that they were in full operation.[1]

7.1 Aspects of Social Inferiority of Woman

Yet, the Indian society of the period shows, indeed, that despite the smothering of the free development of woman and denial of independent personality to her, the influence she wielded, however subtle and-subterranean, was a force to reckon with. But it did not in any way change the stamp of social inferiority she bore. That was visible at each stage in her life from infancy to old age and formed one of the chief characteristics of the then Indian society. Visible in an extreme measure among the Hindus, although Hindu religion had never taught the inferiority of women, there being no parallel in Hinduism to the story of man's fall as a result of Eve's temptation and the stigma attached to womanhood as a whole, it was perceptible as a general trend among the other communities also, including the Muslims and the Parsis. Muslim women did not even take part in prayers at the mosque.

The first display of the social inferiority of woman was at the birth of a baby girl; presenting a striking contrast to that of a boy. May be it was due to the need for obsequies which legally a son only could perform that he was heralded into the world amidst acclaimations of joy and a jubilee was celebrated in the house in honour of his birth. The birth of the daughter was generally observed with a heaviness of heart and a gloomy silence which forcibly expressed sorrow. There would generally be few festivities of any description; little announcing of the birth with the sounding of the conch, no singing and dancing by women in the family, no visitations from the dancing eunuchs, no feast to the Brahmans and no congratulations from friends or relatives. If at all friends visited, they only came with a view to offering a few consoling words. The father would often answer an enquiry about the birth of the baby in most despondent terms if it happened to be a girl that nothing was born. The general gloom that ensued the birth of a girl was indeed due, to a great extent, to prospects of having to face difficulties in arranging her marriage, finding a proper match in the restricted fields at the proper age, and the humiliation of failing to have enough resources to celebrate it with befitting honour. The expenses of a marriage were often disastrous to the family. No wonder the coming of a daughter was looked upon as a great reproach, an encumberance, a source of trouble, in a word, a calamity. The position was, however, different among certain sections and tribes who accepted a bride price. The birth of a girl was welcomed with joy. The vast majority of the people did not show such extreme reactions.

Signs of change in the attitude towards girls were beginning to be perceptible as the century advanced, among the educated few, who no longer viewed the girl with antipathy and indifference, the concern about her future notwithstanding.

The restrictions on marriage, especially those of hypergamy, practised among certain sections of the people, and the ruinous expenditure involved in it, posed serious problems, the solution of which led to customs of a most heinous nature. A daughter to remain unmarried was considered disgraceful and impious; to marry her to one of the same clan was degrading, if not incestuous; to find a suitable match in the higher group was difficult and above all to procure adequate funds for the whole show was often disastrous.[2] The *Kulin* Brahmans of Bengal, a very small section, had found an easy, though hateful and condemnable solution of the problem in the worst type of polygamy, and indulged most unscrupulously in the practice of giving away the daughter to an otherwise suitable match, regardless of his age and the number of wives he might have. The practice, however, was speedily dying out.[3]

There were others, sections of different communities spread in different parts of northern India, who found the answer to their dilemma in the destruction of their female offspring. The practice of female infanticide was associated mainly with the Rajputs of Rajputana who were proud of their lineage and were disinclined to give their daughters in marriage to those lower in rank.[4] Some of their sections such as the *Chauhan Thakurs* suffered from extremely irrational and false pride that they rebelled against the very idea of being a father-in-law or a brother-in-law to anyone since the status of the father or that of the marrying girl would be inferior to that of her husband. The words which express these relations were considered by them the worst terms of abuse and no *Chauhan Thakur* would readily allow any man to call him *soosur* (Father-in-law) or *sala* (brother-in-law). They had also developed a superstition and considered it unlucky to have a daughter alive in the family.[5]

7.2 Female Infanticide

The practice of infanticide, however, was by no means confined to the Rajputs in Rajputana only. It was found in the North Western Provinces, Agra and Oudh, Punjab, Bombay Presidency and Central Provinces, even among some non-Rajput castes. Enquiries conducted in 1856 by an officer appointed for the purpose revealed that the evil was so rampant that in a number of villages in the North Western Provinces not a single girl was found and that there had not been one within the memory of men, nor had such an event as the marriage of a daughter taken place for more than two hundred years.[6]

In the Punjab, strangely enough, the Rajputs, with some exceptions in the cis-Sutlej states and the hill areas, had escaped the taint generally and the dreadful distinction, chiefly belonged to the *Bedis*, the priestly class among the Sikhs. Other tribes also bore a share of the opprobrium such as some of the Musalman sects and some sub-divisions of the

Khatri castes. The inherent pride and supposed sanctity of their order made the Bedis unwilling to contract alliance for their daughters who were consequently doomed to an early death. In certain regions, such as Bombay Presidency, infanticide was more due to exorbitant expenses than to the pride of heritage.[7] The heinous crime was rampant for years, even after it had been detected. Surprisingly, but sadly, it was perpetrated by women at the helm of affairs in most ingenious, but cruel and callous ways.[8] A common method of destruction among the Rajputs of Cutch and certain tribes in Sindh was to drown the children in vessels of milk or in holes made in the ground filled with milk. The signal '*doodh pilao*', feed with milk, was sufficient to secure the infant's destruction. In other cases, the female infants were either given opium, or left uncared for until they expired.[9] Barbarous and heart-rending to the extent of being incredible, the fact remains that it became a custom observed from generation to generation just because their forefathers had done so before them with hardly a feeling that there was anything criminal or monstrous in the practice. Happily, this was confined to small sections only though scattered in different parts.

Efforts to deal with the crime had been made by the government as early as 1841-42 and when in the fifties it was revealed to be widely prevalent, these were considerably intensified, but the evil persisted for some time. The measures, that were taken, were of two kinds. One, which aimed at the removal of some of the causes which led to the committing of the crime, especially the limiting and restricting of the extravagant expenditure on marriage. The others were of a coercive and directly deterrent nature.[10] The success of the first type of measures depended mainly on the people who began soon to respond to the persuasion and inducement from the government officials. These measures were first initiated in Mainpuri in North Western Provinces where some leading *Chauhans* met and drew up a set of resolutions with the object of reducing the marriage expenses.[11] The precedent so set was followed up in other regions also, Punjab, Oudh and elsewhere.[12] Undoubtedly, the move had proved useful in that it had roused a strong sense, among the people themselves, of the extreme folly of spending fabulous sums of money on marriages. It was being proved all around that with a little help and pressure put on them by the officers of the Government, they would be glad to limit such expenditure.

But this alone could not achieve the objective. It was too slow to produce any tangible results. The preventive and coercive measures proved more successful. These consisted mainly in the introduction of an effective system of registration of births and deaths in suspected localities, active vigilance, periodical inspection and enumeration of children. Their success was undoubted for, "in 1842 Mr. Raikes found that there was hardly a Rajput girl living in the district of Mainpuri. Nine years afterwards in 1851, there were 1,458 girls found alive, and in 1855 the number had risen to 2,530."[13] Similar results were observed in Agra District, Punjab and Oudh and indeed in all regions where preventive measures had been taken. This proved in a most unmistakable way, that it was quite in the power of the Government of India to eradicate or at least to diminish the crime. Local authorities in the regions infested with the crime felt that the measures for its prevention needed to be enforced more systematically and continuously; that the existing law was altogether inadequate to meet the situation. Hence the Female Infanticide Act of 1870 (Government of India Act VIII of 1870) was promulgated under which female infanticide was declared a punishable crime.

The Act of 1870, although a comprehensive measure, did not by any means succeed in eradicating the crime immediately. It certainly did prove to be much more effective a check than the measures adopted hitherto. The Government, therefore, subsequently extended the jurisdiction of the Act to areas which had not been included, initially, in the specified regions suspected of the evil, but were later discovered to be equally guilty. The result of the Act, at best, was that it checked the open and ingenuous committing of the murder and a large number of girls escaped an early and unnatural death. Yet the crime was far from being completely extinct.

In the years that followed, it assumed a different form, subtle and slippery, thus difficult to detect. The female baby would often be smothered or suffocated, exposed or just neglected. On the whole, however, female infanticide according to the official reports of 1882 showed signs of dying out. In the Punjab, it was believed not to be practised generally or habitually except in the case of the Bedi families of Gurdaspur and even among them it assumed the form of intentional neglect rather than actual murder.[14] In the districts of the North West Provinces in which the Rajput clans were scattered and greatly mixed with other classes of the population and where the support of clan feeling and clan custom was comparatively weak, there was reason to think that infanticide had almost ceased. But in districts where Rajputs were found in large and homogeneous communities, the suppression of the crime was much more difficult. On the whole, the crime appeared to be slowly, steadily and surely discredited so that by the end of the century the practice of deliberately doing away with female infants was confined to a limited area and even there it was somewhat rare and rather secret. This was possible because government action had the support of the public opinion as expressed by the educated and the vocal sections. The newly arising reformists also gave their countenance to the measure without any reservations.

The vicious practice, however, had prevailed long enough to leave undesirable effects. Female infanticide, naturally, created dearth of wives—girls for marriage, among the castes which practised it. They had, therefore, to look around for a bride among others, and had often to pay heavy price for her. Perhaps this encouraged traffic in girls and may be, kidnapping of children which was a serious menace also received abetment. Brokers in the trade, would procure small girls on payment of paltry sums to poor parents particularly at times of dire need such as flood, famine and draught and then dispose them off for profit. The very castes who destroyed their own females for mere pride of blood and heritage, when in quest of a wife, stooped to purchase a female of whose caste or heritage they had no idea. Nor did they want to make any effort to enquire about it. In fact, they connived with the brokers pretending the girl came of high caste.

7.3 Attitude of Sufferance Towards Girls

There is no gainsaying the fact that in the areas where infanticide had been prevalent, the life of a girl was less valued and as a general rule she received far less care and attention than a boy. This could be seen even in the daily routine of life. A girl would be no less warmly clad and less carefully rubbed with mustard oil as a prophylactic against colds and chills to which the greater part of the mortality amongst young children in India was due. The attitude of sufferance towards girls was common to all the communities, the parental love and warmth notwithstanding. May be it was the practical problems of settling a daughter in life that was responsible for it. The birth of a female child, even among the educated supposed to be changing their attitude, was accepted helplessly as a verdict of fate.

Basically, the Hindu social system proceeded on the assumption that the daughter did not belong to the family and that at the proper time she would go to her husband's family. Hence the difference in the attitudes towards a female child. Distinction was made in her rearing and even in the ceremonies performed for her, since a daughter was raised with a view to preparing her to go to another family to which she was to belong. Marriage for her was imperative, the main ceremony, the only *samskara* she could go through and thus the most important event of her life. Her training in this direction commenced early in her childhood which was actually far too short. Indeed it was not easy to determine when the childhood of a Hindu girl ended and the married life began. At about five years of age she was initiated by the elderly ladies of the family in the preparatory rites of *brata* or vows, the primary object of which was to secure her a good husband and render her religious and happy throughout life. The germs of superstition being thus early implanted in her mind she was more or less influenced by it even after. Formed by nature to be docile, pliant and susceptible, she readily took to the course of religious exercises. The chief '*bratas*' that the girls in Bengal observed indicate that from early age they were trained for a married life. For instance the rite of *Shiva Puja*, the '*brata*' of *Hari* or *Krishna* and the worship of ten images were all meant to seek the blessings for a good husband. The '*sajooty brata*' was a ceremony performed by girls of all classes in Bengal for the purpose of obtaining a husband who would never take a second wife ; while the '*yampookur*' was a worship which blessed a girl never to lose her husband. There were many fasts of the same nature in other parts of northern India also. The worship of the *Tulsi* plant in many parts of Upper India had the same objective, the blessing of a good husband. Unmarried girls, even small children, also observed the fast alongwith the married women of the family on the special day for the purpose of giving offerings for the long life of the husband. Thus at an early age girls were made conscious of the two great misfortunes that might be in store for them, a rival wife to supercede and the loss of the husband whom they were taught to regard as the one blessing of their existence.

7.4 Seclusion of Woman

As enjoined by the *Shastras* and confirmed by custom, a girl of high rank would pass into the marital state as chosen for her by her parents at an early age when there could be no question of her voice or volition in determining her marriage. In the married state, among the high castes, woman lost even the semblance of freedom she enjoyed as an unmarried girl. She became, at once, subject to many restrictions. Even if marriage proved to be an elysium, the beloved wife and the daughter-in-law lived in complete subordination to the mother-in-law in strict seclusion among her own sex within the precincts of the part of the house meant for women. The seclusion of women, though observed much more strictly among the Muslims, was coveted alike both among them as also the high caste and well placed Hindus as a mark of social superiority.

Instead of being resented it was considered a privilege and highly appreciated. It was regarded as a proof of their husband's affection and the father-in-law's concern for them. To be kept in seclusion away from the world, was associated in their minds with ideas of wealth and rank. For them to be subjected to public gaze was the acme of misery. In one word, it was the fashion which the lower ranks tried to imitate to improve their status.

A good bit of diversity prevailed in this regard so that in certain regions such as Bengal and N.W.P., the seclusion of women was more strict and rigorous than in the Punjab, western parts and the hill areas. On the whole, women of higher castes or of moderately good social position in all the communities would scarcely be seen outdoors except in covered conveyances. They would not generally appear in public unveiled, and hold any social intercourse whatever with any man outside the family circle. Even within that, they could not freely move about before male relations older than their husbands, much less talk to them. It was considered highly immodest for a woman to appear unveiled even before her husband in the presence of a third person; while addressing him was inconceivable. His company in the day time was unusual.

These restrictions were confined only to the higher and middle classes. In the lower grades of life, women appeared in public without reserve for they could not afford the luxury of remaining in seclusion. They needed to work out of doors for their daily bread. In fact, women among the lower ranks could be seen doing domestic work such as, sweeping the floor, washing steps of the door, bringing water from the well, making purchases at the bazar, etc. not unusually exposing their faces to view. Troops of them could be seen working as labourers, carrying basket loads of earth. So was it in the rural and tribal areas. Women enjoyed much more freedom in the countryside than their sisters in the cities, the prevailing note of village life being the absence of domestic privacy and the publicity amidst which people lived. Life was largely spent in the open air and there was none of the isolation and seclusion of the women except among the higher ranks. Even among them it was not too stringent.

However, it goes without saying that a life spent in strict seclusion with little education and enlightenment of any description kept most women generally ignorant with an extremely narrow vision and restricted horizon. They were completely absorbed in the routine of the domestic life, looking upon men, the bread-winners, on whom they depended for everything, as their protectors and hence devoted themselves heart and soul to their service and welfare. In well-to-do families, there would not be much to do for young women as all the household work would be done by the older ladies, widows of the family or by servants, so that they led a life of indolence and luxury spending much time on personal embellishment. If at all they did any work, it was in regard to food and its preparation. What kept them occupied and happy was the ritual and the ceremonies connected with the life in the family enriched further by their own ingenuity.

7.5 Female Attachment Towards Ornaments

The instinctive love for jewellery as an aid to the enhancement of feminine charm which is universal even today, had in the absence of other interests become too exaggerated. Women of all ranks would be covered with jewellery made of gold, silver, brass or even wax and glass depending upon the resources of the family. Primarily meant to serve the vanity of women, as also of the men who provided it, jewellery, incidentally, proved to be of much help to the family when in need of funds. In the days when she institution of banks had not developed, perhaps, this was one of the safest devices to save money, which might otherwise be foolishly spent. Besides, for women their jewellery was the main part of their property, the '*stridhan*' over which men normally had no claim.

A woman's social standing was generally determined by her ornaments. Till marriage, a girl among families of good means in NorthWestern Province might wear a silver nose-ring and silver-wristlets. These would be replaced, on marriage, by a small gold nose-ring and glass bangles which alongwith the rings on her toes formed the symbol of her marital state, her *suhag*. The nose-ring changed into a bigger one when she had her *gauna* ceremony, and went to live with her husband. In Bengal, the married women wore an iron bangle as a symbol of their *suhag*.

Jewellery among urban people, on the whole, was elaborate, their being ornaments to adorn every visible part of the body from head to foot, but these were comparatively lighter in weight and less cumbersome in size in contrast with those worn by women in the countryside.

The peasant jewellery had some of the most primitive types. Its material varied widely. Often made of base metal, the weight of the ornaments could be fantastic. A Garo woman was found wearing earrings of 16 lbs. supported by a string tied over the top of her head the friction of which had quite worn away her hair. In N.W.P., in the neighbourhood of Banaras and Patna, the weight of the bell-metal anklets gave the girls a peculiar suffering gait. The Santhal belle normally wore two anklets, twelve bracelets, a necklace, earrings etc. weighing in all 34 lbs. The distinctly savage type appeared among the Nagas of Assam who wore earrings made of tusks of wild boar, neck collar of goat's hair, dyed scarlet and armlets of brass, ivory, plaited cane etc.[16]

The full display of jewellery could be witnessed on special occasions such as fetes, fairs, festivals, feasts and marriages. Even children, boys and girls, would be seen on such occasions gorgeously dressed with jewels on their feet and arms, neck and ears. Women at such times would dress up with a vengeance, so to say, for this was their only diversion from the drudgery of the household routine.[17] A marriage in the family was a source of great entertainment. They would just let themselves go for fun and frolic, singing love songs in rather obscene language and indulging in jokes often of an indecent nature though in exclusively women's gatherings.[18]

7.6 Male Child as a Source of Female Security

A married woman would normally be happy and content with her lot especially if she were the mother of a son. Her status in that case would be considerably enhanced. But if, per chance, she happened to prove barren or bore only daughters, her lot was far from enviable. Living under a constant threat of being superseded by a rival wife, she would become at once a drudge in the family, inviting the contempt not only of the mother-in-law, but often of the husband also. The term for barren woman '*Banjh*' or '*Auntri*', incidentally, was one of the worst abuses in certain regions. The happy lot of a married woman, thus, had hardly any security. The threat to bring a second wife could easily prove to be a real one. Law in this respect was partial to man and woman, no doubt, was the sufferer. This was evident in many ways. The prevalence of the institution of polygamy, though to a small extent yet was assuming monstrous form in *Kulinism* in Bengal as also that of polyandary, restricted to limited areas and small sections of people only, indicates that woman's will or volition could be treated as a secondary matter, some scope for romance and flippancy among certain sections, particularly the tribal and hill people, notwithstanding. Man, in contrast, had unreasonable freedom of action.

Generally speaking, marriage sealed the fate of Indian woman particularly of the higher classes. The dissolution of marriage was looked upon with contempt almost among all the communities even though it was lawful among some. The Muhammadan law allowed divorce but it was far from commonly sought. Besides being considered disreputable, the husband had to pay a large dowry, agrred to at the time of the marriage, to the divorced wife. This was not always easy to procure if the wife desired it. The law, however, was partial to Muslim men in that it was fairly easy for them to get the divorce. A husband had merely to demand it. It was enough for him to say the word '*talaq*' (divorce) three times and the bond was loosened. A Muslim woman, on the contrary, had to get the consent of the husband before she could ask for it.

The Parsi woman obtained the right to get a divorce, if marriage turned out to be unhappy, by the Parsee Marriage Act of 1865. (Government of India Act No XV of 1865). So did the Christian woman by the Act of 1869.

For the Hindu woman generally, there was no redress whatever from an ill-sorted marriage under any circumstances. The law governing these matters had been so completely interpolated that even Manu's sanction for divorce under exceptional circumstances was disregarded.[19] Curiously enough, in this respect, the so-called primitive society among the hill and tribal people as also the lower caste appeared to be more liberal and rational. It recognised the chances of friction between man and wife in domestic life and so had provision for maladjustment. Divorce and separation, in case of ill-sorted union, incontinence, cruelty, desertion, adultery and the like were allowed on the strength of custom, for, "under the Hindu system of Law, clear proof of usage will outweigh the written text of law."[20]

With all such provisions, divorces were surprisingly infrequent. A divorcee, man or woman, did not enjoy public respect. Maltreatment of woman among these classes was not an evil of the type found among certain higher classes of Hindus; nor was woman an absolute non-entity. She enjoyed without doubt a status to be reckoned with. Among the Tharus of Nainital, for instance, the female so dominated that often the husband had no alternative but to pray to God for redress against the ill-treatment by the wife.

For a Hindu woman of high caste, an ill-sorted match was a heavy yoke for the rest of her life. Even if she was put to untold hardships she had to bear them patiently, since marriage being a sacrament, it created an indissoluble tie between the husband and wife. Neither party could divorce the other unless allowed by custom, or by conversion to another religion. In the latter case, a party could be entitled to ask for dissolution of the marriage under the provisions of the Native Converts Marriage Act of 1866. This was a hardship, more to a woman than to a man for whom the institution of polygamy rendered divorce unnecessary. Echoes of a slender voice of the educated few were beginning to be heard in favour of legislation to give the right of divorce to Hindu woman also, but public opinion was too conservative yet to accept a change of this nature. Even death of an ill-matched husband did not give the wife any relief, for that left her a widow and as such in a worse position.

7.7 The Stigma of Widowhood

In a high caste Hindu family the position of a widow, more often than not, was most melancholic. If the widow be a mother of sons she was not usually a pitiable object although she certainly was looked upon as a sinner. The widowed mother of girls was treated indifferently. But it was the child widow or the childless young widow upon whom, in an especial manner, fell the abuse and the contempt of the community as one upon whom Heaven's judgement had been pronounced. From the moment of her husband's death she was taught, regardless of her age, to lead a forlorn life of austerity, abandon every comfort, renounce every desire and abstain from all delicacies. All amusements were strictly forbidden to her. She was not to be present at any festivity or family rejoicing. In fact, her very sight on such occasions was regarded as an ill-omen. One of the common abuses was the term for widow, *Rand* in North Western Province and *Randi* or *Khasam Khani* (one who has eaten her husband) in the Punjab. Even little prattling girls of tender years on losing their husbands were removed from their dolls and toys and condemned to a dull, drab, dreary, dismal widowhood for the rest of their lives. For the welfare of the Manes of her husband with whom she may not have lived at all or even seen, save at the time of her nuptial, a widow was expected after his death to lead a life of complete self-denial. Her manner of life was minutely prescribed so as to destroy totally her personal charm and attraction.

"Not only must she see no man, she must also avoid very approach to ease, finery and pleasure. She must neglect the care of her person

THE POSITION OF WOMAN

must wear no ornaments; her hair must be shaved or at least must be worn dishevelled ; she must not see her face in a mirror, nor use perfumes or flowers, must not anoint her body; and her dress must be coarse and dirty. The use of any kind of conveyance is prohibited, and she must not rest on a bed. Her food is limited as to quantity and quality. She must not take more than a single coarse meal a day ... Besides other fasts, perhaps a dozen in a year, a Hindu widow is required to abstain absolutely from food and drink twice a month, one day and night during every bright and dark period of the month ... from which fasts, not even severe sickness, can give her dispensation."[21]

To the gods, furthermore, she had to be devout, to the Brahmans reverential and to her husband's relatives meek and submissive.

A widow in a family of ordinary means was at once a cook, a menial servant, nurse and a house-keeper. Her services were more commanded than solicited. To the credit of the widow it might be said that she worked hard from simple disinterestedness. She dedicated herself to the family for the shelter and the protection she received.

In many homes, true widows were honoured and loved by the family. In the absence of the *mater-familias*, the widow would often step into her place and wield all her authority, leading not only a contented and happy life but also acting as the guardian angel of the house. In some cases, jealousy of the younger members caused complications and disturbed the domestic peace.

7.8 Rise of Immoral Trafficking

On the whole for all her kind services, the treatment, the window received from those she served, was often improper. She was made the victim of fraud and chicanery. Her jewels, her money would often be misappropriated by some male relatives. She might also be exposed to temptations difficult to resist and find it hard to subdue her natural instincts. In many cases, the severe rules for a life of self-mortification were virtuously observed and demands of flesh sublimated. And yet in many others, a licentious and profligate life in secret was the inevitable result ending ultimately in shame and disgrace for the family and prostitution for the unfortunate widow, but never to graceful remarriage. This was largely true of Bengal. In other provinces such as the Punjab and North Western Province cases of extreme maltreatment were rare, though the life led by a widow was generally devoid of worldly pleasantries.

The conduct of society, in this respect, was not only unkind but unjustifiable and irrational to the point of being ludicrous. This was displayed in the crudest manner in the tolerance, nay, the respect shown to the prostitutes, the *nautch-girls*, as they were modestly called in northern India. While a widow of the family was treated as an inauspicious being and was shunned on propitious occasions in the family, *nautch-girls* were specially invited to grace those functions. In society, they were everywhere. Never being married, they could never be widows. Hence, their presence at weddings was considered auspicious. They were invited as a matter of course on all festive occasions, such as the birth of a son, *yagyopaveet* (thread ceremony) and marriage ceremonies, birthdays and even house-warming. It was a proverbial saying, that without the jingling of their feet-bells, a dwelling place does not become pure. Seeing the dancing girls honoured, gaily and richly dressed with plenty of jewels, their presence regarded propitious, the young widow was bound to feel the contrast with her own position, the pang becoming more poignant. It is not strange that some of them forced by circumstances were tempted to have an easy change in the mode of their lives.

7.9 Widow Remarriage

The miserable condition of the high caste Hindu widows had aroused the pity and stirred the thought of many leaders of the community earlier in the century, but it was only under the championship of Pandit Ishwar Chandra Vidyasagar that the cause found its warmest sympathiser. He raised a voice, at once strong and sonorous, persuasive and appealing, inspiring and convincing in the crusade he started against enforced widowhood. He published a paper showing that Hindu *Shastras* did not prohibit widow marriage which created a great stir and led to much acrimonious discussion for which the *Dharma Sabha* was greatly responsible. Undeterred, he sponsored a petition seeking legislation for the legalisation of remarriage of the Hindu widow. The Act of 1856 was the result, though passed after much agitation and despite the opposition of a huge majority of the orthodox. It legalised the status of Hindu widows contracting second marriage and their children by such marriages. But the law did not preserve for the widow her civil rights. The widow on marrying a second time forfeited the property from her deceased husband "as if", says the Act, "she had then died."

The Act, however, remained merely a permissive one for decades to come. Custom and caste, with its weapon of excommunication, proved much stronger allies of the orthodox public opinion. For all practical purposes law and legislation appeared to be checkmated. Curiously enough, the greatest obstacle in the matter was the opposition and orthodoxy of the woman. "Physical sutteeism had been interdicted by law, but moral sutteeism is still dormant in the breast of every Hindu widow", wrote an Indian author in 1882.

The practical lead given by Pandit Ishwar Chandra Vidyasagar in marrying his son to a widow was followed by some others in quick succession but after that the zeal appears to have languished on account of adverse public opinion and it remained just a beacon light for a long time. It was only with the progress of education and the work of the reformers, later during the century, that a change of attitude among the higher classes was discernible and some widow marriages took place. But the practice never became general.

Among the lower castes, the forest tribes and the hill people all over northern India, the widow normally enjoyed the right of remarriage. Even in Bengal, the hot bed of many evils connected with women, low castes such as the *Chamars, Bagdis, Bauris,* married widows freely; nor did the people of Orissa and Chhota Nagpur place much restraint on widow marriage. In Bihar it was practically universal. So was it in North Western Provinces and the Punjab as also in the Rajputana.

Commonly known as levirate, under which the younger brother married the elder brother's widow, the custom of widow remarriage varied slightly in different regions. And so did the terms used for it, though the practice was, virtually the same everywhere. *Karewa* or *chaddar dalna* as it was known in the Punjab, was freely practised by the Jats and the custom was so extended as to permit a man to marry by *Karewa* a widow of another caste whom he could not have otherwise married by the proper ceremony of *phera* or circumambulation. In Rajputana, besides *Karewa*, it was termed *Natra* or *Dhareja* or *Gharana*. In North Western Provinces it was *Dhareja* or *Karao* or *Sagai*. There was practically no difference in the various provinces in the form of the ceremonial followed by the castes that allowed marriage of widow. The idea that a full marriage ceremony could not be performed more than once for a woman, appeared to hold good and remarriage could take place with much simplified ritual. As a rule no Brahman or priest officiated and the ceremonies were for the most part restricted to the new husband giving the woman new clothes and bangles (*churees*) in the presence of the caste-fellows and taking her to his house generally in the evening after dark.

On the whole, widow marriage was not a question of caste but of status within caste. For instance, the *Jats* almost always allowed widow marriage but families of high social standing and certain tribes among them disallowed it. On the other hand, Brahmans in certain localities practised it and so did the lower grades of *Khatris*.

Among the Muslims, there was no legal inhibition on widow marriage but strong prejudice against it among the higher classes was gaining ground particularly, among the converted classes who were relatively most numerous in the tracts farthest from the Punjab. The number of widows increased steadily in Assam and Bengal. The same appeared to be true of other communities, the Christians and the Parsis.

7.10 Economic Conditions of Woman

Economically, woman was entirely dependent on man, the earning member of the family. However much she might contribute to the resources of the family by way of the domestic work she did, there was no recognition of it. Nevertheless, women of all classes, except the wealthiest, who could afford the luxury of employing servants, did all the household work. Cooking was mostly done by women. Caste prejudices prevented the hiring of cooks, and the training to be given to the daughters necessitated it. Besides, lack of education and absence of other interests, limited the scope of their activity to the household work only. In families of average means, women drew all the water for household purposes, ground flour required for the day's consumption, husked rice and did spinning and cotton ginning. Among the poorer classes, the wife was a real help-mate, doing all the housework as also giving a helping hand in the trade of the man. For instance, in the case of potters, women prepared the earth, and later sold in the market the wares prepared by their husbands; in the case of textiles, women did the spinning, men took care of the weaving; among fishermen, men caught the fish, women sold them in the market. Thus, women joined men in their occupations.

There were, however, certain vocations which women adopted independently, especially those, who either had nothing but their own labour to depend on, or those, who needed to supplement the income of the male members of the family. Chief among these were spinning and grinding corn. In the case of Brahman women, cooking was a popular occupation. For others, some of the common occupations were those of bangle-seller, milk-seller, grain-parcher, dung-fuel-seller, etc. Hair dresser (*Nain*) and mid-wife (*Dai*) were regular professions. In families where females were kept in strict seclusion, poor women, found occupation as water carriers, scavengers, washer-women, etc. Some domestic trades such as *chikan* and other embroidery net-work, basket and fan making, vermicelli making, etc. were also carried on by women. In Bengal and Bihar not few women worked in the indigo and tea plantations.

Among the agricultural classes, who formed the bulk of the population, women bore a good share of the labour, save among those who had the means to keep their women in seclusion. The practice in this respect was largely a matter of tribal custom, their abstention from field work being looked upon as a mark of the highest social status. But it was not wholly regulated by such custom. While poverty would sometimes compel women who, from their caste, would not be expected to work in the fields, to do so, it was still more commonly the case that social pride and pretensions would induce sections of those castes whose women ordinarily did field work of all kinds to affect the exclusiveness of higher castes. The practice, however, varied from region to region, in some parts from tribe to tribe of the same caste, from village to village of the same tribe and even from family to family of the same village.

In the Punjab, for instance, the women of *Jats* and *Rors* of *Kamboks* and *Arains* and similar minor agricultural tribes worked regularly in the fields with the men. The women of the richer Brahmans, Tagas and Saiyad Rajputs did not go into the fields, while those of the poorer families of these castes and of all the Gujars did light work in the fields. In the hills women of all but Brahmans and Rajputs worked in the fields; in the higher hills almost the whole of the field work, not always excepting ploughing was done by women ; the men working as carriers and coolies. On the frontier, the Pathan women worked very generally in the fields. In Assam hills, women performed hard toil working in the fields and carrying heavy loads uphill. They had plenty of spirit and could generally hold their own.

Anomalous though it might sound, the fact remains that quite a number of women took up the profession of *nautch-girls*, virtually prostitution. The most curious point regarding these women was the tolerance with which they were received into respectable homes and the absence of social disfavour. Moral values aside, this was one of the most lucrative occupations for the women who were driven to it.

But a woman's share in the work or her contributions to the income of the family did not make any difference in her position in regard to her rights to the property of the family. These rights, mainly of three kinds, maintenance, succession and inheritance, determined, more than any other part of law, the status enjoyed by women in any community. The legal position of most of the Indian women, in this respect, speaking generally, was rather sad. The law, governing the two major communities—Hindus and Muhammadans—based mostly on religious texts, had been subject to interpretations, and customs, old and obsolete. In the case of the Hindu law, it showed strange departures from its original ideals so that the Hindu woman had come to labour hard under the greatest legal disabilities. The Muhammadan law appeared to be comparatively more liberal and considerate, while the laws governing the Parsis, Christians and certain progressive Hindus, married under the special Marriage Act of 1872 being adopted more or less in conformity with the social necessities or social opinions of the current era, were to a great extent just and liberal. These laws of the minorities did not in any way affect the general position of the woman.

7.11 Right to Inheritance and Property

The right of maintenance as a daughter or married woman was almost uniform in all communities. Law enjoined a father to maintain his unmarried daughter. On the death of the father, the daughter was entitled to be maintained out of the deceased's estate.[22] According to Hindu law, a daughter on marriage ceased to be a member of her father's family and became a member of her husband's family and so, thereafter, she was entitled to be maintained by her husband and after his death out of his estate.[23]

The case of a Hindu widow was exceptional and pathetic. While other legal systems recognised a widow's right of succession and inheritance to the estate of her deceased husband, the Hindu Law recognised her right to maintenance only. This reduced her position to that of dire dependence and made it absolutely pitiable. If the husband left no property, joint or separate, no one in her husband's family except her own sons was under any legal obligation to maintain her. As for the right of succession and inheritance, the legal position of Hindu woman was not only anomalous, but also most deplorable since the law governing these was unjust, inequitable and most unsatisfactory. A Hindu woman could not inherit the property of her husband if the husband had left a son, grandson or a great-grandson who were considered preferential heirs. In the case of a joint-family she was not entitled to inheritance at all under the *Mitakshara* school which governed the major part of Northern India. In Bengal under the *Dayabhaga* school, she was entitled to inheritance provided the deceased husband had left no preferential heirs. The right to whatever she inherited was limited in that she could not dispose of it, but could enjoy its yield for her lifetime.

A woman could, however, own separate property which was from ancient times known as *stridhan*. This commenced at her bridal and consisted of her ornaments and gifts received from her relatives, the bridegroom and his family and relatives. According to Manu, "what was given before the nuptial fire, what was given at bridal procession, what was given in token of love and what was received from a brother, mother or father are considered as the sixfold property of a woman . . ."

Generally speaking, a woman had absolute right over such belongings and could "spend, sell, devise or give it away at her own pleasure."[24] A husband had no claim to *stridhan*, but could in case of extreme distress and dire necessity, such as famine or some indispensable duty use it, but he would be under a moral obligation to restore the value of it when able to do so. This was observed in a general way, since no separate account of *stridhan* was maintained. The right to take his wife's property was purely personal one in the husband. His creditors could not claim it. All other belongings of the woman were subject to her husband's dominion.

The Muhammadan law, contained explicit provisions regarding the maintenance of a daughter or a wife. A Muhammadan father was under statutory obligation to maintain his daughter and the position of a Muhammadan widow was much better than her Hindu sister. The Muhammadan law, though orthodox in many respects like the Hindu law, was more liberal and equitable in its branch of succession and inheritance. A Muhammadan woman was given a definite and certain share and was not excluded from inheriting her father's and husband's property even if the deceased left behind him male lineal descendants.[25] For instance, upon the death of a Muhammadan intestate, his estate devolved immediately upon his heirs in specific shares. A daughter received a share to the extent of half of that of a son, or when there were two or more, to the extent of two-thirds collectively from the estate of the deceased. And, although the daughter did not get a share equally with the son, she obtained it with absolute right without any qualifications. Many sections among Muslims, converted from Hinduism were, however, governed by Hindu law on the ground of custom as prevalent among them.

7.12 Social Reformers at Work

Notwithstanding the fact that women as a rule suffered from disabilities of all kinds and were to a great extent victims of an unjustifiable social tyranny which imposed obligations on them without giving them the corresponding rights, it would be wrong to conclude that they were absolute non-entities. It is surprising how, despite the forces such as the patriarchal joint-family, customs of *Parda*, polygamy and its concomitant *Kulinism*, the property structure, early marriage, permanent widowhood etc., conspiring to smother their free development, the women in India wielded an influence in no way less than that of the women in comparatively more progressive countries of the West during the period. It has been observed by many that devoid of education, submerged completely in ignorance and incarcerated mostly in the home, they were incapable of making any mark on the menfolk, that they were absolutely subordinate to them. And yet, it is undoubtedly admitted, that even so, women were 'in Posse' powerful and supreme. Whatever the intellectual disparity between men and women, with the coming of Western education among the higher classes, the power of the weaker sex remained as strong as ever. It was used often, to thwart the efforts of their own benefactors, men, superior to them in every respect. Yet it also proved to be the source of inspiration to many of the champions of reform. This by itself is a proof that the influence of the fair sex was potent if not omnipotent. Even Keshub Chandra Sen, a man with radical ideas, appears to have admitted the influence of woman when he said, "man is the noun in the objective case, governed by the verb woman."

The influence wielded by woman was equally, if not more, marked among the poorer classes and the peasantry, where the wife was a true partner in life, a help-mate working side-by-side with her husband, in his trade or the field, over and above her hard toil in the house, cooking, spinning, tending the cattle, bearing and rearing children.

The brightest feature in this respect is that during this period of women's degradation there were deep stirrings of conscience among the intelligensia of the country. The tide of degeneracy was beginning to turn in the closing decades of the nineteenth century. But the movement was tardy, stumbling and fattering mainly on account of the feminine influence, however unenlightened. The staunchest advocates of reform felt helpless before their own women, supposed to be otherwise in complete subjection and yet not infrequently wielding their influence in a most subtle manner, somewhat under the garb of stimulated submission.

Paradoxical though it might appear with the gloomy background of the general condition of woman, the fact remains that even during this period there were some outstanding women, who in defiance of all customs appeared to be the true representative of the early ideals. One of the ring-leaders of the mid-century revolt against the foreign rule in 1857, interestingly enough, was a woman, Rani Lakshmi Bai of Jhansi. Coming from the upper strata of society, her normal place would have been in the palace and not on horse-back in the battle-field. The year 1857 also saw a good augury of the change in the birth of a woman in a Brahman family, Rama Bai, who later earned the title of '*Pandita*' for her learning, and proved to be an outstanding example of defiance of convention. She put into practice much of what the reformers of the period were preaching.

References

1. Jha, Vol. III, Part I, verse 147, p. 172.
2. Strachey, p. 290.
3. Risley, pp. 166-67.
4. Ibid., p. 173.
5. *Selections from the Records of the Government of N.W.P.*, Vol. II, p. 186. Female Infanticide No. I, From C. Raikes to W.H. Tayler, 31st May 1848.
6. Strachey, p. 290 ; also, *Proceedings of the Council of Governor General of India*, 14 January 1870.
7. Government of India Selections, *General Report on the Administration of the Punjab proper 1849-50 and 1850-51* ; also Government of Punjab, *Selections from Correspondence*, Vol. I, 1853, No. XVII. Minute on Infanticide in the Punjab, R. Montgomery, pp. 400-02.
8. *Calcutta Review*, Vol. 104, 1898, p. 158; also, Home Public Proceedings, 20 August, 1870, Nos. 96-98A.
9. *Census Report, 1901*, Vol. I, p. 116.
10. *Proceedings of the Council of the Governor General of India*, 14th January, 1870.
11. *Selections from the Records of the Government of N.W.P.* Vol. II, 1868, No. III. From C. Raikes to W.H. Tayler, November 17, 1851.
12. Government of Punjab, *Selections from Correspondence*, pp. 431-35. Report of the meeting of Chiefs at Amritsar.
13. *Proceedings of the Council of the Governor General of India*, 14th January, 1870.
14. *Census Report 1882, Punjab*, Vol. I, p. 374.

15. *Calcutta Review*, Vol. 36, 1861..
16. Crooke, p. 287.
17. Monier-Williams (1887). p. 29.
18. Ishuree Dass, p. 178.
19. Rama Bai, p. 68.
20. *Calcutta Review* Vol. LXXXVI, pp. 220-23; Sherring, Vol. III, p. 84
21. *Proceedings of the Legislative Council of India,* November 17, 1855, pp. 764-65.
22. Mayne, p. 596.
23. Ibid., p. 601.
24. Ibid., p. 755.
25. Amir Ali, pp. 52-70.

8 Pastimes, Festivals and Fairs

    8.1 Male Indoor Pastimes
    8.2 Male Outdoor Sports and Games
    8.3 Children's Pastimes
    8.4 Female Pastimes
    8.5 Jugglery
    8.6 Social Entertainments
        8.61 Dance
        8.62 Puppetry
        8.63 Drama
        8.64 Other Entertainments
    8.7 Hindu Festivals and Celebrations
    8.8 Muslim Festivals
    8.9 Fairs

The means and modes of recreation of a people speak for their character, culture and mental calibre. In the Indian society, of the period under review, the need for reanimation found expression in diverse ways. Sometimes it takes a conscious and deliberate form as in playing games and having group entertainments. At other times, it remains unconscious and is implied in activities organised for purposes other than mere recreation, such as the celebration of festivals, holding fairs and having feasts on festive occasions. The dominant note of these was the social aspect, the corporate feeling, the common merry-making and the enthusiasm with which the community participated. There was no lack of hilarity among people on any occasion, even in the large variety of games, sedentary and hectic, played by men, women and children.

8.1 Male Indoor Pastimes

It appears that there was a large variety of games played by the people, both in urban and rural areas. One of the most universally known games, chess, was held in high esteem. Its original Sanskrit name being *Chaturanga* which means four-numbered, the game represented a battle, each of the two opposing armies arranged in four divisions. It was commonly known by the name *Shatranj* and showed only slight differences with its European counterpart, the chess, in the names of the pieces and the manner in which they moved. In big cities like Bombay and Calcutta, *Shatranj* appears to have been played on the same lines as the modern chess. The upper classes in other cities of northern India were also familiar with this game which implied a fair amount of thinking, planning and skill on the part of the players.

PASTIMES, FESTIVALS AND FAIRS

Chaupar was another popular game played on a board, generally made of cloth and in the form of a cross consisting of four rectangles with their sides so placed as to form a big square in the centre. Each rectangle was divided into 24 squares in three rows of eight squares each, twelve red and twelve black. The cross was called *chaupar*, the arms *pansa* and the squares *khanas*. On this board, two games were played, both having the common name *chaupar* but distinguished technically. The one played with dice was called *pansa* and the other played with *kowries* was called *pachisi*.

Pansa[1] was played with 3 dice called *pansas* or *dals* and sixteen men or *mards*. The men were distributed four to each arm of the cross and were painted red, green, yellow and black. The dice were $2\frac{1}{2}$ inches long and $\frac{1}{4}$ inch square. Their four faces were marked 1, 2, 5, 6. *Pansa* required two players, one of whom took the red and yellow and the other the green and black. The game was played by repeated throws of the dice and moving the men accordingly, until all of them on one side were moved into the large square in the centre of the board. This generally took some time and required considerable skill in adjusting the moves to the throws. Gambling could be done by betting on the various throws and on the result of the game.

Pachisi[2] was played on precisely the same principle, but with seven *kowries* or shell money by four persons and the men were not set on the board, but kept by the players who took their positions opposite a rectangle. Each player would start his men one by one from the middle row of one of his own rectangles, beginning at the division next to the large central place. They then proceeded round the outside rows of the board, passing, of course, through that of the adversaries' rectangle, travelling from right to left until they got back to the central row from which they started. Any piece was liable to be taken up and thrown back to the beginning as in backgammon by any of the adversary's pieces happening to fall upon its square, except in the case of the 12 privileged squares marked with a cross. The movement of the pieces was regulated by the throwing of the *kowries* as dice which counted according to the apertures falling up. The players would throw in turns, the highest throw being twenty five from which the game got its name *Pachisi*.

The board was used as a carpet ornamented and marked with different colours and cloth sewn on it. It was sometimes played by two persons, taking two opposite rectangles with eight pieces each and playing them all from the rectangle next to him. Often one game could last hours. The long duration of the play and the fascination which it produced made it one of the most favourite pastimes.

An allied game played on the same kind of cross-like board was called *chausar*.[3] This could be played either by four players with four counters each or by two players with eight counters each. The basic principle was the same as that of *chaupar*. Starting one by one from the middle line of his own rectangle and from the square next to the central place, the player sent his four men round the outer line of squares till they worked back to the starting point. The game continued till three of the players succeeded in working round the board.

Playing-cards were well known among all classes of people and constituted a happy pastime along with the other games in "the halls of the rich, the *chandi mandals* of the middle classes and under the shades of trees." The cards used were of two kinds, the Mughali and the Western. The former known as the *Ganjifa*, a pack of ninety-six cards, round in shape and divided into eight suits of twelve each. The western type, a pack of fifty-two cards in four suits was, however, coming into vogue as the decades of the century rolled on.[4]

Dice known variously as *pasa* or *dhara* was a common and popular source of amusement and was played in different ways. A four-sided piece of ivory about two inches long and $\frac{1}{3}$ inch thick, the dice, was marked an ace, deuce, cinque and sice. A set of three dice was generally used and when not combined with any other game playing with these was called *Jua* or gambling. Indeed, the dicing had associations with certain festivals such as the *Diwali* when it became something like a religious observance and was not only tolerated, but was considered as enjoined by religion, and hence was freely indulged in.[5] In big cities gambling with dice, cards or *kowry* shells was common. In Bombay, it assumed, at one time, an extent which called for special legislation to control it. A curious form was prevalent in Bombay known as rain-gambling and also had to be checked by legislation, since this form found loop-holes in the law and defied it.[6] The players during the monsoon sat round a vessel placed under a spout connected with the house roofs and bets were made on the event of rain falling in sufficient quantities within a given time to fill the tub.

8.2 Male Outdoor Sports and Games

Kite-flying was enjoyed by all, young and old. The time of the year when this essentially open-air sport was enjoyed varied in the different parts of the country and depended on the congeniality of the weather whose cooperation was essential. Groups of people would collect not only in open lawns but on house-tops and for hours be engrossed in watching this game of human skill making adjustments with the whims of nature, while the flying of the kite depended to a certain extent on the breeze, a perfect game required considerable amount of skill to take real advantage of it. In fact, kite-flying as practised in certain parts of the country, such as the North-West Provinces and the Punjab was quite an art. The object was not merely to fly the kites steadily at great heights, but the main interest lay in having regular kite-flights. Two or more kites would be flown and the fliers would aim at entangling the strings, which coated with pounded glass would be stiff and sharp, capable of cutting each other. The main interest of the sport lay in

PASTIMES, FESTIVALS AND FAIRS

cutting the opponent's strings with a judicious sawing motion of the hand. The detached kite would float with the wind, chased by crowds of boys and men and when falling on the ground would be captured as a free booty by whosoever first laid his hands on it.

Another sport, well-known and quite a favourite in the cities was pigeon-flying. Two flocks would be let loose from different stands at the same time, the owners frantically whistling and waving flags to recall their own or to entice birds of rival sportsmen. The birds would meet and mingle in the air and finally when they returned to their own stands some of them would be enticed away as captives. The objective then would be to ascertain the gain or loss on either side. The winners would go in triumph to the losing party to demand a ransom for the captives.

Besides the pigeons, *mainas* and *bulbuls* were trained to fight. The owners of the birds would challenge one another and fights would be arranged. Much fuss, at times, was made over the *bulbul* fights and sometimes special invitations would be sent for watching them. In certain places cock, ram and bull-fighting was also practised with equal interest.

Wrestling was common in all seasons, though it was specially enjoyed in winter. It was the chief indigenous athletic exercise of the Indians. Nearly every village had its band of wrestlers. Their stadium was usually a small space of ground under a tree where people collected to witness the wrestling. For larger villages, it was not uncommon to have a big house, as village houses go, with all the wall decoration inside and out, to serve as a gymnasium so to say. Besides the wrestling-pit, with its thick layer of soft earth, it often contained Indian clubs and heavy brick-shaped stones with which men excercised after the manner of the dumb-bells. Every village of importance had its annual wrestling day to which people came from many miles. Competitions were held and prizes were given from the sum subscribed by the villagers. It was considered a point of honour that no villager competed in his own village. Wrestling was conducted with much decorum in accordance with exact and well-organised rules. The decisions of the referee were generally accepted without any dispute. In some villages, feasts also took place on such occasions. Modern novelties were creeping into rustic festivities. Aerated water in bright colours formed an attraction for the village youth and children. Swimming in the village pool and boating where a river was accessible were common pastimes.

8.3 Children's Pastimes

Juvenile games had a charm of their own, The girls in their brief childhood played with dolls as they do the world over, but also had games such as *Bahu-Bahu* or *Bow-Bow* in which the mysteries of marriage were emblematically represented. Celebration of marriage of a doll and all the ritual involved in the marriage ceremony was a common pastime for girls in the cities as well as villages. Groups of girls would often play at house-making and would be seen dexterously discharging the normal duties of a housewife. For very small girls, hide and seek, blind-men and *Ful-Kuti* were common games.

In certain parts of northern India girls played a game very much like the Western Jacks or Jackstone. This was played in different ways, though the most common form was one played with small roundish stones, often five in number and was known as *geetee* or *gutta*. Four stones were put on the ground and one was thrown up about nine inches. The skill lay in picking up those on the ground and lobbing the one thrown up with the same hand without dropping any. Elaborate rules had to be followed and the game could be played by any number of girls and often continued for a long time since the four on the ground had to be picked up in several orders, ones, twos, threes and all.

As for boys, a large variety of games was prevalent. Marbles were played in different ways of which two were very popular, *Ekpari-Sabsari*, throwing marbles into a hole, and *Akal Khwaja*, the throwing of marbles into two holes, the player counting one each time he succeeded in striking another or sending a marble into a hole.

Andha Badshah and *Ankh Michauni* were varieties of blindman's buff and were played with great gusto. This had other varieties also such as, *Baro-Chhapja, Ektara, Dotara*. In *Bujha-Bujhi* a child's eyes were tied up with a piece of cloth and was asked who touched him and until he succeeded in guessing he was not released. *Bunti-Chandu*, another game, had two varieties, one *Uran Chandu* in which a cap was thrown up and whoever caught it pelted the others as they ran away; the other *Bama-Chandu* in which a stone was set up against a wall at which each boy aimed his cap three times, and whoever succeeded in knocking it down flung it at the others.

Chakri or *Chakki* was a kind of a bandalore, a small reed with a cord fixed in the centre which wound and unwound itself with the motion of the hand. *Chil-Jhapatta* representing a pounce like a kite was a game in which if a boy raised his hands at the words *Gadha Pharphar* which he was not supposed to do, he was tickled by all the party; in *Ghirka* a stick was fixed in the ground with another across resting on a pivot, and a boy sitting at each end with their feet touching the ground whirled it round the joint-making a creaking noise. *Ghum*, to turn, was another similar game in which boys would hold a rope fastened to a pole fixed in the ground and would run round it. *Gulli-danda* was the tip-cat; *gulli* being the short tipped stick and *danda* the big stick with which the short one was struck. This was played in different ways and was known by different names such as *Haral, Namasadra, Eridari, Eku-duku* and *Kai-Kata*. On several occasions, particularly certain festivals, groups of boys playing these games would be a common sight. A variety of slings known variously as *Gophiya, Gophana* or *Gullel* were kinds of pellet bows used for flinging stones. Boys in cities and villages had much fun with it while they vied with one another in throwing stones at the greatest distance with the slings.[7] This game was put to a practical use in the countryside where the boys were employed in using the *gullel* for the protection of crops also.

Hardu-gudu, Phala, Tora or *Kabaddi* were varieties of the game played on the lines of prisoners-base. It was a simple but a common pastime for children in which boys divided themselves into two parties by drawing a line on the ground representing the boundary between the opposing parties. The sport began with a boy from one party transgressing the line of separation, encroached on the ground of the other and tried to touch some member of the other party. He was expected to do so in one breath and therefore kept uttering some word such as '*Kabaddi, Kabaddi*', to indicate the continuity of one breath. The opposing party being alert all the time tried to avoid his touch. If the boy succeeded in striking an opponent and returned to his own side in one breath, the boy touched was said to die and retire from the field, but should the intruder lose breath before recrossing the line, the struck opponent was not dead, but should the transgresser be seized by his opponents and lose his breath on the other side, he was said to die. The attack was made alternately and the side which managed to save some member or members while all the rivals were dead was declared to have won the game.

In *Jhar-bandar* or *dab-daboli*, one boy would climb a tree and defend his position against the others.[8] In *Kan-chitti*, also known as *sawari*, a boy was held by the ears by another boy who struck a piece of wood supported by two stones and tried to knock it down. *Lattu*, was the game of tops highly popular with children.

Phisal-banda or sliding down the steep banks of a tank, river, slopping stones or hill side was equally enjoyed. This was perhaps the unsophisticated version of the modern slippery slide. In *Qazi-mulla* one boy would act as the chief law officer and the other as the learned divine. *Sat-kudi* or seven steps or *Kiri-kara* was like the modern hop-scotch while *Thikri-mar*, throwing a potshed, was like the ducks and drakee. In schools and colleges, the exotic games like cricket, football and tennis began to find their way, especially as the century advanced while swordplay, fencing, single-sticks and other similar indigenous games began to give way.

8.4 Female Pastimes

Women mostly found pleasure and amusement in the ceremonials connected with the celebration of festivals and events of import in the family life. Indeed, they looked forward to the celebration of any event such as birth or marriage which would give them an occasion for mirth and merriment, doing full justice to every opportunity. For days jovial singing, joyful jesting and joculating would go on among women. However, they were well acquainted with some of the games also. Playing-cards and *pachisi* known as '*das panchish*' in Bengal were by no means the monopoly of men only. Women played these as also several other games with equal interest, chief among them being *Ashta-kashte, mangal patan* and *bagh bandi*, in Bengal.

Ashta-kashte was played on a board of 25 squares with sixteen pieces of small *kowries* which were placed on four sides of the board. For regulating the move, four large-sized *kowries* instead of dice were used. It was played by four individuals and was said to finish when all the pieces traversing through the length and breadth of the board entered into the central square.

Mangal-patan, strangely enough, had a military air about it. It represented a battle between the Mughals and Pathans and was played on a board consisting of sixteen squares with a large square in the centre. Each army consisting of sixteen pieces took its position and the moves of the pieces were regulated by the skill and the planning of the players.

8.5 Jugglery

Among the varied amusements, the performance of the Indian juggler occupied a very important position. An expert in his art, the juggler could then, as now, show all kinds of tricks. He could climb a pole, keep up a number of balls at a time, draw yards of ribbon from his mouth, eat fire or swallow a sword with an adroitness quite equal to his brother artist of the West. Some of his performances were adjudged even more wonderful by the European eye. A half-naked juggler with his arms and shoulders bare, would take in his hand a fresh twig of a tree and running his fingers along it strip off the leaves. To the utter astonishment of the spectator, a number of live scorpions would fall with the leaves to the ground. Next moment the juggler would have his arms in the air, gather up the scorpions in his hand and they would disappear in the same mysterious way as they came.[9] The variety of tricks performed by the jugglers was tremendous. He could exhibit sleights of hands, convert a pice into a mango, a plum into a *kowry*, create an egg in an empty bag and make a dead goat drink water. They could vomit fire and thrust a knife through a man's neck without injuring him. Some were known as *nats* and showed skill no less astonishing than the modern acrobats. Among other feats, they could dance on ropes, walk on it with points of horns tied to their feet, jump up poles 30 or 40 feet high and lie there on their backs, slide on ropes with their heads, the feet being high in the air ; leap a few feet over high camels from the ground, walk fast on their toes over a sheet stretched out at the four corners without letting the weight of their bodies fall on the sheet and tear it ; throw up three iron spikes high in the air, lie down instantly on their backs and receive the descending spikes, iron part downwards, about their thighs without hurting themselves. Strangely enough, there were juggling women also who exhibited feats of all kinds. Some could raise large weights with their eye-lids, bring out scores of yards of threads and cotton of different colours unentangled from a lump of cow-dung and practice a good many other tricks. The youngest and the prettiest of these women was the principal person of the party and was called the 'Phoolmati'.[10]

The Indian juggler assuming another character would appear as a snake-charmer. He would go about in saffron robes with covered baskets containing some snakes and even cobras. He would play the flute and the snakes would look charmed and delighted. Sometimes a number of them would creep out of the basket at the same time, lift up their heads and make rythmical movements keeping time with the music. The snake-charmer seemed to have them completely under control. His playful handling of the snakes would easily collect crowds to amuse themselves.

Another popular amusement was the performances of monkeys and bears. When there were two bears they would wrestle with each other, otherwise the man would himself wrestle with the bear. The monkeys would generally be in pairs; they would be trained to represent a discontented wife and an unhappy husband. The village *nats* and *bazigars* were recognised as great entertainers also.

8.6 Social Entertainments

8.61 DANCE

Among the social entertainments, dancing formed a very important item. Although dancing at one time had been held in great esteem and honour, it had during the course of centuries sunk into disrepute. Among the hill people and forest tribes, however, folk-dancing was a natural pastime in which men and women participated freely. In the Punjab, the *Jats* had folk-dances on festive occasions. The *Jhumir dance* of the Jats of Muzaffargarh was recognised as special entertainment on the occasion of a wedding. The better classes of Indians in the cities did not dance themselves. For amusement, however, troupes of professional dancing girls known as *nautch-girls* were hired on important occasions, such as the celebration of a marriage or some important festival.

In big cities like Calcutta, wealthy people often arranged these dance entertainments and invited friends, including European officials to watch. The *nautch-girls* were paid according to the means of the person who hired them and also to the celebrity of the locality to which the girls belonged. Native princes had this amusement almost daily. Some rich people, to acquire greater celebrity, made them dance on extensive boards, borne by the *kahars* on their shoulders.[11] The dancing would go on for hours and sometimes at the end of the dancing and music, jesters would appear to entertain the gathering. The *nautch-girls* were far from being considered respectable. They belonged more or less to the class of the Western opera dancers who could in many instances be respectable, but as a class were not regarded models of severe virtue. Among the educated classes and high European officials, dancing was beginning to be looked upon as highly undesirable and the voice of the reformer was certainly being raised against it before the century was about to close.

8.62 PUPPETRY

Another form of amusement popular with the people, was a kind of puppet show commonly known as the *kathputlee nautch* in which small figures were brought on the stage and were made to go through certain evolutions in the Punch and Judy style.

The puppet shows held at night would sometimes represent popular historical events such as the court of Akbar, the Great and sometimes they would depict scenes from the life around such as a *bania* with his bundles and a thief watching and taking them away. Often the well-known members of the society, especially the officials and English ladies were satirised. Professional men known as *Bhands* or *Naggals* provided another source of diversion. Rich men, wishing to celebrate some auspicipous event in the family such as a marriage, a birthday or a namesday of a child, would often hire *Bhands* to give a performance at night and would invite friends to witness it.

8.63 DRAMA

The drama, though not highly developed, had its own place. In Bengal it was known as the *Jatras*. The plots were very often the amours and sports of Lord Krishna. The actors were boys to play the part of all characters, both male and female. The equivalent of the *Jatras* in other parts of northern India particularly in North Western Provinces and Rajputana was the *Raslila*, a dance-recital of the story of Lord Krishna and his frolics with the milk-maids.

Very akin to the *Jatras* was the *Pachhali* which was a recitation of a story in measured lines accompanied with singing and music. The stories recited were popular topics taken from Hindu *Shastras*, such as the marriage of Shiva, the battle of Kurukshetra or the lamentations of Radha. For some time, the *Pachhali* was highly popular and very much in vogue. In cities like Calcutta, it was celebrated annually on a grand scale. Bands of *Pachhali* singers could be seen going round the streets during certain festivals. When *Pachhali* recitations were given for women only, they were represented by female actresses. The language and the tone of such recitations not being always too chaste, a voice was beginning to be raised against them in the closing years of the century.

Katha or narration of popular stories from the Epics, the *Ramayana* and the *Mahabharata* was popular not only in rural areas but also among the city people. The *Katha of Satya Narayan* was commonly arranged to be recited as thanks-giving on the achievement of a pious wish or the averting of a danger of some kind. At the end of the

Katha a feast would be given to all friends, relations and caste men.[12]

Often in a village some very old persons, superannuated or having lost eye-sight would be greaty honoured for the stock of folk-tales, mostly derived from the *Panch-tantra* or *Hitopadesh* passed orally from one to the other like the *Smritis*. These narrations of stories was very popular as entertainment in the evenings

Ramlila, the story of Ram, the hero of the great epic *Ramayana* acted in series on nine successive nights preceding the Dussehra festival over a large part in northern India, formed the most prized entertainment. People, both in urban and rural areas alike, participated in these performances with great enthusiasm.

One other form of entertainment was through recitations by songsters knows as *Kavis* in Bengal. They formed a group under a leader from whom the group derived its name. These groups were often composed of songsters from different castes and the leaders could be chosen from any caste. Two bands under different leaders would often vie with each other in winning applause of the audience. This was most popular in muffassil towns in Bengal where some rich person would invite the *Kavis* and have a gathering.

8.64 OTHER ENTERTAINMENTS

In big cities, it appears that a new enterprise was being tried. One comes across specific mention of dramatic companies in certain places giving performances and staging plays on Western lines not only of a religious nature, but others also such as Alaudin and the wonderful lamp. These performances were by no means specimens of perfection by way of dresses or scenery and all roles were played by boys.

The wilder jungle tribes had games and sports of their own, more vivacious than sedentary such as the annual tug-of-war, throwing javelins, playing clubs, etc. and other harvest games. Eastern frontier played *Kon Yon*. It took its name from the seed of a creeper about the size of a horse chestnut. Several of these were set up on end and the players propelling their nuts with the middle finger of the right hand endeavoured to knock down as many of their adversaries nuts as possible. But their most interesting pastime was dancing. Their dances still retained their religious character and were performed at the chief agricultural seasons, seed time and harvest in the belief that the beating of the dancer's feet on the ground would arouse and please Mother Earth and cause the crops to prosper. Hence, the unrestrained merry-making of the jungle-tribes.

Clubs in the modern sense of the word were generally unknown except in cities like Calcutta and Bombay. Life being simple and unsophisticated, the bazaar was a free lounging place where one could meet friends and acquaintances, exchange ideas, pay compliments and discuss current affairs. Often the house of a prominent person served as a meeting place for such informal discussions.

In the rural areas, the village 'Chabutra, under the *Pipal* tree served as the centre place where people could lounge, smoke *hukka* and gossip. As for women, the village well or the tank or the river where they went to fetch water for daily household consumption was the veritable club without any concomitants of modern club life. Women with their spinning wheels, sitting in rows facing each other in the narrow lanes outside their houses in villages and small towns, spinning, talking, gossing, having fun and often singing, where common sight in the Punjab The weekly or bi-weekly village-market known as the *Hat* was one of the most important attractions for the rural people since it served not only as a place for business but also as a place for recreation and amusement.

8.7 Hindu Festivals and Celebrations

Festivals made their own, but, special contribution towards the entertainment for, although mainly religious, they were partly social and seasonal and as such had a very important place in the life of the people in India where the social and religious affairs have always been inextricably intertwined. Whatever the origin of a festival, whether deeply rooted in religious mythology or based on ideas of mimetic magic or connected with agricultural seasons, the celebration had a religious aspect ond hence involved certain ceremonial ritual, and most of the festivals had very much the character of outdoor popular amusement. They formed the peoples' chief holidays, and on the occasion of many of them, special fairs were held. For women these festivals had special charm for they were their main diversion from the monotony of the household duties. A brief description of some of the important festivals might be interesting.

The most primitive Indian festivals are based on ideas of sympathetic or mimetic magic. These fall into two main categories; those intended to promote the fertility of the soil, fall of rain, intensity of sunshine and growth, and due harvesting of by magical rites; and the others performed with a view to expelling evil and the influence of demons. The primitive and backward people of hill and jungle areas had several feasts illustrating this. The *Hos* and *Santhals* had seven annual feasts such as, one representing symbolic marriage of the earth which took place when the *sal* tree blossomed in flowers; a second, at the sowing of rice, the third at the sprouting of the seed; the fourth, at the transplantation; the fifth, at the offering of the first fruit; the sixth, at the clearing of thrashing floor and the seventh, when the granaries were full of grain.[13] The festivals intended to symbolise the expulsion of evil influences covered a wide variety since this formed also in part the motive underlying the agricultural feasts as well as the village and domestic rites. In these performances, men and women and children all participated enthusiastically. "At the time an evil spirit is supposed to infest the place and to get rid of it", wrote Colonel **Dalton**, "women

PASTIMES, FESTIVALS AND FAIRS

and children go in procession round and through every part of the village with sticks in their hands, as if beating for game, singing a wild chant and shouting vociferously till they feel assured that the evil spirit must have fled."[14]

The bewildering variety of festivals had one point in common in that they all provided fun and frolic in some measure and since the principal festivals were conveniently juxtaposed through the year, interest in life was at no stage allowed to dwindle.

The New Year as is customary among all was hailed with much hope and joy and the festival of *Baisakhi*, the first day of *Baisakh*, the first month of the Hindu year falling in the middle of April stood for merriment. While no public religious ceremony inaugurated the New Year, the day began with bath at the river and was marked by festivity The tradesmen and shopkeepers closed their accounts and started new ledgers. In homes, special meals with palatable sweet-dishes were prepared. In the Punjab where the New Year was associated with the harvest, the festival of *Baisakhi* was the occasion of much mirth and excitement. Apart from the usual bath at the river or the tank in the vicinity and the visit to the places of worship, the farmer gave full expression to his joy and jubilations. Fairs were held both in towns and villages though the latter far transcended the former by way of activity and excitement.

In Bombay Presidency also there were great festivities on this day; gifts were presented by the head of the family to various members and all valuables were collected in the room devoted to the family god, and were worshipped.

In Bengal, the worship of *Dhenki*, a large wooden beam working on a pivot by which rice was husked, formed quite an important festival. The *Dhenki* was operated by women and besides its adorations associated with a number of events in the family, this hand-made machine was annually worshipped with much pomp by women in the month of *Baisakh*. The head of the *Dhenki* was painted with vermillion, annointed with the consecrating oil and presented with rice and tender grass leaves.

Dasshera also known as *Ganga Puja* which falls on the tenth day of the month of *Jaistha* (May-June), commemorates the descent of the river Ganges from heaven to earth and is so called because bathing at the Ganges at this time is said to remove all the sins committed during ten different lives. It was also a festival in honour of the monsoon and the first freshes in the river. It was one of the most interesting festivals and was celebrated with great gusto at Haridwar. Thousands of people would bring flowers, fruits and grain to the river and have a bath at the sacred stream. In Bengal, fish would be given as offerings, lamps of clarified butter would be lighted, officiating priests rewarded and Brahmans entertained. It was considered proper to bathe in the Ganges for those who lived near enough, but other rivers could also serve the purpose. Legends showed that their virtues were equally great. In the absence of a river at a convenient distanc,e a tank was considered good enough.

Snan Jatra was one of the three great festivals in Bengal, performed in honour of Jagannath. It falls on the full-moon of *Jaistha* (May-June) and ushers in the great festival of the *Rath Yatra* which takes place seventeen days later.

Although the festival was celebrated with much enthusiasm all over Bengal, it was at Puri, the headquarters of Jagannath's worship that it had its greatest significance. *Rath Yatra* or the car festival was another great day falling on the second day in the bright fortnight of *Asarh* (June-July). It was a very important festival in Bengal and Orissa. The idol of Jagannath was taken out on a huge ponderous car in a procession. Thousands of devotees would join and feel blessed in being able to help in moving the *Rath* so that old men as well as children would be eager to perform the meritorious act. In the early and mid-century years, the deluded votaries of a most diabolical superstition threw themselves under the wheels of the gigantic car and many would be crushed to death in the hope of obtaining felicity in the coming world. This practice, however, was beginning to be discredited as the century advanced. Public opinion was expressing itself and it was practically checked with the help of the authorities. Curiously enough, even caste distinctions on this occaions were at least temporarily ignored. Large crowds would go out to witness the religious ceremony performed on the occasion, and no small portion of these would be there out of sheer curiosity and many simply for an outing and excitement. The whole neigh-bourhood would have the appearance of a fair which actually would begin soon after ther eligious ceremony.

The goddess of *Shashthi* looked upon as the patroness of mothers and the protectress of children, although regularly worshipped at six seasons of the year had a special festival in *Jaistha* (May-June). It was not common to set up an image of this goddess and since the banian tree was regarded as specially sacred to her, she was represented by it on this occasion. Women of the neighbourhood marched with music to the tree. Mothers with sons were happy and joyous while those as yet unblessed were fervent with prayers for the blessing. After the religious ceremony, another interesting feature of the festival followed. The sons-in-law were invited to the houses of their fathers-in-law, entertained hospitably and given presents. This was one of the happiest days of the year and was the occasion of much fun and amusement, especially for the women. A similar festival was celebrated in North Western Provinces also.

Jhulan-Yatra or the Rocking festival, in Bengal and other parts of northern India commenced on the eleventh of the waxing moon in *Shravan* (July-August) and lasted for five days terminating on the night of the full-moon. On this occasion a swing was specially hung, profusely decorated with flowers, flags and buntings and Radha and Krishna were placed in it every night and gently rocked and entertained with music and dancing. This festival was held in considerable estimation and was celebrated with pomp and eclat with only slight variations in details in the different parts of northern India. In Bengal, friends were invited to feasts and *jatras* and celebrations were performed. The *jatras* began at about 11 o'clock at night and continued until six or seven the following morning. Crowds of men, women and children sat to watch them the whole night through and these theatrical representations of the lives of the deities formed a most successful and interesting method of teaching the people the most memorable events of their lives. In the North West Provinces the whole month of *Shravan* was dedicated to festivities in honour of Krishna and other gods and was known as the month of *Hindolas*. Temples were decorated, images were adorned with new outfit and swung while devotional singing and dancing went on.

Raslila was the most favoured pastime of all and sundry at this time. It was performed night after night and sometimes the series would go on for the whole rainy season. Not infrequently a little indulgence in vulgar expressions entered the depicting of the love stories, but against that the voice of the reformist was coming up in the closing decades of the nineteenth century. In Bengal, the *Raslila* was performed as *Ras Yatra* or *Ras Purnima* as an annual festival from the tenth lunar day in the bright fortnight of the month of *Kartika* (October-November) to the full moon day.

For girls the month of *Shravan* (July-August) provided special festivity, particularly in the North West Provinces, Rajputana and the Punjab. Married girls paid visits to their parents so that sisters, cousins and childhood friends got together and enjoyed themselves. Swings were specially improvised and green *sarees* presented by mothers and other older relatives were worn by girls who had real fun swinging and singing folk-songs. The third day of the waxing moon during the month, known as the *Teej*, had special celebration.

A special festival in honour of *Manasa*, the queen of snakes, was also held in the month of *Shravan*. Bengali mothers anxious for the preservation of their children from the bite of the serpents implored the favour of the *Manasa*. On one of the last days of the month, women would go to the village tank with offerings of rice, milk and sugar, and after presenting them on behalf of their children, would help themselves to a good feast. In towns and large villages where women could not easily go out, this ceremony termed, *Ban bhajan*, took place in the house itself. In the North West Provinces and many other parts of northern India, *Nag Panchami* was celebrated with great eclat and had a similar significance.

On the full moon of *Shravana* (July-August) was held another festival known as *Salono* or *Raksha-Bandhan* celebrated in all parts of northern India with some variations, when women tied *Rakhis* or bracelets as charms to avert evil round the wrist of their brothers who in return gave presents in acknowledgement of the honour and as a token of the pledge to protect their sisters. The Brahmans tied a thread round the wrist of those who were under their religious guidance on a similar basis of protection. Closely connected with this festival on the same day or some other day soon after was another known as *Jayi* or *Jawar* in Upper India. This was a simple rural feast for which a most elaborate ritual was developed. However, the common celebration involved the sowing of barley in a pot on the seventh day of the waxing moon and when in three weeks the stalks would be grown the women and girls would distribute them to the men of the family who would tie them in their turbans. A fair was held on this occasion where women and children thronged.

Krishna Janmashtmi or *Nandotsava* (known as such in Bengal), the birthday of Lord Krishna, formed a great festival and was observed on the eighth lunar day in the dark fortnight of the month of *Bhadra* (August-September) in Upper India. Although abstinence was practised on the day previous and on the day itself rigid fast was observed by the pious, rejoicing and merriment was the dominating note of the day.

Anant Chaudas, the worship of Vishnu, was celebrated on the 14th lunar day in the light fortnight of the month of *Bhadra* (August-September). Offerings of fourteen kinds of delicacies were prepared, half of which were offered to the Brahmans while the other half were eaten by the persons who performed the worship. A big fair on this occasion provided an opportunity for fun and frolic, particularly for women and children.

The dark fortnight in the month of *Aswin*, known as the *Pitar Paksha* was devoted to *poojas* performed for the benefit of the souls of the departed forefathers. A period which would have been grim and sad became full of excitement as each day meant a great feast given primarily to the Brahmans in the name of the departed ancestors, but actually shared by all. This meant activity and reverential festivity which kept everybody busy for days, especially women, with the preparation of the feasts.

Vijaya Dashami, commonly known as *Dussehra* and in Bengal as *Durga Pooja*, falls on the tenth lunar day of the light half of the month of *Aswin* (September-October). The variety of legendary tradition connected with the festival and responsible for its different names does not, however, detract from its importance. On the contrary, it adds to the richness of the festivity. In Bengal, it was celebrated to worship the goddess Durga, the female principal under whose influence the universe is created and who, among other things, is said to have killed a giant Mahisa who had maltreated the gods and oppressed the inhabitants of the three worlds. In other provinces *Dussehra* stood for the victory of Ram, the hero of *Ramayana*, over Ravana, the King of Lanka who had kidnapped his wife, Sita. Notwithstanding these differences of tradition, the festival was celebrated throughout with universal rejoicings. Men, women, children, learned and ignorant; rich and poor, high and low; Brahman and *Chandal* all welcomed the approach of this festival for a true holiday. The husbandman laid aside his plough, the merchant his books, the tradesman his tools and the landed proprietor his *Zamindari* cares and all partook of the general mirth. Every village had its music and every house its festivity. The whole period of ten days, beginning from the first day of the light half of *Aswin* and known as *Navratra*, while devoted to religious worship was at the same time full of joy, fun and feasting. The nature of amusement indeed varied according to the tastes and hence the degree of importance given to *nautches, jatras* or pure devotional music.

Deepavali, rows of lamps, commonly known as *Diwali*, and in Bengal as *Kali* or *Shyama-Pooja*, is another festival of great importance with a variety of legendary tradition attached to it, falling on the dark night of the month of *Kartik* (October-November). Whether it was celebrated as Rama's return to Ayodhya after the long exile of fourteen years or Durga's victory in the dreadful war with the demons or in honour of Lakshmi, the goddess of wealth and prosperity, the festival, apart from the religious worship, had ample occasion for merriment. It was the great occasion for a cleansing of the house and purchasing of new equipment. At night, the houses were illuminated and the whole town or city wore a gala appearance with streets and shops profusely decorated, confectioners with ingenious ideas of sugar toys and sweets and fire crackers adding to the excitement. Merchants looked upon this day as the beginning of the new financial year and would start new account books. Gambling on this occasion was looked upon as an auspicious amusement. In fact, the day was particularly devoted to the goddess of wealth and prosperity for which *pooja* was performed and invocation made. For women, the festival meant new clothes and jewellery and an occasion to dress up for the worship of *Lakshmi*.

Two days after *Deepavali*, on the second lunar day of the new moon in the month of *Kartik* (October-November) came another festival known as *Bhratri Dwitiya* or *Bhaiphoja*, or *Yama Dwitiya* or *Bhai-Duj* to commemorate the attachment between *Yama* and *Yami*. According to the legend Yami or Yamuna, the sister of Yama, offered welcome to her brother on this day and thereby secured for him immunity from death. Hence sisters invited their brothers on this day, feasted them, gave them presents after the special ceremony of marking their foreheads with saffron, sandal and rice grains. Brothers in return made suitable presents to sisters according to their means. This festival on account of its emotional touch was one of the happiest occasions.

The festival of first fruits was celebrated in Bengal when it was time to harvest rice crop and the first sheaves of paddy were offered to the gods. The festival was celebrated in certain parts of the province with sports, pyrotechnic exhibitions and entertainments given to Brahmans and friends.

Makar-Sakranti marks the return of the sun to the northern hemisphere and usually falls on the last day of the month of *Pausha* (December-January).

The observances on the occasion were partly of private and partly of public character. The ceremonies consisting of offerings to the progenitors, conducted by the family priests being over, the general rejoicings began with fun and feasting. In the, Punjab the festival coincided with the winter sowing of the crop and happened to be at the coldest time of the year. The celebration, thus, assumed a very joyful character. In the evening, bonfires were built, sweets made with sesame seed, parched rice, pop corn and sugarcane were distributed. This festival was most important in Nepal, hill regions of U.P., and Bihar where it was differently observed. In Bengal, the day was devoted to feasting and great quantities of puddings and cakes made of rice-meal were consumed. The festival was also called *Phool-Sankranti* on account of the custom to place flowers on the threshold of friends and relations who in return gave presents of rice and grain. In the countryside in Bengal a festival known as *Paushali* was celebrated when a number of men would go round from house to house during the day with baskets for offerings. The gifts would then be taken to the village green. Brahmans would be engaged to cook the food and then all would eat together. Sports like *Gulli-Danda, Hadu-Gadu* and swimming matches would form the great attractions of the day.

The fifth lunar day in the month of *Magh* (January-February) was celebrated as a great festival. Although it differed in its legendary origin in different parts of northern India, the enthusiasm displayed on the occasion was universal and did not lack in warmth.

In Bengal, the day was dedicated to Saraswati, the goddess of learning. All who had even the slightest smattering of learning paid their homage, and not only her image but also pens, ink, paper, books, etc., by which knowledge could be acquired, were worshipped. Women had no share in this worship, though curiously enough the patron of learning was represented by a goddess and not a god. In the North West Provinces and the Punjab the festival was known as *Vasant Panchami* and denoted the advent of spring. A general holiday was observed. People wore yellow clothes, visited friends, and open-air sports like kite-flying were enjoyed and feasts were given. The festival was also known as *Shri Panchami* and in certain parts it was incumbent on every religious-minded person to worship the implements or the insignia of the vocation by which he lived. "The soldier worshipped their sword ; the cultivator his plough ; money lender his ledger; the *Thags* had a picturesque ritual for adoring the pick-axe with which they dug the graves of their victims." With the institution of modern mills, this festival assumed rather curious forms. In the jute mills near

Calcutta, the operators bowed down to the foreign-imported engines which worked their looms. In one instance, the orderlies employed by the Government of India and who moved with the government back and forth between Calcutta and Simla furnished a still more interesting but rather grotesque form assumed by the worship on this occasion. Some orderlies in Simla at one time used a large packing case in which office records were transported, to make an alter. They covered it with plantain leaves and branches of the sacred *pipal* tree and put all the stationery in common use in the government offices on it, draping the whole with festoons of red tape. A Brahman priest was employed to perform the ritual of the religious worship with the chanting of Vedic *mantras*. The worshippers made the usual offerings and at the end of the ceremony had a good feast for which a special subscription had been raised.

Dol-Yatra, Dolotsava or the *Holi* festival, falls on the full moon day in the month of *Phalgun* (February-March). The legendary origin though varied, the practical form of the celebration of the festival was very much the same in all parts of northern India. Commonly accepted as commemoration of the sports of Sri Krishna and the milk-maids of Vrindavan, it seemed to be designed to celebrate the spring and in its purest form it was a most delightful and sprightly festival. The fun of the festival lay in the lively and vivacious squirting of colour, often red powder, but also in liquid form through syringes. In big cities, an absolute holiday spirit prevailed and gross licentiousness with impunity was permitted. Groups of people would go round singing songs, often in none too decent a language, and in delirious joy, besmear the passers by with colours. Crowds of people, including some European officials, would collect to amuse themselves watching prostitutes dancing, drinking themselves and giving presents to the dancers. The bacchanalian mirth would go on for days and at night singing with the accompaniment of drums and cymbals, as also dancing in a state of frenzy, would go on for hours. In the countryside, however, the festival was celebrated with moderation and confined itself to playful colour throwing, light singing and dancing. Public opinion, however low and feeble, was beginning to express itself against the indecencies indulged in.

The ninth lunar day in the bright fortnight of the month of *Chaitra* (March-April) was the birthday of Ram. The festival, known as *Ramanavami*, was celebrated with much zeal, especially in the North West Provinces. Primarily a religious festival, there was enough opportunity for amusement such as singing and feasting which played an important role.

Charak-Puja or the hook-swinging festival took place on the last day of the month of *Chaitra* (March-April) and was celebrated in Bengal only. This was in honour of Shiva, the Lord of Kailash and was mainly celebrated by the *Sanyasis*. The peculiarity of the worship was that the devotees of Shiva belonging to the lower castes and the most dissipated characters assumed Sanyasa for a week or ten days living abstemiously and observing austerities for the propitiation of Shiva. While processions of these men paraded the streets leading to the temples of Shiva displaying all kinds of tortuous feats such as piercing the tongue with spears or falling on a row of knives or collecting and playing with fuel, a sort of carnival seemed to go on. Crowds of people gathered just to watch and have fun. Processions were formed and *tableaux vivante* arranged on platforms representing different trades and professions and carried through the streets. On the second day of the *Pooja*, the most cruel part of the ceremony, the swinging took place. Indeed the scenes represented, the gestures employed and the feats displayed, in the former days at least, were all of obscene character and primitively cruel, but towards the end of the century the objectionable and cruel features of the festival were largely either eliminated or curtailed. Instead of inserting a hook in the flesh of men and then swinging them from great heights, a bundle of clothes representing a man began to be swung or a rope began to be tied round the body of a man in which the hook could be hung. It was no easy task to shake off the cruel practices connected with this festival. The importance of public opinion as also of the government, who as early as 1865 had prohibited the hook-swinging, was clear, for the practice continued in all its notoriety for years, notwithstanding the law. The conservatives among the Hindus were highly incensed at the prohibition. Public opinion among the educated during the period of study was definitely becoming more and more hostile to ceremonies which were considered obscene and irrational by them, but formed a necessary part of the celebrations of many festivals as far as the vast mass of people was concerned. The purging of these festivals of some of the practices considered objectionable became a part of the programme of reform.

8.8 Muslim Festivals

The festivals of the Muslims, though fewer in number, were celebrated with equal zeal. *Nauroz* or the New Year's Day, was a festival of great importance. The exact period of commencing the Mussalman New Year is the very moment of the Sun's entry in the sign Aries. This usually happens on the 20th or 21st of March. The exact hour determines the special colour for the clothes worn on the day by all regardless of class or rank. The religious community would have the prayers read in the family and then usher in the New Year, but for the common people, the day was devoted to amusement, having feasts, exchanging presents, paying visits and extending greetings. Women worked for days in preparation and on the actual day set out trays of presents tastefully decorated, vying with each other for the display of novelty and taste. Children received gifts, the servants and the slaves were regaled with dainties and the poor were given clothes, money and food.

PASTIMES, FESTIVALS AND FAIRS

Muharrum, the anniversary of the martyrdom of Hussain, the second son of Fatima, the Prophet's daughter, was commemorated with great enthusiasm. The first ten days of the months of *Muharrum* were observed as the days of lamentation by Muslims in general and *Shias* in particular. Religious and reverential, the celebrations involved a good bit of sentimental and emotional expression. The *Imambaras* were specially prepared for the occasion, sometimes draped in black and special prayers were read. *Taziyas* representing mausoleums erected on the plains of Karbala over the remains of Hussain were built at great expense and taken in procession through the streets, crowded with thousands of people of all communities, presenting a scene of uttar confusion. Men and boys disguised in all kinds of quaint get-ups ran about fencing and jumping. Curiously enough, the Hindus also took part in the ceremonies. Hindu women considered it auspicious to take their children from under the *Taziyas*. Some of the Hindu Rajas celebrated the festival with equal pomp and show.

Idu'l-Fitr, literally the feast of breaking the fast, also called *Id-i-Ramzan* or *Idu'l-Saghir* or the minor feast, commences on the first day of the month of *Shawwal*, the tenth month. It was considered specially a feast of alms-giving and there was a festival of rejoicing after the tension of *Ramzan*, the month of fast. The special sweet dish, vermicelli, prepared on the occassion gives it another name *mithi* or sweet *Id*. People gave alms in accordance with the injunctions in the traditions, wore their best clothes, assembled in the mosques to say their prayers and then spent the rest of the day in visiting, merry-making and picnicing.

Idu'l-Azha or *Idul-Zuha* variously known as *Id-i-Qurban* (the Feast of Sacrifice), *Bakr-Id* or *Bari-Id*, and celebrated on the tenth day of *Zul-Hijjah*, the twelfth month of the *Hejira* year, formed a part of the rites of the Meccan pilgrimage. On the day of the festival prayers were said at the *Idgah* and all those who professed the faith, sacrificed animals according to their means—sheep, goats, lambs, cows and camels. It was considered highly meritorious to sacrifice one animal for each members of the family, but since this meant heavy expenditure, one victim for the whole household was allowed. In extreme cases, several pooled resources and made joint sacrifices. Part of the flesh was distributed to the poor, part among friends and the rest used by the family. Quite apart from the religious ceremonies, the festival was regarded as a day of joyful remembrances; consequently, as one of holiday and festivity among all ranks. Women dressed in their choicest, clothes and costly jewellery to receive or pay visits. The children had their sports and amusements.

Besides the two *Ids*, the great festivals of the Mussalmans, there are some others which are not properly feasts, but were, as now, generally regarded as such.

Akhiri Chadar Shamba, meaning the last Wednesday of the month,

Safar, was observed as a festival in commemoration of the fact that on this day the Prophet, who had been seriously ill showed signs of improvement. The day, therefore, was observed as a day of relief and thanksgiving. It was considered proper to bathe, wear new clothes, use rose-water and make sweet cakes. Prayers were read and sweets were distributed. Some of the lower orders employed dancing girls to sing and dance and drank toddy and other liquors.

Bara Wafaat was the commemoration of the Prophet's death which took place on the twelfth of the month of *Rabi-ul-Awwal*. On this day food was cooked in large quantities and after prayers had been read, it was distributed to the poor. In some parts of the country it was more customary to keep this day not as the anniversary of the death of the Prophet, but as the *Jashn-i-Milad-i-Sharif* or the feast of the Noble Birth.

Shab-i-Barat, meaning the night of the record, was celebrated on the fourteenth day of the month of *Shaban* when a sweet dish, halwa, was prepared and *fatihahs* or prayers were read over it for the benefit of the deceased ancestors. It was believed that God on this night registered all the actions men were to perform during the ensuing year.

8.9 Fairs

Besides the myriads of festivals, of which only the principal ones have been mentioned, there were periodical fairs which provided the people with the much coveted amusement. The fairs were of two kinds; one the village fair where petty articles of food and products of local handicrafts were sold generally by barter, and secondly, the religious fairs in which a visit to a place of pilgrimage was combined with a considerable trade in all kinds of merchandise, including cattle. It is difficult to say as to which appeared first, trade or worship, for the two seemed to be closely tied and the fairs served purposes of a varied nature—social, religious and economic. To the devout, a visit to the holy place was a deed of great religious merit but to the common man the fair had a more practical appeal. For him it had a social and economic significance so that while it afforded a happy meeting ground it also had the important factor of trade in it.

There were numerous local fairs associated with legends and connected with certain religious festivals as also a number of general fairs of great renown. These were held at places of pilgrimage especially during the bathing season when people would collect in large numbers. Every twelve years the planet Jupiter is in the sign of Aquarius and on such occasions special fairs were held. Enormous gatherings of pilgrims collected at the sacred sites along the banks of the holy rivers, such as Haridwar, Prayag, Banaras, Sonepur, Garhmukteshwar on the Ganges, and Mathura and Batesar on the Jamuna. The rivers showing no sectarian or partisan feelings, the fairs were democratic gatherings of all classes of Hindus and sometimes other communities also. For the womenfolk the fair served as a holiday and real outing to which they looked forward eagerly and for which they spent days and weeks making preparations. Whole families would set out in bullock carts sometimes days ahead, if the distance to be covered was long.

The site of the fair with thousands of people, men, women and children dressed in their best, had often the appearance of a camp, especially when the sojourn lasted two to three days. Families would take a temporary abode under some tree — *pipal* or *neem* or mango and have a good picnic. True, the religious aspect of the visit was given its due respect; the families took their bath at the river and made the offerings to the deity at the temple, yet by far the greater part of the time was spent in pure amusement. Women mostly flaunting their finery, went about lightly, haggling over trinkets; men, some just looking around, others busy with gambling tables or doing a brisk business, and children, hovering over shops of sweets and toys as also enjoying the swings and merry-go-rounds. Not that adverse happenings did not occur. The thieves and pickpockets had ample opportunities, but this was all part of the game. The missionary with his magic lantern also hurried to the fair for the crowds gave him an excellent opening and a valuable chance for preaching his faith.

Of the hill regions which had innumerable fairs, the *Nagar-Mela*, a semi-religious fair in Kullu held annually at Sultanpur, was typical of the lightheartedness displayed on such occasions and the type of amusement derived. Not only was the fair the chief market of Kullu, it was a place of rendezvous for young boys and girls as also of entertainment in singing and dancing.

Normally, the different religious communities had their own fairs at the places of pilgrimage sacred to their faiths. The Hindus having them at Haridwar, Prayag, Sagar, Garhmukteshwar and Puri. The Sikhs had them at Amritsar, Sialkot and Anandpur and the Muslims had them at the shrines of their saints, chief among them being at Ajmer, Panipat, Pakpatan and Nigaha in the Punjab. All drew large crowds.

The fair at Nigaha enjoyed special renown. It was held annually at the shrine of the Muslim Saint Sakhi Sarwar and its significance lay in the fact that it was attended by all irrespective of caste and creed. Not only did they share the fun and amusement and contracted useful business, they made offerings at the grave and invoked the divine intercession of the Saint. Like other fairs, vast crowds also assembled merely for the sake of amusement, to listen to music and watch the *nautch-girls* dance.

Another occasion of common interest and a source of recreation to all was an eclipse. Although the Hindus and the Muslims had very different ideas regarding its cause, the reactions and the mode of its celebration was very much the same. Loud cries from the mixed crowd would announce the commencement of the eclipse. The Hindus would thereupon prepare for a bath at the river and offer charity in corn, oil and money to the poor. The Muslims would go to say prayers and then offer alms to the poor likewise. To the recipients of the alms it mattered little as to the source whence it came.

The significant point in all the observances, undoubtedly, was the humanising element which is not always clearly recognised. Social life derived its vivacity, its binding force from these conditions of common joy and festivities, when caste and often, even sectarian differences, receded into the background. At public fairs, the high and the low, the rich and the poor, the ignorant and the learned, mingled and moved about freely. The festival crowds in the closing years of the century, it may be interesting to note, were beginning to be used by different forces such as the reformers and the missionaries to transmit their ideas to them.

The larger number of the domestic festivals of the Hindus displayed the warmth and pathos of domestic tenderness. Their celebration was so ordered as to allow all sections of the community to share it. The Brahman, the Sudra and even a Muhammadan, each had a sort of prescriptive right in any entertainment that might take place in the neighbourhood. Above all, however, they served as forceful stimulus for zest and fervour in life all around the year.

Much of the ceremonials connected with the festivals, however, revealed the credulous ignorance and the intellectual backwardness of the vast masses. Even the voice raised against some of the objectionable practices by the educated few had not proved very effective for the simple reason that the vast majority lacked education and clung to tradition.

References

1. Temple, Richard (1884-86), p. 243.
2. Ibid.
3. Herklots', p. 333-34.
4. Yusuf Ali (1907), p. 25 ; Herklots', p. 335.
5. Crooke (1906), pp. 9-10.
6. Government of India Acts, Act III of 1867 ; also Bombay Gambling Act 1887,
7. *Calcutta Review*, Vol. XV, 1851 , p. 342.
8. Herklots', p. 338.
9. Kerr, p. 190.
10. Ishuree Dass, p. 145.
11. Ibid. p. 148.
12. Ross, p. 71,
13. Crooke (1906), p. 211.
14. Dalton, Colonel : Devil Driving of the Himalayas, quoted by Crooke (1909), p. 213.

9 Perspectives on Education

    9.1   The Shape of Old and New Education
    9.2   Factors Responsible for Slow Progress of Western Education
    9.3   Promotion of Western Education
    9.4   Impact of Western Education
    9.5   Women's Education
    9.6   Work of Missonaries in Women's Education

The importance of education in the life of a people can hardly be overrated. It is one of the fundamental factors by which the worth of a society or even an individual is judged. The lack of education or ignorance is usually held responsible for all kinds of social disabilities. It is believed to produce, often, a rank growth of positive evils which are both a peril and a stigma to society. It places, moreover, a serious embargo upon the industrious enterprise and fixes life in the routine of old and antiquated methods, conventional habits, traditional customs, with little hope or even desire for betterment. Education, thus, as a vital force in human life, is recognised to hold an undisputed precedence among means which contribute to the formation of character and the growth of that feeling of solidarity which is the basis of all progress. Its ideals explain the hidden forces of social life. It checks and restrains, chastens and sublimates the lower and meaner tendencies of human nature; it enlightens and informs the mind, stimulates and stirs the latent qualities and inspires noble ideals. It is a creative and aggressive force so that the social conditions of a people are found to be significantly and closely connected with the type and extent of education among them. In fact, the two so intimately and intricately react on each other that it is difficult to discern the causal relationship between them.

    Taken in the ideal sense, perhaps, education may by found to touch few people in any society. The term, however, is mostly used in the popular sense and is construed to mean the instruction imparted in the schools and colleges. In the early stages, it amounts more or less to literacy, the outward expression of education, and at best the initial tangible step towards it. Yet, it is in this first step, the schooling, as it is termed today, that much is done for society, its future—not as much the immediate, as the distant future, for education takes at least a generation to begin to yied its results.

    The state of education in northern India during the later half of the nineteenth century was far from complimentary, in any sense of the term. There was no general education worth the name. The bulk of the people lived in a blissful condition of crass ignorance. Credulous and superstitious, they appeared to be content with their traditional ways. Any change in the grooves in which they moved was regarded as serious encroachment on the sanctity of their social system. Even an effort at improvement or an enquiry into the state of affairs was more often than not looked upon with suspicion by the masses considering it to be a precursor of some fresh assessment. During the 1871-72 census, a man detected trying to hide his babies gave the explanation that they were too young to be taxed.[1] In Murshidabad, the general feeling was reported to be that the surplus population was to be blown away with guns; in other places it was believed that it would be drafted to the hills where coolies were wanted.

9.1 The Shape of Old and New Education

Sadly and strangely a people credited with knowledge and learning of a superior order and achievements of a rare quality, a people, "so acute in intellect, so remarkable for erudition, so successful in industrial arts" at a time when the Western civilisation was not even born[2] had degenerated in the course of centuries to an exceedingly low ebb. Learning had become stagnant and stereotyped, but happily not extinct. Nor had northern India become totally illiterate. The indigenous system of education developed by the spontaneous efforts of the different communities, Hindus, Muslims and Sikhs, believed to have existed from time immemorial, was still fairly widespread alongside the new schools established by the government, and maintained a general uniformity of character. The educational organisation was not different, but only less complete and successful in some parts of the area than in others. It had continued to function unmindful of the political vicissitudes and uninterrupted by the queer concatenation of circumstances which had led to the establishment of the British regime in India. Village schools under this system taught, not only the three, but often the four Rs, the fourth being religion. In fact four distinct methods of education were in operation with slight variations according to local conditions. Instruction, as imparted in the seats of Sanskrit learning better known as *tols* in Bengal, in the *maktaba* and *madrassas* attached to the mosques, in the large number of village schools known as *pathshalas*, and by the Brahmans to their disciples. In the Punjab, the Sikhs had their elementary village schools where elementary education was imparted in *Gurmukhi*. The indigenous schools were more or less religious in character, particularly the higher class schools—whether it be the Hindu *tol* or the Muhammadan *maktab*, though the religious element was more marked in the Muhammadan *maktab* and the *Gurmukhi* school than in the *pathashala* or elementary school of the Hindu village community. These were mainly secular in character and the children of any of the villagers could be admitted to them except those who belonged to the castes which it was pollution to touch. The higher schools of the Hindus were practically closed against all, but Brahmans.[3] The Muhammadan *maktabs* and *Gurmukhi* schools of the Sikhs, on the other hand, were completely democratic.

The general illiteracy prevailing throughout the period with only slight improvement as the decades passed was appalling. Official figures at the end of the century, though for the whole country showing only 53 literate persons per thousand, one male in every ten and one female in 144,[4] are an eloquent reflection on the condition of education in northern India, the most thickly populated part of the country. Among the provinces in the area, Bombay and Bengal with 125 and 109 literates per thousand, respectively stood far ahead of the Punjab and United Provinces with 67 and 59 literates respectively. In larger cities people were better educated than in rural areas. The statistics at the end of the period show the number of literates in the cities as 339, 324, 212, 196 per thousand for Bengal, Bombay, Punjab and United Provinces respectively. Of these, women formed a very small proportion, being 63, 63, 27 and 20 only.[5] In other respects, there was no connection between the spread of education and the density of population. Nor did race as such seem to have any relation with it. In the extreme North West of India where the Aryan element in the population was believed to be the strongest the people were found to be far more ignorant than in the East. Kashmir in educational matters was the most backward tract while Central Provinces enjoyed only a slightly better position with 56 per thousand as literates.

Community-wise the educational results were most favourable to the Parsis, a high percentage of whom amounting to nearly two thirds of their total strength were able to read and write. The others may be placed in the order as Christians, Jains, Sikhs, Hindus, Muslims, with the Animist tribes at the bottom claiming only eight males per millennium as literate.[6]

Caste-wise, generally speaking, it was the higher castes who appreciated or who could make use of the advantages of education so that the professional and trading groups among them, everywhere took the lead. There were, however, noteworthy exceptions among the lower castes who as a general rule were largely illiterate owing mainly to social taboos, but partly to lack of practical use for education. The opportunities opened to them by the missions were working a social upturning of unexpected magnitude so that in some localities they were beginning to press hard on those of the upper ranks.[7] The proportions of the literates varied in different tracts and the high castes in one part might be more backward from the point of view of literacy than castes of far lower ranks elsewhere. For instance, the Babhans and Rajputs of Bihar were outsripped in the race for education by the Chasikaibarthas of Bengal proper. Although normally the degree of education varied directly with the special position of the caste, the Brahmans, it is noteworthy, did not always lead. In Bengal proper, they were headed by the Baidyas; in the provinces as a whole the Baidyas and the Kayasthas followed by Karans Subarnabanika, Gandhbaniks and Aguris showed a higher proportion of literacy than the Brahmans.[8] In Bombay, the Vanis were ahead of the Brahmans and the Prabhus were treading very close to them; in Central India and Rajputana the Mahesris were leading; in United Provinces the Kayasthas held a high position and though they constituted barely 1 percent of the total number of persons who could read and write and 20 percent of the aggregate of the literate females.[9] This was helpful in obliterating, though slightly, the artificial distinctions which favoured and puffed up the Brahmans who in many instances were marking time, while the lower castes such as the Mahars of Nagpur and Santals of Assam were marching briskly and hopefully coming forward.[10] These examples, though striking and cheering were exceptions to the general trends. The Brahmans were, nowhere, surpassed by any caste of the same locality, which did not claim a twice-born origin. Other castes of this status almost invariably possessed a larger proportion of literate persons than any clean Sudra caste; the latter again ranked higher in this respect than the unclean Sudras, and the unclean Sudras than those who were altogether outside the pale of Hindu society, with some exceptions such as the Shahas of Bengal who were far better educated than their social position would indicate. This was due, in most such cases, to the prosperous conditions they enjoyed. However, the encouraging aspect of the otherwise lamentable state was that there was a steady increase in literacy as indicated by the statistics. From 66 literate males in 1881 to 87 in 1891 and 98 in 1901 with corresponding proportion for females being 3, 4 and 7[11], was no doubt progress, although far from satisfactory when reckoned with the vast populace completely unlettered.

9.2 Factors Responsible for Slow Progress of Western Education

The slow progress of education was due to many factors of which the political causes aside, the social conditions were equally important. Among the inherent characteristics of the social system of the Hindus, the majority community, caste hindered the advance of education. Its influence with its system of hereditary occupations was responsible to a great extent for the traditional indifference of the people at large towards education. The pride and selfishness of the Brahmans, who had from ancient times secured the monopoly of all learning and felt that the maintenance of their intellectual supremacy, no less than the promotion of their material interests, depended on their excluding the *profanum vulgus* from access to it, still prevailed to a considerable extent. They had never discouraged the communication of mere rudimentary instruction to the people in the vernacular, but instruction in the sacred Sanskrit, the repository of their literature, religion, science and law had ever been reserved for their own sacred order. The belief that the whole human knowledge was contained in the Sanskrit writings and learning anything other than the *Shastras* was useless had restricted the field of education and rendered it static and stagnant. The learned professions were not only the monopoly of a few castes, but the imparting of knowledge to certain others such as the Sudras was strictly forbidden. Again, there were only a limited number of castes whose traditional occupations necessitated a knowledge of reading and writing. The great mass of the people, who lived by agriculture or manual labour, who had for many generations been illiterate, who were regarded by higher castes as unfit for education and who had become indifferent to its advantages saw no reason why their children should be sent to school or taught things of which they were totally ignorant and for which they could perceive no practical use. Nor did they have the means, for they were generally too poor to be able to set aside the sum required to meet the fees, even if they could spare their children for the purpose and dispense with the help they received from them in various ways, such as herding their cattle collecting fuel, etc. Furthermore, the prejudice of the higher castes against those considered unclean deterred the admission of their children to the schools and sit with those of the privileged classes.

The problem was, thus, complex. Its solution could have been easier if the government had followed a positive policy and not faltered and floundered as it did. It had taken the British government almost a whole century of oscillation and vascillation, from the time its first foothold was established in Bengal in 1757, to decide on its educational policy A. Howell, a British officer in the Bengal Civil Service wrote in 1871 :

> "Education in Indian under the British Government was first ignored then violently and successfully opposed, then conducted on a system now universally admitted to be erroneous and finally placed on its present footing."[12]

9.3 Promotion of Western Education

The East India Company was a trading rather than a ruling corporation, and as such education was no part of the programme of its early administrators. It was only during the later times of its government, when its administrative needs demanded that the promotion of education, as such, in India was considered one of the duties of the State. The same motive determined the type of education to be imparted. Hence, the change-over from the encouragement of oriental learning which for long had been acknowledged to be a matter of importance to the promotion of Western education. The decision in 1835, of the acrimonious controversy between the two lines of thought, respecting the claims of Oriental and English education, in favour of the latter, had the support of some sections of the higher classes of the Hindu society especially in Bengal. The demand for English was notable even in the provinces then not

British, such as the Punjab. The years that followed saw a marked invigoration of the process of anglicising education which had profound effects on society. The opening of new seminaries and a series of corresponding measures for the promotion of English studies such as the abolition of Persian as the court language in 1837, the introduction of the scholarship scheme in 1839, and the declaration of the policy in 1844 enjoining the selection for government service of candidates who had received English education, gave it much impetus. But English could not have been imposed on the millions of unlettered Indians. It was a necessary corollary that pupils were to be sought from among a special class, through whom it was expected to filter downward to the masses. This policy not only failed to yield the desired results, but added to the social problems by creating a new class that of the English educated, which small to begin with was destined to grow into a force to reckon with.

English education had, however, been given its value in terms of livelihood and so had become an object of ambition as the only avenue to good appointment and to improved status in society. It was not merely a question of learning English language; it was a question of new knowledge, new ways of thought, new attitude to life. The Hindu society, the first to respond to the new trends in education, in its thinking strata had, thus, been profoundly stirred and quite early in the century its reactions against some of the social customs had been astoundingly rebellious. The voice against the practice of *Sati*, for instance, had come from those who had been educated under the new system and were becoming a powerful force that played a significant role in the social field.

The failure of the downward filtration theory was in the fitness of things. The literary classes whether they were Brahmans, learned in the sacred literature of ancient India, or men primed with the most modern knowledge that the English colleges could impart, agreed, for the most part, in the rejection of the idea that education ought to be extended to the masses of the people.[13]

The change in the policy that was necessary, was embodied in the historical Despatch of 1854 commonly known as the charter of education in India. Synchronising almost with the beginning of the period of study, it stands as a landmark in that it was the first authoritative declaration of policy on the part of the sovereign power responsible for the administration of British India accepting education as a state duty.[14] It outlined a complete and systematic organisation of education from the university to the elementary school. The policy defined therein controlled the system of education in operation throughout the period under review. It evidently recognised the failure of the two experiments made earlier, one stressing classical languages of India, the other emphasising English as an exclusive medium of instruction. The special characteristic of the new policy was the importance assigned to the vernaculars as also a happy balance between the two extremes.

The Despatch of 1854 declared emphatically that the education which was to be extended in India was that which had for its object the diffusion of the improved arts, science, philosophy and literature of Europe, in short of European knowledge, but it explicity repudiated any aim or desire, "to substitute the English language for the vernacular dialects of the country."[15] European knowledge was to be "diffused through the medium of vernaculars which alone are understood by the great mass of the people." A befitting tribute, nonetheless, was paid to the antiquarian and historical interests of the classical laaguages of India as also to the honourable and influential position of those who maintained the traditional learning. The new policy, further, stressed the importance of primary education, which had been, hitherto, too much neglected. It declared that it was specially necessary to place the means of acquiring useful and practical knowledge within the reach of the great mass of the people who were utterly incapable of obtaining education worthy of the name by their own unaided efforts. It also acknowledged the need of fostering in every province of India the indigenous schools which had existed from time immemorial.[16]

Measures prescribed for the carrying out of the policy such as the constitution of separate departments of instruction in the different provinces, foundation of universities at the Presidency towns, the establishment of training schools for teachers, the maintenance of existing government schools or colleges linked by a scheme of scholarships, increase in the number of schools when necessary and finally the introduction of a system of grants-in-aid were speedily adopted. Education in the modern sense of the term may be said to commence with the opening of the period under review. Indigenous schools began to be sought for and endeavours made by the offer of pecuniary aid and official advice to induce school masters to improve their methods and follow a system of education approved by the state. This endeavour met with a degree of success which varied greatly from place to place and from time to time[17]. In Bengal, for instance, the sustained efforts of the Department of Public Instruction contributed, but little to the network of primary schools already in existence; and there still remained an outer circle of indigenous institutions not greatly inferior to those which had been absorbed in the state system of primary instruction. In Bombay Presidency, on the other hand, in 1858 no less than 90% of the villages were without any indigenous schools. The Department of Public Instruction made independent efforts. In the whole country, a large number of indigenous schools were brought within the new scheme but the progress made in the successive decades was not uniformly steady. The highest increase in the number of schools and pupils was seen during 1871-81.

Primary education, nevertheless, remained a formidable job. There were about 98,535 public schools with 3,268,726 pupils in 1901-02, in the whole of the country. Private agencies like the missionaries and progressive and philanthropic Indians along with the government toiled and panted at the colossal task. Certain sections such as the aborigines numbering some 4,720,000 in Bombay, Bengal and Central Provinces alone in 1882 who had no schools of their own and the low castes who were denied access to schools were reached with difficulty by the ordinary educational agencies.[18] Valuable efforts were being made by others, particularly the missionaries, but the progress remained slow. The population was vast, the diversity of caste, creed and language bewildering and the desire for elementary education among the masses almost nil. They had yet to be convinced of the practical utility of primary education which did not open any careers. Nor were the British authorities prepared to apply the dogma of democracy that primary education should be gratuitous. Free, compulsory, universal education for the people of India was not even an ideal to be aimed at. Elementary education, which had to be paid for did not find willing purchasers. It advanced, but slowly more especially in the countryside. Rural India stoutly disbelieved in education[19] since it appeared to serve no useful purpose Even where schools existed many places remained vacant solely because the peasant preferred to keep his sons at home for more useful purposes and dreaded the effects of books on their habits and character. Parents considered education useful only when it led to public office.

This was not the case with secondary and higher education which was therefore much sought after. In fact, secondary education had developed earlier than primary education. The British Government had commenced its efforts in this direction much earlier, and with better results—the main object being training auxiliaries for its administrative work.[20] The task here was limited and the classes to whom education was offered were attracted by the prospect of government employ. At the beginning of the period, in 1854 there were, under the direct control of the department some 20 English schools both high and middle. By 1871 the number of schools had gone up to 42 equating no less than 5,600 pupils.[21] The decades that followed saw much growth, the most rapid being in the seventies. Even in regions like Bihar, known to be backward, the demand for English education during these years was unprecedented and remarkable

As for college education, the picture was still more encouraging since it offered better prospects for careers. From the outset, there was a close connection between college education and government service, and the hope that their sons would procure good posts had operated as a strong motive in favour of the preference for English education which the educated Indians especially of Calcutta had displayed earlier.[22] The Hindu Gains of Learning Act of 1855 gave an additional stimulus to the young boys to go in for English education as their earnings could, thereafter, be used by themselves in preference to being pooled or merged in the family resources, if they so desired.

The increasing number of students at arts and oriental colleges as well as professional colleges like the medical colleges at Calcutta and Bombay and the Engineering College at Roorkee were a convincing proof of the popularity of English education. The opening of the Universities in Bengal[23] and Bombay[24] during the tumultuous year 1857 gave higher education great impetus which was further accelerated by the addition of two more, one in the Punjab in 1882, and the other at Allahabad in 1887. In point of mere numbers, the strength of the students sharing English education, increased from year to year with a keen desire to pass examinations so as to be qualified to get into government service. Figures for the twenty five years (1857-1882) are an eloquent testimony to this.[25] The total number of students who passed the different university examinations in the fifteen years 1857-71 in Bombay, Bengal, N.W.P., Punjab and Central Provinces were 2,725. In the decade that followed, the number was more than doubled, being 5,844. The increase kept up the pace with slight fluctuations here and there, and by the end of the nineteenth century the quantitative extension of education was an accepted fact though it was infinitesimal as compared with the vastness of the population. The need for more to be done was recognised even by the Goverment. The appointment of the Education Commission in 1882 was made with a view to reviewing progress and to determine further steps to be taken in regard to sections particularly backward in education, such as the aborigines and the low-castes; among the communities, Muhammadans, and girls of all communities whose education had hardly been touched.

Misgivings regarding the quality of education had begun to be expressed both by Indians, some educated and some of those who had not taken any advantage of the facilities for education, as also officials among the authorities, quite early, during the period of study, leading to a survey of the system by another commission at the end of the period sponsored by the then Governor General Lord Curzon in 1902.

9.4 Impact of Western Education

Whatever the intent and worth of English education and, however, small the fraction of those who received it, its effects were undoubtedly tremendous. Strictly speaking, education in the modern sense had not been in operation long enough for a just and fair assessment of its results. It was, at best, barely fifty years old and that too the outcome of different agencies working with different objectives in view, yielding a variety of results. The government interest was mainly in the preparation of a *Karani* class, i.e., the clerks, and to this end education was directed in government institutions.[26] The missionaries had wider ideals, but their main object was religious proselytism and education imparted in their institutions was accordingly conducive to that purpose. In the institutions run by the progressive Indians, a wide variety of trends was growing. The object with which English education was pursued, regardless of the institution in which it was imparted, was the openings it provided for earning livelihood.

The educated few formed a class by themselves. Although a mere sprinkling among the vast multitude of unlettered people they were becoming a distinct section. Heterogeneous in its composition, consisting of representatives of different communities, castes, creeds and following different professions, besides the public service, such as bar and other legal pursuits, private practice in medicines, commerce and banking, civil engineering, mechanical industries and the like, it enjoyed a unique homogeneity. It comprised men brought up under a common system of education, who developed a common plane of thought and a broadening of vision from a common source. This peculiar class, the literati, very different from the traditional class of the learned Brahmans, was an addition to the already numerous classes in society and stood distinctly apart. English education became the dividing line. In fact, a wide gulf began to be yawning between the educated and the uneducated. The new-born intelligentsia and the old-fashioned people, the few and the many among the Indians themselves. The profits of English education also created a distance between the Hindus and the Muslims as communities, the latter having for many generations lost the start taken by other communities in English education. A similar gulf began to divide town and country for education spread mainly in urban areas. Since the English educated professional classes gained in importance the intelligence of the countryside began to be attracted to town and town occupations.

English education, however, proved to be the accelerating cause of progress, albeit confined to the educated class to begin with. The fermentation of ideas that set in the small section in the first instance began to show results affecting society in many ways.

The simplest and the most natural effect was on education itself. The dazzling success in life, normally, of the educated, acted as a powerful incentive to others to follow their example to better their prospects in life. Peculiar reactions, in this respect, were also noticeable. The poorer people appeared to be beginning to think that education, on however small a scale, would raise their status; and the wealthy seemed to think that attending schools would lower their dignity. In any case those who gained from education became its staunch advocates and endeavoured to see that their sons were educated. The enthusiasm and the enterprise of the highly educated did much to rouse self-effort in the process of education. Their munificence was responsible, to a very great extent, for the extension of education. It was on this account that the Indian press became active and views on social problems began to be expressed freely. Public opinion, however meek and mild, modest and moderate, was beginning to be formed[27], and by the end of the century had grown powerful.

Speaking generally, the English-educated generation differed from that which preceded it in its attitude to life and social problems. An assertive self-importance, a questioning outlook, a tendency to reason, to look into the why and wherefore, even negation and defiance of the accepted ways, were their outstanding traits. In the opinion of the British officers, the English educated public servant had higher integrity than others. Whether this was gained from an education which was purely intellectual and which abstained absolutely from moral and religious teachings or from the sense of responsibility of the public office, it is hard to say. However, the increased number of the educated later did not give the same satisfaction on this score as the few had initially done.[28]

The intellectual and secular education had its good points as well as those that were undesirable. The absence of all religious instruction carried to the extent of absolute neutrality became a grave defect in regard to the higher welfare of society so that "the man was often confounded with the stomach." The pupils, not unnaturally, received the impression that their religion, their history and old traditions, completely neglected in the curriculm, were unimportant.[29]

In any case reverence for the current forms of religion seemed difficult when face to face with dogmas which science had exploded. A disposition to scoff, and a sense of superiority amounting to conceit, were leading to the faith of the young students in their own religion, being shaken and unhinged without their being anything to take its place, This was a little more true of the Hindus than of the Muslims. "The western education", wrote R.C. Temple in 1882, "has not affected the Muhammadan faith. It has subverted the Hindu faith or the Brahmanical religion among the educated classes of Hindus, but not among the masses who continued to follow the ancestral idolatry with the same simplicity as of yore."[30] Actually, the faith was becoming dubious with those who had some tincture of education while with some of the highly educated it was being somewhat shattered. Many of them had lost faith in mythology but they did not become irreligious men nor atheists nor materialists. They, in many cases, reverted to the primeval faith, or adopted some form of theism, and questioned social practices which were supposed to have religious sanctions. In other words, the desire for the quest of the true and the pure in religious and social customs was leading the educated to form new sects and societies.

The individualism taught in Western education was very different from the way in which the sense of self-interest was subdued in the Hindu system. The spread of English education and the example of the English society was bringing the individual into greater prominence and not infrequently causing conflicts. A mighty transformation, not commendable in its entirety was taking place. Monier-Williams' comment on the change that was coming is significant.

"We teach a native to believe in himself. We deprecate his not desiring to be better than his father. We bid him beware of merging his personality in his caste. We imbue him with an intense consciousness of individual existence. We puff him up with an overwhelming opinion of his own sufficiency. We inflate him with a sublime sense of his own importance as a distinct unit in the body politic."[31] The self-confidence thus gained often led to a tendency of insubordination and lack of regard for the elders. In their anxiety to cast off the reproach to subservience, the educated class often mistook rudeness of behaviour for dignified independence. As a result some of the basic principles were shaking. The traditional idea of education in India was based on reverence for the teacher whose word was law and who was almost worshipped by his pupils. There was no equivalent of this sentiment in the new set-up of education. The teacher lost his status and had no *locus standi* which the *Guru* had enjoyed.

The distance created by education between the few and the many was in itself undesirable for there could not be a sympathetic understanding between the higher and the lower classes. The unequal mental and intellectual development of the people led to a great many anomalies in social life.

In the family, the new spirit inculcated by English education was injecting maladjustment. It often happened that a family had one or two individuals who on account of their education were advanced in ideas, habits and tastes, the others being backward intellectually with the result that they felt they were misfits. Elements representing different levels of development could not but be ill at ease. School or college life and home life were two separate circles. They lacked a convincing sense of reality. For instance, a student would read and might dream of romantic love, but at home, "a little girl in wifely adoration" held the key of his future and had locked it fast against sentimental experience. The liberty of conscience which the English classics expounded and which he read avidly was wholly inconsistent with the rules of his caste; his mother would suffer agonies of shame were he rebelliously and traitorously to desert her cherished traditions. Education thus created two worlds—one at school or college or the place of occupation, the other at home, in the caste and community, the latter being the real world of absolute values in which the social life proceeded undisturbed and the occupational world where ideas possessed of only relative value moved.[32]

In family life education became often a source of much internal strife between the young and the old male members disturbing the peace and homogeneity, and challenging the traditional submission of the members to the head of the family. Further, the tendency to support the idle and the distantly related in the family, was, under the influence of education, considerably getting diminished.[33]

Education thus was beginning to rouse the spirit of rebellion against the thraldoms from which the people, particularly the Hindus suffered. A feeling of revulsion against the tyranny of caste was noticeable among the educated especially in Bengal, the others also chiming in with them. As years moved, inroads in various directions into the well-guarded pale were visible. The domination of the hereditary priesthood was beginning to be questioned and not merely resented. Irksome superstitions and customs were often examined, ignored and sometimes set aside by the educated who appeared to be rational and even defiant. The educated lower caste in many localities were pressing hard upon those of the upper ranks. In some parts, many posts formerly held by educated Hindus in government service on the railways, in collieries and in private establishments were held by Christians converted from among the educated low castes, such as the Santhals.[34] Barriers, hitherto insurmountable to the mixing of caste in educational institutions, were beginning to show signs of liquidation. In this respect, medical education stands out as most noteworthy. High caste medical students, though few in number, faced with the problem of touching dead bodies for dissection had decided in the early part of the century against the caste rules and renounced all prejudices. "Most certainly", said a young Brahman who had been under Duff's instruction, "I for one would have no scruples in the matter. It is all prejudice, old stupid prejudice of caste of which I have got rid." Many others gradually appeared to be echoing this utterance.

Restrictions about food were losing their stringency and a movement towards greater freedom in the choice of food was noticeable. Educated men and even others travelling on railways found it impossible to follow strictly the rules regarding food and so did men who had to remain away from home for long hours on business and occupation. Convenient relaxing of rules was being accepted and connived at.[35] The earliest educated youths had gone to the extremes. Not only content with eating beef, a group of them in Calcutta had gone to the extent of throwing bones and remains into the house of an inoffensive orthodox neighbour. The orthodox Hindu openly dined at the table and portook of forbidden animal food cooked and served by non-Hindus or low-caste or practically no caste Hindus. The use of English drinks was also becoming popular. Aerated water was getting more and more common among students and complaints were coming up that even strong drinks were finding their way among them.

In the daily routine, the tendency among the educated was to adopt the habits, mannerism and mode of living of the ruling class. The educated considered it more dignified to wear western style clothes and to introduce western type furniture in their homes, particularly in that part which wae open to visitors and strangers.

The small section of the educated, however, appeared to be exceedingly out of place in the whole set-up. The general mass looked upon them as *sahibs* and shunned them just as much as they did the English people who in their turn termed the Indian *sahibs* as Baboos and ridiculed their efforts to copy them. Nevertheless, these changes followed in the wake of English education helped to bring some educated Indians into closer contact with some Englishmen encouraging some mutual regard and esteem and promoting social intercourse. The feelings of aversion and contempt on the part of both the rulers and the ruled tended to be weakened, for the English educated as government servant was found almost everywhere—as a clerk, as a subordinate judicial and revenue and police-officer, as a professor in a college or a teacher in a school, in various capacities in the Department of Public Works, the forest department, the telegraph, the railway, the medical service, etc.[36] The acceptance of each other on sufferance and having formal relationship, however, did not mean the closing of the gulf between the rulers and the ruled. The mutual indifference, if not antipathy began to assume a different form—political aspirations on the part of the educated Indians and distrust on the part of the British officials.[37]

The liberal ideas developed by English education, to which much of the primitive beliefs were yielding, were also the source of inspiration to see things in their right perspective. They brought about a state of mind on which other influences of a creative or reformative nature could work. The result was unprecedented activity on an intellectual level leading to the founding of various societies, literary and scientific as also those for religious and social reform. All the reformers of the period were English educated and the opponents of reform generally without it. The Brahmo Samaj, which had come into being with the first wave of the English education in the first part of the nineteenth century, was forging ahead. The Prarthna Samaj in Bombay and the Arya Samaj in the N.W.P. and the Punjab were expressions of a similar urge among the educated in those provinces. Rational probing into the ideas, ethics and primeval religion had commenced. The earliest literature on Hinduism began to be studied with renewed veneration; the later and more elaborate writings of the Hindu priesthood were being disregarded. Customs and social traditions accepted for centuries were now beginning to be re-examined and rationalised. The importance of education, and that of the right type, was being recognised and was being stressed by the new societies that were rapidly coming up. Some of the caste communities such as the Kayasthas, Bhargavas and Aroras were organising their own associations with a view to introducing reforms in their communities and providing special facilities for education to the members of their own castes.

This spirit was manifest among the advanced sections of the educated irrespective of their religion. Even Muslims who were considered backward and had not responded to western education as some of the others had, were by the third quarter of the century waking up. Sir Syed Ahmad Khan's sedulous efforts to rouse his community became a movement by itself, and the founding of the Aligarh College proved to be an eloquent testimony to the inspiration drawn from English education.

There was on the whole an upheaval of the mind among the educated especially in Bengal, consequent on the spread of secular education; but while an advanced party was springing up with contempt for irrational beliefs and institutions that seemed to be absurd on the face of them, the society was not yet prepared for a real change. Education and enlightenment, or even instruction and information had not gone far or deep enough. It had touched just a fringe of the vast mass. The educated few were like a drop in an ocean. Hence, the impact of the new ideas could not be far-reaching.

9.5 Female Education

This was bound to be so, for the whole policy and procedure had been a total neglect of the most potential half of society. 'The mind and heart of the most important agent of instruction, woman'[38] had not been given proper recognition nor enough attention. All statistics of the period indicate appalling illiteracy among women. Even at the end of the century, the percentage of literate women as compared to men, in the country as a whole was lamentably small—one literate woman to fourteen literate men.[39] It was almost vain to educate boys when they had to go home to an ignorant mother.

It is indeed no paradox to maintain that in any society the education of girls is a problem which is probably more complex and important than that of boys. The wife and mother have a decisive influence over the husband and children, over the public and private conduct of the former and the moral and intellectual development of the latter. The impress of the mother on young minds is, indeed, in many cases ineffaceable; the mentality of the mother shapes that of the children. These are truths that apply universally. To the British officers and others in authority familiar only with conditions prevalent in cities and that too among certain higher or perhaps it would be better to say well-placed classes, their application seemed to be less apparent in northern India of the period of study. The influence of women, as strong and potent in the Indian family as anywhere else, was considered to be ineffective in the society where they were not seen. Their education, a matter of vital importance for the general well-being of society, deserving first claims, remained largely unattended. No notice of female education as a recognised part of the government scheme had been taken prior to 1850. It had been left entirely to the fostering care of individuals and private societies. This was partly due to the strong prejudice of the people against the education of women, founded not on any direct precept of the Hindu faith but rather on immemorial custom and tradition.

In certain provinces among certain classes, little girls occasionally attended the indigenous village schools and learnt the same lessons as their brothers. Many women of the upper classes learnt the legends of the *Puranas* and the epic poems which supplied impressive lessons in morality and in a way formed the substitute for history. Among the lower orders the keeping of daily accounts fell in some households to the mother or chief lady of the family. The arithmetic of the homestead was often conducted by primitive methods, addition and subtraction done by means of flowers or any rude counters which came to hand. Among the more actively religious sects and races, the girls received education as a necessary part of their spiritual training. In the Punjab, they could be seen seated in groups around the venerable Sikh priest learning to read and recite their scriptures or the *Granth Sahib*. The Brahman tutor of wealthy Hindu families did not confine his instruction to the sons alone. In fact, there had always been and were, even during the period under review, some women of outstanding talents and accomlishments. The state of Bhopal was ruled by ladies for two generations; many of the most ably managed of the great landed properties of Bengal were entirely in the hands of women.[40] In commercial life also, some women conducted through their agents lucrative and complicated concerns.[41] Nevertheless a large mass of women were sunk in absolute ignorance. The idea of giving girls school education as a necessary part of their training in life was consicuously absent for the most part of the period. Their life was so strongly dominated by superstition that even to touch books by girls was considered inviting misfortune. In fact, a feeling existed in most Hindu families that a girl who learnt to read and write committed a sin which was sure to bring down a judgement upon herself and her husband. She would probably have to atone for her crime by early widowhood, the greatest misfortune that could befall her.[42] In any case, the girls were supposed to become vile and wicked, unruly and indisciplied under the influence of education. Moreover, reading and writing had come to be associated with prostitutes and *nautch-girls* so that the prevalent idea was that education was not for respectable women.[43]

With such prejudice connected with female education, the Government was probably unwilling to interfere. But other agencies, like Christian missions who had no dominions to safeguard had started working in this direction in the early decades of the nineteenth century. For a long time education of girls remained in the hands of missionaries, especially in Bombay.

Government efforts in favour of female education synchronised with the opening of the period, when Lord Dalhousie, the then Governer General, took definite steps to extend to it Government patronage by instructing the council of education that thenceforth its functions were definitely and systematically to embrace female education. The Governor General thought it was possible to establish female schools in which precautions could be taken to maintain conditions in conformity with the prevalent customs. He also directed that all possible encouragement should be given to any attempt made by the Indians in this direction. The first female school recognised by the Government was established under a committee of Indians at Barasal.

Female education, however, proved to be much more arduous a task than that of boys, there being many factors that impeded its progress. In the first place, the effective desire for education as a means of earning livelihood did not exist in the case of girls. Among the richer classes there was no need for women to work in order to earn. At best they looked after the household work. Among the poorer classes the type of labour they put in to earn their living did not require the type of education given in the schools. The demand for education, therefore, did not exist. Parents, except among Parsis and Indian Christians, who were the first to change their attitude, attached no importance to their daughters obtaining knowledge. Nor was a husband affected by the ignorance of his wife. Government schools as they began to be opened attracted but few to receive the instruction they imparted. It was only after long years of hard labour and strenuous efforts on the part of the missionaries, the educated Indians and societies such as the Brahmo Samaj and the Arya Samaj that a demand for girls' education in schools began to be visible.

Secondly, social customs proved to be the greatest impediment in the way of female education. The practice of early marriage left the duration of school-going age for girls much shorter than that of boys. It usually terminated at 9 and seldom extended beyond the 11th year. At such a tender age, there could hardly be any education. It could scarcely be said to begin when the girl would disappear into seclusion. The married girl among higher classes could in very rare cases have the opportunity of continuing with her studies after she left the school. Under such circumstances where it was not easy to bring girls to schools, it was even more difficult to have a sufficient number of women teachers. This dearth greatly hampered the progress of girls' education, for the few women teachers available belonged to classes in which the system of child marriage did not prevail and were objected to on grounds of caste or religion. Consequently, men were employed as teachers in most of the schools and this caused parents to withdraw their daughters even earlier than they might have done if female teachers were employed. Moreover, the State system of instruction was conducted in a large measure by the male staff primarily for boys so that the special needs and requirements of girls did not receive the attention they deserved. In smaller towns, the difficulties in persuading parents to send their daughters to school were still greater. A district officer in Assam wrote, "It is very difficult in the *Muffassil* to get parents to educate their girls. They are too useful in the house and parents think they will forget and despise ordinary household duties if they learn how to read and write. Girls thus qualified are said to become '*Dushta*' which means they are less likely to submit to their parents' choice of husbands."

Notwithstanding the difficulties, female education progressed considerably during the period under review, and despite the setback it received from the tumults of the year 1857, the number of schools under the Department of Instruction as also the management of other agencies increased steadily. So did the number of pupils in almost all parts of Northern India.[44]

The pace at which female education moved, however, was neither uniform nor adequate, but it was progress nevertheless. The statistics of the period bear eloquent testimony to this. Had there been proper records of the indigenous schools, the figures might have been higher.

Province-wise, the Presidencies of Bengal and Bombay were leading. Bombay at the beginning of the period in 1854 had 65 girls schools with, 3,500 pupils and 593 girls attending boys' schools. In 1864, the number of girls' schools had gone up to 639. In 1871, there were 218 girls schools with 9,190 pupils.[45] In Bengal in 1854, the number of girls' schools was 288 with 6,869 pupils. Under the grant-in-aid system, the girls' schools in 1862-63 were 35 with 1,183 pupils. In 1870, the number of such schools had risen to 274 and the pupils, 5,910. In 1881, the number of girls under instruction in Bengal were 35,760 being 1 girl in 976 of the female population.[46] In the North West Provinces, the progress was rather erratic. In 1854, there were 17 missionary girls' schools with 386 pupils. By 1870-71, the number of schools had gone up to 640 with 13,853 pupils; but this rise was followed by a great decrease in the subsequent years. In 1875-76, there were 400 government primary schools for girls with 9,000 pupils and in 1880 only 160 schools remained with 3,757 pupils. In 1882, the total number of girls under instruction was 9,771 being one girl to 2,169 of the female population.[47] In the Punjab in 1854, the work of female education under the government had hardly begun. In 1856, there were 17 schools for girls known to the Department of Instruction with 306 pupils. By 1865-66, there were 1,029 schools with 29,561 girls on the rolls, though most of these schools were merely rudimentary schools which had existed from time immemorial for the purpose of conveying religious instruction. Returns of 1870-71 showed 465 schools with 11,819 pupils. The census reports of 1881 indicate 6,101 girls under instruction being 1 girl in 1,416 of the female population. In the Central Provinces in 1870-71, there were 137 government girls' schools with 4,494 pupils, 2 aided schools with 169 pupils and two unaided with 58 pupils. Census Reports of 1881 returned 3,171 girls under instruction or 1 girl in 1,539 of female population together with 4,187 women able to read and write, but not under instruction.[48] In Assam, female education showed rapid development after its separation from Bengal in 1874. The Census Report of 1881 returned 1,068 girls under instruction or one in every 2,226 of the female population together with 1,786 women able to read and write, but not under instruction.[49] At the end of the nineteenth century, the extent of female education was 9 per thousand in Bombay, 5 in Bengal, 4 in Assam, 3 in Central India Agency, Berar, Punjab and 2 in United Provinces.[50] There is a possibility of under-statement in this since there was a strong prejudice among certain classes, chiefly the higher ones, against admitting that their women were able to read and write. The popularity of education in the case of girls like that of boys, was more visible in cities than in the villages. The proportion per thousand being 63 in Bengal and Bombay, 27 in the Punjab and 20 in the United Provinces.[51]

Looked at community-wise, the Parsis topped the list. One tenth of their women could claim to be literate.[52] Then came the Indian Christians followed by Hindus, Sikhs and Muslims.[53] In the Punjab and Berar, the Muslims, although as a community backward, showed a higher percentage of girls in education.[54] The newly rising small communities, the Brahmans in Bengal and the Arya Samajists in U.P. and the Punjab had distinctly higher number of literate girls as compared to the Hindus.[55]

Caste-wise, there was no strictly uniform pattern applicable to all parts of northern India. On the whole, the higher castes and the upper strata of society were averse to allowing their girls to go to attend schools except as very young children. Non-Brahman castes gave the lead in this field. For instance, the Kayasthas had the largest number of literate girls in Assam, Central Provinces and the United Provinces; the Baidyas in Bengal; the Prabhus and Vanis in Bombay.[56]

It need hardly be stressed that education on the whole among girls was of the most elementary type. It could hardly be otherwise. It was only towards the end of the nineteenth century that a few women in big cities were found going in for higher education. The number of women at the universities was smaller still. It was only in 1878 that the first Indian girl matriculated from the Calcutta University and thereafter in 1884 took the degree of Master of Arts.[57] At the end of the nineteenth century, the number of girls at the University did not exceed 171 in the whole country and 143 in Northern India.[58]

The progress, however, meagre, was the result of the tremendous effort on the part of the different agencies at work to foster female education. The Department of Instruction offered prizes and scholarships to successful girls and rewards to vernacular school masters who would form girls' classes in their school.[59] In Bengal, special steps were taken and rewards of Re. 1 for every four girls under instruction were offered to *Gurus* in improved Pathshalas.

In some parts of northern India, surprisingly enough, a large number of girls, most of them undoubtedly very young, were found in mixed schools. The Report of the Education Commission of 1882 mentioned 42,000 girls in mixed schools in the whole country. And since the establishment of a girls' school in every village was found to be impossible, the Department of Instruction favoured the opening of schools where boys and girls under seven years of age could be placed under trained mistresses.

Efforts were also being made to provide facilities for training women teachers needed for the girls' schools. Female normal schools were established at the principal cities, such as Bombay, Ahmedabad, Poona,

Calcutta, Jubbalpore, Lucknow and Agra. But the class from which women teachers could be drawn was limited. The profession of a teacher was not looked upon as a normal career for any Hindu or Muslim lady. The students at the normal schools were, for the greater part of the period under study, Europeans, Eurasians and Indian Christians. It was only towards the end of the nineteenth century that some Brahman ladies were coming forward to be teachers. In 1881-82, there were 515 girls at normal schools thoughout India. Of these 138 were in the Punjab, 73 in Bombay and 41 in Bengal. In the United Provinces female teachers were still more scarce. "The same difficulties which hindered the spread of female education operate even more unfavourably on the supply of female teachers. There is a prejudice against women following this profession and by many it is regarded as hardly respectable," wrote an inspector of education.[60] At the Normal School in Lucknow, special facilities were provided for ladies who observed *Parda*. In Bengal, the Department of Instruction tried another method by offering to utilise female votaries of the *Vaishnava* sect as teachers.[61] At one time female *Vaishnavas* seemed to have contributed a good deal to the instruction of their country-women and in the early part of the 19th century many families of the higher classes had preceptresses from this sect. But the attempt to train them as teachers for girls' schools proved unsuccessful. Efforts to persuade widows to adopt teaching as profession also proved futile except in rare cases which aroused severe public criticism. In some parts, however, young teachers were beginning to be inclined to allow their wives to be trained as teachers and to take up similar duties in girls' schools attached to those for boys where they taught. The majority of girls' schools, therefore, conducted by male teachers of fairly advanced age even though there was a growing feeling against the employment of men.[62]

9.6 Work of the Missionaries in Female Education

The efforts of the government were more than supplemented by those of the missionaries. Their arduous labours and novel methods, devised as the result of the lessons they learnt from their experiments and activities in the first half of the nineteenth century, achieved much more than the mere opening of schools in the routine could ever have done. They had, no doubt, been successful in attracting sufficiently large number of girls from lower castes to their primary schools, and their orphanages also found enough inmates from among the poor sections—particularly those picked as waifs during calamities like floods, famines and epidemics; but they had met with no success as far as women in the higher castes and upper strata of society were concerned. In the second half of the nineteenth century, the Christian Missions in India intensified their work for women.[63] Receiving encouragement and assistance, both moral and material in personnel and funds from the various missionary societies in England, they gave a decided impetus to the movement for education which grew steadily thereafter. In addition to the new schools that they continued to open, the new campaign they started was to find access to Indian women in their homes. Whatever their objective, direct evangelisation or indirect cultural conquest, the approach was to be through education. If girls would leave school at a young age to be married and disappear in seclusion, the missionary women teachers decided to follow them into their homes, offering to teach whatever was acceptable—knowledge of the three Rs or handiwork such as knitting or embroidery of the western style. In the homes where men were educated but were not ready to break the traditions and send their grown up daughters or wives to schools, it was easy for the missionary women to get to them. In the case of orthodox families where education had not made much headway even among men, it was indeed an uphill task to penetrate the sacred precincts of the women's apartments. But the missionary women teachers persevered, patiently and persistently, undeterred by failures, taking heart from whatever little success they achieved. *Zanana* teaching gradually became a regular practice. Thus the system of education in India, where the caste spirit of ostracism and exclusiveness had reigned for centuries, was helped considerably by missionary activity, and a large number of girls were being educated at home.

Some effort was being made for *Zanana* teaching on non-missionary basis by secular agencies among which the National Indian Association with its headquarters in London, was the most important. Miss Mary Carpenter who paid a visit to India specially to collect data as to what could be done in the field of education for women made laudable efforts.

The progress made by female education might not have been steady if the Indian public opinion had not given it the requisite countenance. The munificence of individuals, however few, serving merely as a drop in an ocean was undoubtedly an important factor. Instances are not wanting of single donations worth thousands of rupees for opening schools for girls. The endeavours of the educated few with progressive ideas and a zeal for the betterment of social conditions were equally important. The closing decades of the period under review witnessed a distinct acceleration of the pace at which new societies were being formed and the question of female education was being discussed and debated in public, in press, and in private homes. A vital question like the education of women involved the very fundamentals of Indian society and aroused deep emotions of the people. The supporters as well as detractors of the movement were growing. The press reports of the period are full of comments both for and against the issue. The conservative elements of society were apprehensive of the undesirable effects education might have. It was felt that educated women were neglecting household duties, considering them a drudgery, and were forsaking their kitchens looking upon cooking as a "coarse common place sickening craft."[64] Criticism on this score was most vehement in the Bengal press. A few comments that appeared in the press might serve as interesting illustrations. One detractor of female education wrote :

"English education has already worked the ruin of native boys, and it is very much to be feared that if education of the same character is given to native girls, native girls will be ruined. Female education should be of a character which will suit their social and domestic position.... Hindu girl should be brought up on strictly Hindu principles and her faith in her religion should not be shaken. Her education should make her a good housewife, an affectionate mother, a loving sister, a gentle neighbour and an angel of charity to all ... The present system of education does more harm than good. The Bengali girl spends her time in reading novels and knitting comforters, while her aged mother performs all laborious domestic work."[65]

Another typical comment ran:

"... The money spent on female education is waste. The girls brought up at school generally imbibe luxurious habits of life, treat their domestic superiors with disrespect, hate their proper domestic occupations; in short lose every amiable trait in character and take great delight in imitating English habits and customs."[66]

Yet another comment in the same strain indicates the strong feelings of the orthodox against education of girls:

"... English education has worked serious mischief among poor Bengali women; they have lost that peace and contentment which made them so happy and enabled them to be a source of happiness to their dearest and nearest relations ... The men of this country have already lost all that was good in them and it will, therefore, be most undesirable to deprive its women by means of an English education of their peculiar excellencies."[67]

People were particularly apprehensive of the motives of the missionary women teachers intruding into the homes and opposed the movement of *Zanana* teachers for fear of girls being converted to Christianity. The press was full of criticism on this score in almost all parts of northern India.[68]

The supporters of female education gave vent to their views in equally strong language and advocated more vigorous efforts on the part of the government so as to provide greater educational facilities to girls.[69] Big cities like Bombay and Calcutta became the centres of activity for the enthusiastic champions of the cause.

The tangible results of all the efforts towards female education, both quantitative and qualitative during the period of study, were at best meagre but there was a definite change in public opinion in its favour. Education of girls was finding tacit encouragement, if not active support from the elderly ladies of the family. This disposition was gradually increasing and naturally influenced the attitude of men.[70]

Comments in this respect in the newspapers fully substantiate it. As early as 1877, one paper in Bengal wrote:

> "There is hardly one respectable native family in Calcutta the female members of which are not able to read and write... At the present time every native of Bengal whether educated or semi-educated is an advocate of female education ... No matter whether they themselves can read or write, or not, they are anxious that their wives and sisters should be able to do so. Even the elderly females are no longer seen to be opposed to education as formerly. Many an old female is seen reading through the aid of spectacles the *Mahabharata* or the *Ramayana.* Many are found to regret that they did not acquire this privilege in their youth."[71]

Education and accomplishments of the girl were becoming an important part of the considerations in the negotiations for arranging marriages since some educated boys were beginning to show courage of their convictions and were asserting their views in wishing to marry only educated girls.[72]

By the closing decade of the nineteenth century, educated women, although very few in number, were coming forward in all parts of northern India to work actively for the women's cause. Outstanding among these were Surendra Bala, Dr. Premvati, Mai Bhagwati and Rama Bai. The career of Rama Bai, who came to be known as Pandita Rama Bai by virtue of her learning, is a fascinating illustration of what education could achieve in the case of a woman. A Brahman by birth, she adopted the Christian faith by conviction. Educated in Sanskrit and Indian lore by her learned father, she acquired knowledge of English through self-effort. Her marriage at the age of eighteen to a Bengali gentleman, after the death of her parents, was unconventional. But when she lost her husband a year later, she challenged the trammels of tradition and not only travelled abroad in England and America and educated herself but dedicated her life to the cause of Indian women. She toiled and laboured with a missionary spirit for the cause of education of girls, particularly of the child widows. The establishment by her of the 'Arya Mahila Samaj' in Poona in 1882 became a landmark in the advancement of women and their education.

The period under review, looked at from the educational angle, witnessed much change. Generally speaking, till after the the mid-nineteenth century female education had not extended beyond the lowest of the population while male education had not extended below the higher classes. By the end of the nineteenth century the position had changed considerably. The quick strides taken by education as a whole had altered the perspective. The proportion of the literate community was still small, but most caste-groups of importance could claim to have at least some persons who could read and write. A generation or two back this could not have been asserted of more than a small fraction of such groups.

Educational work in such volume and variety as was done under different auspices revealed itself as a "social influnence of transforming efficacy, with facile power to create a new and stimulating environment." In a word, education opened up new channels of social influence.

References

1. Monier-Willams, (*1887*), p. 279.
2. Ibid, pp. 286-87.
3. *Report of the Education Commission, 1882*, pp. 56-57.
4. *Census Report, 1901*, Vol. I, p. 158-61.
5. Ibid.
6. Ibid.
7. Dennis, Vol. III, p. 231.
8. *Census Report, 1901*, Vol. I, p. 166-69.
9. *Census Report, 1901*, Vol. I, pp. 176-75.
10. Dennis, Vol. III, p. 231.
11. *Census Report, 1901*, Vol. I, p. 161.
12. Howell, p. 1.
13. Strachey, p. 247.
14. Richey, Part II, p. 364.
15. Ibid., p. 367.
16. Ibid., pp. 367-68.
17. *Fourth Quinquennial Report on the Progress of Education, 1898-1902.*
18. *Report of the Education Commission, 1882*, p. 147.
19. Holderness, p. 224.
20. Chailley, p. 493.
21. *Moral and Material Progress Report 1879-80*, p 88.
22. *Fourth Quinquennial Report on the Progress of Education 1898-1902*, p. 45.
23. Act II of 1857, 24 January, 1857.
24. Act XII of 1857, 18 July, 1857.
25. *Report of the Education Commission, 1882*, p. 269.
26. Chailley, p. 493.
27. *Report of the Education Commission, 1882*, pp. 300-04.
28. Strachey, p. 259.
29. Alston, p. 123.
30. Temple, p. 130.
31. Monier-Williams (*1887*), p. 304.
32. Fuller, p. 367 ; Ballu Ram, p. 177.
33. Temple, p. 128.
34. Dennis, Vol. III, p. 231.
35. Basu, pp. 91-93.
36. *Report of the Education Commission, 1882*, pp. 301-02.
37. Morrison, pp. 88-89 ; Karkaria, p. 94.

38. Hunter, p. 167.
39. *Census Report, 1901*, Vol. I, p. 158.
40. Strachey, p. 523.
41. *Report of the Education Commission, 1882*. p. 250.
42. Ballu Ram, pp. 103-04.
43. Fuller, Mrs. B., p. 128.
44. *Census Report, 1901*, Vol. I, p. 161.
45. *Report of the Education Commission, 1882*, p. 523.
46. Ibid., p. 525.
47. Ibid.
48. Ibid.
49. Ibid., p. 528.
50. *Census Report, 1901*, Vol. I, p. 58.
51. Ibid., p. 160,
52. Ibid., p. 161.
53. *Census Report, 1891*, Vol. I, p. 223.
54. *Census Report, 1901*, Vol. I, p. 170.
55. Ibid.
56. *Census Report, 1901*, Vol. I, pp. 168-170.
57. Croft, p. 278.
58. *Statistical Abstract Relating to British India*, No. 35, 1891-1900, pp. 148-49.
59. *Report of the Education Commission, 1882*, p. 523.
60. *Fourth Quinquennial Report on the Progress of Education, 1898-1902*. p. 322.
61. *Report of the Education Commission, 1882*, p. 538.
62. Ibid., pp. 538-39.
63. Dennis, Vol. III, p. 12.
64. Ballu Ram, p. 107.
65. Report on Native Press Bengal, 1887. *Bharat Basi*, 3rd September 1887.
66. Report on Native Press Bengal, 1887. *Dainik Samachar Chandrika*, 21st July 1887, p. 753.
67. Report on Native Press Bengal 1887, *Dainik Samachar Chandrika* 2nd April 1887. p. 398.
68. Report on Native Press Punjab 1884, *Akhbar-i-Am*, Lahore, 10th November 1888 p. 284; Ibid, 8th September 1888, p. 257,
69. *The Tribune 1886*, Vol. VII, pp. 3-4, Reports of Social Conference.
70. Ballu Ram, p. 105.
71. Report on Native Press, Bengal 1877. *Sahchar*, 6th August, 1877, p. 11.
72. Ballu Ram, p. 104.

10 Social Reformers at Work

    10.1 Abolition of Sati and Widow Remarriage
    10.2 Female Infanticide
    10.3 Native Marriage Act, 1872 ; and Abolition of Child Marriage
    10.4 Raja Rammohun Roy and His Work
    10.5 Voice of Dissent
    10.6 Indian Reform Association
    10.7 Social Reforms in Bombay
    10.8 Swami Dayanand and the Arya Samaj
    10.9 Social Reforms among the Parsis
    10.10 Social Reforms among the Muslims
    10.11 Opposition to Social Reforms
    10.12 National Social Conference
    10.13 Kayastha Conference
    10.14 Social Reforms in Punjab
    10.15 Social Reforms in Rajputana

The most important result of the diffusion of education, however small its extent, was the mighty stir of thought it caused in the otherwise placid dovecots of society. It produced men, few in number as compared with the vast populace utterly unlettered, but some among them sufficiently aroused and enthused to examine critically the conditions in which they lived. Many of them, sprung from the sacerdotal class itself with eminent scholarly attainments, high moral principles and unblemished characters as well as practical useful career, were in the fore-most ranks of society.[1] They made no secret of their dissatisfaction with the faith they inherited from their fathers as also their desire to purge it of the impurities that had crept in. Their opinion and suggestions carried weight and commanded respect both with the people as well as the government. That all was not commendable. That certain aspects of social life were undoubtedly anachronistic was realised quite early in the century. Right in the initial stages of the development of education, a voice, loud and clear, resonant and irresistible, had been raised against practices, which could not by any stretch of the word, claim to be termed as civilised. The struggle to create public opinion in favour of change and to enlist government support to legislate, marked the beginning of the movement among the educated which was at once rational and reformative, destructive as well as constructive. It began against one of the practices—the custom of *Sati*—prevalent among the high classes of the Hindus conspicuously in

SOCIAL REFORMERS AT WORK

the province of Bengal, first to come into close contact with the West. The leader of the movement, Raja Rammohun Roy, though not a product of English education, was surely an admirer of it and certainly its ardent advocate. He saw the salvation of the decrepit social structure of the Hindus only in the promotion of English education and the ideas resulting from it.

10.1 Abolition of Sati and Widow Remarriage

The government, though fully aware of the practices that could then as now be termed as evils, followed a policy that perhaps any alien government would, that is, a policy of safety first of its dominions. The waves of liberalism in England were, however, felt in India and although the state was for the most part inert, it showed a tendency sometimes to be actively helping the social and religious reformers. Government legislation in 1829, in response to the long-felt need and demand under Indian leadership for the abolition of *Sati*, one of the serious blemishes on the Hindu society of the times, involving pathetic conditions where widows were forcibly burnt on the pyres of the deceased husbands, was the first deliberate step of its kind. The hand of legislation, touching the practice of slavery in 1843 and human sacrifice in 1845 were good auguries.

The period under review opened with a great encouragement from the Government with two Acts in quick succession to each other. The year 1855 saw the prohibition of gross obscenities under the garb of religion in the streets, and 1856 legalised widow remarriage. But the state chose to go slow and remain neutral to the extent of being partial to its interests so that many usages, equally grave and serious, and perhaps much more condemnable, and of which, the Government was fully aware, continued to be practised till such time as popular disapproval became loud and widespread agitation was launched against them. The government became even more cautious and wary in regard to legislation concerning social life after 1857, the year of the upheaval which almost challenged the very existence of British authority. It acted only when it became absolutely imperative, when popular demand could no longer be ignored or resisted. Government, however, appeared often to evade responsibility, by throwing it upon the people with the excuse that the measure proposed was ahead of public opinion or that it must be "asked for by a section sufficiently important in influence or in number, to justify the course proposed."[2] Even when it did act, the legislation met with the immediate situation without following it up with provisions for the implications that might ensue with the result that legislation often remained a half-measure. The prohibition of *Sati* in 1829, hailed as a courageous and noble act, left the position of the widow in the class, among whom the practice had prevailed, in most pathetic and pitiable state. Rescued from the flames, she was left for the next twenty seven years to the fate of what has been appropriately termed 'Cold Suttee'. And when after hard toil, tremendous agitation and potent persuasion, the Government did move and passed an Act in 1856 to legalise the status of the Hindu widows contracting second marriage and their children by such marriage, it did nothing to preserve for the widow her civil rights as the widow on marrying a second time forfeited all her property from her first husband. Again, the implementation of the Act lacked the force one might expect from any government, leaving it an abortive measure. In the forty five years that followed the Widow Re-marriage Act 1856, a paltry few hundred widows had remarried and even these not without suffering strictures. Caste excommunicated them for it and sometimes all their friends with them. This awful persecution and the public stigma attached to remarriage made the Act practically inoperative throughout the period.[3] Having given the widow the permission and made it lawful for her to remarry, the Government did not follow up the action to give her protection after marriage. Excommunication for doing a lawful act was tantamount to flouting government authority but nothing was done about it. Injuring rights of a member of the community was as grave as a criminal act but apparently it was not treated as such.

10.2 Female Infanticide

State action, however, was taken against female infanticide in 1870.[4] The evil was so widespread among high castes in certain parts of northern India, comprising N.W.P., Punjab, Rajputana and Gujarat that it needed hard effort and long years of vigilance on the part of the government agencies to eradicate it completely. The Act proved a success wherever it was strictly and regularly applied. The root cause of such a criminal practice remained unchecked and was left to the gradual development of public opinion through diffusion of education.

10.3 Native Marriage Act, 1872 ; and Abolition of Child Marriage

On two other occasions during the period of study, the Government responded to public demand. Once in regard to the new ritual, eschewing idolatry and unnecessary ceremonial, adopted by the members of the Brahmo Samaj to celebrate marriages. As the number of such marriages increased the question of their legality was raised. Legal opinion being against the validity of the new ritual, an appeal was made to the Government to recognise it for those who were in its favour. This led to the subsequent Native Marriage Act of 1872 which provided a civil form of marriage and made it applicable to all non-Christians who objected to be married according to any of the current religious forms.[5] It was a measure with very restricted field of operation and remained so for the rest of the period of study. The other important matter in which the Government was constrained to move was the question of child marriage. The law as it stood was insufficient to

SOCIAL REFORMERS AT WORK

protect child wives. As early as 1856, Chevers in his book entitled *Medical Jurisprudence for Bengal* had called attention to the crying need. By 1870, the year girl babies obtained security of life, and recommendations were beginning to be made to the government for an increase of the age of consent by an amendment of the Penal Code which since it had become operative in 1860, had stood at ten years. It took over two decades of agitation, official and non-official, in India as also in England to move the Government. It was only in 1891 that the Age of Consent Bill was passed fixing the age of girls at twelve instead of ten. State activity, ready or tardy, willing or hesitating, had undoubtedly helped in the eradication of some of the social evils. The greater share in rousing public opinion against social abuses, inequalities or inequities, was taken by private individuals and bodies in the different provinces. The natural or spontaneous effect of western learning upon the revival of the old Sanskrit Vedic literature and philosophy, which had been for a long time almost a sealed letter to most of the Brahmans themselves, was a theistic movement beginning in Bengal and spreading thence to other parts of the country. The hold which the Brahmans had exercised for centuries was being lost among the ignorant masses. With the spread of education, the loosening of the Brahmanic hold was going on '*pari passu*'. The educated Hindu tended to become either a theist or a sceptic. As a theist, he would either remain so in theory or take same part in the religious movement by becoming member of the theistic associations or starting new groups or *samajas* for the worship of one God and for prayer meetings. The urge came from the rational thinking and was expressed in the effort to expunge the idolatrous practices from their religious ceremonies. These theistic bodies had significant reflections on the social life of their members. In course of time, they became important agencies through which change and reform were brought about. This tendency proved to be common to the educated of all castes, creeds and communities, expressing itself, sooner or later, though somewhat differently in the different parts of the region.

10.4 Raja Rammohun Roy and His Work

The first reactions of this nature were palpable among the Hindus of Bengal, the province in the vanguard of effort for education and topping the list in the suffering from the worst of abuses. The pioneer in the field was a learned *Kulin* Brahman, Raja Rammohun Roy who founded the Brahmo Samaj (The Society of the Worshippers of the one True God). It represented a body of men who were struggling to establish the worship of the Supreme Being in spirit as opposed to the prevailing idolatry. The Brahmo Samaj, as a sternly theistic society, opposed to polytheism, mythology and idolatry, was the first of its kind and the most influential of the religious movements of the nineenth century. In an age of general degeneracy when northern India especially the province of Bengal was steeped in the most debasing forms of idolatry, when the moral and spiritual aspects of religion and its elevating influence had been lost sight of and in their place the grossest superstitions reigned, the opening of a place of worship where there was no image of god or goddess was itself a revolution. But, this was only one aspect of its programme; religious reformation did not absorb the whole attention of its founder. His exertions in the other spheres of reform were equally incessant and arduous. He realised, more than any other leader of his age, the need of social reform particularly in regard to the disabilities from which the women among the high castes suffered. The object form of social slavery in which the women, especially in Bengal lived and the misery and degradation of womanhood as such, had a strong appeal to his sympathetic heart. In him, women found the greatest champion of their rights. He defended the legal rights of females, advocated their education, and, above all, devoted all the energies of his noble soul to save them from a cruel death. The agitation he carried on for the abolition of the custom of *Sati* in his Bengali journal '*Kaumudi*', by proving from ancient Hindu scriptures that self-immolation of widow was nowhere enjoined as a duty and that, a life of piety and self-abnegation was considered virtuous, strengthened the hands of the Government and served as the basis of the preamble of the anti-Sati decree. His death in 1833, was a serious blow to the reform movement in that the pace set by him could not be kept up. It slowed down considerably, and for a time social reform receded into the background, since the Brahmo Samaj had neither been properly organised nor had it received a properly chalked out programme for social reform. The keen interest that the founder had evinced in the social problems and his ideas, however, remained alive and were taken up by his friends and co-workers. In the opening years of the period under study, 1850-56, the programme of the Brahmo Samaj was going through a reorientation. The doctrine of scriptural infallibility accepted by the founder and upheld even by his successor Maharshi Devendra Nath as the Acharya of the Sabha, was being questioned and renounced by the younger members of the Samaj, majority of whom came from among the English educated. With this arose a tendency, not only to broaden the basis of Brahmoism, by advocating new social ideals, but also to rationalise the fundamental articles of religious belief. The new spirit began to manifest itself in the columns of the *Tattvabodhini Patrika*, where articles began to appear advocating female education, supporting widow remarriage, crying down intemperance, denouncing polygamy, trying to rationalise Brahmo doctrines, and seeking to conduct the affairs of the church on strictly constitutional principles. The views of Devendra Nath, one of the older leaders of the Samaj, on social questions were not quite in harmony with those of the younger party who were thinking impatiently and wished to move fast. Branches of the Samaj were being opened in the suburbs of Calcutta, as also in the provincial towns, and efforts made for the implementation of the general programme. The development of controversies among members, the rationalistic agitation and the adoption of methods of discussion and decision by voting even in the case of religious issues indicated the influence of western education which became still more acutely felt after 1857, the year a new and very young member Keshav Chandra Sen joined the Samaj. Under his influence, the activities of the Samaj were not only passing into the hands of the younger party, but they were assuming a more practical form. To propagate the idea of widow remarriage, he organised in 1859 the performance of a sensational drama called *Bidhawa-Bibhaha* (Remarriage of widows) which attracted large gatherings and was highly appreciated. Domestic ceremonies began to be celebrated by the members of the Samaj according to the new ritual known as the Brahmo *Anushthan*, specially drawn up with a view to expunging the impurities from the celebrations. The marriage ceremony of the daughter of the old leader Maharshi Devendra Nath and the *jat karma* ceremony of Keshav Chandra Sen's first son were outstanding examples of the new move. A loud voice was being raised against caste and idolatry with warm response from the educated community. The result was not only marriages according to the non-idolatrous rites of the Samaj, but some inter-caste marriages as well as cases of widow remarriage.

The importance of female education was realised and as early as 1861, Keshav Chandra Sen made a passionate appeal to the members of the Brahmo Samaj to make it an important part of their programme. The younger party responded warmly. They started a regular scheme for *zanana* education and went even further than their leader's intentions. Being in favour of equality, they began to given education to their daughters and wives and began to take them out openly. In 1862, Keshav Chandra Sen took his wife to visit the Tagores. Later, he took some Brahmo ladies to visit some European families also. A new magazine, the *Bambodhini Patrika* was started for the benefit of ladies. In 1865, the Brahmika Samaj—prayer meeting exclusively for ladies was organised. This gave further impetus to the cause of female education, thus commencing a new era of female emancipation. Soon after this, provision began to be made for ladies to sit at the general meetings behind *chicks* (reed-screens).

10.5 Voice of Dissent

This hectic activity of the younger group aroused much opposition. Within the Samaj, it meant cleavage giving rise to two hostile camps, the conservatives and the progressives who appeared to have radical views. The latter, in course of time, suffered further fission for similar reasons.

Opposition to social reform agitation had started as early as 1830 when the Pandits of Calcutta had formed the Dharma Sabha to agitate against the abolition of *Sati*. The new ferment, leading to radical changes, roused the hostility of old Hinduism. "Put them down. Put them down", was the cry raised everywhere by the orthodox. Those who sent their children to Calcutta became apprehensive lest they should come under the influence of the new reformers. The engines of social persecution were set in motion in every part of the province. In 1863 in Bhagalpur, the leading members of the Hindu community combined to put down the new spirit of Brahmoism, threatening every one who dared to join the reformers with excommunication. It only meant a slight slowing of the process of change without any adverse effects on the resolution of the younger party.

10.6 Indian Reform Association

In 1870, the Indian Reform Association was formed under the presidentship of Keshav Chandra Sen. This represented the purely secular side of the reform programme of the Samaj carried on by its missionaries. The Association was open to non-Hindus and was started with a view to promoting the moral and social betterment of the people through special attention to the amelioration of the condition of women. The programme included education and temperance. Night schools were opened for working people and technical schools for industrial education for the middle classes. An adult female school opened for the wives and daughters of the Brahmos was indeed the highlight of the period. Vigorous propaganda was carried on against intemperance by means of lectures and discussions organised from time to time. Started in the early sixties by Baboo Pearey Charan Sircar, this programme under Keshav Chandra Sen made common cause with the temperance reformers in England. Among children, at this time, was organised the 'Bands of Hope'. But the most important reform activity of the Samaj was regarding the marriage which, under the progressives, had been shorn of many features they considered unnecessary. In place of the '*Sampradan*'—gift of the bride—mutual vows alone were introduced, thus making the ceremony more western than eastern. The question of its validity finally led to the passing of the Act of 1872. It abolished early marriage, made polygamy penal, sanctioned widow and inter-caste marriage and was rightly hailed with joy by the progressives. It became, however, the principal cause of alienation of Brahmos from the orthodox. Marriage with reformed ceremony, thereafter, was no longer unknown. In fact, the number of such marriages was gradually increasing.

10.7 Social Reform in Bombay

Social reform in Bombay, commenced fifteen years later than Bengal under almost similar circumstances, though the two movements were not alike in all respects. The people there proved more practical and less impulsive than their brethren in Bengal and worked with the definite aim to put down caste without any ostentatious bravado as shown by medical students in Bengal in 1835, going in for beef-steak, though not always free from tactless enthusiasm. Like Bengal, the progressive movement sprang from the educational and religious effort and views, similar to those as Rammohun Roy and these appeared to be reflected in Bal Sastri's endeavours, who was inwardly moved by the same spirit and looked to the devotional element inherent among the Hindus through which alone Hindu society could be gradually enlightened and elevated. The earliest organisation was a secret society, the *Gupta Sabha*, formed for purposes of worship and religious discussion. It was succeeded in 1849, under the influence of Dadoba Pandurang, by another organisation, the Param Hansa Sabha, an eclectic society. This too was a secret society but social reform held a more prominent place in its discussions than religious questions. Almost the first act of the society was a challenge to Hindu orthodoxy through forcible occupation of a house when the tenant was away and removal of the idols to one corner, without any ceremony. The pledge taken by the members was unprecedented and radical in that they had to vow that they would not observe the distinctions of caste, would taste bread prepared by Christian bakery and drink water at the hands of a Muhammadan. The liberalism of the society attracted a large number of youth and, by 1860, it reckoned some 500 members on its rolls. Branch societies of the Param Hansa Sabhas were established in some of the prominent *mufassil* towns such as Poona, Ahmedabad, Khandesh etc. The members were inspired by a sort of *espirit de corps* and appeared to work in unison, but were rather hasty and acted too fast. Strict secrecy was maintained about the weekly meetings as also about other activities such as the annual dinners when Param Hansas from the entire Presidency came to join at the table without distinctions of caste. Spirituous drinks and forbidden food were strictly excluded from these convivial gatherings. The sole object of keeping the activities secret was to bring men together and promote union secretly till such times when they would have enough number of adherents to profess it openly and declare a formal renunciation of caste. The enthusiasm of the members sometimes got the better of their discretion in fighting the gigantic evil—the caste—and the society, did not last long. It had to be dissolved in 1860, after a brief span of life. The dispersion of the Sabha acted on different people differently. Some became apathists, some orthodox bigots, some changed from fanatics into atheists and only a few reconciled themselves to the lost cause by hoping to work anew on a different plan. All traces of the Param Hansas were lost. The only legacy left was the continuance of the vicious system of eating forbidden things on the sly and the idea of social reform confused with the idea of license in eating and drinking.

The more earnest men maintained their convictions and watched with interest the Brahmo movement in Bengal. The birth in 1867 of another theistic society in Bombay—the Prarthna Samaj—was the result of

Keshav Chandra Sen's visit and the impression he made on the leading men of the day. This was formed under the guidance of Dr. Atma Ram Pandurang. The aims of the society were theistic worship and social reform. Its rules and regulations regarding membership and the weekly prayer meetings were liberal and open. The society thus stood on a sure footing. Its programme of marriage by theistic rites as also inter-caste and widow remarriage was very much similar to that followed by the Brahmo Samaj which wielded influence through visits by its leaders.

The first marriage celebrated according to reformed rites in Bombay took place in 1868. To young educated men of outstanding ability and vision, the Prarthna Samaj had the same appeal as the Brahmo Samaj in Bengal and as the years moved, bands of them joined the Samaj. In the seventies, R.G. Bhandarkar and M.G. Ranade joined, followed in the eighties by S.P. Kelkar and N.G. Chandavarkar. These are some of the outstanding names among those who were destined to play an important role in the reform movement. Valuable contributions were made by Pandita Rama Bai who worked among the women and founded the Arya Mahila Samaj or the Ladies' Society in 1882.

The pace set by the Prarthna Samaj was slow but it was steady. The movement did not spread widely, nor did it produce much literature as compared to the Brahmo Samaj. But it had definite aims, the abandonment of caste, the introduction of widow remarriage, the encouragement of female education and the abolition of child marriage. Though, some of the diffidence of the Parma Hansa Sabha appeared to be clinging to the members all through the period.

"The Prarthana Samaj may be said to be composed of men paying allegiance to Hinduism and to Hindu society with a protest. The members observe the ceremonies of Hinduism, but only as mere ceremonies of routine, destitute of all religious significance. This much sacrifice they make to existing prejudices. Their principle, however, is not to deceive any one as to their religious opinions, even should an honest expression of views entail unpopularity."

The Samaj thus carried on work of preliminary nature which proved useful later when greater stress came to be laid on purely social reform.

10.8 Swami Dayanand and his Arya Samaj

In the North West Provinces and the Punjab the reform movement began still later, but conformed to the general pattern and was connected with another religious organisation, the Arya Samaj. Founded in 1875 in Bombay, by Swami Dayanand, the Arya Samaj had the largest membership in the Punjab. Actuated by the same urge as that of the founders of other religious bodies, that is, to purge the Hindu faith of the abuses and the impurities that had crept in. Dayanand had implicit faith in the perfection of the order, social and religious as prescribed by the Vedas.[6] He denounced idolatry most vehemently and preached reform on those lines. His attitude to social problems was definite and explicit and he gave to his organisation a programme in clear and definite terms. The Arya Samaj thus repudiated caste by birth, condemned the numerous sub-divisions into which Hindu society had been split up by reason of castes and sub-castes, considering these as artificial barriers, created to divide men, highly pernicious and harmful; though it recognised the inherent inequality of physical powers and mental as well as intellectual faculties, created by nature. The influence of heredity and environment was also acknowledged. Nevertheless, the Arya Samaj favoured equal opportunities to all men and women to acquire knowledge and to qualify themselves for whatever position in life they would like to fill. The lower castes, better known in more recent times as the depressed classes, had never before found a greater champion fervently advocating their admission into the Hindu society, thereby giving them a status they had hitherto lacked. But the field in which the Arya Samaj did yeomen service was in regard to women. Their position among the higher classes at the time, despite what had been done for them, was most deplorable. The disabilities from which they suffered being nowhere sanctioned in the scriptures, the Arya Samaj tried to bring home to the people the fact that women were highly wronged, that the rights given to them not only in the Vedas but by Manu also, had been denied and gross injustice was being done to them. The stress laid on education and an appeal to ancient Hindu religion in regard to the relation of sexes, helped considerably to change the attitude of men towards women.

The Arya Samaj strongly opposed child marriage. It carried on a most vehement crusade against it and achieved much success in rallying public opinion in favour of its views. It fixed minimum marriageable age at sixteen for girls and twenty five for boys, the highest that was being suggested by different leaders and bodies at that time. The Samaj encouraged celebacy even to later ages. In 1880, when Dayanand wrote on the subject of marriage he suggested an exchange of photographs between the contracting parties instead of a marriage arranged by parents or guardians without consulting the parties.

As for domestic ceremonies, the founder of the Arya Samaj laid down a ritual compiled in detail on the lines prescribed in the scriptures and termed it the *Sanskar Vidhi*. He enjoined the members of the Samaj to perform the rites of all the *sanskaras* strictly in accordance with it.

The Arya Samaj gained precedence over the other organisations of its kind by virtue of the earnestness with which it tried to combat the root cause of the evils — mass ignorance. The eighth principle of the Arya Samaj enjoined the members to endeavour to "diffuse knowledge and dispel ignorance." The Samaj as a body and its members in their individual capacities engaged in educational work of considerable importance. In the Punjab and N.W.P. its work in extent and volume was second to no other agency except the government. Christian missions maintained a large number of schools of all kinds, but no single mission could claim to have as many schools for boys and girls as the Arya Samaj. The distinctive feature of the institutions opened by the Arya Samaj was the stress laid on the Hindu religious teaching. In fact, the Samaj suffered a rift among its members over the issue as the conservative group wished to encourage the teaching of oriental lore independent of official control while the progressives believed in giving western education along with religious instruction in institutions affiliated with a government university. The Dayanand Anglo-Vernacular College, opened in 1887 was an impressive and solid result of the efforts of the Arya Samaj to diffuse modern type of education with a view to enlighten the people and improve the social conditions.[7]

It was, however, in regard to the education of girls that the Samaj made the most outstanding contribution through a large number of schools, both primary and secondary. As for their higher education, Jullundur in the Punjab became the centre. A band of young members of the local Arya Samaj, led by Lala Dev Raj and Munshi Ram (later known as Swami Shraddhanand) opened the first women's college in the Punjab, the Kanya Mahavidyalaya. This gave a tremendous impetus to female education and in the long run helped in social matters also. According to the report of the College by the Secretary Shri Badri Das for the year 1893 seven years after its inception, the number of girls on the rolls of the Mahavidyalaya was 129 of whom 108 were unmarried and 11 were widows. The fact that mothers and daughters, mothers-in-law and daughters-in-law came together to receive instruction in the Mahavidyalaya indicates how public opinion was changing in favour of female education.

The movement spread far and wide and the institution began to attract girls even from the backward provinces. In 1904, the founder of the institution is reported to have taken the youngest girl of the institution to a public meeting and made her recite Vedic *mantras* to the gathering. This was a five year old girl from Peshawar in North West Frontier Provinces. Women were stepping forward and beginning to participate in the Arya Samaj activities. At the anniversary of the Arya Samaj in Lahore in 1886, Mai Bhagwati delivered a speech on the rights of women though she spoke from behind a screen, and a seven year old girl recited a Vedic poem.

The Arya Samaj, through its programme of social reform was revolutionising the intellectual and social thought of the Hindu society, the full significance of which could hardly be realised during the period under review.

10.9 Social Reforms among the Parsis

The Parsis, having a good deal in common with the Hindus, suffered from somewhat similar evils. Child marriage, and the *Zanana* were universal, polygamy was not uncommon and domestic etiquette with all the superstitions was more or less a prototype of that of the Hindus. In the early part of the nineteenth century, the community was living in great ignorance and the ordinary Parsi received little education and did not understand a word of his prayers or of the liturgy of Parsi worship. The priesthood being hereditary, very few of the priests were scholarly. The urge for reform among them also sprang from a feeling of disapproval of some of the customs and usages in their rellgious life.

In 1853, the *Rahnumai Mazdayasnan Sabha* or the Religious Reform Association was started which had for its object "the regeneration of the social condition of the Parsis and the restoration of the Zoroastrian religion to its pristine purity." Notable among the movers were Dadabhai Naoroji, S.S. Bangali and Nowrozjee Furdoonji. The community was stirred to its depths through lectures, meetings and literature bringing forth proposals of reform. The *Rast Goftar*, their weekly journal, proved a powerful instrument in their hands for the formation of sympathetic public opinion.

The early reformers among the Parsis were "cautious, discreet, sagacious and tactful in their movement. They rallied round them as many leading Parsi priests of the day as they could and submitted to them in a well-formulated form specific questions under specific heads, asking their opinion if a particular, dogma or creed, ceremony etc. was in strict conformity with the teachings of the religion of Zoroastra or contravened those teachings."[8] They succeeded in reforming certain customs pertaining to marriage and death ceremonies. Practical steps, however, were taken by Khurshedji Rustomji Kama soon after his return from Europe. In 1863, a college for the education of Parsi priests was founded with a view to giving them proper instruction in the Avesta so that they might show the adherents of the faith the authority for casting off the many superstitious accretions which religion had gathered in the course of the centuries. The college did not yield the expected result and was far from successful since younger generation of educated Parsis showed a lurking tendency of indifference to religious questions.

On the purely secular side, the leaders of the community realised fairly early that the basis of all reform was female education. Parsi women were as much the emblem of ignorance and superstition as their Hindu sisters. Framji Cowasjee Banajee was the first Parsi who had the courage to brave the prejudice of his time in this respect by giving his daughter English education. His example was soon followed by many others, chief among them being Manockjee Cursetjee and Jamsetjee Jeejibhai. Although not a man of liberal views, Framji's contact with Europeans enabled him to take a sober view of social questions. He understood what was the right way of working for the cause, without offending the susceptibilities of the opponents. This quality he had shown as early as 1847 when Grant Medical College was established and bigoted Parsis, whose number was legion, could not tolerate the idea of Parsi youth joining the college because cutting dead bodies was against their religion. As a member of the board of education, Framji saw the harm that would be done to the community if the Parsi youth were prohibited from receiving medical education. At the same time he knew he could not make any radical changes. He worked out a tactful expedient by providing separate rooms where Parsis after dissection could have bath and go through purification ceremonies as were deemed necessary according to Parsi ideas.

The popular basis of female education, however, could not be devised that easily. It involved a struggle on the part of a persevering band of enlightened men dedicated to the cause. The conservatives saw no use of female education. Their leader Dosabhoy is reported to have said in reference to Dadabhai Naoroji, "the young man wants to educate females. But what do females want education for ? It will only spoil them. You see you should not supply more oil to a lamp than it can bear for otherwise the light is sure to extinguish itself."[9]

The reformers, undeterred completely by such remarks, went on with their plans, opening schools for girls, providing other facilities needed and thus giving female education an active start. The Parsi Girls' School Association, organised by Framji Nuseerwanji Patel, Nowrozjee Furdoonji and Sorabjee Shapooji Bangali did excellent work for the promotion of education of women which helped in the speedy advancement of the community.

The social progress of the Parsis was further facilitated by the diffusion of knowledge and propaganda done through the press by means of tracts and publications. The first effort in this direction had been made in 1840 when '*Vidyasagar*', a periodical in Gujarati started publishing. Its success was encouraging and another periodical in Gujarati, *Jagat Mitra*, was started in 1850. In 1857, *Stri Bodh*, a special paper for women was started. These helped to diffuse progressive ideas and create public opinion favourable to change.[10]

One other organisation which materially helped social reform among the Parsis was the Parsee Law Association, founded at a meeting of the Parsis in 1855. The object was to secure for them in the Presidency towns and the *mufaasil* a uniform law relating to inheritance and marriage as also to raise the legal status of Parsi women. Most of the older Parsis looked upon it with suspicion. Some even opposed the attempt to ask for a law against bigamy and other similar practices which were prevalent among the Parsis. After several years of patient and steady perseverance, going through a period of difficulties and anxieties, the young workers succeeded in inducing the Government in 1865 to give the Parsis a special law of inheritance and divorce, suited to the changing conditions of their social progress.

The educated Parsi proved a decidedly wiser and steadier reformer than the educated Hindu. Both started about the same time on the mission of social and domestic reform and at the end of about the same period while the Parsi reformer could point to his labour and well exclaim that in his struggles with the religious and social ignorance he had carried and won a victory over blind faith in old customs. The Hindu reformer, on the other hand, had to admit that he had been more or less worsted in the contest with orthodoxy and social abuses. The Parsi met with greater success partly because of the smaller number of the community concentrated in small contiguous areas and partly on account of their consistency and faithful adherence to the cause, undeterred by the obstacles and difficulties in their way. The early reformers among the Hindus, on the other hand, began zealously, but after the heat of youthful enthusiasm had exhausted itself, succumbed to the trials and tribulations to become lukewarm, lacking courage to stand up to their principles, some of them "to degenerate into seeming bigots, cold materialists or self-seeking apathists." Even Keshav Chandra Sen, towards the later part of his career retraced steps. The want of mental and moral poise affected the progress of social reform adversely. Moreover the early Hindu reformers unlike the Parsis committed the serious mistake of attempting too much at once. Instead of concentrating on the removal of the root cause—ignorance, the educated Hindus rushed headlong to declare a crusade against the social evils around them. Instead of beginning with home, they began with society thinking caste to be the main evil. In trying to tackle an institution of that nature, they failed to achieve much but aroused enough opposition and in years of struggle lost heart. They omitted to pay heed to the prime necessity, female education, promote domestic reform and widen popular culture, which issues, if given proper attention at the early stages of the reform movement, would have facilitated the removal of other serious evils.

10.10 Social Reform among the Muslims

The Muslim leaders though late in their efforts at reform had the advantage of the experience gained by others. They began with correct analysis of the cause of the backward nature and the suffering of the community. The fundamental evil, as spotted by Syed Ahmad Khan, among the Muslims was the general ignorance and lack of education.[11] It was to the removal of this that he directed the whole might of his effort. He felt that other evils would die a natural death. He had early realised the value of English education and set about making plans for persuading his brethren to realise the worth of his ideas. He launched active propaganda through pamphlets and books, talks and lectures and formed an association for the study of western science. He established English schools and endeavoured in every possible way to convince his community of the wisdom of learning English and absorbing the culture of the West. His monthly journal in Urdu, *Tahzib-ul-Akhlaq* or Reform of Morals, which he started after his return from England in 1870, became his powerful organ. It dealt with religious, social and educational subjects and through this periodical Sir Syed combated the prejudice against western science, advocated greater social reform and sought to rouse the Muhammadan community to self-confidence and vigorous effort. He urged that there was no religious reason why Muslims should not dine with Europeans provided there was no forbidden food on the table and boldly put his teaching into practice, living in European style, receiving Englishmen as his guests and accepting their hospitality in return. He had to face all possible slandering for it, being excommunicated and also called an atheist and a renegade. But like other reformers he held bravely on.

Sir Syed Ahmad Khan's educational effort culminated in the Anglo-Muhammadan College at Aligarh with an idea to create an institution on the lines of Oxford and Cambridge Universities, with this difference that education in it rested on religion. The College gave an opening to the community and soon proved a success. Interest in modern education appeared to have been aroused so much that in 1886 Sir Syed started the Muhammadan Educational Conference with the object to spread high education among Muhammadans, to make arrangements for the introduction of good religious education in Muhammadan schools, to improve Muslim schools where classics were taught and to improve the *maktab* system. The programme was to hold annual sessions at different centres of education. It is needless to stress that this did much to awaken the Muslims towards their backward condition.

10.11 Opposition to Social Reforms

Much credit goes to these movements spread over a good part of the latter half of the nineteenth century, for what little was achieved by way of reform, though a great deal remained yet to be combated. Society was no longer somnolent. It was stirred up and a variety of reactions was manifest. But opposition to reform grew simultaneously, mounting in intensity with the activities of the reformers. The *Sanatan Dharma Rakshini Sabha* was organised by the opponents incited by the reforms carried out and considered as serious breaches of the old faith. In 1875, *Bharat Varsha Arya Dharma Prasarini Sabha*, an association for the spread of the Aryan religion in India, was organised in Monghyr. The opposition was not only from the conservative and uneducated sections, but even among some of the educated there was a great social reaction and their watchword was that whatever was Indian was perfect and as such required no change or improvement. This doctrine was being preached wildly in Bengal and in resonant echoes in Bombay. In this reactionary movement, strangely some Indian Christians also participated and did propaganda in favour of practices like infant marriage. The opposition to reform was open and often unsubdued. "In the bathing ghats, at the river side, in market places, in public squares, in the drawing rooms of influential citizens, everywhere the rivalry between the two sections became the subject of talk."[12] The reformers were ridiculed and scoffed at. "Lines of comical poetry, caricaturing the principle of reform were composed by the wags of the time and passed from mouth to mouth till the streets rang with laughter and ridicule."[13] In 1892, the *Bharat Dharma Maha Mandal* was formed with a view to bringing about a complete religious reformation.

Opposition to reform was cropping up in another form—a bid in defence of the orthodox faiths—and was visible in the different communities through various organisations. Nonetheless, the net result of this was that the reform movement assumed a secular role, independent of the religious movement with which it had been hitherto associated. Caste societies and reform associations were being organised in the different provinces, each working for and concentrating on the special need of the particular group concerned. Activity appeared to be at its peak during the 1880s. The reformers were assailing, from various points, with diverse motives and sometimes with dissimilar aims and different degrees of force, the fortress of long established Hindu customs. There was general agreement among them as to the need of reform but there were differences of opinion, sometimes irreconcilable, regarding the methods to be adopted and the extent of change to be sought.[14] Some believed in compulsion and coercion and felt it was the duty of the educated to exercise the utmost pressure on the masses to make the desirable changes. Others believed that the *Shastras* should be so interpreted as to convince the masses that change was rightly needed. Another group felt that those who believed in change should make it regardless of opinion against it and act according to their convictions even if they were isolated. The idealistic view was that the reformers should appeal to the sentiment of the people and arouse their conscience to the wrongs in the society and thus urge to rectify the position. Many felt that the government should act boldly and legislate to make some of the evils illegal. The more cautious and wary among the reformers felt that public opinion was the most important factor, that no reform could be welcome unless there was demand for it and for this education was most essential which undoubtedly required time. According to them hasty steps were to be avoided.[15]

10.12 National Social Conference

To whatever view they subscribed, individuals and organisations in different parts of northern India felt the need of a common platform even for the discussion of social problems and the co-ordination of efforts that were being made to solve them. A great amount of intelligent thought, feeling and energy existed and it required to be focussed in an organised manner. It was in Bombay that the idea began with some of the members of the Prarthna Samaj stimulated by the formation in Sindh of the Social Reform Association in 1886. The idea was further developed on a wider basis when in 1887 after four years of preliminary efforts and meetings, the formation of the National Social Conference was announced.

The first session of the National Social Conference was held in the South, in Madras, but the movement gained momentum in northern India, where eleven out of its fourteen sessions between 1887 and 1900, were held at different principal towns. The methods of the Conference were practically the same as those in use with the Indian National Congress, a body with a purely political programme. To begin with, the Conference held its sessions in the same place as the Congress and immediately after it so as to take advantage of the gathering of the intelligentsia and the arrangements made for it.

The National Social Conference was open to all irrespective of caste or creed and some Muslims and Parsis also attended but the great majority of those who took part in the proceedings were the Hindus. At the close of the Conference, the members usually dined together regardless of caste, race or religious distinctions. The programme though wide and varied, however, tended to be Hindu in its affinities and interests. At the very first meeting, it was chalked out in a general way so as to give a start to the functioning of the Conference. It included, *interalia*, disabilities of women in all respects, a subject which had agitated the intelligensia for over fifty years. It was decided that the Conference might take up issues such as the sea-voyage, the ruinous expense of marriage, the limitations of age below which marriage should not be allowed, the re-marriage of young widows, the evils of remarriage of old men with young girls and inter-marriage between sub-divisions of the same caste. Local problems, it was admitted openly, had to be dealt with by local bodies. This was stressed in 1888, when M.G. Ranade, one of the chief leaders of the movement explained the scope and position of the Social Conference, pointing out how the customs of one province differed from the other even in regard to the main evils. For instance, caste organisations showed differences in the details of their working; polygamy prevailed in one province while it was unknown in others; the widows' unhappy disabilities effected different castes in different ways; infant marriages were unknown in many castes and communities, while they represented a great evil in other classes; the prohibitions against foreign travel were operative in one place while they were practically not of much moment elsewhere.

The function of the Social Conference was to strengthen the hands of local associations and to furnish information to each association, province or caste as to what was being done by the others, similarly situated and to stimulate active interest by mutual sympathy and cooperation. Local associations working for reform were to be affiliated with the Conference to which reports were to be sent through delegates. Within three years of its inception, the Conference had no less than seventeen Reform Associations in northern India affiliated to it, besides some others not yet formally recognised but doing good work in the same direction.

While cognizance was taken of the differences, emphasis was laid on the common background and it was stated that efforts were to be made to eliminate the differences and correct perversions which had sprung up and obscured the nobility of the common stock and ancient origin.

The method of work was well-thought out and, as early as 1889, the Conference decided to have a social reform fund through membership subscription and donations. For the propagation of the programme and for educating public opinion preachers, preferably knowing scriptures and able to quote from them in support of their contentions, were to be employed; literature on social reform was to be published and widely circulated; periodical lectures were to be organised and the formation of local or caste associations encouraged. To avoid the possibility of the decisions of the Conference remaining purely pious intentions, members were required, according to a resolution of the Conference in 1888 to take pledges to implement their chief aims—one not to marry their children below a certain age and the other to educate all their female relations to the best of their ability and in case of breach to pay a prescribed penalty.

The programme was taken up in earnest and as years moved it was expanded considerably. The Conference discussed at its sessions a variety of subjects, chief among them being, the age of consent, the unsatisfactory working of the widow-remarriage Act, the disfigurement of child widows, restitution of conjugal rights, ill-assorted marriages, exacting money in consideration of the gift of girls in marriage, polygamy and *Kulinism*, curtailment of expenses on marriage and other ceremonials, female education, fusion of sub-castes, admission of converts back into Hindu society, anti-*nautch* and purity movement, *Siapa* system, use of obscene language and singing immoral songs at marriages, temperance, sea-voyage and social relations with foreign travelled men.

The reform of marriage customs being the most crying need of the society, it no wonder engaged the attention of the reformers, and year after year resolutions were passed bearing on some aspect or the other of the evils involved. Efforts made from within to ameliorate the condition of women sufferers from long ages of unjust treatment had hardly led to any tangible results. Public discussions had given rise to controversies between the progressives inculcated with western notions and the old school of orthodoxy, the discord being especially pronounced where the proposed departures from time-honoured customs affected the position and obligations of women in the Hindu social system.

Behramji Malabari, a Parsi journalist of Bombay, devoted himself with rare energy and determination to the removal of what appeared to him to constitute the most palpable evils in Hindu social life, infant marriage and enforced widowhood. Through the medium of press and also by means of lecturing tours and even by direct personal appeals to the highest British authorities, Malabari created in England a sympathetic public opinion and in India a great sensation stirring up Hindu society to a remarkable degree, exciting no inconsiderable ill will against himself. Not that Malabari was a pioneer in the cause. Many other worthy Hindus of great ability and good social position had preceded him. As early as 1870, Keshav Chandra Sen had raised the issue of fixing the minimum age of marriage of girls and had approached eminent doctors and other renowned leaders for opinion.[16] Even though many notable worthies were in favour of the age being fixed at twelve, even fourteen, orthodox ranks bitterly arraigned the suggestion as open sacrilege. Many, however, were working contemporaneously with Malabari for the objective he had in view. In fact, there was a dual reaction to his efforts. While many leading Hindus were brought by his crusade against infant marriage and enforced widowhood to a full realisation of the cruelty and manifold harms of these customs, there were others so irritated by his attacks upon their ancient, well-established social life as to resent his meddling with their affairs and to vigorously deny both the accuracy of his facts and the validity of his conclusions.[17] In this respect, the reactions of the Muslims were exactly of the same kind, the Maulvis denouncing the move and the progressives supporting it. The issue was discussed in full detail at several sessions of the Social Conference and the consensus of opinion was vehemently in favour of the proposal. At the third Conference at Bombay, in 1889, the first resolution passed on the subject, "that in the opinion of this Conference, the distinction made by the the Penal Code, between the general age of consent (12 years) laid down in Section 90 and the special age prescribed in Clause 5 and the exception in Section 375 is both unnecessary and indefensible and that with a view to prevent early completion of marriages, which leads to the impairment of physical health of both husband and wife and to the growth of a weakly progeny, cohabitation before the wife is 12 years old should be punishable as a criminal offence and that every effort should be made by awakening public conscience to the grave dangers incurred to postpone the completion of marriage till the age of 14 at least, as being in accordance with the dictates of our ancient medical works and modern science, and countenanced by the approved sentiment and practice of the country that every member joining any of the social reform associations connected with this conference should be asked to pledge himself not to complete in his own case or in the case of his children who are minors any marriage before the bride completes her 14th year", indicated the pulse of the section of public which counted. The pressure on the Government was such that despite orthodox ranks bitterly opposing, legislation could no longer be withheld, particularly after the distressing sensation caused by the death of Phulmani Dassi, a girl of ten reported to have been due to the outrage committed by her husband a man of 30. The Age of Consent Bill finally became an Act in 1891 and was indeed an outstanding triumph for the reformers.

The long-drawn out controversy over the age of consent and the dissemination of new ideas gave rise to many interesting cases effecting incidental reforms. One such case was that of Rukma Bai who was married at eight but was unwilling to go and live with her husband when she came of age. The husband filed a suit against her and obtained a decree in his favour. The girl refused to live with her husband even at the cost of penalisation. This was a challenge both to traditionalists as also to the seekers of reform. The former utilised the case in doing propaganda against female education which, they had apprehensions, would encourage girls to be bold like Rukma Bai. The latter took up the issue and appealed to the Government that there should be no compulsion when either party, the husband or wife, refused to live with the other. The Social Conference passed a resolution in 1891 to the effect that imprisonment in the case of the execution of decrees for the restitution of conjugal rights, even as a last resort, should be abolished.

The question of child marriage, apart from other issues, had been very much under discussion and the Conference was making all the effort it could to create public opinion against it. At the Calcutta Session in 1890, a place very appropriate for the discussion of a custom widely prevalent among the high castes of Bengal, a resolution was passed expressing its denunciation and appealing to the society to discourage the practice. It also said that within the sphere of the various castes and communities strenuous efforts be made to postpone the celebration of marriage rites till 12 in the case of girls and 18 in the case of boys and the consummation of the marriage till after they attain the age of 14 and 20 respectively, and that the members of the various social reform associatians in the country should pledge themselves to see those limits of age were observed in actual practice and public opinion educated in favour of even higher age.

To achieve the objective soon, radical suggestions kept coming up such as the imposition of restrictions on the admission of married students to the universities and appeal to the government for legislation, but the consensus of opinion rejected them.

The condition of widows aroused not only sympathy but a feeling of utter helplessness against the callousness of the higher levels of society. The Conference reiterated approbation of widow remarriage and condemned social persecution and ill-treatment of widows. The issue was taken up in detail at the 3rd conference in 1889 at Bombay, attended by no less than some 4,000 members, including some women, among whom was the illustrious Rama Bai, a learned young widow dedicated to the cause. The position was stated succinctly in a resolution regarding the inadequacy of the law as a protective measure for the widow who chose to marry; and the Conference recommended a thorough enquiry into the working of Act XV of 1856 with a view to suggesting further improvements in the matter. It also resolved that the disfigurement of child widows before they attained the age of 18 and even after that age without the consent of the widow, recorded in writing before a *Panch* or a magistrate, be deemed an offence and prohibited by law.

The reformers' concern and interest in the matter were further expressed in the resolutions passed in the subsequent years. In 1892, for instance, at Allahabad, the Conference decided that caste organisations be formed to arrange for social penalties to be inflicted on those who aided in disfiguring child widows without their consent.

The situation improved but little and the discomfiture of the reformers was evident from a resolution passed at the Amraoti session of the Conference in 1897. It was felt that the working of Act XV of 1856 for forty years had established the fact that the Act had failed to secure to the remarrying widow the full enjoyment of her rights in many ways. She forfeited her life interest in her husband's immovable property for doing a lawful act, when such forfeiture would not have resulted if she had misconducted herself. Even in respect of *Stridhan* proper, over which her power of disposal was absolute, there was a general impression that she lost proprietary rights over her moveables in favour of her husband's relations who otherwise could not have interfered with her free disposal of the same. In many cases, she and her husband were not only excommunicated, but the right of worship in public temples had been denied to them and no relief had been given to them in civil courts. In some parts of the country, she was subjected to disfigurement before she arrived at the age of majority without any freedom being given to her to exercise her choice. The Conference suggested that steps be taken by the social reform associations to adopt measures to relax the stringency of caste usages and also to secure a reconsideration of the principles of the Act with a view to remedying its defects.

The practical effect of these efforts was that some people, though very few, had the courage to arrange marriage of young widows of their family. The year 1896 reported 25 widow-marriages, of which ten were in the Punjab, six in Bombay, four in Central Provinces, one in Bengal and one in N.W.P. In 1900, the total number of widow-marriages in the whole country, since the movement began, was reckoned to be 300.

The subject which found comparatively easy concurrence among members was the reduction of expense on marriage and simplification of ceremonials. At an early stage in the programme of the Conference, important recommendations were made in this regard, leaving to each local association the choice to adopt such of them as suited its circumstances. These included reduction of expenses of ceremonies at birth, marriage, death and other similar occasions and prescription of scales for persons of various means, as well as for presents made by a bride's family to that of the bridegroom. These recommendations were successfully adopted by many caste organisations.

With regard to the baneful practice of the sale of girls for marriage or arranging marriage on *Badla* or *Golawat* or *Batta-Satta* (barter system) prevalent among certain castes in the N.W.P., Oudh and the Punjab, the Conference expressed its condemnation, stating that it was fraught with the degradation of the marriage tie and should be discouraged by all means, by gradually enlarging the circle of sub-castes eligible for the choice of marriage alliances.

The Conference denounced no less strongly the abuse of polygamy as prevalent in certain regions, particularly Bengal, and recommended that all social reform associations should discourage the practice as at once degrading and pernicious in its consequences, that steps should be taken to enforce that no second marriage would take place without an adequate provision being made for the discarded wife and children, if any, that the associations should pledge their members not to encourage such marriages by their presence and support; and that wherever *Kulinism* prevailed the reform associations in those provinces should make every effort to educate public opinion in regard to the evil consequences resulting therefrom and promote inter-marriage independently of the artificial distinctions of *mels*, *garhs*, etc.

Ill-assorted marriages with great disparity in age, as was prevalent especially in Bengal under *Kulinism*, were denounced in no uncertain terms. The Conference pointed out that the practice of naive girls of 12 or under being yoked to old men with one foot in the grave was opposed to the spirit of the *Shastras* and was extremely prejudicial to the interests of the community. The necessity of actively discouraging all marriages where the difference of age between the parties exceeded thirty years was strongly affirmed.

The cause of most of the evils being the caste-restrictions, the Conference endeavoured to combat that evil. An appeal through a resolution to local associations, recommended fusion of sub-castes and inter-marriages between those of them who could inter-dine. It also recommended re-admission into the Hindu community of the converts to other faiths. Punjab took a prominent part in this activity, where in 1897, some 200 persons were received back into the Hindu society. Reports of stray instances of such re-admissions were received from other provinces also.

Besides the abuses which involved *Shastric* injunctions and had pseudo-religious elements about them, there were other objectionable practices which called for strenuous efforts to eradicate them. The prejudice against sea-voyage, highly detrimental to progress, was absolutely unfounded on any religious authority. It was objected to because it involved caste-restrictions on food and touch. Strangely, no disability was attached to those who undertook journey by sea to Asiatic countries. The Conference resolved that it was not desirable to excommunicate persons who undertook distant sea-voyages and requested social reform associations to take active steps to welcome foreign travelled men without any persecution and *Prayschit* (repentence) offered by them.

Public opinion, in certain sections at least was growing strong against the custom of having *nautch-girls* on festive occasions in the family. Curiously, no caste restrictions appeared to apply to these women and they seemed to be honoured in all homes alike. Propaganda against them showed signs of success and in 1895, at the Poona session, the Conference recorded its satisfaction at the general support the anti-*nautch* movement had found in the different parts of the country, but felt greater effort was needed to achieve complete success. Local social reform associations were recommended to continue making efforts to persuade their members to pledge themselves personally against having *nautches* in their houses and to see that festivities in families were carried on without any obscenity. This, in a way, covered the practices of using obscene language, singing immoral songs and indulging in vulgar jokes at the time of marriage festivities. The cultured opinion considered these practices objectionable and the Conference launched a drive against them by open condemnation.

At the time of death, the expression of mourning particularly among women, showed utter lack of control, succumbing completely to emotion. Loud mourning expressed by beating of the chests known as the '*Siapa*' system, prevailed widely in Sind, the Punjab, N.W.P. and Gujarat. The Conference made special appeal to the local reform associations to take active steps to stop it. Needless to mention that these resolutions were far from adequate measures to fight these practices. The root cause of most of the evils and the obstinacy with which society was clinging to them was rightly diagnosed to be the lack of education among women. The reformers took up the cudgels against ignorance, the real obstacle to change and advancement. At almost every session of the Conference the importance of female education was stressed. It was openly admitted in one of the resolutions that the permanent progress of society was not possible without further spread of female education. Efforts were directed to measures which would facilitate its promotion, such as opening of training schools for female teachers and organising home classes for grown-up ladies who could not attend regular schools.

The efforts made by the Social Conference were diverse and, notwithstanding the fact that they were, to a great extent, pious resolutions, their value as guiding and co-ordinating agency to the local associations, apart from arousing public interest and building considered opinion, is undeniable. In fact, the Conference served as incentive to many castes to take up the reform activity and forge ahead.

There was not a province from where encouraging reports were not coming about the activities of the caste associations. Even the backward areas, including some of the states, hitherto known to be impervious to change were falling in line with the others. Chief among the castes, to organise their associations and to make efforts to implement the programme laid down by the Social Conference were the Kayasthas spread widely all over northern India,[18] the Vaishyas, Sarins and Aroras of Punjab,[19] Bhatias of Bombay and Jains of Gujarat. Some castes even among Brahmans, such as Audich, Gaur and Bhargavas followed the example of the others.[20]

10.13 Kayastha Conference

The main object of these organisations was to work for the moral and material well-being of the community concerned, through education and the introduction of reform on the lines suggested by the Social Conference, implementing as far as possible the resolutions passed by it. The earliest effort in this direction originated in North West Provinces, an area otherwise considered backward, by the Kayasthas who proved to be most active and served as a model to others. The idea was sponsored by Munshi Har Govind Dayal, a pleader of Lucknow where the first Kayastha Conference met in November 1887. Valuable efforts to bring the Kayasthas together were made by Swami Shagan Chand who toured all over the areas where the Kayasthas were found to awaken them to the need of reform and concerted action. No less than 800 delegates attended the first conference, of whom 600 were local and 200 came from other parts of the country. The aim of the Kayastha Conference was to bring together the Kayasthas by organising Kayastha Sabhas in every town and place of importance, having a sufficient Kayastha population, and to improve the educational and moral status of the community, as also to encourage commercial enterprise by its members.

By 1890 more than 300 Sabhas had been established covering all the principal towns in N.W.P., Oudh, Bihar, Central Provinces, Rajputana and the Punjab. Education received attention as the first item of the programme. Efforts were made at once to raise the Kayastha Pathshala of Allahabad, which had been opened in 1872 through the munificence of wealthy Kayasthas, to a college and to open more schools. Female education, prevalent on a considerably large scale as compared to others, also received attention. Almost all the upper and middle classes gave elementary education to their girls. The Valmiki Kayasthas gave free education to their females.

Kayastha literary associations and clubs were established and were doing good work at Lahore, Lucknow, Agra and other towns. A series of pamphlets known as the 'Kayastha Social Reform Series' as also some useful books were published by them. For the convenience of students, boarding houses were being opened.

As early as 1888, the Kayastha Conference passed a resolution and took steps to stop money stipulations at marriages, extravagant expenses on weddings and other ceremonies and early marriages. Cases where money had been received secretly or in some new form were severely dealt with by the Sabhas and subjected to harsh criticism. Marriage expenses were sought to be curtailed and revised rules were framed fixing expenses according to income. Child marriage, generally speaking, was not found among Kayasthas except among the very wealthy on whom the Sabhas kept a watchful eye. To help poor students and those who wished to pursue higher education, the community started a fund by means of a monthly or annual subscription or donation in proportion to their income. The Rajputana and Punjab Provincial Sabhas helped students going to England, the Central Provinces Sabha assisted a law student. Some 100 students and 35 widows received pecuniary assistance for training from the local Sabhas.

The Kayasthas started temperance clubs and endeavoured to discourage drinking by doing propaganda against it.

By the end of the century, the Kayastha Conference could claim to have been positively successful in creating to a certain extent an *espirit de corps* among the various sections of the Kayastha community. A Valmik Kayastha of Bombay had begun to look upon a Bihari Srivastava as one of his own kith and kin.

How this caste-feeling might eventually prove detrimental to the national solidarity, the social reformers of the period perhaps did not pause to think. It was, however, not long before some of them, equally interested in the political emancipation of the country, realised the harm it would do.

10.14 Social Reform in Punjab

The Punjab though late to start, began to simmer with activity in no time. There was hardly a town of any importance which did not have at least one or two of the caste associations, chief among them being the Sarin Sabhas, Bunjahi Khatri Sabhas, Aggarwal Sabhas, Kayasthas and Arora Bans Sabhas.

The Sarin Sabha was one of the most important associations and held conferences from time to time at different places in the Punjab, the first having met in 1887 at Lahore. By 1895, the Sarins could well claim the credit of banishing wine and the *nautch-girls* from their marriage parties. Unequal matches were not only being condemned, but made punishable by the *Biradari*, caste fraternity. The marriageable age of girls had been raised; the expenses incurred on festive occasions had been curtailed and regulated and a healthy opinion on many social questions created. Practical steps were taken to have widows remarried without any stigma attached to such marriages. Diwan Sant Ram, a leading reformer re-married his own daughter thereby giving a lead to many others.

Outstanding work was done in the Punjab in other directions also. The Punjab Purity Association worked strenuously to remove some of the very palpable abuses. Doing propaganda through its fortnightly paper, 'The Purity Servant', it did a lot of practical work. The removal of prostitutes from the main street in the shopping centre of Lahore was due primarily to the pressure exercised by it. Special gatherings, known as the *Pavitra Holi* meetings were organised to do away with obscene jokes on the occasion of Holi festival. Widow relief work was undertaken and one rupee per month was given to each deserving widow. In 1890, the number of widows who received such help was forty.

Through the columns of its paper, devoted to discussions on moral and social subjects beneficial to the interests of the public, propaganda was done against drinking. Several temperance associations in the different parts of the province worked for the cause by circulating temperance literature and organising lectures on the subject.

The Amritsar Temperance Society was the most active with a hectic programme. Besides the publication and distribution of tracts, leaflets and booklets, lectures were delivered. Propaganda was continued by taking out processions and showing pictures exhibiting the deplorable condition of the drunkard's life. To take the message of temperance to the common man, preaching was conducted in streets as also at fairs and on occasions of festivals like *Basant, Baisakhi, Diwali*, etc. Temperance Dramatic Clubs and reading rooms formed important items of activity. Special prizes were given for articles, poems and essays on temperance.

10.15 Social Reform in Rajputana

Among the states, Rajputana took the lead by forming the Walterkrit Rajputra Hitkarni Sabha in 1888 under the guidance of Col. Walter, the British Resident at Ajmer. Marriage customs being the bane of social life in Rajputana, involving exorbitant expenses with disastrous effects on families, detailed rules were drafted for regulating them with punitive consequences for those who violated them.

The Walterkrit Rajputra Hitkarni Sabha met annually, discussed reports on the working of the reform scheme, from the branches spread all over Rajputana. The Sabha did practical work and the members adhered to their own rulings. Its success served as an incentive to other backward sections.[21]

The multifarious activities in favour of reform, chiefly at principal centres of education and administration, signified a conscious effort on the part of the progressive sections. However small the numerical strength of the people among whom the reforms to whatever little extent were being adopted, the fact remains that a beginning had been made for sure in the principal fields. Woman, the greatest sufferer from time-old social tyranny, found her shackles loosening up. Her wrongs were beginning to be righted. The number of families giving education to their girls, preferring the marriage of the daughter to a slightly higher age was growing. Names like Rama Bai, Anandi Bai Joshi, Sorabji

Cornelia, Toru Dutt and Mai Bhagwati shone like bright stars and proved that the trend of the age among the progressives was to let woman have the right and freedom to fend herself. So was it in other spheres. Even inter-caste and widow-marriages, however few in number, were accepted. In short, the attempt at reform made a successful headway in every sphere. In any case, it created an awareness of the need for change that there was social deformity which required reform. It brought into being, in all parts of the country, the forces of innovation which worked, with considerable success, for the awakening of the social conscience, thus portending a unique evolutionary revolution.

References

1. Bose, S.C. : Shib Chander, p. 189.
2. Fuller, Mrs Jenny, p. 184.
3. Ibid., p. 194.
4. Government of India Acts 1870, Act No. VIII.
5. Sastri, Shiv Nath, p. 246.
6. Lajpat Rai, p. 13.
7. Ibid. p. 184-94.
8. *Indian Social Reformer*, Vol. 32, p. 113.
9. *Indu Prakash* Vol. III, March 23, 1885, p. 3.
10. Ibid.
11. *Report of the Education Commission, 1882*, pp. 505-07.
12. Sastri, Shiv Nath., p. 42.
13. Ibid.
14. *Hindustan Review and Kayastha Samachar*, September 1903, pp. 225-26.
15. Ibid.
16. Government of India Selections from Records, No. 69-82. Also, Circular letter of Babu Keshav Chandra Sen to certain medical men, 1st April 1871, inviting opinion on the marriageable Age of native girls. Miscellaneous Papers in Indian Social Reform edited by. Chintamani, p. 260.
17. Ibid. pp. 211-17.
18. *Tribune*, 24 December 1890, article on Kayasthas. Also, Social Conference Reports 1889-94, 3rd Conference Report 1889, Appendix 1, p. 107.
19. Chintamani, p. 385 ; Diwan Sant Ram's speech at Social Conference, Lahore, 1900.
20. Chintamani, p. 209.
21. Report of the Walterkrit Rajputra Hitkarni Sabha. Also, Social Conference Reports, 1889-94, Summary of the Progress of Social Reforms in Different Provinces, Rajputana, pp. 53-54.

11 The Old Order Changeth

An overall review of the social conditions of northern India, during the half century from 1850 to 1900, is at once interesting and baffling, fascinating and bewildering, stimulating curiosity and inspiring investigation. It is difficult, however, to make statements of general application for fear of immediate and blatant contradiction in some form and in some part of the region which implied, by virtue of the immensity of its size, a vast variety of caste, creed, custom and convention all juxtaposed haphazardly through urban as well as rural areas With the changed political and economic conditions, the many facets of society appeared to present a kaleidoscopic view, contradictory in certain respects, but maintaining a general uniformity.

The consolidation of the British rule and the organisation of the administration during the period had been accompanied by the extension and development of education on western lines. Affecting in the first instance a very infinitesimal fraction of the people, attracted by the material gains it offesed, western education proved a powerful force. The diffusion of ideas it involved served as a leaven and caused a mighty fermentation in thought, the impact of which proved highly potent even portentous. In the social field, it proved most puissant, affecting, social institutions with a unique force, at once devastating and revivifying. It gave a new orientation to the Indian mind. The period, thus, was significant for change, though not always salutary for alteration in ideas and outlook. It was an age of intellectual fermentation, an era of transformation in social conditions and adjustments, hence highly complex.

The introduction of western education, according to the policy framed in the early part of the nineteenth century, had not remained a simple case of imposition of a western mould on the Indian mind of the privileged few who took to it. It had, on the contrary, caused a profound change of ideas which was making itself felt more and more as years and decades passed. The period under review, synchronising with the establishment of universities and expansion of education, reflected this crystal clear. The changed forms of thought of the recipients of the English education indicated that the leaven was working. The fermentation of ideas that resulted proved tantamount to a mighty intellectual revolution, unparalleled and novel, in that it was silent, often imperceptible, unplanned and unobtrusive to a certain extent. It was the product of the relationship between two civilisations fundamentally different and at unequal stages of development coming into contact with each other. It was, in a way, the resultant of a clash between the eastern and the western outlook. To a certain extent it was artificial and exotic, superficial and unnatural but it was momentous and serious. The impact of the west disturbed the disposition of the existing forces in the Indian society and brought into being new elements, creating new conditions resulting in an unprecedented social turmoil. Two opposing norms, the western and the eastern stressing the rights of the individual and the rights of the community or society respectively, warred with each other. This Homeric struggle in the domain of thought upset the old stratification and brought about a new bifurcation of society on a very uneven basis. A small, negligible fraction of people, the educated, more properly termed the literate, emerged as a group favouring the western norms. The vast unlettered majority clung steadfast to the eastern. English education being the dividing line, these two divisions of society centred roughly in the urban and rural areas, respectively, adding thus one more division to the innumerable social strata already in existence. The results were paradoxical in nature.

A motley host of heterogeneous types, the educated, comprised men of different castes, creeds, communities and callings, scattered but forming pockets in different parts of the region. They derived their strength not from their numbers, but from the common plane of their thought and attitudes. Ideas which had remained confined to small groups at centres of education only were, during the period under review, spreading fast. They received impetus from many factors. Difficulty of means of communication no longer retarded their movement. It was, on the contrary, considerably accelerated by the development of railways, the posts and telegraph system as also the rise of the press and the growth of education. To a certain extent, all diversity among them appeared to subordinate itself to the affinity of their ideas, in the sense that the members of the group thought somewhat alike regarding the major issues and problems that perplexed them. Reason, with them, was beginning to be looked upon as the touchstone for testing all accepted notions. The overwhelming power, hitherto, exercised by religion was giving way to a more or less secular attitude. The sense of community life which had in the past characterised Indian life was being disturbed and in its place was coming the individualism of western thought. The changed outlook was leading to destruction of old sanctions and repudiation of old values, although, this was more often than not, in theory only. Profession and practice, not infrequently, appeared to be at variance with each other.

The literate intelligensia, growing in number, eager and restless in thought, inquisitive and impatient in stirrings, defiant and aggressive in conduct, self-confident and assertive in views, however, had no roots in the life of the people. A sophisticated outer layer, they formed, nevertheless, a force to reckon with.

The vast majority of the people, the masses, rural as also urban, unlettered and unsophisticated, ignorant and superstitious, immobile, and immutable they remained more or less placid and complacent. Deeply imbued with the sense of community life, they stood steadfast for the ways of the past. With elements of granite strength, they upheld all that was traditional, whether pristine and primeval or perverse and distorted. Their life, particularly in the villages, flowed along ancient channels, unruffled on the whole, except occasionally when the temptation of material gain proved too strong to resist adoption of the urban ways of life, or convenience got the better off tradition and the use of imported objects like machine-made cloth, kerosene oil, umbrellas, etc. began to creep into the village world.

The mental distance that education created between the small minority, the literati, and the vast mass, the unlettered, became the most conspicuous and outstanding social anomaly, notwithstanding the innumerable incongruities of the social pattern in existence. This disparity of class was incomparable to any other of caste, creed, status or rank and pervaded the whole social pattern.

The influence of the west stimulated an ideological change undermining the faith in the indigenous religions and institutions. Not only were the young educated becoming sceptical, but some of the enthusiasts were losing their bearings and becoming sedulous apes. In fact, the first fruits of western education in India had been riotous excesses and wild license. By the light of their newly acquired knowledge young India had begun to feel that everything which was Hindu, in origin, since majority of them were Hindus, was bad. Unable to discern the later accretions and deformities of the social structure, they had nothing but wholesale condemnation for it. Falling blindly for the western system, they failed to see any good in the Hindu institutions. For them, the caste-system was totally bad even if it was based on the first essential principles of division of labour; the joint-family system was bad, despite the fact that it was, at one time, and could still be, the living school for the teaching of self-abnegation and a sense of duty. It had the rudiments of practical socialism, even communism. The Hindu system of marriage, treated as a necessary sacrament and a spiritual union between man and woman, to them was absolutely bad. In short, for them everything of indigenous origin was bad and, everything western seemed good in proportion. Moral courage, in the form young India learnt, was the necessary outcome of western education. And young India began to indulge in undesirable practices to assure themselves and the world that their English education had borne fruit in developing their hitherto latent moral courage. Disrespect for age, irreverance for superiors, conceit and arrogance in conduct, appeared to be part of their new learning. The iconoclastic education of the West, thus, by emancipating the Hindu intellect from the thraldom of superstition and Brahmanic supremacy had brought about a state of extreme leaning in the opposite direction of uncritical adulation of the foreign culture and social life which shocked the sense of propriety of the more sedate sections of society.

Voice against the crude, rather confused admiration, to the extent of indiscriminate imitation of western ways of life had been raised quite early. Raja Rammohun Roy's efforts, by giving an exposition of the philosophic side of the religion, which, under the spell of western influence, had been so summarily condemned and superciliously rejected, had checked considerably the undesirable trends though not completely stemmed the wave of anglicising India. The agitation he sponsored against the gravest of the social evils, the practice of *Sati*, had aroused a spirit of unrest and enquiry into the basis of social usages. This spirit had grown more and more intense as years and decades passed. In the post-Mutiny period when the ascendancy of western thought and ideas became the dominant feature, it inspired new quests for spiritual truth and relaxation of old social tyrannies. It found new channels of thought and expression, it gave new interpretation to old practiees. It facilitated the comingling of ideas, leading to a process of currents and cross-currents, resulting sometimes in serious and futile conflicts.

The sense of individuality fostered by the western environment was a fruitful source of important change in the attitude of the literati so that the general trend among them was one of doubt and scepticism. The implicit faith in social institutions and respect for conventions was shaken. These, no longer, commanded the rigid adherence they had enjoyed from time immemorial. The butteresses of faith, tradition and superstition were being undermined. This change was clearly noticeable, though in varying degrees in regard to different practices. In social polity, it was most conspicuous in respect of caste, known to be the bedrock of Hindu society, with infectious influence on other communities. While it was still a powerful force and while new social rings were being formed through the working of the spirit of exclusiveness, the general idea of caste was undergoing change. It was facing an irresistible challenge in the new forces of western ideas marshalled against it, so that it was rendered no longer impregnable and unvulnerable. Incompatible with the changed conditions of life, it was beginning to be regarded as a social anomaly and a ban to progress. Maintenance of extreme orthodoxy was becoming difficult, nay, well-nigh impossible. In the school room, in the railway compartment, on board the steamer, at mills, in newly coming—up factoriest,he stringency of caste rules was diminishing. In respect of most of the offences against caste such as those regarding food, personal contact, sea-voyage, in all large centres of population the general attitude was rapidly changing. The breaches were tolerated more liberally even among the uneducated in their daily life. Travelling by train, for instance, was far too convenient to be abstained from even by the orthodox. Using water from the taps that were being installed in cities like Calcutta, was proving much easier than fetching it from the river with all the trouble involved in it. Getting medicine from the hospital, in spite of the contactual contact it involved with those of the lower castes, was far too beneficial to be eschewed. Caste rules were, therefore, being ingeniously relaxed to suit the situation. Even the most punctilious would be seen, not only sitting in the same compartment in close proximity with those whom, normally, they would not like to have near them, but also eating food sometimes at the hands of those not permissible by caste-codes. Indulgence in forbidden food no longer exposed one to excommunication in the strict sense, and foreign travel was becoming more or less an accepted fact. Instances of people going abroad and on return being admitted into society readily or reluctantly were growing. Many venturesome Indians, visiting foreign lands, on return rebelled against the humiliating requirements which alone according to caste-rules could purify them from the polluting indiscretion of a visit to those lands. This spirit was growing more and more valiant, although the vast majority of the people remained unaffected. Reports to the National Social Conference at Amraoti in 1897, from different parts of the region, regarding foreign-travelled young men being admitted into society are significant. Several Saraswat gentlemen returned from England and though the *Guru* of the caste had refused admission to them the reform party succeeded in openly showing their sympathy with them. Raja Nowlojee Rao Gujar, a scion of the princely house of Nagpore, returned from England and was well-received. Messrs Booti and Alonikar of Nagpore, Mr. Krishna Rao Bhola Nath of Ahmedabad, Professor Gokhale of Poona and Mr. Kelkar of Gwalior were similarly, though not formally, admitted by some of their caste people and the opposition did not dare to place any difficulties in their way. Two Bhatia gentlemen, for the first time in that community, left for England with the full support of their caste. In the Punjab, several young men in the orthodox castes, who had been to England, were admitted back without any opposition. Two young men from the Arora caste-group went to England. The liberal section of the Kashmiri Pandit Sabha strongly favoured foreign travel.

As for the adoption of another religion, the general attitude was likewise changing. In large towns, at least, the convert to Christianity was no longer so rigidly or instantaneously excluded from society as he used to be.

The superiority and the supremacy of the Brahman was facing a challenge in many ways. Knowledge was no longer his sole monopoly, nor did he enjoy entirely the leadership in society. Education was bringing non-Brahmans into prominence. Society was being familiarised, as never before, with non-Brahman leaders, religious and social. Neither of the Brahmo leaders, Keshav Chandra Sen and Pratap Chandra Mozomdar was a Brahman; B.M. Malabari of Bombay was a Parsi, nor was Swami Vivekananda who represented Hinduism at the Parliament of Religions at Chicago in 1893, a Brahman. Interestingly enough, the Theosophists who championed Hinduism and supported social reform and were highly respected by the educated from among whom later they drew their members, were, far from being Brahmans or Hindus, not even Indians. Curiously enough, the most outstanding among them, was a woman—Mrs. Annie Besant, who received respect from the Indians, in equal measure with her male colleagues, without any reservation.

Even in regard to the most grievous and unpardonable offences against caste, those concerning marriage—marrying below caste, out of caste or marrying a widow—on which the force of caste was concentrating, strangely its adamantine bonds were showing signs of loosening. Cases of inter-marriage, though exceedingly few in number were beginning to be reported in the nineties. Bengal papers announced an inter-marriage at a high level between two sub-divisions of the Kayastha community which had hitherto kept aloof. In the Punjab, a betrothal was announced in 1896 between two sub-castes of the Sarin community. This was the first instance of an inter-marriage between these two sub-divisions. The same year, for the first time, inter-marriages between ladies and gentlemen from Bengal and Madras took place. A few instances of similar unions could be cited from the Kayastha community in the North-West Provinces and some sub-castes in Gujarat. It might be interesting to note that the marriage of Mrs. Sarojini Naidu *nee* Chattopadhyaya, one of the renowned leaders in the freedom movement of the country, to Dr. Govindarajulu Naidu took place in 1898. It was a conspicuous instance of the new trends and marked an epoch in the history of the endeavours at reform.

Child marriage among the educated community was beginning to be deprecated and was becoming a little less common. The struggle for existence getting harder, and the joint-family system which made the burdens of child marriage lighter, being adversely affected, young men who were beginning to assert their views in the matter that concerned them most intimately were getting averse to undertake marital duties and responsibilities until they could be in a position to discharge them properly. When they did marry they preferred a grown-up girl. The consciousness among educated parents of the harm early marriage did to girls and the change of their views resulting in giving education to the daughters, even though not general yet, automatically helped raising the age of marriage. By the end of the century, infant marriage was not only looked down upon among the educated, but efforts were being made to persuade the government to pass legislation against it and also to make such regulations that would deny married boys admission to universities. By the last decade of the century caste organisations like the Arora Bans Sabha in the Punjab and the Walterkrit Rajputra Hitkarni Sabha in Rajputana were actively working to raise the age for marriage by framing rules to be followed by their members. The assets of success to their credit were commendable in that the members of these caste associations observed the rules strictly.

The movement in favour of widow remarriage was beginning to show some practical results Instances of valiant young men who had the courage to take the bold step of marrying a widow were beginning to appear even in the papers. Even advertisement in newspapers by youngmen willing to marry a widow and seeking one were not altogether unknown. At the annual Social Conference, the number of widow marriages, however few, was reported with pride. In fact, there was not a single province in which the supporters of the cause were not active. More and more caste groups and influential persons were enlisting their support to the widow remarriage movement.

As for polygamy among the educated, Muhammadans excepted, public opinion disfavoured it. Second marriage required a convincing justification. At best polygamy was hiding itself. Even *Kulinism*, the most perverse form of it, was being openly censured and had considerably gone out of favour.

Change in views, regarding the position of woman, was particularly noteworthy. Not only was the daughter beginning to have equality in treatment but also care, concern and some education along with the sons. Her traditional seclusion was being disfavoured and the custom of *Parda* was in some cases yielding to western ideas. The rigidity of seclusion could hardly be maintained, for instance, on railway trains, steamers and in public hospitals. In big cities like Calcutta places of amusement like the museum and zoological gardens were an attraction where the strictness of *Parda* was affected. Women were beginning to participate in the activities of the new religious sects. At the meetings of the Arya Samaj and the Brahmo Samaj, women were beginning to come and sit behind reed screens. Advanced ladies in Calcutta were even organising fancy fairs and theatricals. Towards the end of the century, some women mainly Hindus, Parsis and Indian Christians could be reckoned who had graduated from the universities and a few who practised medicine. One Parsi lady had taken to law as profession. However small the number, women were definitely coming out in some fields. Some of them had even started attending mixed parties. Some women were participating in the Social Conference sessions also. In big cities, even clubs for women were coming up. The Hindu Ladies' Social Club in Bombay, founded in 1894, was an outstanding example of its kind. Within five years of its existence, the Club stood well organised and its membership ran into a few hundreds.

Another conspicuous change was in regard to the joint-family. The influence of self-interest, imbibed in the young through western education, was of a disintegrating nature. Western ideas of individuality and notions of family responsibility which were being gradually adopted by the educated community did not harmonise with the joint-family system. The tendency was to ignore responsibilities beyond the circle of the nearest relations. The moral cohesiveness which bound the members of the family together was losing its strength. The increased cost of living as well as the standard of living without corresponding increase in the means to attain it, had strengthened the sense of limited self-interest. With the education of girls, problems in the family were increasing. The tendency of the young men was more and more against the joint-family system of which they were prone to see the disadvantages only and these too in an exaggerated manner. The strength and sanctity of the traditional family system showed signs of being shaken. Along with this was visible another deleterious change without any measure of relief to those who were affected by it. The disposition to charity, extolled as one of most commendable traits of Indian social conditions, was succumbing to new utilitarian trends.

Apart from the ideological changes that were coming the educated were consciously or unconsciously, directly or indirectly, voluntarily or involuntarily, imbibing the materialism of western civilisation and the western view of its superiority over the eastern. They were eager to pursue the western path of progress and reform. They were getting obsessed, so to say, by the western ideas of decency and of rise in the standard of living as the essential perquisites of advancement. There was indeed a maudlin rage for rise in the standard of living on the western pattern and adoption of English customs. This was especially the case with Indian christians, so many of whom of higher ranks were living in close touch with English people. In big cities a considerable number of the educated were beginning to copy the manners and fashions of the European rulers. In some of their forms of politeness, there was a tendency apparent to adopt European ways. In Bombay, the educated Parsis were far ahead of the others in this respect. In Calcutta and the neighbourhood these tendencies were equally marked. They were conspicuously perceptible in the dress, one of the most unstable part of the Indian institutions, particularly in the case of men. At Presidency towns, individuals among the wealthier classes were adopting the European style of dress. It was well-known that Indian boys neatly clad in English style had a much better chance of getting work and at a higher rate of pay than would be the case if a boy made his application dressed in Indian style garments. His English dress also secured him many little concessions and courtesies especially when travelling. One of the first changes adopted by the young educated was to put on white socks and English shoes in place of the indigenous slippers. Then he would discard the loose *dhoti* in favour of the English trousers and wait for a while before introducing another change. After some interval he would put on an English shirt which for sometime would be worn hanging down the knees outside the pants. In due course, he would assume a waist coat and then a sort of surtout coat. Variation was noticeable in the adoption of the English dress, for some adopted it in toto, some in part; some without its head dress, some without its neck-appendages and some without both. In a large gathering in a

THE OLD ORDER CHANGETH

big city, a bewildering variety could be witnessed—English dress in all its integrity as well as its various fanciful modifications and Indian dress, *chapkan* with or without *choga*; the indigenous *dhoti chaddar*, sometimes with shirt or coat or without either in Bengal and Bombay; the varieties of *pajama* and shirt and *chapkan* in North West Provinces and the Punjab, turbans or caps for head and sometimes bare-heads.

On the whole female dress did not witness much change. Only in the case of women of very advanced families, who were taking to education and were emerging from their seclusion and beginning to make appearance in public, that some changes were taking place. The tendency was to drape the body more carefully. For instance, in the parts of the region, such as Bengal, Bombay and where women wore *saree*, a jacket was added. Women of respectable families while going out would cover the whole body with a big scarf or a *chaddar*. In the North West Provinces and the Punjab where under the influence of the Arya Samaj women were taking to education and went more frequently out of the house, a similar tendency was noticeable. To the indigenous skirt, shirt and veil was added a bigger *chaddar* to cover the whole body, before appearing in the presence of strangers. English dress was not favoured even among the highly anglicised families except in the case of Indian christians. Among the Parsis, in some cases, it was adopted for small girls. But even in this case the typical cap was retained.

Western contact, however, influenced the taste for ornaments and jewellery worn by women among the educated without in any way affecting diminution to the instinctive desire for personal adornment. The decorative taste among the older ladies was formed as much by aesthetic as by prudential considerations. In their ornaments, therefore, weight and purity of metal were combined as far as possible with elegance. With the younger generation the cumbersome old fashioned ornaments, not harmonising well with European taste were losing favour and were either being discarded or replaced by lighter, better finished though less pure articles. The introduction of European ideas of propriety had, probably, much to do with the rejection of the various leg and foot ornaments, the rhythmic jingle of which delighted the ears of the sterner sex who had not received the full light of western civilisation. Nose ornaments and heavy ear ornaments as also those for the waist were becoming obsolete. Bangles and necklaces, however, not only continued to hold their own but were being adopted even by Anglo-Indian ladies.

The influence of western ideas was visible in the homes of the educated in the mode of living. Tables, chairs and sofas and other articles of European furniture were finding their way into the households of the well-to-do educated in large towns. Hand fans in use from ancient times were being superseded by swinging fans suspended from the ceilling and pulled by servants. Domestic utensils were equally being affected by western contact among the upper educated class. Brass plates and tumblers were giving way to China and glassware with forks, knives and the usual paraphernalia of the western type. Eating at table was being preferred to squatting and eating on the floor in the kitchen. Among the advanced, the whole family including women were beginning to have their meals together. In this respect the Indian Christians and the Parsis were changing more rapidly than the others.

Restrictions about food were, to a great extent, losing their rigidity and a tendency towards greater freedom in the choice of food was noticeable. Western dishes were gaining popularity in the homes of the heterodox who openly dined at the table and partook of food cooked and served by non-Hindus or very low-caste or practically no caste Hindus. The example of British officers was proving infectious for many among the educated, and the use of drinks was increasing as it was considered fashionable and adding to their status. The demon of drink was claiming many victims from classes who had always been noted for their abstinence. As for smoking, not only were cigarettes replacing the indigenous and less harmful *hukka*, but their use was increasing among the students. Even the pleasures, traditional ways of amusement and entertainment were changing in form. Such agencies as the *yatra* the *pachali* and the *kathakata* in Bengal which served both as entertainment, as also to propagate the high ethical and spiritual ideas of the *Ramayana* and the *Mahabharata* were becoming obsolete. They were being replaced by the theatre and circus. The celebration of festivals and the ceremonial of the rites in the families among the educated was losing its old zest and significance, though the traditional routine was mostly kept up. The traditional games and exercises were giving way to those imported with western education, cricket, football, tennis, etc. Indigenous toys no longer delighted the children and the fashion of giving imported trinkets as presents on festive occasions, such as birthdays and weddings, was gaining ground. The infatuation of the educated for the material development of western civilisation was intensifying at a terrific pace.

The contrast between the two sections of society was tremendous and although it was only the men in the first instance who were affected by the change, the new western ideas could not remain confined entirely to them. It was but natural that women would sooner or later fall in line with them. The educated man began, indeed, to have a desire for companionship with his wife on a mental plane also. The foreign travelled, particularly, with his experience of the difference in the family life with women equally educated and enlightened. yearned for a change in that direction. Some venturesome enthusiasts were teaching their wives to read and write despite the mockery and scoffing they met with. Many allowed the missionary ladies easy access to their women in their homes to teach them the three Rs Some even employed them to teach the women in the family.

Their attitude to their daughters was altering completely. While at the beginning of the period under review, it was a scandal to educate girls but by the closing years of the period it was beginning to be considered desirable. With the development of female education, even though it was on a very small scale, a new force of tremendous potential had entered the social arena. The number of women, who graduated from the universities, and took to some kind of profession, was negligible. and yet the difference it made to the general tone or the outlook was remarkable. A consciousness of the social injustice and a desire to fight for their rights as also to uplift the position of the down-trodden and tradition-shackled sisters was growing rapidly. The determination of Rukma Bai in 1880s to take a firm stand, to take up cudgels with the law and to remain undaunted even in the face of adverse verdict is only an instance of the type of consciousness that was developing among women. She exercised her right to decide for her life and refused to obey the law ordering her to go and live with her husband. A single instance of its type, undoubtedly, it reveals the seeds that were being sown.

Pandita Rama Bai's bouts with destiny proved that women were beginning to think and shake off the fetters and be not only the makers of their life but the shapers of the social pattern also. Her own fate and early widowhood had revealed to her the pitiable state in which a young widow could be and she thereafter dedicated herself to the uplifting of the young widows. Mai Bhagwati in the Punjab became conscious of the need for education of girls and worked in the field created by the Arya Samaj.

The number of women coming out to attend the meetings of the Arya Samaj and the Brahmo Samaj, even though they sat apart from men and behind reed-curtains, was slowly and consistently increasing. The industrial schools and training centres for girls, which were being opened by the missionaries of different denominations in different parts of the region were being filled and need for more was being stressed. The widows' homes started by different agencies were being freely availed of. This was not only because the educated men had changed their views but because the women were also awakening. Some were beginning to take up professions such as teaching, medicine and even law. The Indian Christian and the Parsi women, no doubt, were in the vanguard, but their Hindu sisters were beginning to look up to them. The leaven of ideas, the infection of example, was beginning to work. The traditional devotion of women to religious ceremonies, the observance of fasts and their dedication to service in the family were in many instances ridiculed. The contrast, however, between the very small number of the enlightened in big cities and towns and those of the villages, steeped in ignorance was even greater than the one presented by similarly placed men. The gulf between the women of higher classes, and those of the lower classes hitherto on account of the customs which only rich could afford to observe, was changing its form.

The paradox of the whole situation was not only in this that the life of the small section of the educated was changing rapidly while the vast majority appeared to remain immutable, except however, when some ideas filtered through and caught the fancy of the masses but in the opposing trends that were noticeable. Currents and cross-currents were flowing at the same time. For instance, while the educated and the higher classes were definitely beginning to encourage the raising of age for marriage, the tendency in the lower strata of society was in the opposite direction. The example of the higher castes, indicative of the higher status, was being followed, thus lowering the marriage age in the humbler castes so that there was rapid extension of child marriage among them. A similar trend was in operation in regard to widow remarriage. The lower castes were prone to favour prohibition of widow remarriage. The Chandallas in Bengal, for instance, the lowest caste in the social scale used to allow their widows to remarry but gradually had forbidden it. This opposing wave was also noticeable with regard to the seclusion of women. The lower castes felt it was a sign of respectability to keep their women in seclusion and, therefore they strove to keep them in *Parda*. A matter of their financial means determined their attitude.

Even in regard to caste, two opposing tendencies were operating side by side—one in the direction of relaxation of the rules of contact, food and other ceremonial advances and fact, the other in the reverse direction, in tightening up the restrictions. The lower castes were tending up-wards ; the upper castes were tending downwards. They were forfeiting their status by engaging in trades and occupations which formerly would have been regarded as beneath them.

Thus many silent changes could be noted and many diverse ideas observed side by side in a strange chequer. The complexity of the whole situation became more confounding because the educated Indian found himself living in two worlds—one at home and the other at work or business. He developed two selves, an Indian and the other partly English, the former to a large extent being smothered by the latter. The pro-western attitude was stronger and more marked because of the glamour of the material achievements of the West. Perhaps, in subject India, it could not have been otherwise. Yet, the habits of milleniums through generations could not change at once. This led to another anomaly. The profession and practice were often conflicting with each other. The reformer practised at home what he vehemently denounced in public, sometimes for reasons beyond his control, but often on account of change or the ignorance of the women in the family. There were, therefore, differences in the degree in which the change in ideas and theory was in actual practice.

The more enthusiastic idealists were not content merely with the slow change that was taking place as a natural result of western influence, They were neither happy at the suggestions of the cautious and the moderates that with education and change of public opinion the social evils would take care of themselves nor did they subscribe to the view of those who stressed reform of religion as a necessary precursor or accompaniment of social reform. They fretted and fumed, strove and struggled, laboured and toiled to accelerate the process of transformation. The social inequities were looked upon by them as deformities which could be treated and reformed. Believing in rapid and deliberate change, the group of the advanced school of social thought, the reformers dedicated themselves to the cause and were working to reform society. They stressed the dangers of the social inequities and set to work for their removal. In their eagerness, sincerity and enthusiasm they failed to realise the delicate ground they treaded and often hurt the susceptibilities of the orthodox who developed a defensive attitude towards all that was traditional. The impact of the West that had aroused a critical impulse and a reformative activity had also stimulated a sense of pride in belonging to an ancient culture and a feeling of its superiority along with a desire for its preservation. These two opposing currents of thought were flowing simultaneously, clashing and conflicting at times in the opposition that the orthodox put up against the reform proposals and the legislation passed by the Government. As the reform movement gained momentum, the reactionary wave also gained in strength. It was not merely opposing reform but was developing a revivalist mentality as a reaction against the extreme position taken by the over-enthusiasts who appeared to be radicals heading towards a revolution. They condemned everything western and looked only to the undesirable effects of western education. They posed questions regarding the inherent worth of the two systems stressing the good in the indigenous culture. Everything western to them was condemnable. They wished to purify society of all that was alien and to revive its pristine form. This feeling for purging society of all customs adopted from foreign culture was not confined to the majority community only. It was shared by the others also—Muslims, Parsis and even Sikhs.

The earliest stirrings of the reactionary spirit were noticeable in the seventies in Bengal where one Raj Narayan Bose started propaganda delivering lectures on the superiority of Hinduism over all other forms of faith.

In this, the Hindus were facing a complex situation because of their long past of millenniums. The revivalists were at sea as to where the point for reversion was to be fixed. Vaguely the general cry was to return to the past, a widespread desire to strengthen the old faith, a sort of an uprising of certain sections of the educated in defence of Hinduism.

The Arya Samaj raised a voice in favour of 'back to the Vedas' and while it had some common points with the reformers' programme it was sternly opposed, in the first instance, to western knowledge from which the reformers drew their inspiration. In the closing decade of the century, even among the followers of the Arya Samaj a cross-current was taking shape in that a section of them had partly accepted western education.

The Sanatan Dharma Mahamandal looked upon English education and the reforms as serious encroachments on the ancient culture. The Ramakrishna Mission, a purely religious organisation, made a bid against western ways through its stress on certain aspects of the Hindu faith, thus becoming a considerabie force in the social field also. The Theosophists with their special efforts to encourage oriental learning, more particularly Hindu religion and culture added to the strength of the revivalists. They went to the extent of justifying every custom and usage of the Hindus and identified themselves with the wave in favour of everything Hindu and against everything western.

A similar reactionary wave was noticeable in the Muslim community in that a spirit of revivalism or puritanism prevailed. The Wahabi movement gained pace and voice was raised in favour of purging the Muslim life of all that had crept into it through contact with other communities particularly the Hindus. All superstitions, customs and practices, attributed to Hindu influence were considered as factors sapping the vigour of Islam and were to be swept aside. A reaction against their own progressives, the Aligarh school of thought was no less vocal.

The reactionary section among the Parsis regarded certain parts of the programme of the *Rahnumai Mazdavasnan Sabha* rather radical and dangerous. They were afraid that the elimination of certain practices from the traditional system as superstitions would weaken the religion and shatter the faith of the masses. The reactionary society, the *Rahe Rust* or True Way, opposed the reformerr. The two prominent papers of the Parsis, the *Suryodaya* or sunrise and the *Rast Goftar* presented the true picture of opposing views of the reformers and reactionaries.

Among the Sikhs an effort was being made in favour of puritanism by the Kukas. They worked against the Brahmanic hold on the masses and to re-introduce the circumambulation of the 'Granth' instead of the sacred fire. This was all a part of the move favouring everything indigenous.

Side by side with these two opposing currents of reform and revival, a third was emerging and beginning to assume concrete shape. This was the voice of those educated who had sense as keen and critical as that of the reformers and pride and esteem for Indian culture as strong as that of the revivalists. Their reviving Indian spirit was face to face with novel conditions and ideas and the urgent necessity of understanding and assimilating them. They turned a new eye on their past culture, re-awoke to its sense and import but also saw it in relation to western knowledge and ideas. They were, in a way, weighing and balancing the two systems, the eastern and the western, and were working for a synthesis of the two in the social and the religious field. In the intellectual field, having a close bearing on the social, the writings of young men like Bankim Chandra Chatterjee and Rabindra Nath Tagore, etc. were noteworthy contributions. On the religious side, which had even greater influence on the social life of the people, both the educated and the masses, Vivekanand stood as the best example. Mrs. Annie Besant worked in the same direction with stress on certain aspects of Hindu culture.

The synthesis that was beginning to emerge was neither wholehearted nor comprehensive. It barely touched an extremely limited section of the educated. The masses remained entirely unaffected. They were accustomed to take refuge in the stability and the protecting conservatism of the ruling public opinion as a check upon any irresponsible force and showed no signs of change. Superstitions, prejudices and fears, traditions and customs, moods, fancies and tastes, modes of thought and hereditary tendencies, backed by invincible habit, dominated and shaped social conditions among them to an extraordinary degree.

In contrast, the educated few were restless and astir. Among them deep-rooted prejudices and superstitions were becoming obsolescent; the adamantine bonds of caste were loosening, women, however few, were beginning to be awakened. Such evil customs as early marriage, prohibition of widow marriage were being definitely discredited and even done away with and the idea of equality was gaining ground.

The period, thus, was one of transition. Crowded with activity of a varied nature, of radical change, reform, revival and even synthesis, it presents a picture somewhat like a kaleidoscope. The influence of the activities, however, remained on surface only. It did not penetrate deep enough into the general passivity and complacency of Indian life though it caused enough restlessness among the classes which suffered from social inequities and among whom social evils were glaringly rampant. The simmerings of unrest and clamourings of better conditions among them were signs of a social awakening which stimulated new hopes and aspirations with visions of a new order. These stirrings in the life and thought were evidence that society was going through a reorientation, a unique rejuvenation. By the end of the period, a new social order was already, it appears, in the offing. Elusive and evasive it could not be pinned to a concrete, stable and uniform shape. It was haphazard, rather vague, with much of the old order and some of the new. It was a period of slow transformation in which the twentieth century conditions appeared to be jostling here and there, with those of the earliest—first, second centuries.

Bibliography

RECORDS AVAILABLE WITH THE NATIONAL ARCHIVES OF INDIA

Manuscripts

Proceedings of the Home (Public) Department, 1860-1900.
Proceedings of the Home (Education) Department, 1860-1900.
Proceedings of the Legislative Department, 1860-1900.

Printed Documents

Selections from the Records of the Government of India, Nos. 2, 5, 6, 18, 54, 57, 60, 66.
Selections from the Records of the Foreign Department, Nos. 205, 214, 223, 290, 311, 337, 345 and 354.
Selection from the Records of the Government of Bengal Nos. 18, 23, 26 and 34.
Selection from the Records of the Government of North Western Provinces, Nos. 1-6.
Selection from the Records of the Government of Punjab, Nos. 1-6.
A Collection of Despatches from Home Government on the subject of Education in India, 1854-68.

PARLIAMENTARY PAPERS

Year	Nos.
1850	41 (191)
1851	4 (145), 453 (531)
1852-53	69 (988)
1857	11 (111); 29 (295); 42 (190)
1860	52 (35)
1861	44 (72 I, II & III); 45 (291); 45 (373)
1862	39 (C 2985)
1867-68	50 (244)
1868-69	47 (351)
1870	52 (397); 53 (163)
1880	53 (C 2732); 53 (2735)
1881	71 (C 3086)
1884-85	60 (289)
1888	5 (134); 19 (227); 58 (281)
1890	53 (6089)
1892	58 (318), 57 (C 6793)
1893	66 (39); 66 (97); 65 (150)
1894	60 (C 7313); 61 (C 7397); 62 (7473)
1895	42 (C 7723)

1898	64 (C 8921)
1899	31 (C 9178); 65 (C 9180); 68 (C 9369)
1900	58 (C 232)

GOVERNMENT REPORTS

Census Reports of India, 1881, 1891, 1901, 1911 and 1921.
Census Reports of Bengal, 1872, 1881, 1891 and 1901.
Census Reports of Bombay, 1864, 1872, 1881, 1891, and 1900.
Census Reports of N.W.P., 1872, 1881, 1891, 1900 and 1911.
Census Reports of Punjab, 1881, 1891, 1901, and 1911.
Census Reports of Rajputana, 1872, 1881, 1891 and 1901.
Census Reports of Central Provinces, 1872, 1881, 1891 and 1901.
Moral and Material Progress Reports, 1866-1900.
Report on Native Newspapers (Bengal), 1863-1900.
Report on Native Newspapers (Bombay), 1868-1900.
Report on Native Newspapers (Central Provinces), 1896-1900.
Report on Native Newspapers (Punjab), 1864-1900.
Report on Native Newspapers (N.W.P.), 1864-1900.
Note on the state of Education in India, 1865-66; 1866-67.
Review of Education in India in 1886.
Progress of Education in India, 1887-88 to 1892-93.
Progress of Education in India, 1892-93 to 1897-98.
Progress of Education in India, 1897-98 to 1901-02.
Report of the Indian Education Commission, 1882.
Punjab Administration Reports, 1840-1900.
Reports on the Administration of Rajputana, 1865-67.
Central India Agency Reports, 1866-1900.
Report on the Working of the Thugee and Dacoity Department, 1874.
Report on Measures adopted in Zilla Mynpoory for Prevention of Female Infanticide, 1866.
Report on the Prevalence of Female Infanticide in Bustee, 1869.
Report on Female Infanticide in Jaunpur District, 1870.
District Gazetteers, all districts of the Punjab, 1884-85.
District Gazetteers, all districts of N.W.P., 1884-86.

REPORTS OF OTHER AGENCIES

Missionary Conferences Decennial Reports, 1872, 1882, 1892.
Social Conference Reports, 1887-1900.
Walterkrit Rajputra Hitkarini Sabha, Rajputana, 1889-1900.

JOURNALS

Indian Antiquary, 1881-1900.
Indian Magazine.
Social Reformer, 1885-1900.

Quarterly Journal of the Poona Sarvajanik Sabha, 1886-1900.
Hindustan Review and Kayastha Samachar, 1898-1904.
English Opinion on India, 1890-1900.
Calcutta Review, 1844-1900.
Asiatic Quarterly Review.
Journal of the Royal Asiatic Society, 1890-1900.
Journal of the Bombay Branch of the Royal Asiatic Society, 1890-1900.
National Indian Association Journal, 1871-75.
Nineteenth Century.

NEWSPAPERS

Indian Spectator, 1883-1900.
Indu Prakash, 1883-1900.
Tribune, 1885-1900.

BOOKS

Abhedananda Swami. *India and her people.* New York; Vedanta Society, 1906.
Acland, Charles. *A popular account of the manners and customs of India.* London: John Murray, 1847.
Aitken Edward Hamilton. *Behind the bunglow.* Calcutta; Thacker and Co., 1889.
Aiyangar, K.V. Ramaswami. *Brihaspati Smriti (Reconstructed).* Baroda; Baroda Oriental Institute, 1941.
Aksaya Kumari Devi. *Fundamentals of Hindu society.*
A Lady Resident. *The English women in India.*
Allen, D.O. *India, ancient and modern.* 1856.
Alston, Leonard. *Education and citizenship in India.* London; Longman, 1910.
Ameer Ali, Syed. *Legal position of women in India.* London; University of London, 1912.
Ameer Ali, Syed. *Mohammedan law.* 1894.
Ameer Ali, Syed. *Spirit of Islam.* 1906.
Anand Charlu. *Remarriage of Hindu women.*
Anand Charlu. *The elevation of Hindu women.*
Argyll (Duke of.) *India under Dalhousie and Canning.* 1865.
Arnold, Edwin. *India revisited.*
Arnold, Edwin. *The Queen's Justice : A true history of Indian village life.*
Arnold, Edwin. *Marquis of Dalhousie's Administration of British India.* 2 vols.
Atkinson, George Francklin. *"Curry and Rice" on Forty Plates or the ingredients of social life at "our station" in India.* London; Day and Sons, 1859.
Baijnath, Rai Bahadur. Fusion of subcaste in India In. Chintamani's, ed. *Indian Social Reform.* 1901.
Baijnath, Rai Bahadur. *Social reform for the N.W. Provinces : Proceedings of public meetings for the abolition of child marriage held by*

Baijnath, Rai Bahadur. *Beharamaji Mihrbanji Malabari.* Bombay; Voice of India Printing Press, 1886.

Baines, Jervoise Athelstane. *Ethnography, castes and tribes, etc.* Straussbu, rg1912.

Balfour, Elizabeth Edith. *The history of Lord Lytton's Indian administration 1876 to 1880.* London; Longmans, 1899.

Bandopadhyaya, Krishna Mohan. *Prize essay on native female education, etc.* Calcutta, 1841.

Bandopadhyaya, Krishna Mohan. *Hindu caste : An essay.* Reprinted from Calcutta Review, Vol 40, 1851.

Banerjee, Guru Dasa. *Hindu law of marriage and stridhan.* Calcutta; Thacker, Spink and Co., 1879.

Barth, Auguste. *Religions of India.* Translated by Rev. J. Wood. London, 1882.

Basak, C. G. *Caste system in Bengal : Its baneful effects and its remedy.*

Bawa Chhajju Singh. *The life and teachings of Swami Dayanand Saraswati.* 2 vols. 1903.

Bell, Thomas Evans. *English in India : Letters from Nagpore written in 1857-58.* London; John Chapman, 1859.

Bell, Thomas Evans. *Our great vassal empire.* London; Trubner & Co., 1870.

Besant, Annie. *Hindu ideals.* 1904.

Bevan, Major H. *Thirty years in India or a soldier's reminiscences of native and European life in the Presidencies from 1808 to 1838.* 2 vols.

Beveridge, Henry. *A comprehensive history of India, civil, military and social, from the 1st landing of the English to the suppression of the Sepoy Revolt including account of the early History of Hindustan.* 3 vols. London; Blackie & Sons, 1858-62.

Beveridge, William Henry. *India called them : A biography of author's parents Henry and Annette Susannah Beveridge.* London; George Allen and Unwin, 1947.

Bhattacharya, J.N. *Hindu caste and sects.* 1896.

Billington, Mary Frances. *Women in India.* London; Chapman and Hall, 1895.

Blanchard, Sidney Laman. *Yesterday and today in India.* London; W.H Allen, 1867.

Blunt, Edward Arthur Henry. *Caste system of northern India, etc.* London; Oxford University Press, 1931.

Blunt, Edward Arthur Henry. *Social service in India.* London, 1938.

Bose, Pramatha Nath. *A history of Hindu civilization during the British rule.* 4 vols. Calcutta; W. Newman and Co., 1894.

Bose, Pramatha Nath. *National education and modern progress.* Calcutta; Kar Majumdar & Co., 1921.

Bose, Pramatha Nath. *The illusions of new India.* Calcutta; W. Newman & Co., 1916.

Bose, Shib Chunder. *Hindu as they are : A description of the manners, customs and inner life of Hindu Society in Bengal.* London, Calcutta; E. Stanford, 1881.

Bower, Henry. *An essay on Hindu caste.* Calcutta; Calcutta Christian Tract and Book Society, 1851.

Bradden, Edward Nicholas Coventry. *Life in India : A series of sketches showing something of the Anglo-Indian, the land he lives in and the people amongst whom he lives.* London; Longmans, 1872.

Brahmo Samaj. *Century of service.*

Brown, Charles Hilton. *Sahibs : The life and ways of the British in India as recorded by themselves.* London; William Hodge and Co., 1948.

Browne, John Cave. *Incidents of Indian life.* 2nd ed. Mardstone, 1895.

Buck, Cecil Henry. *Faiths, fairs, and festivals of India.* Calcutta; Thacker, Spink and Co., 1917.

Buck, Edward John. *Simla, past and present.* Calcutta; Spink and Co., 1904.

Buckland, Charles Thomas. *Sketches of social life in India.* London; W.H. Allen and Co., 1884.

Buller, Major John. *Travels and adventures in the provinces of Assam during a residence of fourteen years.* 1855.

Burton, Richard Francis. *Sindh and the races that inhabit the Valley of the Indus with notices of the topography and history of the province.* London; W.H. Allen and Co., 1851.

Burton, Richard Francis. *Sind revisited with notices of the Anglo-Indian army, past, present and future.* 2 vols. London; R. Bentley, 1877.

Buyers, William. *Recollections of Northern India, etc.* London; John Snow, 1848.

Caird, James. *India, the land and the people.* London; Cassell and Co., 1863.

Campbell, George. *India as it may be : An outline of proposed government and policy.* London; John Murray, 1853.

Campbell, George. *Modern India.* London; John Murray, 1852.

Cameron, Charles Hay. *An address to Parliament on the duties of Great Britain to India in respect of the education of the natives.* London; Longmans, 1853.

Cape, Charles Phillips. *Benaras, the stronghold of Hinduism.* London; Robert Culley, 1908.

Capper, John. *Three Presidencies of India. A history of the rise and progress of the British Indian possessions.* London; Ingram, Cooke and Co., 1853.

Carpenter, Mary. *Six months in India.* 2 vols. London; Longmans, 1868.

Carstairs, Robert. *Human nature in rural India.* Edinburgh and London; W. Blackwood & Sons, 1895.

Carvey, W.H. *The good old days of the Honourable John Company giving curious reminiscences, illustrating manners and customs of the British in India during the rule of East India Company.* 2 vols. 1906-07.

Cavenaugh, Orfeur. *Reminiscences of an Indian official.* London; W.H. Allen and Co., 1884.

Chailley, Joseph. *Administrative problems of British India.* London; Macmillan, 1910.

Chakravarti, Ram Dayal. *A lecture on early marriage.*

Chandar, Bholanath. *Travels of a Hindu to various parts of Bengal and Upper India.* London; Trubner & Co., 1869.

Chapman, Mrs. E.F. *Sketches of some distinguished Indian women.* London; W.H. Allen and Co., 1891.

Chattopadhyaya, Nishi Kant. *Social and religious reformation in India.*

Chattopadhyaya, T.H. *Memo on judicial and other reforms.* 1863.

Chimnabai (Maharani of Baroda) and S.M. Mitra. *Position of women in Indian life.* London; Longman, 1911.

Chintamani, Chirravuri Yagneshvara, *Indian Social Reform.* 2 pts Madras; Thompson and Co., 1901.

Chirol, Valentine. *Indian unrest.* London; Macmillan. 1910.

Clarke, S.E.J. *India and its women*, 1894.

Clarke, S.E.J. *India and its people.*

Clemens, Mrs. *The manners and customs of society in India*, 1841.

Coley, James. *Moral and social emancipation of the native females of India : A sermon, etc.* Calcutta; W. Palmer, 1851.

Collet, Sophia Dobson. *Brahmo year book 1876.* London, 1876.

Collet, Sophia Dobson. *Life and Letters of Raja Rammohun Roy.* Compiled and edited by late S.D. Dobson. London; Harold Collet, 1900.

Compton. *Indian life in town and country.*

Cooper, Elizabeth. *The Harim and the Parda : Studies of oriental women.* London; T. Fisher Unwin, 1915.

Cotton, Henry John Stedman. *New India or India in transition.* Rev. ed. London; Kegan Paul, 1907.

Cotton, Sydney John. *Nine years on the North West Frontier of India 1854-64.* London; Richard Bentley, 1868.

Cowell, Herbert. *Hindu law being a treatise on the law administered exclusively to Hindus by the British Courts in India.* 2 vols. Calcutta; Thacker, Spink and Co., 1870.

Cox, Edmund Charles. *My thirty years in India.* London; Mills and Boon, 1909.

Craik, Henry. *Impressions of India.* London; Macmillan, 1908.

Crooke, William. *Islam in India or the Qanun-i-Islam.* Rev. ed. 1921.

Crooke, William. *Northern Western Provinces of India : Their history, ethnology and administration.* London; Methuen, 1897.

Crooke, William. *Religion and folklores of Northern India.* London; Humphrey Milford, 1926.

Crooke, William. *Things India, etc.* London; John Murray, 1906.

Crooke, William. *Tribes and castes of the N.W. Frontier Provinces and Oudh.* Calcutta; Office of Superintendent of Government Printing, 1896.

Crooke, William. *Notes on Northern India.* 1907.

Crooke, William. *Rural and agricultural glossary for N.W. Provinces and Oudh.* 1886.

Cust, Robert Needham. *Picture of Indian life 1852-81.* London; Trubner & Co., 1881.

Cust, Robert Needham. *Notes on missionary subjects.* 4 pts. London; Elliot Stock, 1889.

Das, D.N. *Sketches of Hindoo life.*

Datta, H.C. *An address on native female education.*

Datta, Sasi Chandra. *Realities of Indian life : Stories collected from the criminal reports of India to illustrate the life, manners and customs of the inhabitants.*

Dayananda Saraswati. *English translation of the Satyartha Prakash, being a guide to Vedic hermeneutics* by Durga Prasad. London; Virjanand Press, 1908.

Dayaram Gidumal. *The status of women in India or handbook for Hindu social reforms.*

Dennis, James. *Christian missions and social progress: A sociological study of foreign missions.* 3 vols. Edinburgh and London; Oliphant, Anderson and Ferrier, 1897-1906.

Del Mar, Walter. *India of today.* London; Adam and Charles Black, 1905.

Duessen, Paul. *My Indian reminiscences.*

Desai, A. R. *Social background of Indian nationalism.* London; Oxford University Press, 1959.

Desai, N. *Women in modern India.* 1957.

Deshpande, D. Y. *Women, family and socialism.*

Dewan, Douglas. *Bygone days in India.*

Dey, L.B. *Bengal peasant life.*

Digby, William. *Prosperous British India : A revealation from official records.* London; T. Fisher Unwin, 1901.

Digby, William. *India for the Indians—and for England.* London; Talbot, 1885.

Dubois, Jean Antoine. *Hindu manners, customs and ceremonies.* Translated from French by H.K. Beauchamp. 3rd ed. Oxford; Clarendon Press, 1906.

Dubois, Jean Antoine. *Description of the character, manners, and customs of the people of India.* 2nd ed. 1862.

Duff, Mountstuart E. Grant. *Notes of an Indian journey.* London, 1876.

Dufferin & Ava, (Marchioness of), *A record of three years work of the National Association for supplying female medical aid to the women of India,.* Calcutta; Thacker, Spink & Co., 1888.

Durkarl, J.B. *Indian education.*

Dutt, N.K. *Origin and growth of caste in India.*

Dutt, R.C. *England and India.* 1897.

Dutt, R.C. *Speeches and papers on Indian questions,* 1897-1900.

Dutton, Charles. *Life in India.* London; Allen and Co., 1882.

Early Travels in India. 1864.

Eden, Eleaner. *Letters from India.* 2 vols. 1872.

Eden, Emily. *Up the country : Letters written to her sister from* Upper Provinces of India. 2 vols. London, 1866.

Edwards, H.B. *A year on the Punjab frontiers.* 2 vols. 1850.

Edwards, S.M. *Folk tales from northern India.*

Elwin, Edward Fenton. *India and Indians.* London; John Murray, 1913.

Elesmie G.R. *Thirty five years in the Punjab, 1852-1893.* 1908.

Essays relative to the habits, character and moral improvement of Hindoos. Undated.

Everest, I. *Observations on India.*

Farquhar, John Nicol. *Modern religious movement in India.* New York; Macmillian, 1915.

Farquhar, John Nicol. *Primer of Hindusion.* 2nd ed. London; Oxford University Press, 1914.

Fateh Chand. *High education for women.* 1891.

Forbes, James. *Oriental memoirs : A narrative of seventeen year residence in India.* 4 vols. London, 1813.

Forsyth, James. *Highlands of Central India : Notes on their forests and wild tribes, natural history and sports.* London, 1872.

Framji, Bomanji. *Lights and shades of the East or a study of the life of Baboo Harish Chandra and passing thoughts on India and its people, their present and future.*

Framji, Dosabhoy *History of the Parsees, etc.* 2 vols. London, Edinburgh; Macmillan, 1884.

Framji, Dosabhoy. *The Parsees : Their history, manners, customs and religion.* London, 1858.

Fuller, Joseph Bampfylde. *Empire of India.* (All Red Series). 1909.

Fuller, Joseph Bampfylde. *Studies of Indian life and sentiment.* London, John Murray, 1910.

Fuller, (Mrs.) Jenny. *The wrongs of Indian womanhood.* Edinburgh and London ; Oliphant and Co., 1900.

Ghose, Aurobindo. *Renaissance in India.* 1920.

Ghurye, Govinda Sadasiva. *Caste and race in India.* London; Kegan Paul, 1932.

Ghurye, Govinda Sadasvia. *Family and kin.* 1955.

Ginwall, Nasvaranji Shehriyar. The Parsee girl of the period. Reproduced from the *Times of India,* 19th April 1884. Bombay. 1884.

Gordar, John Digby. *Work and play in India and Kashmir.* London; Eden Remington and Co., 1893.

Gore, Frederick St. John. *Lights and shades of hill life in the Afghan and Hindu highlands of the Punjab.* London ; John Murray, 1895.

Gorst, M.E. *Curse of education.* 1901.

Graham, General, *Sir Syed Ahmad Khan.* 1909.

Grand, George Francis. *Narrative of the life of a gentleman, long resident in India.* Cape of Good Hope ; Author, 1814.

Grant. *Anglo-Indian domestic life.*

Griffith, Ralph Thomas Hotchkin. *The hymns of the Rgveda.* English translation. 2 vols. Benares; E.J. Lazarus, 1896.

Griffiths, P. *Modern India.* 1957.

Gupta B.A. *Hindu holidays and ceremonials.* 1919.

Hansard, Vols. XXV, XXVIII, XXX and XXXVI.

Har Dayal. *Our educational problem.* 1922.

Har Dayal. *Thoughts on education.*

Hardevi. *Pamphlet on female education and female rights.* Allahabad; Queen Press, 1893.

Harwell, E.B. *Benares, the sacred city.*

Hassan Ali, Mrs. M,, *Observations on the Mussulmans of India.* London; Humphrey Milford, 1917.

Hedges, William. *Diary of William Hedges during his agencies in Bengal as well as on the voyages.* 3 vols. London ; 1887-89.

Herklots' *Islam in India* by Jafar Sharif also referred to as *Quanoon-e-Islam* by Jafar Sharif translated by Herklots and revised by William Crooke.

Hodgson, Brian Houghton. *Miscellaneous essays relating to Indian subjects.* 2 vols. 1880.

Holderness, Thomas William. *Peoples and problems of India* (Home University Library of Modern Knowledge). London; Butterworth. 1912.

Hopkins, Edward Washburn. *India, old and new, with a memorial address in honour of Professor Salisburg.* 1901.

Hopkins, Edward Washburn. *The mutual relations of the four castes according to the Manava Dharma Shastra.* Leipiz, 1881.

Howell, Arthur. *Education in British India prior to 1854 and in 1870-71.* Calcutta; Office of Superintendent of Government Printing, 1872,

Hunter, William Wilson. *History of British India.* London; Longman & Co., 1899-1900.

Hunter, William Wilson. *The Indian of the Queen and other essays.* London; Longman & Co., 1903.

Hunter, William Wilson. *The Indian Empire : Its people, institutions and products.* London; Trubner, 1882.

Hunter, William Wilson. *Indian Musalmans : Are they bound in conscience to rebel against the Queen.* Edinburgh, 1871.

Hunter, William Wilson. *Marquis of Dalhousie.* (Rulers of India). Oxford; Clarenden Press, 1890.

Hunter, William Wilson. *A statistical account of Bengal.* 20 vols. Edinburgh, 1875-77.

Hutton, James. *A popular account of the thugs and dacoits—the hereditary garotters and gang-robbers of India.* London, 1875.

Hutton, John Henry. *Caste in India : Its nature, functions and origins.* Cambridge University Press, 1946.

Hyder, H.B. *Parochial annals of Bengal, 1901.*

Ibbetson, Denzil Charles Jelf. *Punjab castes.* 1916.

Irving, Benjamin Atkinson. *Theory and practice of caste.* London, 1853.

Ishuree, Dass, *Domestic manners and customs of the Hindus of the northern India and more strictly speaking of the North-West Provinces of India.* 1866.

James, Henry Rosher. *Education and statesmanship in India.* London; Longmans, 1910.

Jha, G.M. *Manu smriti. The laws of Manu with the Bhasya of Medhatithi.* Vol. III, Part I, Calcutta; 1922.

Johnstone, James. *My experiences in Manipur and the Naga hills.* London; Sampson and Co., 1896.

Jones, Oliver John. *Recollections of a winter campaign in India in 1857-58.* London, 1859.

Jones, P. John. *India : Its life and thought.*

Kapadia, K.M. *Marriage and family in India.* 1958.

Kapadia, K.M. *Hindu kinship.*

Karaka, Dosabhai Framji. *History of the Parsis.* London; Macmillan, 1884.

Karkaria, Rustom Pestamji. *India, forty years progress and reform, being a sketch of the life and times of Behramji M. Malabari.* London; H. Frowde, 1896.

Kaye, John William. *Christianity in India : An historical narrative.* London, 1859.

Kaye, John William. *History of the Indian mutiny of 1857-58.* London; W.H. Allen and Co., 1888.

Kaye, John William. *Administration of the East India Company : A history of Indian progress.* London; Richard Bentley, 1853.

Keen, Henry George. *A servant of John Company, being the recollections of the Indian officials.* London; W. Thacker and Co., 1897.

Keith, Arthur Berriedele. *Speeches and documents on Indian policy 1750-1821.* 2 vols. London, 1922.

Kerr, James. *The domestic life, character and customs of the natives of India.* London, 1865.

Ketkar, Sridhara V. *History of caste in India.* 2 vols. Ithaca, New York; Taylor and Carpenter, 1909-11.

Khattri. *Conference proceedings of the Special Khattri Conference held at Bareilly, 1901.*

Kincaid, Dennis Charles Alexander. *British social life in India, 1608-1937.* London; G. Routledge and Sons, 1938.

King, (Mrs) Robert M. *Diary of a civilian's life in India.*

Kitts, Eustace John. *A compendium af the castes and tribes found in India.* Bombay; Education Society's Press, 1885.

Knowlson, Thomas Sharper. *Origins of popular superstitions and customs.* London; T. Werner Laurie, 1930.

Kothare, Balaji Sitarama, *Hindu holidays.* Bombay; Times of India Press, 1904.

Lajpat Rai, Lala. *Arya Samaj.* London; Longmans, 1915.

Lajpat Rai, Lala. *Problem of national education in India.* London; George Allen and Unwin, 1920.

Lang, J. *Wanderings in India.* 1859.

Lethbridge, Roper. *High education in India : A plea for State colleges.* London; Allen and Co., 1882.

Leonowens, Anna Harriette Crawford. *Life and travel in India, being recollections of a journey before the days of railroad.* Philadelphia; Porter and Coales, 1884.

Lilly, William Samuel. *India and its problems.* London; Sands and Co., 1902.

Long, Rev. J. *Five hundred questions on the social conditions of the natives of India.* Calcutta, 1862.

Low, Sidney James Mark. *Vision of India as seen during the tour of the Prince and Princess of Wales.* London; Smith, Elder and Co., 1906.

Lyall, Sir Alfred Comyns. *Asiatic studies, religious and social.* 2 vols. London; John Murray, 1899.

Mackey, G.R. Aberigh. *Twenty days in India.*

Mahmood, Syed. *History of English education in India.* 1895.

Maine, Henry James Sumner. *Ancient law.* London; John Murray, 1887.

Majumdar, D.N. *Races and cultures of India.* Bombay; Asia Publishing House, 1958.

Malabari, Behramji Mehrbanji. *Gujrat and the Gujrati : Pictures of men and manners taken from life.* London; W.H. Allen and Co., 1882.

Manu. *Ordinances of Manu.* 1891.

Manu. *Manusmriti with the commentary of Kulluka.* Bombay, 1906.

Manucha, K.M. *Hindu home life.* 1890.

Marshman, John Clark. *History of India.* 3 vols. London, 1867.

Marshman, John Clark. *The story of Carey, Marshman and Ward.* (Bunyan Library). 1864.

Mayhew, Arthur Innes. *Education of India : A study of British educational policy in India 1835-1920 and of its bearing on national life and problems in India today.* London; Faber and Wyer, 1926.

Mayne, John Dawson. *A treatise on Hindu law and usage.* Madras, 1878.

Mayer, J.E. *Humours and pathos of Anglo-Indian life.* London; E. Stock, 1895.

MacCosh, John. *Advice to officers in India.* London, 1856.

Mehta, R.V. *Thesis on the legal rights of women under different communal laws in vogue in India.* 1839.

Mill and Wilson. *History of British India.*

Misra, B.B. *The Indian middle classes : Their growth in modern times.* London; Oxford University Press, 1961.

Mitra, S.M. *British rule in India.* Undated.

Monier-Williams, Monier. *Modern India and Indians, being a series of impressions, notes and essays.* London; Oxford University Press, 1878.

Monier-Williams, Monier. *Religious thought and life in India : An account of the religions of Indian people.* London; John Murray, 1883.

Monier-Williams, Monier. *Modern Hinduism.* London; Oxford University Press, 1885.

Morrison, John. *New ideas in India during the nineteenth century : A study of social, political and religious developments.* Edinburgh; George A. Martin, 1906.

Mozoomdar, Pratap Chandra. *Faith and progress of the Brahmo Samaj.* Calcutta; Calcutta Central Press Co., 1882.

Mozoomdar, Pratap Chandra. *Life and teachings of Keshub Chander Sen.* Calcutta; J.W. Thomas, 1881.

Muller, F.M.   *India, what can it teach us.*   1919.
Mullick, Bulloo Ram.   *Essays on The Hindu family in Bengal.*   Calcutta; W. Newman and Co., 1882.
Mukerji, A.C.   *Ancient Indian fasts and feasts.*   1930.
Murdoch, John.   *India, past and present.*   Madras; SPCK Press, 1903.
Murdoch, John.   *The women of India and what can be done for them.* 1895.
Murdoch, John.   *Indian Year Book 1861 ; A review of social, intellectual and religious progress in India and Ceylon.*
Murzban, M.M.   *The Parsis in India: Their customs, usages, etc.* 2 vols.
Natrajan, S.   *A century of social reform.*
Naoroji, Fardunji.   *The personal bearings of Europeans in India towards the natives.*   1874.
Nesfield, John Collinson.   *A brief view of the caste system of the North Western provinces and Oudh, together with an examination of the names and figures shown in the Census Report, 1882, being an attempt to classify on a functional basis all the main castes of U.P.*   Allahabad, Oudh Government Press, 1885.
Nivedita, Sister.   *Aggressive Hinduism.*   Madras; G.A. Natesan, 1918.
Nivedita, Sister.   *Cradle tales of Hinduism.*   London; Longmans, 1913.
Nivedita, Sister.   *Studies from an Eastern home.*   London; Longman, 1913.
Nivedita, Sister.   *Web of Indian life.*   London; William Heinnman, 1904.
Nolan, Edward Henry.   *Illustrated history of the British Empire in India and the East from the earliest times to the suppression of Sepoy Mutiny in 1859.*   2 vols.   London 1857-59.
Nolan, Edward Henry.   *History of the British Empire in India aad the East.*   3 vols.   1878-79.
North India Notes and Querries.   5 vols.   1891-95.
Observations on India by a resident there for many years.   1853.
Old Punjabee, Pseud.   *Punjab and North-West Frontiers of India.*
O'Malley, *History of Bengal, Bihar aad Orissa.*
Oman, John Campbell.   *Brahmans, theists and Muslims of India.*   London; T. Fisher Unwin, 1907.
Oman, John Campbell.   *Indian life, social and religious.*   London; T. Fisher Unwin, 1889.
Pal, Bipin Chandra.   *The present social reaction : What does it mean ?*
Panikkar, Kavalam Madhava.   *Educational reconstruction in India.*   Madras; Ganesh and Co., 1920.
Panikkar, Kavalam Madhava.   *Hinduism and the modern world.*   Allahabad; Kitabistan, 1938.
Parry, Roy Edgardo.   *Sikhs of the Punjab.*   London; Dranes, 1923.
Patterson, A.J. *Caste.*   1861.
Patterson, A.J.   *Caste considered under its moral, social and religious aspects.*
Pears, Stuart Adolphus, *Over the sea, or letters from an officer in India to his children at home.*   London, 1857.
Peggs, James.   *India cries to British humanity relative to infanticide, etc.*   London; Simpkin and Marshall, 1832.
Podfield, J.E.   *The Hindu at home : Being sketches of Hindu daily life.*

Powell, Baden Henry Baden. *The Indian village community, examined with reference to the physical ethnographies and historical conditions of the provinces chiefly on the basis of the revenue settlement records and district manual.* London; Longmans, 1895.

Pricehard, Iltudus Thomas, *Chronicles of Budgepore or sketches of life in Upper India.* 2 vols. London, 1880.

Princep, V.C, *Imperial India : An artist's journal.*

Puckle, Bertram Saward. *Funeral customs : Their origin and development.* London ; T. Warner Laurie, 1926.

Punjabi, pseud. *Short essays on social and Indian subjects.* Calcutta; Central Calcutta Press, 1869.

Raikes, Charles. *Englishmen in India.* London, 1867.

Raikes. Charles. *Notes on the North Western Provinces of India.* London, 1852.

Rama Bai Saraswati. *The high caste Hindu women.* 2nd ed. Philadelphia, 1887.

Ranade, Mahadev Govind. *Religious and social reform.* 1902.

Ranade, Ramabai. *Miscellaneous writings of the late Hon'ble Mr. Justice M.G. Ranade.* 1915.

Rao. S.V, *Remarriage of Hindu women on shastric basis.* 1929.

Ray Choudhari, J,K. *Hindu customs and manners.* 1888.

Rees, John David. *Modern India.* London ; G. Allen and Sons, 1910.

Rees, John David. *Real India.* London ; Methuen, 1908.

Richey, James Alexander. *Selections from educational records.* Part II, 1840-1859. 1920.

Risley, Herbert Hope. *The tribes and castes of Bengal.* 2 vols. Calcutta, 1891.

Risley, Herbert Hope. *People of India, etc.* 2nd ed. Calcutta; Spink and Co., 1915.

Rose, Horace Arthur, *Glossary of the tribes and castes of Punjab and North West Frontier Provinces.* 3 Vols. London ; S.T. Weston, 1811-1814, 1919.

Ross, Edward Denison. *An alphabetical list of feasts and holidays of Hindus and Musalmans.* 1914.

Roy, Raja Rammohun. *English works.* 3 vols. Calcutta, 1885-87.

Russell, Robert Vane. *The tribes and castes of the Central Provinces.* 4 vols. London; Macmillan, 1916.

Russell, William Haward. *My diary in India.* 2 vols. London, 1860.

Sarkar, Benoy Kumar. *Folk element in Hindu culture : Contribution to socio-religious studies in Hindu folk institutions.* London ; Longmans, 1917.

Sastri, H. *Social reform on shastric lines.* 1909.

Sastri, Siva Nath. *History of the Brahmo Samaj.* Lahore, 1911.

Samuelson, James. *India past and present : Historical, social and political* London ; Trubner and Co., 1890.

Sen, K.C. *Brahmo Samaj : Lectures in India.* 1899.

Sen, K.C. *Essays, theological and ethical.* 1885.

Sherring, Mathew Atmore. *Hindu tribes and castes.* 3 vols. Calcutta, 1872-81.

Share. John. *The private record of an Indian Governor-Generalship.* Massachusetts, 1933.

Sleeman, William Henry. *Rambles and recollections of an Indian official.* 2 vols. London, 1844.

Sleeman, William Henry. *Journey through the Kingdom of Oudh in 1849-50.* 2 vols. London, 1858.

Smith, J. *India and its problems.*

Smith, J. *Sketches in Indian ink.* 1880.

Sorabji, Corneha. *Love and life behind the pardah.* London ; Freemantle, 1901.

Steeves, C.M. *In India.* 1899.

Stock, Eugene. *History of the Church Missionary Society.* 4 vols. London ; Church Missionary Society, 1899-1916.

Strachey, John. *India.* London ; Kegan Paul and Co., 1888.

Strachey, John. *India, its administration and progress.* 3rd ed. London ; Macmillan, 1903.

Stray leaves from the diary of an Indian officer. 1865.

Sushila Devi. *Ideal of Hindu womanhood.* 1907.

Tagore Law Lectures, 1879.

Tavernier, Jean Baptista. *Travels in India.* 2 vols. London; Macmillan, 1889.

Taylor. W. *Thirty eight years in India from Junagarh to the Himalaya Mountains.*

Temple, Richard Carnac. *India in 1880.* London; John Murray, 1880.

Temple, Richard Carnac. *Bird's eye view of picturesque India.* London ; Chatto and Windies, 1898.

Temple, Richard Carnac. *Legends of Punjab.* Bombay; Education Society's Press, 1884-86.

The women of India and what can be done for them: Papers on Indian reform. 1895.

Thomas, Lieut. F.S. *Silent India.*

Thorton, Douglas Montagu. *Parsi, Jaina and Sikh or some minor religious sects in India.* London; Religious Tract Society, 1898.

Ticklemore. *Humour and pathos of Anglo-Indian life.* 1895.

Tilak, Bal Gangadhar. *Writings and Speeches.* Madras ; Ganesh and Co., 1919.

Tod, Colonel James. *Annals and antiquities of Rajasthan.* 2 vols. London; Smith Adder and Co., 1829-32.

Trotter, Lionel James. *History of the British Empire in India, etc.* 2 vols. London. 1866.

Trotter, Lionel James. *History of India under Queen Victoria from 1836 to 1880.* 2 vols. London; W.H. Allen, 1886.

Tucker, Henry St. George. *Memorials of Indian Government.* Edited by John William Kaye. 1853.

Twining, Thomas. *Travels in India.* London ; Osgood McIlvaine and Co., 1893.

Urguhart, M.M. *Women of Bengal.* 1926.

Valbezen, E. De. *English and India.* London ; W.H. Allen and Co., 1883.

Vidyarthi, M.L. *India's culture through the ages.* 1952.
Vidyasagar, Ishwar Chandra. *Marriage of Hindu widow.*
Vivekananda (Swami). *Speeches and Writings.* Madras; G.A. Natesan, 1912.
Wallace, R.G. *India in 1887.*
Walter, H.A. *Ahmadiya Movement.* 1918.
Ward, Thomas Humphry. *Reign of Queen Victoria : A survey of fifty years of progress.* 2 vols. London; Smith and Elder, 1887.
Ward, Rev. W. *India and the Hindus.* 1853.
Watkin, Edward William. *India, a few pages about it.* London; C.F. Roworth. 1889.
Westermark, Edward Alexander. *History of human marriage.* 5th ed. 3 vols. London ; Macmillan, 1921.
Whitehead, D.D. *Indian problems.*
White, Col. S. Dune. *Travels in India.* 1844-66.
Wilkins, William Joseph. *Modern Hinduism, etc.* London; T. Fisher Unwin, 1887.
Wilson, A.C. *After five years in India.*
Wilson, John. *Indian caste.* 2 vols. Bombay, 1877.
Woodruff, Philip, pseud. Philip Mason. *The men who ruled India.* 2 vols, London; John Cape, 1953-54.
Yusuf Ali, Abdallah. *Life and labour of the people of India.* London; John Murray, 1907.
Yusuf Ali, Abdallah. *Cultural history of India during the British period.* Bombay; D.B. Taraporevala, 1940.

FICTION

Translated Works

Ayodhya Singh Upadhyaya	*Venice ka Banka* (English).
Baboo Gopal Ram Gahabhari	*Naye Baboo.* Sam. 1950.
-do-	*Dau Bahin.* Sam. 1959.
-do-	*Devrani Jethani.* Sam. 1958.
-do-	*Bara Bhai.* Sam. 1951.
-do-	*Theen Patochu.* Sam. 1961.
-do-	*Sasa Patochu.*
Baboo Kartik Prasad Khatri	*Ila*
-do-	*Pramila*
-do-	*Jya*
Baboo Ram Chand Verma	*Chhatrasala*
Baboo Ram Krishna Verma	*Thuga Vritantamala.* Sam. 1946.
-do-	*Akbar, Amala Vritantamala.* Sam. 1951.
-do-	*Chittor Chataki* **(Bengali)** Sam. 1951.

Bankim Chandra Chattopadhyaya	*Durgesh Nandini*
-do-	*Rajni*
-do-	*Kapal Vish Vriksha*
-do-	*Rahasya*
-do-	*Krishna Kanta ka Vasiyatnama*
-do-	*Shekhar*
-do-	*Anand Math*
-do-	*Radha Rani*
-do-	*Raj Singh*
Dvijendra Lal Rai	*Bharat Ramani*
Gajadhana Singh	*Banga Vijeta*
-do-	*Durgesh Nandini*
Ganga Prasad Gupta	*Poona me Halchal*
Michael Madhu Sudan Datt	*Meghnath Vadha*
Rabindra Nath Tagore	*Teen Sathi*
-do-	*Ankh ki Kirkiri*
-do-	*Gora*
-do-	*Rasmani ka Larka*
-do-	*Tapasivini*
-do-	*Cabulliwala*
-do-	*Ela Didi*
-do-	*Do Bahan*
-do-	*Master Sahab*
-do-	*Bahu Rani ka Hut*
-do-	*Chir Kuwara Sabha*
Rakhal Dass Vandhyopadhaya	*Shashank*
Sarat Chandra	*Sati*
-do-	*Srikanta*
-do-	*Grihdah*
-do-	*Anandi ka Swarga*
-do-	*Vilasi*
-do-	*Viraj Bahoo*
-do-	*Suprabhat*
-do-	*Shesh Prashna*
-do-	*Path ke Davedar*
-do-	*Parineeta*
Tara Shankar Bandopadhyaya	*Saptapadi*
Vibhooti Bhooshan Bandopadhyaya	*Bandopadhyaya*
-do-	*Deja Loka*
-do-	*Vana Phool*
-do-	*Avarana*

STORIES

Banga Mahila	*Dulai Vali.* Sam. 1964
Chanderdhar Sharma Guleri	*Usne kaha tha.*

BIBLIOGRAPHY

Girija Dutta Vajpeyi	*Pandit aur Panditani*. Sam. 1960.
Jai Shankar Prasad	*Gramya*
-do-	*Indrajal*
Jainendra Kumar	*Apna Apna Bhagya*
-do-	*Bahu Bali*
Master Bhagwan Dass Mirzapur	*Pluque ki Churaul*. Sam. 1959
Prem Chand	*Bade Bhai Sahab*
-do-	*Shatranj ke Khilari*
-do-	*Bade Ghar ki Beti*
-do-	*Idgah*
Vishambhara Nath Kaushik	*Raksha Bandhan*
-do-	*Rani Mata*
-do-	*Chitrashala*
-do-	*Kahani Sangraha*

Hinai ke Maulik Upanyas

Ambika Dutta Vyasa	*Ashcharya Vrittanta*
Ayodhya Singh Upadhyaya	*Theth Hindi ke Thath*
-do-	*Adha Khila Phool*
Bal Krishna Bhatta	*Sant Ajan Eko Sujan*
-do-	*Nutan Brahmachari*
Kishori Lal Goswami	(*Upanyasa Masik Patra*)
-do-	*Rajiya Begum* (1904)
-do-	*Tapasvini Meera Bai*
-do-	*Leela vati*
-do-	*Lavang Lata*
-do-	*Lucknow ki Khabar*
Lajja Ram Mehta	*Dhoorta Rasik Lal*
-do-	*Hindu-Grihastha*
-do-	*Adarsh Dampati*
-do-	*Bigare ka Sudhar*
-do-	*Adarsh Hindu*
Prem Chand	*Gaban*
-do-	*Sevasadan*
-do-	*Nirmala*
-do-	*Karma Bhoomi*
-do-	*Ranga Bhoomi*
-do-	*Karbala*

Index

Age of Consent Bill 122, 222
Aggarwals 126, 228
Agra 13, 41, 140, 198
— and Oudh 138
Aguris 182
Ahirs 71, 75
Ahmedabad 54, 192, 211, 235
Ajmer 59, 177, 229
Aligarh College 192
— School of Thought 244
Allahabad 55
Almora 48
Alwar 12, 67
Amritsar 177
— Temperance Society 229
Amroha 58
Amusements 27
Anglo Indians 19-20, 23
Anglo Indian ladies 239
— — Society 21
— Muhammadan College 218
Annie Besant 236, 245
Arora Bans Sabhas 228, 236
Aroras 126, 192
Arya Dravidian 41
Arya Mahila Samaj Poona 201, 212
Arya Samaj 122, 192, 195, 212-14, 239, 241-43
Arya Samajists 104, 197
Ascetics 51
Assam 41, 54, 182, 197
Assamese 40, 45
Assyrians 64
Astrologers 58
Atkinson, Franklin 22
Atmiya Sabha 8
Attock 13
Awadhi 44

Badri Dass 214
Bagheli 45
Bagri 75
Baidyas 182
Baloch 44

Banajee, Framji Cowasjee 215
Banaras 43, 55
Banias 70
Bankers 67
Bankim Chandra 245
Bansphors 72
Barter 97
Basor 72
Beliefs 66
Bengal 7-8, 12, 20-21, 41, 44, 54, 70, 71, 98, 180-82, 185-87, 196-97, 205, 207, 225, 239
Bengali 8, 40, 44
Bengali, S.S. 215-16
Bentinck, Lord William 6-7, **9**, **14**
Berar 54
Beveridge, Lord 22, 27
Bhagwati, Mai 201, 214, 241
Bhand 72
Bhandarkar, R.G. 212
Bharat Dharma Mahamandal 219
Bharat Varsha Arya Dharma Prasarini Sabha 218
Bharatpur 67
Bhargavas 192
Bhat 126
Bhojpuri 44
Bhutan 21
Bihar 20, 41, 75
Bikaner 12
Bishnois 125
Black vs. Whites 34
Blacksmiths 67
Bombay 13, 21, 23, 54, 70, 75, 138, 156, 165, 181, 186-87, 196-97, 200, 219, 239
Bose, Raj Narayan 243
Brahmans 8, 58, 68-69, 71-72, 126, 182
Brahmo Samaj 122, 192, 212, 267
Braj 44
British Community 19
British Policy 5, 186
Buddhists 47

Calcutta 13, 23, 30, 54-55, 70, 77, 156, 163, 165, 186-87, 191, 198, 200, 208-09, 234, 238
Calcutta University 197
Cards playing 158
Carpenter, Mary 199
Caste 63
Caste, Change of Custom 26
Caste Disabilities Removal Act 1850, 12, 87
Caste groups 68
Caste restrictions 70, 225
Castes, Nation Type 76
Castes, Occupation in Caste System 3, 65-67, 77, 80
Celebrations 166
Census Report 1881, 196
Census Report, Bombay 64
Central Provinces 72, 138, 186, 197
Ceremonies 101, 103, 106
Chamars 71-72
Chandavarkar, M.G. 212
Chaupar 157
Chausar 157
Chhatisgarhi 45
Chhota Nagpur 124
Child marriage 121, 212, 273
Child marriage abolition 206-07
Children's pastimes 160
Christian Marriage Act 1852, 115
Christian missionaries 6, 14, 214
Christians 50, 72, 181
Christianity 116
Civil Mairrage Act 1872, 116
Connubial restrictions 73
Contractual restrictions 72
Costumes 43
Cursetjee, Manockjee 215
Court language 184
Curzon, Lord 187
Customs 60

Dalhousie, Lord 11, 14, 194
Dalton, Colonel 166
Dance 163
Dancing girls 148
Darjeeling 21, 28
Dayal, Munshi Hargovind 227
Dayanand Anglo-Vernacular College 214
Dayanand, Swami, 212-14
Delhi 54-55
Department of Instructions 185, 197
— — Public Works 192
Devendra Nath, Maharshi 208-09
Dharma Sabha 209
Dharma Sabha Calcutta 14
Dharkar 72, 126
Dhobi 72
Dholpur 67
Dhuniya 72
Dialects 185
Disabilities Removal Act 12, 87
Discrimations 34
Divorce 145
Doms 71-72, 75
Doongarpur 12
Dosabhoy 216
Dosadh 75
Dowry system 128
Drama 164
Dravidian 42
Dravido-Munda 45
Dress 42
Dustoor 130
Dutch 40

Earth God 9
East India Company 15, 20
Education 14, 179-80
Education Commission 1882, 187, 197
Education, Western 182
Educational Despatch 14
Egyptians 64, 69
Ellenborough, Lord 13
Endogomy 124
Engineering College, Roorkee 187
England 7, 32

INDEX

English 8, 45, 184-85
English colleges 184
English customs 238
English education 45, 184, 186, 205
English schools 186
English-speaking community 20
Entertainments 163, 165
Eurasians 19
Europeans 19
European Society 30
— traders 20
Exogomy 125

Fairs and Festivals 60, 176
Family ceremonies 101
— dwellings 99
— life 55, 98
— members 95
— priests 97
— servants 97
Fatehpur Sikri 59
Feasts 129
Female education 193, 198, 209
— infanticide 138-39, 206
— — Act 1870, 140
— normal schools 197
— ornaments 143
— pastimes 162
— security 144
Festivals 60, 156, 174, 176
Food restrictions 70
Functional castes 75
Furdoonji, Nowrozjee 215-16

Gambling 28, 157
Gandhbaniks 182
Gandharva marriage 116
Ganges 8
Ganjifa 158
Garhmukteshwar 177
Garhwal 21, 48
Gaur 71
Germans 40
Girls 141
Goldsmiths 67
Grant Medical College 215

Greeks 20, 40, 64
Grihni 94
Guga Pir 58
Gujarat 11, 43-44
Gujarati 40, 45, 71
Gujars 71, 75, 124, 126
Gupta Sabha 211
Gurmukhi 180
Guru Nanak 59

Hardinge, Lord 12
Haridwar 177
Heredity 67
Hierarchy 68
Hill Stations 78
Himalayas 41
Hindi 44
Hindu College, Calcutta 8
Hindu Gains of Learning Act 1855, 186
Hindu idolatry 7
Hindu Joint-Family 91
— Ladies Social Club, Bombay 237
— Law 114, 151-52
— Muslim affinities 58
— mythology 3
— orthodoxy 14
— population 46
— religion 3
— Saints 58
— Society 184
— superstitions 57
— Widow 151
— Women 152
Hissar 58
Howell, A. 183
Human sacrifices 9
Hunter, W.W. 9
Hypergamy 126

Ibbetson, Danzil 57
Idolatry 2, 7
Ilbert Bill 1882, 35
Illiteracy 181
Immoral trafficking 147
Indian Christians 195, 239

Indian Reform Association 210
— Society, Upper Strata 32
Indo-Aryan 41, 44
Indo-Chinese 45
Indo-Gangetic 45
Indo-Tibetan 45
Indus 13
Infant marriage 221
Inheritance and Property Right 151
Intellectual stagnation 4
Intelligenstia 232
Inter-marriage 40
Islam 3, 45, 116

Jabalpur 198
Jagannath, Lord 177
Jainism 116
Jains 48, 181
Jaipur 43, 67
Jats 67, 70-71, 75, 126
Jeejibhai, Jamsedjee 215
Jews 20
Jijhotia 126
Joint-family fissures 97
— — system 92
Jugglery 162
Jullundur 214

Kali, Goddess 11
Kanauj 75
Kanauji 44
Kanaujia Brahmans 70
Kandh districts 10
Kangra 21, 98
Kania, Khurshedji Rustomji 215
Kanpur 54-55
Kanyakubi Brahmans 126
Kanya Mahavidyalaya, Punjab 214
Karans Subarnabaniks 181
Kashmir 41, 48, 54, 181
Kashmiri 44-45
Kathaks 3
Kayastha Conference 226
— Pathshala 227
— Sabha 227
— Social reform 227

Kayasthas 69-71, 182, 192, 197, 228
Kelkar, S.P. 212
Khandesh 211
Kharwar Khatri 126
Khatris 70, 126
Khattua (circumcision) 105
Kidnapping children 141
King, Robert 25
Kite flying 158
Koli 75
Kulin Brahmans 126
Kulinism 225
Kumaon 21
Kumhar 75
Kurmi 71

Ladakh 48
Lahore 43-44, 54, 214, 229
Liberalism 205
Life pattern 57
Lingayats 125
Lucknow 54-55, 198, 228

Madras 220
Madrassas 180
Mahadev, the God 11
Maharajas 33
Mahars 75, 182
Mahesries 182
Maithil 75
Makar Sakranti 171
Maktab 180
Malabari, Behramji 221, 235
Malda 44
Male child 144
Male indoor pastimes 156
Mangal Patan 158
Maratha families 126
Marathas 43, 70, 75, 126
Marathi 45
Marriage 5, 105, 114
—Act of 1872, 151
— auspicious months 13
— concept 115

INDEX

Marriage customs reforms 221
— dissolution 155
— expenses 128
— forms of Hindu 116
— religious injunction 114
— rites 116
— rituals 130
Marriageable age 117
Marwar 67
Match-making 123
Matrimonial bargaining 127
Maulvis 14
Mecca 59
Medical Colleges 187
Meo 75
Mercantile class 20
Middle class 55
Midwife 97
Military 19
Minas 67
Missionary Societies (England) 198
Mitakshara School 152
Mithla 75
Mongolo-Dravidian 41
Mongoloid 41
Monier-Williams, M. 26, 47, 189
Moral courage
Mount Abu 28
Mozamdar, Pratap Chandra 235
Muhammadan 152
Muhammadan Educational Conference 218
Muhammadan Schools 218
Muhammadan widow 152
Muhammadan woman 152
Muharram 61, 174
Murree 28, 44
Musahar 72
Muslim converts 99, 124
— names 58
— priests 58
Muslims 49, 58, 72, 179, 181, 197
Mussoorie 28

Nagar Mela 177

Nagpur 182, 235
Naidu, Govindarajulu 236
Naidu, Sarojini 236
Nainital 28
Namakchashi 104
Naming 104
Nanak, Guru 59
Naoroji, Dadabhai 215-16
National Indian Association 199
National Social Conference 219-25, 235
Native Marriage Act of 1872 116, 206-07
Nauroz 174
Nautch girls 226
Newari 44
Nigha 177
Nikah 130
North Western Provinces 40-41, 105, 227, 236
North west 181

Occupation 81
Occupational restrictions 73
Omens and superstitions 109
Orissa 9, 41
Orthodoxy 7
O'Shaughnessy, William 15
Oudh 140

Pachmarhi 28
Pachisi 157
Pak Patan 59, 177
Panchayats 78
Panch Pir 58
Pandurang, Atma Ram 212
Pandurang, Dadoba 211
Param Hans Sabhas 211-12
Parliament of Religions, Chicago 1893, 235
Parsee Law Association 216
Parsee Marriage Act 145
Parsi 195
Parsi Girls School Association 216
Parsi women 43

Parsis 50, 181, 239
Pashto 44
Pathshala 180, 197
Pastimes 156
Patel, Framji, Nauseerwanji 216
Persian 44
Persians 69, 184
Peshawar 214
Pigeon-flying 159
Pilgrimage 59, 177
Polygamy 8-9, 133, 225, 237
Poona 197, 211
Population 18
Postal services 13
Potter 75
Prarthna Sabha 192, 211-12
Prayag 177
Presbyterian ministers 20
Premvati 201
Priesthood 3
Primary education 185
Privy Council 14
Professions 54
Public Schools 185
Punishment 79
Punjab 11, 21, 41, 75, 105, 138, 140, 181, 184, 239
Punjab Purity Association 228
Punjabi Khatri Sabha 228
Punjabi 197
Punjabis 40, 44
Puppetry 164

Qalandar 58
Qazi 130

Radhia Brahmans 75
Rahnumai Mazdavasnan Sabha 215, 244
Railway reservations 35
Railways 13
Rajas 33
Rajasthan 43
Rajasthani 40, 45

Rajputana 41, 54, 67, 75, 138, 182
Rajput girls 139
Rajputra Hitkarini Sabha 236
Rajputs 67, 70, 72, 124, 126, 138
Rajput widow 12
Raikes 139
Rama Bai, Pandita 201, 212, 228, 241
Ramakrishna Mission 244
Ramlila 165
Ranade, M.G. 212, 220
Rath Yatra 168
Reform associations 220
Religious and moral improvement 6
— diversity 45
— groups 51
— identities 44
Remarriage 12
Reservation of compartments 35
Restrictions of privileges 72
Rituals 108
River-bathing 58
Robert, King 30
Rohtak 98
Roman catholic priests 20
Romans 64
Roy, Raja Rammohun 6-8, 15 205, 207-09, 211, 234
Rukma Bai 223, 241
Russell, D.W.T. 28
Rulers and the ruled 19, 32, 34
Rural occupations 56
— organisations 57

Sacrificial ritual 2
Sagar 177
Sahib culture 21
Saiyad Saar at Bahraich 58
Sakhi Sarwar Sultan 58, 177
Salaaming and Spilting Act 34
Sanatan Dharma Mahamandal 244
Sanatan Dharma Rakshini Sabha 218
Sanskrit 44
Sanskrit literature 7

INDEX

Santhals 124, 182
Sant Ram, Diwan 228
Saptpadi 130
Sarin Sabha 228
Sati Abolition 8, 205-06
Schools 185
Scytho-Dravidian 41
Sectarian castes 76
Self-immolation 10
Sen, Keshab Chandra 183, 209-210, 212, 222, 225
Shab-i-Barat 176
Shagan Chand, Swami 227
Shah Mina's Dargah 58
Shaikh Saddo 58
Shakar Ganj, Baba 58
Shashthi 168
Shatranj 156
Shillong 28
Shore, John 31
Shradhha 108
Shraddhanand, Swami, (Munshi Ram) 214
Shravan 169
Shrine 59
Shrines of Saints 51
Sialkot 177
Sikhism 116
Sikhs 48, 59, 177, 181, 197
Simla 28-29
Sircar, Baboo Pearey Charan 210
Sirohi 67
Slavery 10
Social and cultural diversities 40
— classes 55
— conditions, 19th century 2
— Conference 237
— institutions, unifying force 53
— intercourse 32
— laws 5
— reformers 153
— reforms 6, 86
— Reforms Association Sindh 219
— reforms Bombay 210
— in Punjab 228
— in Rajputana 229

Social Reforms Muslims 217
— — opposition 218
— — Parsis 214
— reforms, voice of dissent 209
— Traditions, decline of 2
Special Marriage Act 1872, 87
Sports and games, male outdoor 158
Stridhan 152
Sudras 67, 69
Sultanpur 177
Sumerians 64
Superstitions 2, 3, 60
Surendra Bala 201
Syed Ahmed Khan, Sir 192, 217

Taga 71
Tagore, Rabindra Nath 245
Taziyas 61
Temple R.C. 189
Territorial Castes 75
Theosophists 235
Thugs 11
Tols 180
Tribal castes 75
— names 44
Turko-Iranian 41

Udaipur 12
United Provinces 41, 48, 181, 197
Universities 187
Upanishads 7
Upnayan ceremony 104
Uprising of 1857, 14
Urban life pattern 53
— professions 54
Urdu 55, 217

Vaishyas 69
Valmik Kayastha 227
Vanis 70, 182
Vedic religion 2
Vernacular 185
Vijay Dashmi 170
Vivekanand, Swami 235
Vocations for woman 150

Wahabi Movement 244
Walter, Colonel 229
Western education 8, 233
— — impact 187
— — promotion 183
Widow 87
— remarriage 148, 205-06, 209
Widowhood 146, 221
Widows 223
Woman, economic condition 149

Woman seclusion 142
— social inferiority 137
Women 136
Women's status 136
Worship of Saints 58
Wrestling 159

Zanana teaching 199
Zorastrianism 116